Mormons & Gentiles

For Gene, George, and Leonard:
friends, teachers, and colleagues

Mormons
&
Gentiles
A History of Salt Lake City

Thomas G. Alexander   James B. Allen

Volume V
The Western Urban History Series

PRUETT **P**PUBLISHING COMPANY
Boulder, Colorado

First Edition
1 2 3 4 5 6 7 8 9

Printed in the United States of America

Library of Congress Cataloging in Publication Data

Alexander, Thomas G.
    Mormons and Gentiles.

    Bibliography: p.
    Includes index.
    1. Salt Lake City (Utah)—History.   2. Mormons—
Utah—Salt Lake City—History.   I. Allen, James B.
II. Title.
F834.S257A44   1984   979.2′25   84-15884
ISBN 0-87108-664-6

Endpapers:

Artist's rendering of the Salt Lake Valley as it will appear with the completion of the Triad Center and the International Center. Courtesy of Triad Utah.

Acknowledgements

A t the completion of a project like this one, authors are always aware of debts they owe that can be repaid in no other way than recognizing invaluable assistance. A great part of the research was done by assistants who helped immeasurably with bibliographic searches, note-taking, and oral history interviews. We particularly appreciate the help of Kenneth Cannon, Harvard Heath, Kim James, Brian Champion, Brian Dunsmore, Bruce Lott, Bruce Van Orden, and Frank Bruno.

We appreciate also the assistance and encouragement of the Brigham Young University College of Family, Home, and Social Sciences. Dean Martin Hickman and Assistant Dean Ted Warner have supplied research support as have the Charles Redd Center for Western Studies and the history department. Marilyn Webb and the staff of the college's Faculty Support Center have typed and proofed the study. Lori Warren, Natalie Ethington, Jennifer Dean, and Kyra Swain of the Redd Center and Mariel Budd and LuAnne Park of the history department provided various types of assistance, and Karen Acerson of the history department helped with final proofing.

We are especially appreciative of the help and assistance of the staffs of particular libraries. Jay Haymond and the staff of the Utah State Historical Society Library have been of immeasurable assistance. Everett Cooley and the staff of the Western Americana department of the University of Utah Library have been very cooperative, as have Chad Flake and his associates in the Special Collections department of the Brigham Young University Library. Donald Schmidt and the staff of the LDS Church Archives also helped us by providing material. Harold Jacobsen and the staff of the Utah State Archives were very kind in supplying microcopies of minutes of the city council.

We are grateful for the assistance and suggestions made by others who have worked on the history of the city. Particularly helpful have been John McCormick and Larry Gerlach who shared with us preliminary versions of important papers. John McCormick and Ronald W. Walker also read the manuscript and provided some most helpful input. Kathryn MacKay and Peter Wiley gave some helpful suggestions, as did Melvin Smith and many others on the staff of the Utah State Historical Society.

We appreciate the time and assistance of a number of knowledgeable people. Particularly helpful were former mayors Jake Garn, John Wallace, and Conrad Harrison, and Mayor Ted Wilson. Former commissioners L.C. Romney, Grant Burbidge, and Jennings Phillips, Jr. also provided interviews and suggestions. We appreciate the assistance of Howard Marcus in supplying papers of his father Louis Marcus, and the suggestions of Earl J. Glade, Jr. and other members of the Glade Family. William Smart, editor of the *Deseret News*; Fred Ball, of the Salt Lake Area Chamber of Commerce; and Emanuel Floor, president of Triad Utah, provided valuable information.

Gerald Keenan and Lyle Dorsett provided encouragement and suggestions, and without their cooperation the project would probably never have gotten under way. We are also grateful to Merilee Eggleston who handled the copyediting chores with consummate skill. And we appreciate the patience of our wives and families who waited as we wrote, discussed, and argued over the content of the book.

Thomas G. Alexander and James B. Allen
Provo, Utah

Contents

1. Similarities and Differences:
   Salt Lake City and the Urban Experience   *1*

2. "This is the Right Place"   *17*

3. The Mormon Commonwealth, 1850-1870   *45*

4. Mormons and Gentiles, 1870-1892   *87*

5. The Americanization of Salt Lake City, 1893-1911   *125*

6. Progressive City, 1912-1930   *163*

7. Depression Decade   *197*

8. War and Prosperity, 1941-1945   *231*

9. Growth and Stagnation, 1946-1960   *251*

10. The Changing Face of a Mature City, 1960-1983   *273*

11. From Today to the Future: The View from 1984   *303*

    Bibliographical Note   *319*

    Index   *349*

The Old Clock Corner, Main Street and First South. For almost a century, Salt Lakers have depended upon the old clock, said to have been brought to Salt Lake by ox team and wagon. Courtesy, Utah State Historical Society.

——1——

Similarities and Differences: Salt Lake City and the Urban Experience

Several years ago the Lutheran church assigned a new minister to Salt Lake City. Naturally concerned about taking over a congregation in the midst of a Mormon-dominated community, he visited Temple Square and went to hear the Mormon Tabernacle Choir. What a surprise, he reported later, suddenly to hear the choir singing Martin Luther's "A Mighty Fortress is Our God." "I knew I had found a home," he said, and instead of spending his time in Salt Lake City in conflict with the Mormons, he felt a peculiar sense of community with them.

Of course, such accommodation does not occur with every minister who comes to town. This story, nevertheless, illustrates one of the central themes in the history of Salt Lake City: much is similar to and much is different from other cities. Like many other cities such as Philadelphia, Washington, D.C., and Cincinnati, Salt Lake City is a planned urban community; unlike most cities of the United States, however, it was organized as a spiritual and religious center. Built on a grid pattern like other planned cities in the United States, it was, unlike most others, designed with streets wide enough to meet the needs of twentieth-century motor vehicles, providing room for public convenience rather than emphasizing the more profitable sale of building lots. A center of capitalism like both Denver and San Francisco, it also served as the focus of a unique if short-lived communal experiment generally associated with villages of much smaller size. In this book we will examine the differences as well as the similarities, in the hope that this balanced view will leave an understanding of Salt Lake City as both a distinctive religious capital and a significant regional center.

Like many other cities of the American West, Salt Lake City was what Gunther Barth has called an "instant city." It was brought into existence suddenly and by design, and it grew in an area where no other settlement existed. Founded in 1847, it reached nearly 1,700 people in four months. By its first anniversary, Salt Lake's population stood at nearly 5,000—twice the number needed for urban status. Within two decades, it had reached 12,000 people—a city of no mean proportions in nineteenth-century America. Each decade between 1850 and 1890, its population soared more than fifty-five percent as migrants from the East and Midwest and immigrants from Europe and Asia moved to the city for religious, social, political, or economic reasons.

Like the cities of the midwestern Ohio and Mississippi valleys Richard Wade has studied, Salt Lake City preceded the frontier. It was founded before any frontier-type economy had developed in the region. It is true that fur traders and Indians had crossed the area before, that explorers like John C. Fremont had visited and reported on the region, and that migrants had passed through what was to become Salt Lake City in the year before the Mormon pioneers arrived. Nevertheless, the Latter-day Saints selected the site on the basis of studies they made before they arrived, and the Great Basin frontier developed in part because Salt Lake City was there first. The city did not grow in any haphazard way from a farming village or trading post; it was a planned community, created by the Mormons as the religious, governmental, and cultural center of their region.

Many American cities, in fact, were planned in a similar way. The people who came knew they wanted to build a city, had a site in mind for its construction, and had brought a plan they expected to use in laying it out. Their plans often had to be changed or modified, as in the case of New Amsterdam (present-day New York City), but the fact that they were planned cities made them part of a significant pattern in the history of urban America.

Actually, the idea of town planning was one of the traditions Europeans brought to the new world, and while they modified it, they never abandoned it. Both in theory and practice, the design of the early modern European planned city was ordinarily quite regular. Usually, the pattern was based on either a radial-circular or a rectangular-grid pattern. In those towns designed with the grid patterns, boulevards sometimes cut diagonally through the blocks to provide passage through the city and access to points within it without the necessity of following a stairstep pattern through the grid.

In the United States, the grid pattern prevailed. Colonial cities like New Orleans, Philadelphia, and Williamsburg were all laid out that way. The crooked streets of Boston were the exception. Farther west, the grid pattern was used in cities like Pittsburgh, Chicago, and San Francisco. In some cities, like Indianapolis and Washington, D.C., boulevards were planned to cut through the grids. Thus, while Mormons tend to think of the grid pattern of the "plat of the City of Zion" as unique, it was in fact an adaptation of the usual town pattern used in many cities of the United States.

For those places planned for agriculture, the pattern was different. Many New England towns were planned as agricultural villages with strips of farm land stretching away from the houses. In the Midwest, however, farmers located their homes on land separate from the urban places, and public land laws required actual residence on the farm for homesteading. Under such conditions, agricultural villages were impossible—perhaps even unwanted.

Salt Lake City was never an agricultural village. Brigham Young envisioned what the German historical sociologist, Max Weber, called an *ackerbürgerstadt* (best translated perhaps as "garden plot city"). That is, it became a city where, inspite of its commercial character, a substantial proportion of the inhabitants grew a majority of their own foodstuffs. It was never meant to be an agricultural village in the New England sense, however, for from the beginning a minority of citizens earned a living from agriculture.

Salt Lake City also shares much with other urban centers. In 1921, Weber published his classic study, "The Nature of the City," in which he outlined certain characteristics he believed were associated with cities. Using a technique he often adopted, that of analysis by ideal types, Weber tried to answer the question: What constitutes a city and what differentiates it from other types of human settlement? In his analysis, he argued that a city was a fortification and a market, it had a court of its own, and at least partially autonomous law. It had a related form of association which could unite it into a corporate unit.

In many ways, Weber's analysis provides a useful model for interpreting the history of Salt Lake City. The Mormon metropolis had all the features Weber identified plus others we associate with more recent cities, such as industrial plants, communications facilities, and a wide range of services not found in rural areas.

For one thing, it was a fortification. At an early time, the Saints constructed a fort to protect themselves from possible Indian raids. Later, during the Civil War, the federal government established Fort

3

Douglas on a hill on the eastern outskirt of the city, like an acropolis overlooking the valley.

Salt Lake City was also a market. From the time of its founding, it was the leading commercial and financial center of Utah. Merchants purchased and exchanged agricultural commodities, minerals, and manufactured goods, sold them in the city and shipped them to other areas. Its banks became the financial centers of the Intermountain region, and the Intermountain Stock Exchange was located in Salt Lake to trade principally in mining stocks. In the 1920s, the Federal Reserve Bank of San Francisco established a branch there.

Most importantly in this connection, the inhabitants of the city lived from trade, commerce, and manufacturing rather than from agriculture. In the census of 1850, taken less than three years after the Mormons arrived, only a third of the heads of household were farmers. By 1870 that number had declined to sixteen percent. Beginning with the gold rush of 1849, overland migration served to cement Salt Lake's position as a commercial center, particularly since it was the only major settlement between the Midwest and the Pacific coast. The completion of the Utah Central railroad from Ogden on the Union Pacific to Salt Lake in 1870 and the later addition of a railroad network stretching to Denver on the east, to Oakland and Los Angeles on the west and to Portland, Seattle, and Montana on the north helped consolidate that position. Later, the Lincoln Highway, the national highway system, and the Interstate system provided connections with principal outside markets. By the late 1970s, Salt Lake City had become, in addition, a major airline market, no longer subordinate to Denver as it had been in the 1960s and early 1970s.

Like all cities in Utah, Salt Lake City enjoys partial autonomy in its governmental functions. This too is part of the criteria Weber suggested was necessary for urban life. Governed at first by the hierarchy of the Mormon church, Salt Lake City enjoyed a variation on the mayor-council form of government until 1912, when it adopted the commission form. Since 1980, it has been governed again by a mayor and council. It has always enforced its own internal regulations, and has traditionally exercised a great deal of latitude in its judicial and administrative system, even though they are actually regulated by state law.

Most importantly, Salt Lake City has served since the beginning as Utah's administrative center. With the exception of one year in the 1850s, the legislature has met there and the governor and other administrative officers have been housed there. Moreover, it is the administrative center of the LDS church. In the nineteenth century this was perhaps not as important as it has recently become, since many members of the Council of the Twelve lived in settlements outside Salt Lake City and many church functions were decentralized. Since the 1950s, however, centralization has moved ahead quite rapidly and the development of a church bureaucracy now housed in an imposing skyscraper at 50 East North Temple assists in that centralization.

But Salt Lake developed characteristics beyond those suggested by Weber. After its initial success as a market, the city advanced rapidly as a manufacturing center. In the nineteenth century, ZCMI had its operations center in the city, and its workshops manufactured for the local cooperatives throughout the region. In the 1870s, primary metals manufacturing began in the valley, and in the late nineteenth and early twentieth century it became a major source of the city's prosperity as the mines of Bingham, Park City, Mercur, and Tintic poured their ores into Salt Lake Valley for processing. Following a decline after World War I, manufacturing revived during World War II as plants in the city produced such products as munitions, oil, aluminum, and radio tubes for the war effort. In recent years, so-called clean manufacturing has expanded in importance as companies like Litton and Sperry have opened plants producing for the electronics industry.

In recent years, tourism has increased rapidly in Utah. Salt Lake's Temple Square, rather than the national parks or ski resorts, has become the largest single tourist attraction in the state. The traditional visits to the April and October conferences of the LDS church are no longer as crucial to the business community as they once were. More important are the conventions, tourist visits, and business meetings held throughout the year.

Salt Lake City has experienced periodic booms that have shifted the economic life of the city. At first it was an entrepot for immigrants and a commercial center. After 1870 it became the mining and smelting center of the Intermountain region. Additional railroad links enhanced that position, and its role as a market. During the 1920s and 1930s, the city's economy languished to some degree. Though it retained its importance as a market and financial center, the depressed condition of the minerals and agricultural industries affected the city's prosperity. World War II started another boom, as Salt Lake played host to war industries heretofore unseen on the Wasatch Front. In recent years, the city has experienced a post-industrial boom not only in tourism, but also in corporate communications centers and energy company headquarters.

Spatially, Salt Lake City has changed little since its boundaries were defined by Congressional enactment in 1870. Annexations have taken place to the west and to the southeast, but the mountains and the Davis County line on the north, the mountains on the east, and South Salt Lake on the south have restricted its geographical growth. Continued development and annexation could take place to the west beyond the Salt Lake airport, presumably to the Tooele County line, since no incorporated cities exist there, but this area has generally been less desirable for residences and mostly used for industrial and commercial development.

Since Salt Lake City was an "instant city," its internal spatial differentiation developed more quickly than in older cities of the East and Midwest. Manufacturing came rapidly upon the heels of commercial development, and the post-industrial service and communications age has been the principal force in Salt Lake's development since World War II.

Neighborhood differentiation occurred in the same way. In the initial core city, little differentiation on the basis of class seems evident. While Mormon church leaders tended to locate east of Main Street and north of South Temple, some of the finest early residences, like the Devereaux house, were located west of Temple Square in what is now the most run-down portion of the city.

Gradually, however, particular areas were recognized as less desirable residential locations. By the 1880s, the non-Mormon population had tended to congregate in the area south of South Temple, especially between Third and Sixth South and Main and Third West, although there was a significant population of Mormons in the area as well. During and after the 1890s East South Temple became the elite residential area, and the upper-middle class began to locate in the northeastern avenues region and the southeast portion of the city. At the same time, the west side began to take on the flavor of a lower-class ghetto as immigrants from Southern and Eastern Europe poured into the city. In recent years, the benches east of the valley floor have been the most desirable residential sections.

Innovations in transportation abetted the development of class-oriented spatial growth. The streetcars allowed people to live at a greater distance from their places of work, as long as they could afford the fare. Middle- and upper-middle-class citizens could live in detached houses with some yard and garden space in the more desirable northeast or southeast section of the city. As the automoblie challenged the streetcar for supremacy on the streets, even farther outlying areas were readily accessible. More recently lower-middle-class housing has become available in the northwest section of the city at Rose Park. Today, the city resembles an amphitheatre designed for the benefit of the upper-middle class. Their homes are perched on the mountain sides, almost in concentric arcs and below them lie the homes of the less wealthy, and the core city. Further to the west are the poorest citizens. Increasingly the auto and urban mass transit have allowed the city's expansion into a metropolitan area covering virtually all of Salt Lake County and stretching northward into Davis County as well.

Salt Lake City developed its urban services at about the same time and in about the same way as other cities in the United States, except it lagged in public health services. Private entrepreneurs provided services when they perceived the possibility of earning a profit. Their development went ahead rapidly. The city offered other services traditionally provided by city government or for which no profits seemed available, and these services developed more slowly. As a result, while Salt Lake citizens could ride to work in relative ease, call each other on the telephone, and light their houses with gas or electricity, they also suffered from typhoid fever, smallpox, and other communicable diseases brought on by lack of sewer, water, and public health facilities.

By the 1890s, this had begun to change. The city had started to expand its street paving and to install water and sewer mains. It had also begun to pay attention to the health of citizens and the purity of food and beverages sold within its boundaries. Not until the late 1920s, however, were even the rudiments of zoning and building codes inaugurated.

More recently, some formerly franchised services that could not pay a profit to privately regulated monopolies have been taken over by the government. Probably the best example is urban transit. The automobile cut so heavily into streetcar services that private companies had practically withdrawn from the field by the late 1950s. The metropolitan region has recently organized the Utah Transit Authority to provide bus services throughout the area. The state legislature authorized the imposition of an additional sales tax for the purpose, and fares are held relatively low.

Like other American communities, Salt Lake City has been subjected to periodic waves of structural reform—to use the nomenclature of Melvin Holli in his study of Detroit. City government has shifted from Church organization to mayor-council form, to city commission, and finally again to mayor-council. City departments have been rationalized, professionalized, and subjected to civil service reform. The internal organization of departments has been periodically restructured in the name of efficiency.

At the same time there have been only two periods of significant social reform in the city, and in both instances the efforts of the city paralleled those of the LDS church. During the early years, as the church attempted to establish a cooperative commonwealth in the intermountain empire, Salt Lake City was the location of many efforts related to this objective. The city's Public Works department, under Daniel H. Wells, cooperated with the church in various projects for new immigrants. In order to protect Salt Lakers from predatory pricing policy and from the immediate impact of the transcontinental railroad, the church undertook price fixing, boycotts, and cooperative merchandising. In order to protect the Saints from themselves as well as from becoming dependent on outsiders, the church inaugurated a moral reformation, and reemphasized its opposition to liquor and tobacco.

Again, in the 1930s, both the city and the LDS church made efforts at social reform. The city relied on the federal government for help in solving problems caused by massive unemployment. It received grants from the PWA, the WPA and other federal agencies to assist in constructing public works and providing employment for distressed citizens. At the same time, the LDS church inaugurated its Welfare Plan, largely on the basis of an experiment begun by President Harold B. Lee in the Pioneer Stake in Salt Lake City. With more than half its adult members unemployed in 1932, the Pioneer Stake inaugurated various projects to provide food, clothing, and bedding for its members and employment for those able to work.

In neither the 1850s and 1860s nor the 1930s, however, was social reform a longstanding success. By the 1880s, the LDS business community had given itself wholeheartedly to a market economy, while providing some help for the indigent. By the 1940s, the employment program of the earlier period had gone by the board. Thus, the most long-lasting reforms have been structural rather than social. Governmental efficiency and effective administration rather than compassionate social services have been the major legacies of reforms in Salt Lake government.

Some American cities have been called "island communities" because of their relative isolation from outside forces. Salt Lake City was scarcely, if ever, that. If any semblance of an island community did exist there, it was eliminated by the impact of the railroad in the 1870s and of nationally integrated business systems after the turn of the twentieth century. Throughout the nineteenth century, however, the majority of the city's population consisted of the foreign born and their children. Barely two years after its founding, forty-niners inundated the city as the first wave of westward migrants crossing the plains to the West Coast. That migration continued throughout the century. In the late 1850s, the city was again disturbed by Albert Sidney Johnston and the Utah expedition. On the heels of Johnston's army came Patrick Edward Connor and the California Volunteers. A center of mining activity from the early 1870s, much of the city's economy has been shaped by outside capital and absentee ownership.

Moreover, by the 1880s, Salt Lake City had developed at least on a rudimentary level what Gunther Barth has called a "modern city culture."

That is, its divided space, its newspapers, its department stores, its ball park, and its theatres were like those of other American communities. The city's baseball teams aped the styles and forms of nationally known performers. The *Deseret News*, the *Salt Lake Herald*, and the *Tribune* reported national and international news, vied with each other for local advertising, reported local events, commented on local and national conditions, and represented local and national mores. ZCMI and other department stores served not only Salt Lake's citizens but those in the surrounding territory through their various outlets. Local and national companies played in the Salt Lake Theatre and later in the vaudeville houses. Literary and general interest clubs discussed ideas, customs, and scientific developments.

Nevertheless, the city changed internally, and a useful device for understanding the changes seems to be provided by Claude Fischer's subcultural theory. Salt Lake saw the introduction of ever greater diversity of cultural groups, and the tendency of persons within the city to belong increasingly to more than one subculture. Mormons of the 1850s and 1860s would have been somewhat limited in the number of subcultural groups to which they could belong. Besides belonging to the LDS Church, they might have been members of one of the literary societies or singing groups, or they might have been patrons of the theatre. Non-Mormons might have belonged to one of the small churches, attended the same theatre, and they might have belonged to a similar singing organization. By the late 1880s, the differences between Mormon and non-Mormon communities began to diminish. Both Mormons and non-Mormons might have belonged to the Commercial Club (predecessor of the Chamber of Commerce). They associated together in joint business ventures, in labor unions, and in private voluntary associations. Both might have gone to baseball games. Only at religious services were their lives separate. By the first decade of the twentieth century, new subcultural groups entered the city with the Southern and Eastern Europeans. With them came the coffeehouses, restaurants, churches, and fraternal organizations unique to their cultures. While they retained these organizations, within a generation or two they also joined the Chamber of Commerce and the Commercial Club, or the more recently organized Rotary or Kiwanis.

A major differentiation between the subcultural groups, however, has come increasingly on the lines of class and wealth. In the early years, a given church had members from both the lowest and the highest classes. But with the increasing size of the city, wards, congregations, and parishes have tended to divide on socioeconomic lines—the poorest people have moved into the central city and the city's western quarter and the wealthiest have migrated into the eastern, southeastern, and northeastern quarters of the city. Thus, geographic dispersal has helped to promote subcultural division within the city.

This diversity of subcultures has developed at the same time as the city has experienced a decreasing degree of social control. In the 1850s, the church leadership could physically restrain people from leaving the city. In 1868, Brigham Young could exert enough control to make certain that the regular church candidate had no competition in his candidacy for alderman. As late as the 1920s, the city could enforce prohibition with a relatively high degree of success. By the 1970s, however, attempts to close down theaters screening pornographic movies achieved only minimal success. By the early 1980s, the variety of subcultures was even greater. Homosexuals have organized religious groups and patronize gay bars. The preservationist Utah Heritage Foundation coexists with the developmentalist Associated General Contractors, and the church's *Ensign* magazine flourishes in the same city where the independent journals for Mormon intellectuals, *Dialogue: A Journal of Mormon Thought* and *Sunstone,* as well as the avowedly anti-Mormon publications of Jerald and Sandra Tanner are produced.

With the diversity of subcultures, one might wonder whether there is any warrant for considering Salt Lake City a community. The major problem in doing this is to determine what we mean by the term "community." If we used the term in the restricted sense Robert Redfield used it in *The Little Community: Viewpoints for the Study of A Human Whole*, which requires virtually every institution and experience to be shared and distinctive, then with the exception of the first few years, Salt Lake City was never a community. While it was distinctive, the distinctiveness was never shared by all inhabitants. Non-Mormons, for instance, have generally seen Salt Lake City in a much different way than Mormons have seen it. It is neither small, homogeneous, nor self-sufficient. It has also never been a community in the sense in which Martin Buber used that term in *Paths in Utopia*, since "every point of its being" does not possess, even potentially,"the whole character of community."

It is, rather, a community in the sense René König uses the term: *"a more or less large local and social unit in which men [and women] co-operate in order to live their economic, social and cultural life together."* Under such conditions, it is often difficult to determine where community ends and society begins. In a large city such as Salt Lake became early in its history, the existence of community has been a matter of degree. It has depended upon what the people shared or what they agreed upon and what had to be regulated by contractual and legalistic means.

In retrospect, its seems that at least three things are necessary for the existence of community. First, there must be love of and attachment to place. For Latter-day Saints, that was easy to achieve. Converts were drawn to the center of Zion like a magnet. Charles W. Penrose, a British immigrant who had never seen Salt Lake City, wrote the poem, later put to music, "Oh Ye Mountain High," in praise of the land to which he planned to immigrate. For non-Mormons, however, there also developed the same sense of love of place. Wallace Stegner, though he has lived much of his life on the West Coast, still considers Salt Lake City his home. It is a place associated in his memory with pleasant things. Much of his writing has drawn him back to Salt Lake and the people of the city.

In part, the love of both Mormons and non-Mormons is tied to the second prerequisite for community, which is shared historical memory. Josiah Royce suggested this criterion in the late nineteenth century. It is not at all surprising that at the recent inauguration of construction of the Triad Center in Salt Lake—a project financed by the Saudi Arabian Khashoggi family and presided over by a native Utahn of non-Mormon extraction, Emanuel A. Floor—images of Brigham Young, community responsibility, historic preservation, and city planning were evoked. These are part of the collective memory of the city. So too are the mining magnates of South Temple Street, Maurice Abravanel and the Utah Symphony, Utah's governors and the state capitol, the athletic contests at the University of Utah, and the visits to Hogle Zoo.

The third prerequisite for community is a set of shared ideals. In the case of Salt Lake City, these ideals have been a commitment to what Robert Bellah has called the American civil religion, a term he borrowed from Jean Jacques Rousseau. The American civil religion consists of a number of elements. It is a general belief in the necessity of religion and morality based on conventional religious belief. It is a commitment to the ideals of the Declaration of Independence. It is the belief in the need for civic virtue, and the concern for the common good under the norms of "equality, life, liberty, and the pursuit of happiness."

This commitment has developed in the American consciousness under one or both of two structures, biblical or utilitarian. That is, it is either sanctioned by a belief in covenant with God or a belief in social contract. As Bellah has noted, one can read the tenets of civil religion from either or both of these two perspectives. Equality can be seen either as "a condition for the fulfillment of our humanity in covenant with God or ... [as] a condition for the competitive struggle to attain our own in-

11

terests." Freedom may be seen as "almost identical with virtue—the freedom to fulfill lovingly our obligations to God and our fellow men—or ... [as] the right to do whatever we please so long as we do not harm our fellow men too flagrantly." The pursuit of happiness and life can be seen equally from both perspectives—virtue and covenant or interest and utilitarianism.

In the nineteenth century, as both Mormons and gentiles in Salt Lake City shared a love of place and a historical memory, albeit with differing interpretations of the meaning of that history, they also shared a commitment to the American civil religion—again to differing interpretations of the content of that religion. To the Mormons, freedom and pursuit of happiness meant liberty to practice their religion as they saw fit and to direct the membership of their voluntary organization in political, social, and economic matters if they chose to do so. To the non-Mormons, it meant freedom under the rule of law to believe what one chose, but to practice only those things sanctioned by the general culture of the United States.

In the early twentieth century the two cultures merged. Mormons generally accepted the moral and cultural norms of Evangelical Protestantism. Today, both Mormons and Evangelical Protestants tend to see themselves as the last preservers of the civic virtue and morality of American civil religion. This is ironic since public opinion polls indicate continued widespread acceptance of these traditional values. Nevertheless, these ideals, together with love of place and shared historical memory, form the basis of the sense of community which has existed and which continues to exist in Salt Lake City.

During the history of the city there have been breaches of community norms. Most obvious are the numerous instances of criminal and antisocial behavior which citizens have dealt with through formal and informal means. Salt Lake residents have seen everything from vice and fraud to violence. The city will undoubtedly continue to witness those things. Their existence, however, does not mean that the sense of community has vanished. It simply means that some people place themselves outside the community, and the existing sense of community provides a focus for dealing with them. The salient fact is the general agreement on the means of punishing such people, not the existence of such behavior.

More serious, however, have been the times when public officials, nominally representing the ideals of the community, have violated standards of the community and diminished public virtue. In all too many cases, the police department—ostensibly sworn to maintain public norms—has been guilty of breaches. From the attempt by Brigham Y. Hampton and his fellow officers to use prostitutes to attack the gentile community in the 1880s through corruption in the department during the early 1900s to payoffs from prostitutes in the 1930s and even questionable activities in the city-county consolidation issue in the late 1970s, the Salt Lake City police department has been involved in breaches of public virtue.

Most serious have been those times when elected public officials have violated community norms. These range from relatively innocent practices such as profiting in the construction of public utilities to more serious offenses such as embezzlement. One would be surprised not to find examples of such practices in a city the size of Salt Lake, but one nevertheless understands the damage done to the sense of community in these circumstances.

Another subject which deserves some comment is the shifting composition of the elites of Salt Lake City. By elites, we mean those persons who by virtue of their position and personal persuasiveness are able to influence significantly the formulation of public policy in the city.

From the very beginning, leaders of the LDS church who have taken an active interest in Salt Lake City affairs have belonged to this group. These included people like Brigham Young, Jedediah M. Grant, and Daniel H. Wells. In the late nineteenth century and after the turn of the twentieth century luminaries such as George Q. Cannon, Joseph F. Smith, and Heber J. Grant were influential. More recently, such leaders as David O. McKay, Nathan Eldon Tanner, and Gordon B. Hinckley have exhibited considerable personal prestige.

To this group must be added a set of Mormon and non-Mormon merchants and bankers in the late nineteenth century. These included William Jennings, W.S. McCornick, and Joseph R. Walker and his brothers. In the 1890s and the early twentieth century, mining magnates like Thomas Kearns, Samuel Newhouse, and David Keith joined the city's elite. This group was often at odds with the LDS leadership, at least initially. Similar breaches between the two groups took place during the 1920s as those associated with the George Wilson, Ernest Bamberger, and the Order of Sevens split with Heber J. Grant and other members of the church's hierarchy.

Shortly after the turn of the twentieth century the city's elites expanded to include people other than religious or business leaders. Most important were a group of people who usually came from the second echelon of business or the professions, but whose status derived from their position in city government or as the spokesmen for influential voluntary organizations. Such political figures as Richard P. Morris and Clarence Neslen, and representatives of voluntary organizations like the Social Welfare

13

and Betterment League, or, since World War II, the Chamber of Commerce would be included.

At least in the period since World War II, the various components of the elite structure of the city seem generally to have been reconciled to one another. Meetings between David O. McKay, Gus Backman, head of the Salt Lake City Chamber of Commerce, and John F. Fitzpatrick of the *Tribune* were extremely important in monitoring policy and developments in the city. They represented the three major cultural groups in the city: the Mormon, nominal Mormon, and non-Mormon communities. In recent years, Fred S. Ball, Backman's successor with the chamber of commerce, John W. Gallivan of the *Salt Lake Tribune*, William Smart of the *Deseret News*, Emanuel A. Floor representing development interests, and Wendel J. Ashton representing the business community and arts patrons must be added. Political leaders of citywide and statewide stature such as Governor Scott M. Matheson should also be counted as members of the elite.

In summary, Salt Lake City exhibits both unique features and some that it shares with other cities. Like many American cities it was a planned city. It has experienced all the features of the ideal type city outlined by Max Weber as well as other features generally associated with modern cities, such as industrial and communications centers. Its development has passed through stages largely associated with shifts in economic activity within the city and the region it serves. It has experienced internal spatial differentiation like most cities in recent times. The development of urban services has paralleled that of other cities. It has housed a variety of subcultural groups which have grown more diverse in recent years. Like many other cities of the United States, it's growth has transformed the city into the center of a metropolitan region. The sense of community in Salt Lake City is based on features similar to those found in other cities. Its elites are often drawn from the business classes and representatives of voluntary associations like other cities.

The notable unique feature has been the presence of the Church of Jesus Christ of Latter-day Saints. The church not only represents the majority of Salt Lake City citizens, but it is a large landowner in the downtown area and is therefore vitally interested in decisions relative to urban planning and development. Beyond this, the interpretation of its religious tenets by members of the church's hierarchy affects the way they perceive the formulation and application of public policy. Any consideration of the city must include the role of the LDS church, the tension and cooperation between the Mormon and non-Mormon communities, and the effect of the beliefs and practices of the Latter-day Saints.

From the beginning, non-Mormons who came to Salt Lake found themselves dubbed "gentiles." This came from the Mormon belief that the church was really God's modern Israel. Utah's fourth state governor, Simon Bamberger, saw the ironic humor in the situation when he remarked that this was the only place in the world where a Jew could be a gentile! And that, significantly, represents a central theme in Salt Lake City's history: the effort of both Mormons and gentiles to build a community in the Intermountain West.

*Charles B. Hall engraving of the Great Salt Lake Valley, July 1847.
Courtesy, LDS Church Archives.*

2

"This is the Right Place"

B efore 1847 the fertile strip of land nestled between the Wasatch
Mountains and the Great Salt Lake was, to anyone who knew
about it, a place to pass through but hardly a place for permanent
settlement. Nomadic native Americans followed game across it and, in
the right seasons, paused to gather whatever food and stores Mother
Nature provided. For some it was part of the trail that led them into
trading contact with people of other tribes, with the Spaniards and,
later, with the people of Mexico. The Spaniards heard tales of this
northern region from various Indians, though not until the famed Dominguez-Escalante expedition of 1776 did any explorers even come close
to the Great Salt Lake. The two padres stopped their northern progress
some fifty miles short, in Utah Valley, but only after they had heard
some interesting accounts of Salt Lake Valley from the Indians and
written the earliest extant description. A half-century later British and
American fur traders invaded the borders of present-day Utah and set
up caches and rendezvous in its northern and eastern sections. One of
them, Jim Bridger, discovered the Great Salt Lake during an expedition
in the fall and winter of 1824-1825 in which he also found the mouth
of the Bear River. After that several trappers, including the famous
Jedediah Smith, spent time in the Salt Lake Valley, and some of their
information filtered back to the United States and, eventually, to the
eager ears of the Mormon pioneers of 1847.

By the mid-1840s Salt Lake Valley was no longer the exclusive
domain of Indians and mountain men. The area belonged to Mexico—
part of an ill-defined and poorly protected northern region loosely called
"Upper California"—but Americans were casting acquisitive looks in
that direction. They also were eyeing Oregon Territory, where their

joint occupation agreement with Great Britain had become increasingly unsatisfactory, and the independent Republic of Texas. In 1845 Texas became an American state, and in 1846 the United States acquired the southern half of Oregon by abrogation of the joint occupation treaty. That same year the United States and Mexico entered into a war that eventually ended in the cession of all the territory now comprising California, Nevada, Utah, most of Arizona, and major portions of New Mexico, Colorado, and Wyoming. Few people had much accurate information about the vast inland region between the Rocky Mountains and the California coast, but already explorers and trailblazers were crisscrossing it and beginning to provide considerable information—some of it quite accurate—for those who cared to search it out.

One reason for the increased activity was Oregon fever which, by the early 1840s, had infected many westward-looking Americans and had a direct effect on preparing the way for the Mormons to find a western refuge in the Salt Lake Valley. During that decade thousands of people traversed the Oregon Trail, pioneering the route for the Mormon Trail. In 1841 John Bartleson led the Bartleson-Bidwell Party across Utah, skirting the northern end of the Great Salt Lake and attempting to find the mythical Buenaventura River flowing out of the lake to the West Coast. Two years later Captain John C. Fremont appeared in the Salt Lake Valley during his second western exploring expedition on behalf of the American government. According to his report, his first view of "the waters of the Inland Sea, stretching in still and solitary grandeur far beyond the limit of our vision...was one of the great points of the exploration." He and his party were enthusiastic about the area. They made a boat trip to the large, treeless island (later named Fremont Island), made numerous scientific observations, searched in vain for the Buenaventura, eventually made their way to California and finally, in May, returned to Utah on their way back to the United States. The report and map of this expedition, published in 1845, provided the most important scientific information yet on the whole Great Basin region and became a significant factor in the Mormon decision to settle in the valley of the Great Salt Lake. In 1845 Fremont returned again, and this time actually camped where Salt Lake City now stands.

Other explorers and western migrants followed, but none became so famous as the Donner party of 1846. Bound for California, this ill-fated group tried to follow an alternate route described by Lansford W. Hastings. With great difficulty they hauled their wagons through the Wasatch mountains, down Emigration Canyon, and past the site of Salt Lake City. After experiencing tragic delays in crossing Utah and Nevada, the

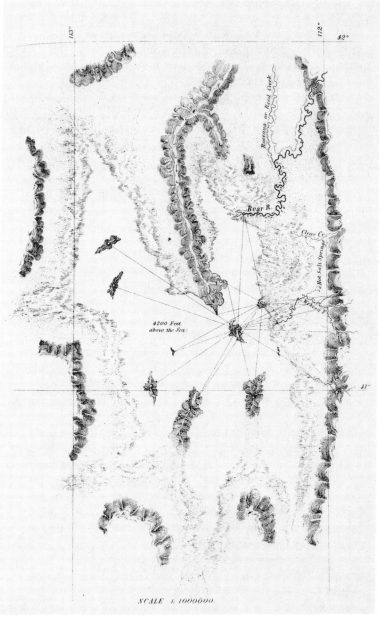

Sketch of Salt Lake Valley from John C. Fremont's report. Courtesy,
Brigham Young University.

19

party finally was trapped by a winter storm in the Sierra Nevada, where most of its members succumbed to exposure and starvation.

Such early passersby looked at Salt Lake Valley as a place to pass through, a place to explore, or, more often, a barrier. But in 1847 someone came to stay. Perhaps decades before any other forces would have created permanent, thriving settlements along the Wasatch front, the religious motives of the Mormons brought them there and compelled them to remain.

The Church of Jesus Christ Latter-day Saints was founded in western New York state in 1830. Ten years earlier, in an atmosphere sparked with revivalism, restorationism, and millennialism, its founder-prophet, Joseph Smith, Jr., had reached a crucial point in his personal quest for religious truth. Retiring to a grove of trees near his father's farm, he prayed for light and saw a heavenly vision in which two "personages" (identified by the Mormons as the Father and the Son) appeared to him and instructed him not to join any church, for they had become corrupt and were not teaching the true ancient gospel. He was assured, however, that at some future time he would receive the fullness of the gospel. Later, through the instrumentality of another heavenly messenger, he obtained a set of ancient records, written on metal plates that had the appearance of gold, and was given the power to translate them. The resulting publication, The Book of Mormon, gave the religious history of certain ancient inhabitants of the American continent, and of the visit of the resurrected Christ to them. While its teachings clearly paralleled those of the New Testament, it also added new insights into many matters of concern to the Christian world and became a keystone of the Mormon faith.

Life was not easy for the Mormon prophet and his followers. As soon as they organized the church, harassment began, and in less than a year most New York Mormons fled to Ohio. There, because of the conversion of a Campbellite minister named Sidney Rigdon and many of his congregation, it seemed as if a place of refuge had been prepared and they could hope to build and propagate their faith in relative peace. In Kirtland they established a seemingly prosperous community, built a magnificent temple, began a communal enterprise known as the "law of consecration," and sent missionaries to various parts of the United States and Canada. At the same time, Joseph Smith received a revelation that Independence, Missouri, was really the "center place" of Zion, and they quickly began to build an ideal community there. But the exclusiveness of the Mormons, their strange doctrines, and political concerns of the older settlers as they seemed to be taking over the area, aroused the older citizens of Jackson County, Missouri, and resulted in their being driven out. Those who were in Ohio also experienced economic and religious difficulties, as the bank founded by Joseph Smith and others failed, and most of them fled or were driven from Kirtland during a period of trial and apostasy. The Saints found temporary refuge north of Jackson County, but could not stay for long, since in the winter of 1838-1839 mobs supported by the state militia drove most of them from the state. Their next refuge was in Illinois, where they built the city of Nauvoo, with its magnificent temple, that soon became one of the two largest cities in the state. Again, however, their growing political power as well as their unusual religious doctrines and practices led to jealousies, bitterness, and conflict with other settlers. On June 27, 1844, a mob murdered Joseph Smith and his brother, Hyrum, while they were being held prisoners in the jail at Carthage.

Over the years Joseph Smith presented a distinctive body of doctrine and practices to his followers. There is no space here to mention all of them, but a few became especially relevant to the settlement and history of Salt Lake City. The Mormons believed wholeheartedly in the divinity of Christ and considered Him the head of the church. They believed, in fact, that the Church of Jesus Christ of Latter-day Saints was actually the authorized restoration of the ancient Church of Christ. At the same time, they revered Joseph Smith as God's prophet and the only person on earth with the right to receive direct revelation for the edification and guidance of the Kingdom of God on earth (i.e., the church). The practical application of this belief was that Joseph Smith's successor, Brigham Young, was viewed with the same reverence, and thus faithful Mormons were not only willing but anxious to follow his direction—even if it meant pulling up stakes and moving to the isolation of the Great Salt Lake Valley. If the direction came from Brigham Young, then it was God's will, and this faith not only provided much of the impetus for the Mormon move west but also accounted for much of the success of Brigham Young's superb community planning and colonizing efforts after the Mormons arrived in Utah. This faith, coupled with the Mormon belief that they were actually building the Kingdom of God on earth, in preparation for the millennial rule of Christ, took on certain political overtones. The church became the dominating influence politically, economically, and socially in Utah, and it was this influence that contributed to continuing charges that the Mormons were somehow anti-American in their attitudes and loyalties.

Another religious practice that caused difficulty for the Mormons was plural marriage. Joseph Smith, who felt he must persuade the most trustworthy leading Mormons before he could open it up to the general membership of the church, taught the doctrine secretly. Joseph himself took several plural wives, and by the time the Saints arrived in Utah most top church leaders as well as other leading men had accepted and were living "the principle," as they called it. Not until 1852, however, did they announce the doctrine publicly.

Sometime before his death, Joseph Smith looked to the West as another place of refuge, and even began to plan the westward movement himself. He sought information on Oregon, California, and Texas, and even authorized an exploring party to scout out possible places for settlement. After Smith's death, Brigham Young and the Council of the Twelve took over church leadership, though the Council of Fifty, a nonecclesiastical, politically oriented group set up by Joseph Smith in 1843 and dominated by church leaders, actually did the major planning for the final western move. At first they continued to look at various alternatives, from Vancouver Island to Texas, and they even attempted to negotiate with the federal government for financial assistance. In 1845 both John C. Fremont's report of his 1843-1845 expedition and Landsford Hasting's *Emigrant Guide to Oregon and California* were published, and by December Mormon leaders were thoroughly digesting them. They also know of the earlier expeditions of Charles Wilkes and B.L.E. Bonneville, and several maps hung on the wall as they met in the Nauvoo Temple planning their western strategy. At least as early as January 1846, they had narrowed their search to the valleys along the western slopes of the Wasatch Mountains, and were planning an expedition that year to select the final site.

That expedition never went, though a group of Mormons left New York in February, bound for California by sea. Instead, the Mormons began the total evacuation of Nauvoo in February and the year 1846 found them in scattered camps across the plains of Iowa preparing for the big push the following year. The main body camped at Winter Quarters, near the present Council Bluffs, and in April 1847, a vanguard company of 143 men, three women, and two children finally led the massive migration to the Rocky Mountains.

As they approached the mountains, members of the vanguard company queried everyone they met about prospects for settlement. Moses Harris, an Oregonian returning to the United States, was pessimistic about any possibilities but thought Cache Valley, to the north, provided the best chance. Jim Bridger, on the other hand, was fairly enthusiastic about agricultural possibilities south of Salt Lake, in Utah Valley, and worried only that the early frost might kill corn. Miles Goodyear, who owned a trading post on the site of present-day Ogden, was even more encouraging though, as William Clayton reported, the pioneers suspected that he wanted them to build a road to his place and that he harbored selfish motives.

No one knows precisely when the decision was made to establish their first settlement at the present site of Salt Lake City, but at least by early July the pioneers were leaning strongly in that direction. They were particularly concerned with finding fertile soil and ready access to water for irrigation, and Salt Lake Valley, with streams running from various canyons, certainly provided that. As they caught their first glimpse of the valley most were delighted with what they saw, for, in fulfillment of the best they had been led to expect, it seemed to offer all they wanted in agricultural potential. "We could not refrain from a shout of joy ... the moment this grand and lovely scenery was within our view," wrote Orson Pratt. Wilford Woodruff, reflecting the deeply felt Mormon view that they were about to settle a God-given place of refuge, called it "the Land of Promise, held in reserve by the hand of God as a resting place for the Saints," and waxed idyllic as he wrote of the "wonder and admiration" with which they gazed upon "the most fertile valley spread out before us for about twenty-five miles in length and sixteen miles in width, clothed with a heavy garment of vegetation, and in the midst of which glistened the waters of the Great Salt Lake, with mountains all around towering to the skies, and streams, rivulets and creeks of pure water running through the beautiful valley." "If the land be as rich as it has the appearance of being," wrote William Clayton, "I have no fears but the Saints can live here and do well while we do right." It was with similar feelings that the ailing Brigham Young gazed for the first time into the valley on July 23 and, according to later reports, said to the small party with him, "This is the right place, drive on."

Most of those who gazed on Salt Lake Valley in 1847 had the same initial impression: fertile soil, good vegetation, a generally favorable climate, plenty of timber in the mountains, abundant water in the mountain streams, and a place that promised golden opportunity for agricultural success. There were exceptions, especially among those who were eager to press on to the coast of California, but for the most part the Mormon pioneers were optimistic—and correctly so—about the potential of the area chosen by their leader. Their success was such, however, that later generations grew up with a mythological impression that their forefathers had taken up the impossible task of taming an infertile, barren wilderness. As expressed by Utah historian Orson F. Whitney in 1892:

> Aside from its scenic splendor, which was indeed glorious, magnificent, there was little to invite and much to repel in the prospect presented to their view. A broad and barren plain hemmed in by mountains, blistering in the burning rays of the mid-summer sun. No waving fields, no swaying forests, no verdant meadows to refresh the weary eye, but on all sides a seemingly interminable waste of sagebrush bespangled with sunflowers—the paradise of the lizard, the cricket, and the rattlesnake....

> Silence and desolation reign. A silence unbroken, save by the cricket's
> ceaseless chirp, the roar of the mountain torrent, or the whir and twitter
> of the passing bird. A desolation of centuries, where earth seems heaven-
> forsaken.

Perhaps such writers were responding to certain environmental changes
that the pioneers themselves observed and participated in creating. Even
though the soil was well suited to their needs, the pioneers confronted
an arid climate and could not depend on rainfall to water their crops,
as they had in the East. They must put water on the land, and their
irrigation projects, that indeed required backbreaking, wearisome toil,
created the new environment needed for planting settlements as well as
crops. Secondly, they confronted a cold climate, and had been warned
that certain crops, including fruit trees, might not mature. While the
settlers could hardly take credit for taming the weather, within a few
years it was clear that corn, fruit, and other crops would mature, and
they gave God the credit for changing the climate as a reward for their
righteousness. Finally, their descendents who perpetuated the "barren
desert" myth may not have been aware of the "heavy garment of vegetation" observed by Wilford Woodruff and others, for within a few
years the rapidly increasing population and the heavy grazing herds of
livestock resulted in a third environmental change: destruction of the
natural vegetation. Lamented Orson Hyde in 1865:

> I find the longer we live in these valleys that the range is becoming more
> and more destitute of grass; the grass is not only eaten up by the great
> amount of stock that feeds upon it, but they tramp it out by the very
> roots; and where grass once grew luxuriantly, there is now nothing but
> the desert weed, and hardly a spear of grass is to be seen.

All this, together with a natural human tendency to glorify the pioneer
generation, resulted in a myth that would have surprised the early Mormon settlers. In their minds, they had found the fertile valley "which
God for us prepared," according to their favorite hymn, and they were
ready to subdue it.

By the time Brigham Young caught his first glimpse of the valley,
the settlement that became Salt Lake City was already begun. Two days
earlier an advance party, under the direction of Apostle Orson Pratt,
entered the valley and rode around some of its perimeter. The next day
they explored further, and on July 23 began plowing the hard, dry
ground. Already familiar with the concept of irrigation, they also began
to build a dam in City Creek, and by the time Brigham Young rode
into camp they had plowed several acres of land, planted corn and
potatoes, and were irrigating the newly planted land as well as flooding
other land in order to make it easier to plow.

Four days later, after more scouting, most generally agreed that this was, indeed, the best place for settlement and an official decision was made. Brigham called together the members of the Quorum of Twelve who were present, waved his hand over a spot between the two forks of City Creek, and designated a forty-acre spot for a new temple. (Later the size was reduced to ten acres, which became the standard size for city blocks in Salt Lake City and most Mormon communities in Utah.) From this center spot, the church leader declared, the city would be laid out perfectly square with ten-acre blocks, eight lots in each block, streets eight rods wide with twenty-foot sidewalks on each side, a house set twenty feet back on each lot, and four blocks set aside in the city for public purposes. The apostles agreed to all this by vote, and in the evening the entire company of pioneers met on the temple ground and unanimously approved the decision of their leaders. Significantly, the plan bore a resemblance to Joseph Smith's concept of the "City of Zion," promulgated a decade and a half before in Independence, Missouri. It also followed the grid pattern traditional with European urban planners.

Salt Lake City had been born. It was one of America's "instant cities," founded suddenly and by design in a spot carefully chosen for its potential ability to sustain thousands of emigrants who would shortly arrive. By the end of the year it was estimated that there were some seventeen hundred of them. And the infant city had an impressive name: Great Lake City of the Great Basin, North America. Its parents quickly shortened its name to Great Salt Lake City, and in 1868 the territorial legislature took away the "Great."

In at least two ways the founding of Salt Lake City was unique in the history of American urbanism. While most American cities were founded for economic reasons, and deliberately located where they would have access to the economic life of the region or nation about them, the Mormon city was founded primarily out of religious motives, and with the idea that it would provide its people with a high degree of splendid isolation from the machinations of the society they sought to escape. In addition, Mormon cooperative enterprise, under the direction of the church's governing councils, was out of the ordinary so far as its influence on early planning and growth was concerned. At the same time, Salt Lake City followed certain traditional patterns clearly seen in the growth of American settlement. In many, if not most, agricultural regions, towns were settled first and became bases from which farmers spread out to subdue the land. Salt Lake City was no exception, as Utah's rural areas were, by design, settled and developed largely as satellites to the central city. Smaller towns such as Provo,

Logan, and Fillmore, became regional centers, but Salt Lake City remained the major population center and continued to dominate the Wasatch Front economy. Equally important, the geographic location of the new settlement, like that of cities such as St. Louis, Chicago, and San Francisco, was a natural spot for external economic forces to combine with the industry of the settlers to make the city a success. Even though Mormon leaders initially envisioned effective social isolation, their city lay on a natural trade route that quickly put them in contact with travelers and merchants from other American cities, and their economy was never really independent of the rest of the nation. In its uniqueness, the history of Salt Lake City becomes an interesting study in community planning and cooperative enterprise; in its sameness it becomes a significant example of the growth of urban communities in the American West.

The Salt Lake Valley had much to commend it as the location of a permanent settlement. The Mormons envisioned themselves as setting up an inland agricultural empire, and the resources of the area were well suited. The soil on the eastern side of the valley was rich, loamy, and fertile, and a great variety of grasses attested to this even before the pioneers took their plows to the ground. Even though the climate was arid, so that traditional eastern farming methods could not apply, several small creeks poured from the canyons to provide water for irrigation. Game and fish seemed readily available. There were few trees in the valley, but nearby mountains contained timber enough for firewood and building needs.

This did not mean that creating a new civilization would be easy. In the minds of some Saints, the area was still a desert, for the treeless valley, the arid climate, and the hard, dry soil were all uninviting. Putting water on the land, getting timber for building and fuel from the mountains, finding forage for the cattle: all this and more was much more difficult than the kind of agricultural life any of them were used to. But the favorable geographic elements together with the faith and dogged determination of the Mormon settlers augured well for success.

They lost no time. On August 2 Apostle Orson Pratt began a survey of the city, and five days later church leaders began selecting their own lots. Brigham Young chose the block east of the temple site, as well as others farther south in the city. Other members of the Twelve each chose several lots in good, convenient locations, which they eventually distributed among their numerous families and friends. These church leaders were preparing to leave the valley as quickly as possible in order to return to the main body of Saints camped at Winter Quarters and other places along the Missouri. The rest of the lots were distributed the following year, after the pioneers began to move out of the original fort. Since the Great Basin was still a part of Mexico, no American land laws applied and, in fact, there would be no legal landholding in Salt Lake until the townsite charter of 1872. In the meantime, the Mormons attempted to promote their own idealistic, cooperative system as announced by Brigham Young on July 28. Each man would be given enough land to till, but only that much, and he would not be allowed to divide it up and sell part of it. "Each man must keep his lot whole, for the Lord has given it to us without price." After the initial selection of lots in 1847, people arriving during the summers of 1848 and 1849 were allowed to choose their land by lottery, and after that land was distributed by the bishops of the various ecclesiastical wards. In this way the pioneers used church organization and discipline for the purpose of promoting effective economic cooperation. Ideally, the Mormons looked at themselves as stewards over land that they did not own, but carefully surveyed and recorded each lot, and after county government was established they paid the county clerk $1.50 per lot (usually in labor or goods) for his work.

The first settlers had a bleak and difficult winter. They had settled in Indian country, and it seemed prudent to protect themselves against possible dangers by building a fort on one of the ten-acre lots. Appearing much like other western forts, its houses and other buildings were made of logs and adobe, but the flat roofs often leaked, making the winter and spring rather unpleasant for the occupants huddled inside. Late in the fall they built a grist mill on City Creek for grinding the wheat brought in by arriving immigrants. It was a relatively mild winter, but supplies ran out all too quickly. The pioneers shared as much as they could, but by spring many of them were living on anything remotely edible, such as rose hips, sego lily roots, thistle roots, and even wild animals and birds. Even if they killed one of their own animals for beef, it was of rather poor quality, for the cattle had reached the valley late in the season and had been worked hard in preparation for winter. The presence of wolves in the area, which killed some of their cattle, only added to the difficulties of the season.

Outside the fort the pioneers enclosed a large field for planting crops, particularly winter wheat, but as they looked forward to an early 1848 harvest, two disasters struck. A late spring frost injured much of the crop, then in May and June hordes of ugly, black, wingless crickets appeared in the fields and began to devour the rest. For some of the settlers this was the last discouraging straw, and they began making plans to move on to California. Others went out to fight the menace, but seemingly to no avail. Then, providentially, flocks of seagulls appeared, and at what seemed to be almost the last possible moment began to devour the crickets, fly away and disgorge them, and come back for more. At least enough was saved that the settlers could plan on surviving the following winter.

In 1848 the Mormon migration began anew, as the Saints camped along the Missouri River began moving across the Great Plains and pouring into Salt Lake Valley. By the end of the summer the population jumped to 5,000. At the same time, city building began in earnest as the settlers broke up the old fort, moved log structures to other locations, and took the adobe bricks to build new houses. Quickly the huge village with its uniform, ten-acre blocks began to take shape. At first each block contained eight lots, and houses were arranged on alternate sides of each block so that none of them faced each other. Each lot contained enough land for family crops, though the main farming was done in the big fields surveyed and enclosed outside the city.

Salt Lake City grew, then, as a planned community, intended to accommodate a population largely of a predetermined nature: that is, it would mostly be made up of devoted Mormons and thus followers of Brigham Young. Because of this, there was little opposition to the plan or to the method by which it was carried out—new immigrants took the lots they drew or were assigned willingly, and also took the direction of their leaders with respect to other community activities. But such cooperation was needed if Salt Lake City were to succeed in accommodating the thousands who would pour in and, at the same time, grow according to the plan.

The impressive achievement of Salt Lake's city planners is seen, in part, by a colorful description of the new community written by Calvin Taylor, a California-bound pioneer who passed through in August 1850. To quote part of his observations:

> The Great Salt Lake City is handsomely laid out—situated on the north side of the valley at the foot of a high bluff or bench of the Utah range of mountains, the ground falling gradually toward the river Jordan between one and two miles distant. The streets are of great breadth and cross each other at right angles, forming large squares which are cut at regular distances by streets of a smaller size, dividing the square into equal parts.... The city is not compactly built, being unlike all other cities in this respect. To each house is allowed one and a quarter acre of ground which is enclosed and sufficient to produce all the necessary garden vegetables in the greatest profusion, besides a considerable quantity of wheat and corn, quite adequate to the wants of each family. This arrangement of houses and lots gives to the city quite a pleasant and rural appearance, and might with propriety be called an agricultural city. The city is watered from the mountains by means of ditches which convey the water through every part of the city; each principle street having a

28

stream upon each side, from which are sluice ways to conduct the water into the gardens for irrigation and other purposes whenever required.

The houses are built of adobes or sundried bricks which are much larger than the ordinary brick, being 12 inches long, 6 inches wide, and 21 inches thick. They are of a lead color and have the appearance at a distance of being painted. There are no bricks burned here owing to the great scarcity of wood.... The houses are generally moderate sized and from one to one and a half storys high and built in modern style. There is a large public building called the State House now being finished [i.e., the Council House, located on the corner of South Temple and Main streets]. It is a square building two storys high. The first story is built of a reddish sandstone with sills and caps of the same material. The second story is built of adobes. It is altogether quite a respectable building and situated upon the corner of one of the principal streets. Besides there are several stores—a post and printing office, and mechanic shops of various kinds, and a large number of buildings now in the process of erection. Opposite the state house is the church, an immense building of a temporary character designed only for present use, it being the intention of the Mormons to build a magnificent temple far surpassing in splendor and magnitude the far famed temple of Nauvoo, of which no doubt they have the energy and ability to accomplish, judging from what they have already achieved during the short time which has elapsed since their arrival and settlement in this valley. [Burton J. Williams, ed., "Overland to California in 1850: The Journal of Calvin Taylor," *Utah Historical Quarterly* 38:328-29.]

Along with planting crops, digging irrigation ditches, building the fort, and taking care of numerous other immediate needs, one of the first orders of business in the new community was to establish some sort of government. On August 26, barely a month after their arrival in the Valley, Brigham Young and the apostles left to return to Winter Quarters. Brigham Young called John Smith, Joseph Smith's uncle, as president of the valley, to govern along with a high council of twelve men. The people accepted the plan at a church conference in October and thus the first governing body of Salt Lake City was actually also an arm of the church government. In practical terms, of course, this is the only way it could have been, at least for the first year.

The minutes of this early theo-democratic government provide fascinating insight into some aspects of life in the first year of Salt Lake City's history. John Smith was usually present, but when he was not someone else took over. The meetings were rather open, and on occasion, when the full High Council was not present, bystanders were drafted to take the place of the absentees. The meetings opened with prayer, and it was always clear that church considerations were paramount when it came to making long-range decisions. The council appointed committees to lay out farm lands, draft laws for the community, and perform

Groundbreaking Ceremony for the Salt Lake Temple, February 14, 1853. Courtesy, LDS Church Archives.

Salt Lake Temple Stone Quarry, Little Cottonwood Canyon. Courtesy, LDS Church Archives.

a myriad of other important tasks. It also assumed the authority to designate who could build roads and mills and who could take timber from the canyons. It decided what fees were to be paid for certain work such as building gates for the fort, and it levied and collected taxes for community purposes. Salt Lake City's first speeding ordinance was passed on July 8, 1848. By that time the fort consisted of three parts, and the council ruled "that no person shall ride or drive through the Forts or their lanes faster than a slow trot under a penalty of $1.00 for each offense."

The council also divided the fort into five ecclesiastical "wards," with a bishop presiding over each. Later, in February 1849, the whole city was divided into nineteen wards, and the bishops became the chief secular magistrates in each ward.

Personal controversies could be settled by the arbitration either of a bishop or the High Council. One wonders how often the bishops added a certain religious indignation to their judgements in the same way John Smith and the High Council sometimes did to theirs. On December 18, 1847, it was reported to the High Council that Albert Carrington's cow had been found dead, but no one could be found who knew how she died. After considerable discussion, "President Smith sealed a curse upon the person or persons who killed Carrington's cow, until they came forward and made restitution. The curse was sanctioned unanimously by the Council."

As might be expected, even under church government there was not complete harmony among the very human Saints, and considerable stress quickly became apparent. As early as October 7, 1847, John Young reported that at least three men, "not considered by himself and President John Smith to be of good faith," had gone northward with their families. Apparently the marshal was assigned to bring them back, for on October 11 he reported that the group had agreed to return, but only after some harsh remarks and the charge that they "did not like so much bondage." On December 26 the council discussed at length still more "disaffected spirits" and instructed the marshal to stop five people who were planning to go to California with Miles Goodyear. Parley Pratt and Henry Sherwood were sent to Goodyear to explain why their people could not leave. The marshal and three deputies found the dissidents leaving the valley, but had no difficulty persuading them to return. They presented themselves to President John Smith, however, and he finally permitted them to go with Goodyear. The Saints were concerned with order in the Kingdom, and leaving without permission during this first year seemed very much out of order. Exactly why is not clear, but it is significant that in July Brigham Young had rejected Samuel Brannan's plea for the Saints to move on to California where, near present-day San Francisco, Brannan believed they would become rich and powerful in no time. Perhaps church leaders were afraid that the lure of easy farming, warm climate, and possible wealth (even before the gold rush) would tempt even more settlers to leave and thus kill aborning their hopes for creating a mountain refuge. Perhaps, too, they were concerned that the "disaffected spirits" might perish in the winter weather or even be massacred by Indians, and they would hardly want to have a story such as that go out to oncoming immigrants.

There was also controversy between individual Saints. On November 6 Chauncy Turner brought charges against a man named Lawson for "killing a three year old heifer of mine, without my knowledge or consent, on Wednesday last." Turner still had the meat from the dead animal, but the council required Lawson to "restore three fold" and instructed the marshal, John Van Cott, to collect the debt and to see that the members of the council were paid for their services in the case. The heifer was appraised at $17.00, but when Van Cott went to take enough property from Lawson to pay three fold, Lawson flew into a rage and declared that "The Council might go to hell and be damned." A month later the case was still not settled, and only on December 16 did the marshal appear before the council to report that Lawson had given him $17.00 cash for Turner and had also given him a yoke of steers worth $34.00 for the payment of the council. The steers were traded for an ox, which was killed and divided among seventeen men: John Smith, his counselors, the High Council, the clerk, and the marshal.

Though this case took longer to settle than most, such disagreements were not uncommon and the council spent much of its time considering them. As in this case, the decision of the council was often very pragmatic, and the fines were used for practical purposes. On July 8, 1848, for example, the council fined David Wilkie $5.00 for illegally turning some water, assessed another $5.00 for "insulting the Council," and levied $1.50 against Tarlton Lewis. All three fines were applied to a fence then being erected by the community.

Church government continued in Salt Lake City until 1849 when an elected Legislative Council of Great Salt Lake City took over. Later that year, as Mormon leaders attempted to get their region admitted as a state in the United States, they wrote a constitution for the provisional "State of Deseret." The effort at statehood failed, and Utah was made a territory under the compromise of 1850, but for nearly two years Deseret operated as if it were a state and, among other things, passed an ordinance incorporating Salt Lake City. It called for a city council consisting of a mayor, four aldermen, and nine councilors. The council

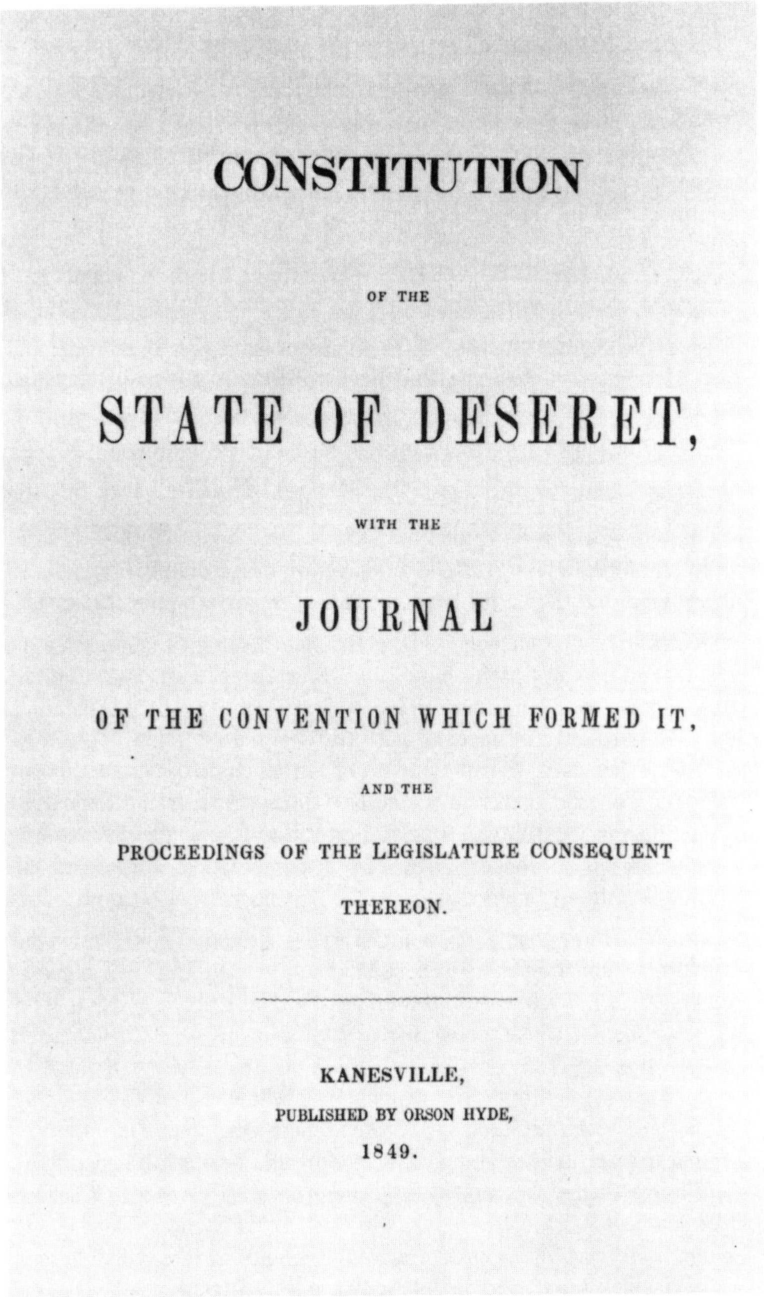

CONSTITUTION

OF THE

STATE OF DESERET,

WITH THE

JOURNAL

OF THE CONVENTION WHICH FORMED IT,

AND THE

PROCEEDINGS OF THE LEGISLATURE CONSEQUENT

THEREON.

KANESVILLE,

PUBLISHED BY ORSON HYDE,

1849.

Constitution of the State of Deseret. Courtesy, Brigham Young University.

itself held both executive and legislative responsibilities, and its members were also to act as justices of the peace. In 1851 the new legislature of the Territory of Utah incorporated this and other acts of the State of Deseret into territorial law, and in this way legal civil government came to Salt Lake City. It would be impossible totally to separate it from church interests, however, for the Mormon people soon elected their bishops, stake presidents, and other church leaders to be their civil officers also.

The new settlement's most urgent business was to provide for its own economic well-being. Under the direction of the council, by the spring of 1848 the Saints had over 5,000 acres of land in cultivation, and several irrigation ditches were under construction. As farming expanded and more ditches were needed, the bishops supervised not only the distribution of land but also the use of the water. There was no private ownership of water. Rather, each man was required to work on the development of the irrigation system as well as on its repair and upkeep, and he received a right to use the water in proportion to the work he put in. A similar system, under the direction of the county courts, was incorporated into law after Utah became a territory.

Meanwhile, in Kanesville, Iowa, Brigham Young was sustained as president of the Mormon church on December 27, 1847—an action ratified by the Saints in Great Salt Lake City in April 1848. On September 20, 1848, the church leader arrived back in the city, never again to leave Utah Territory. From that point on, in spite of any city, territorial or federal governmental power, the new "prophet, seer and revelator" was the leading and most influential citizen of Salt Lake City. So far as the Saints were concerned, his word was practically law, and his vision of the future molded what Salt Lake City was to become.

Born in Whittingham, Vermont, in 1801, Brigham Young received little formal education but had excellent practical training. Always industrious, he was in business for himself as a painter, glazier, and carpenter at age sixteen. He was converted to Mormonism in 1832, and soon went on a proselyting mission to Canada. He quickly found favor in the eyes of Joseph Smith, and eventually became one of the founding prophet's closest associates. In 1835 he became a member of the church's original quorum of twelve apostles, and in this leadership capacity he spent much of the next nine years doing missionary work and setting in order the affairs of the church in the United States, Canada, and England. He was on a mission in New England, in fact, when Joseph Smith was murdered, and quickly returned to Nauvoo to lead out in the debates over succession.

In Utah, Brigham Young became the first governor of the territory, as well as superintendent of Indian affairs. Recognized by historians as one of America's great colonizers, he directed the founding of over 350 communities within the boundaries of present-day Utah, Idaho, Wyoming, Colorado, Nevada, and Arizona. Not afraid of innovation, he was also a superb planner and administrator. He participated in the founding of two present-day universities as well as a now-defunct college, led out in the development of agriculture and business enterprise in Utah, and was constantly involved in reforming the church as well as defending it before the gentiles. He had a reputation for both tenderness and firm judgment, depending upon the circumstances, and his vigorous, unyielding defense of the church earned him, early on, the sobriquet "Lion of the Lord." At the same time, he had a good sense of humor, he obviously loved the Saints, and the affection they returned to him was genuine. Almost invariably they referred to him as "Brother Brigham" instead of using more formal titles such as President, Governor, or even Brother Young. He frequently visited outlying settlements, and on these trips often demonstrated his penchant for practical detail. Recalled C. R. Savage, a photographer who sometimes traveled with him, he carried "rawhide to mend the wagons, marbles for the children, and tobacco for the Indians."

As church leader, Brigham Young set the example so far as the peculiar doctrine of plural marriage was concerned: he married twenty-seven wives and fathered fifty-seven children. But such was not his most important legacy. Rather, as his biographer has demonstrated, that legacy was a combination of many things: the foundation for a durable, self-sufficient, egalitarian commonwealth of Saints; his nourishment of cooperative institutions; his infusing into Mormon doctrine the necessity of "working out one's salvation" by practical temporal labor; and his fundamental attitude that Mormonism was synonymous with truth—all truth, whether scientific, philosophical, theological, or doctrinal, must be part of it. As Brigham himself declared, Mormonism "embraces all truth in heaven or on earth, in the earth, under the earth, and in hell, if there be any truth there." It was Brigham Young, as much as anyone else, who incorporated into Mormon thinking the idea that the gospel "holds out every encouragement and inducement possible, for them to increase in knowledge and intelligence, in every branch of mechanism or in the arts and sciences, for all wisdom, and all the arts and sciences in the world are from God, and are designed for the good of His people." It was such teaching that encouraged Mormons to seek higher education and ultimately encouraged their strong support of higher education in Utah.

Brigham Young, President Church of Jesus Christ of Latter-day Saints and the great Mormon Colonizer. Courtesy, Utah State Historical Society.

At the same time, Brigham Young was no theologian, though he held strong opinions and often disagreed openly with the more systematic theology of Orson Pratt. He seemed to enjoy personal speculation, even on doctrinal matters, and sometimes advanced extremely innovative doctrines that never became official teachings of the church, in spite of his role as prophet.

The diversity of his contributions, moreover, is futher illustrated by the fact that while he was developing a foundation for egalitarian ideology, he was also laying the foundation for Utah's modern business community. He helped construct the Union Pacific and Central Pacific railroads, for example, and encouraged the development of many other capitalistic enterprises.

All this was part of a marvelous complexity of character that, as Leonard Arrington has observed, helps explain how he could function in so many different capacities and still retain the loyalty of the "wide variety of persons who made up the Mormon community." He was quick to judge, yet sensitive and warm-hearted; practical and also idealistic; logical and also, at times, mystical; romantic as well as pragmatic. His speculative mind once even led to the innovative suggestion that the Salt Lake Temple should be built with adobe brick instead of native stone for, he reasoned, everything was either "composing or decomposing" all the time and, since stone had reached its zenith it was now in the process of decomposing. Adobe, on the other hand, would continue to "compose," or harden, and stand long after the stone had gone. He quickly changed his mind, however, and it hurt no one's faith in him to see him indulge in such conjecture from time to time.

The people of Salt Lake Valley knew him as both a man and a prophet, and saw elements of both the human and the divine in his leadership. When it came to things that really mattered, they generally followed in the spirit of Herbery C. Kimball who said, in October 1852, "I have to do the work he tells me to do, and you hve to do the same, and he has to do the work told him by the great master potter in heaven and earth. If brother Brigham tells me to do a thing, it is the same as though the Lord told me to do it." As if to emphasize Kimball's words, at that same October conference Brigham Young called upon the people to vote on a particular way of controlling the canyons by allowing selected individuals to build and maintain toll roads into them. When the Saints voted his way unanimously, he then declared, "Let the judges in the county of Great Salt Lake take due notice, and govern themselves accordingly. The same thing I say to the judges of any of the other counties of the territory. Take notice, and govern yourselves accordingly.... Now this is my order for the judges to take due notice of; it does not come from the Governor, but from the President of the Church." As expected, his policy was adopted throughout the territory.

The first two years of Salt Lake City's history also saw the beginnings of certain industries. Mostly on a home level, the enterprises established then sometimes became the roots for larger businesses later on. Sometime before 1850, for example, Samuel Mulliner manufactured the first leather in the valley, and later he became one of the prominent tanners in the city. In 1849 a California gold seeker passing through Salt Lake City noted that such services as fixing wagon wheels and mending watches could be obtained here as cheaply, and with as much quality, as anywhere in the states. Grist mills, saw mills, a foundry, and every other enterprise needed for building a new community quickly sprang up; carpenters

The Eagle Emporium, founded by William Jennings, later merged with ZCMI. Visiting Indians in the foreground. Courtesy, LDS Church Archives.

and other tradesmen either sold or bartered their skills as new houses went up. In addition, the church itself promoted a number of public works projects, usually accomplished by able-bodied men donating "tithing labor" (one day in ten). These included a wall around the temple block, an adobe church office building, a public bathhouse at the nearby warm springs, and an armory. By 1850 Salt Lake City was a beehive of small industry as well as agriculture.

Though most business was conducted as private enterprise, Salt Lake City's early economy was not totally free from regulation. The council not only determined who could build the mills and the roads, but also began to set the prices millowners and other basic entrepreneurs could charge. Such an arrangement preserved the idea of private ownership, but at the same time provided the kind of community planning and regulation the Mormons considered necessary for success. But the early entrepreneurs probably had little to complain about for, on October 13, 1847, the council agreed in at least one case to "sustain whoever built the Mill in labor, good pay, and as much grain as the people could be persuaded to spare." It was this kind of economic cooperation, enforced by the authority of the council as well as the general willingness of the Saints to follow the direction of the council, that helped the infant city survive its first few years.

Ironically, the most important economic boon to Salt Lake City in these early years was the California gold rush. Its impact came in various ways. First, there were actually several Mormons in California in 1848. Some were members of the Mormon Battalion, who had marched from Fort Leavenworth, Kansas to California in 1846 as part of the Army of the West in the war with Mexico. They remained there to earn money before joining their friends and families in the Salt Lake Valley, and some were actually involved in the discovery of gold at Sutter's Mill in 1848. Other Mormons had sailed to California with Sam Brannan in 1846, while still others had left Salt Lake with the permission of the church after deciding they did not want to cast their economic lots in the Great Basin. But these good Saints could not escape the requirement that they pay their tithes and offerings, and two apostles, Charles C. Rich and Amasa Lyman, were sent to California to collect. Between 1848 and 1850 over $60,000 in gold coin and dust came into Utah from various California Mormons.

In the fall of 1849, curiously enough, church leaders even secretly authorized a few young Mormons to leave Utah and go to the gold fields. Understandably reluctant to let many people go, they nevertheless felt that if there was money to be gained, then someone should get it and bring it back for the benefit of the economy as a whole. The "gold missionaries" were sponsored by certain leading churchmen, and on their return were to share their wealth with their sponsors. Unfortunately, very little was realized from the curious venture, but at least after the missionaries returned in 1850 their failure could be seen as proof of the folly of chasing after wealth in California.

The gold rush had its most dramatic effect, however, in the way the Mormon settlements prospered from the gold-seekers of 1849 and 1850. Salt Lake City was on one of the best routes to California, and it is estimated that some fifteen thousand people went through each year. It was an economic windfall for the Saints. Fresh horses and mules normally sold for $25 to $30 each, but the hurried gold-seekers were willing to pay as much as $200 by the time they got to Salt Lake City. They also willingly paid extremely high prices for scarce vegetables, flour, and other goods. At the same time, there were certain things, such as surplus wagons and harnesses, that they were willing to sell to the Mormons at greatly reduced prices—often as much as fifty percent below the prices in eastern cities. Mormon blacksmiths, wagonsmiths, teamsters, millers, laundresses, and others with various skills found plenty of employment during the gold rush summers, and further east Mormons operated ferrys across the North Platte, Green, and Bear Rivers. To the Mormons who spurned the gold rush for the sake of their spiritual salvation, gold actually helped bring economic salvation. As Leonard Arrington has written, "the most important crop of 1849–1851 was harvested, not in the Salt Lake Valley, but at Sutter's Mill, near Coloma, California."

Another impact of the gold rush was to provide a circulating medium for Salt Lake City and the settlements fanning out from there. As early as December 1848, the church attempted to mint the gold dust brought in by members of the Mormon Battalion, but faulty equipment forced the abandonment of that effort in favor of a form of local paper currency. From September 1849, until early 1851, however, another church mint was in operation, which coined about $75,000 in gold pieces. But these coins developed a bad reputation, for it was discovered that through a mistake in determining weights, they were worth ten to fifteen percent less than face value. The church mint closed, and the supply of gold coming into the valley rapidly dwindled away, but at least for a time the local economy was boosted through the minting of California gold.

By 1850, then, Salt Lake City was already becoming integrated with the national economy. It was on the overland route to California, and would never really be isolated. Even though they thought ideally of economic independence and self-sufficiency, the settlers were clearly dependent upon the outside world for many goods and supplies. Almost from the beginning, gentile (i.e., non-Mormon) merchants found ready customers among the Mormons. In 1849 Livingston and Kinkead opened a store in a small adobe house and brought $20,000 worth of goods to the valley, and the following year another store was opened by the firm of Holladay and Warner. As early as the winter of 1849 the government established a post office at Salt Lake City, and the next year a four-year contract for carrying the mail was let to Samuel H. Woodson of Independence, Missouri. The resultant service was poor and irregular, but at least it was there as one more link between the Mormons and the people they had tried to get away from.

While all this was going on, the people of Salt Lake City tried not to ignore their own cultural development. The pioneers brought school books with them, and in the fall of 1847 Mary Jane Dilworth opened

Great Salt Lake City, 1851. Rendering from a daguerrotype. Courtesy, Utah State Historical Society.

the town's first school. The only place she could find to conduct it was an old military tent, set up within the walls of the fort. There was no furniture, but slabs and sections of logs seemed adequate under the circumstances. There was no paper for the students to write and draw on, but they made do with dry bark and fine, colored clay. Other schools followed, and in 1850 the newly incorporated "University of Deseret" began instruction at the secondary level.

In addition to all this, some Mormons seemed fond of going to meetings—religious and otherwise. Significantly, one of the first public constructions was a 20-by 40-foot "bowery" on the temple block, and there the pioneers of 1847 regularly heard exhortations from church leaders and held Sunday worship services. By winter another bowery was erected inside the old fort, where weekly church meetings and all other major public assemblies were held for nearly two years. One such assembly was the "harvest feast" of August 10, 1848. It was a sumptuous feast indeed, with beef, dairy products, grains, vegetables, and pastries all being served. Prayer, songs, speeches, music, and dancing were the order of the day, as the people reaffirmed their faith that indeed they were making the desert "blossom as the rose." The following year a larger bowery was constructed on the temple block.

By 1850 the square blocks and streets of Salt Lake City covered an area nearly four miles long and three miles wide, and it was growing rapidly. More than eleven thousand people had migrated to Utah, and though many were beginning to locate in other settlements, over half were still in the vicinity of Salt Lake City. According to the U.S. census, there were 6,157 people in Salt Lake County, including fifteen free blacks, and these were almost evenly divided between males and females. The youthful nature of the population is seen in the fact that fifty-six percent was under twenty years of age, and thirty-eight percent was between twenty and fifty. In general, the county was characterized by relatively young families, with 232 babies under one year and 2,760 children, or forty-five percent of the population, under fifteen.

Nearly every family had its garden plots and some general farming was done inside the city, but most agricultural activity took place outside its limits. The economies of the urban and rural areas complemented and served each other, and the impressive agricultural statistics of the valley provide an insight into the rapid growth of the pioneer economy. Ninety-two hundred acres of land were under cultivation, and during the year ending June 1 that land produced 58,500 bushels of wheat, 5,200 bushels of corn, 5,000 bushels of oats, 25,900 bushels of potatoes, 1,100 bushels of barley, various other grains and produce, 2,200 tons of hay, and even 70 pounds of tobacco. Pioneer life was not easy, but the economy was becoming viable and the founding fathers had every reason for optimism as they envisioned the future growth of their inland metropolis.

Frederick J. Piercy sketch of Salt Lake Valley, 1853. Courtesy, Utah State Historical Society.

—— 3 ——

The Mormon Commonwealth, 1850–1870

B righam Young had great plans for Salt Lake City, not just as an important metropolis in its own right, but also as the hub from which settlements would be planted throughout the Intermountain West. Mormon immigrants poured into Utah at the rate of thousands per year, and by 1869 over 80,000 people inhabited some 200 towns in the territory. Salt Lake City was vitally important to all these communities in at least three ways: (1) it was the gathering place from which exploration proceeded and from which pioneers were "called" to settle other places; (2) most of these settlements were planned and governed according to patterns already set in Salt Lake City; and (3) the city became the major religious, economic, and political nucleus for the region and in this way had a direct impact upon the well-being of every community within its orb. Probably no other American city has been so directly and immediately involved in the development of so many other communities.

The rapid influx of population was the result of effective organization of immigration by Mormon agents in both America and Europe. Through the church-sponsored Perpetual Emigrating Fund, well-organized pioneer companies, the handcart experiment, and church wagon trains assisted the immigrants in their westward trek until the arrival of the railroad in 1869. But taking care of the immigrants once they arrived in Salt Lake City was equally important, and here Mormon authorities were equally adept. Newcomers were greeted warmly, taken to a spot called Emigration Square, treated to good food, sometimes entertained by music and dancing and, through the good graces of the Salt Lake

City bishops, temporarily housed until they could make better arrangements or were assigned to settle someplace else. According to a report of the arrival of one group in 1864, the bishops had a "stirring time …enormous quantities of meat, pies, bread, potatoes, and other consumables having been 'taken up' through the wards and 'put down' with considerable gusto by the arrivals."

Often authorities held a "placement meeting" in which the immigrants and their families were assigned to various wards for the winter, and also were provided with work through a variety of community tasks. These might include painting, gardening, irrigation, or a variety of building projects. From 1850 to 1870 Daniel H. Wells served as Superintendent of Public Works, which was really a church appointment, and under his direction several projects provided both employment for needy immigrants and some important buildings for Salt Lake City. These included the Council House, the Social Hall, the Endowment House, a tithing store and storehouse, an arsenal, and even the early stages of the Salt Lake Temple. It was not long, however, before many new arrivals found themselves on the move again, as they heard their names read from the pulpit or in some other way discovered that they had been "called" by their leaders to one of the outlying settlements or to be among a company that would establish a new community somewhere in the ever-expanding Mormon commonwealth.

In 1860 there were 8,200 people in the city, and by 1870 the population had grown to 12,800. Some characteristics of the population suggest certain general Mormon influences. In 1870, over sixty-five percent

Residential Area in Southeast Salt Lake City from the top of City Hall, 1868. Courtesy, Utah State Historical Society.

was foreign born, mostly from the British Isles, reflecting the missionary and immigration patterns of the church. Nearly ninety percent of the American-born population came from the North, again demonstrating the northern origins and general missionary patterns of Mormonism.

There were also groups of non-English-speaking immigrants, particularly from Scandinavia, and in the 1860s the *Deseret News* catered to some of them by carrying material in both Welsh and Danish. By that time there were also some forty adult Jews in the city, who got along very well with the Mormons and, through the willing help of Brigham Young, obtained the use of a Mormon building for their worship services.

Employment patterns in Salt Lake County reflected the urbanizing tendency of the population. In 1850, 33.6 percent of the heads of households were farmers, but this dropped to 27 percent in 1860 and 16.1 percent in 1870. Small, though significant, increases came in the percent of professional workers (2.4 to 3.1 in two decades), merchants (1.1 to 2.7), clerks (1.4 to 3.9), and transportation workers (.9 to 3.1). In spite of the fact that Utah remained primarily rural and agricultural throughout the century, Salt Lake City became an urban oasis in the Great Basin.

Even though Salt Lake City was the central city for the territory, there was a chance, in the early 1850s, that it would lose its status as the territorial capital. In October 1851, Anson Call lead a group of thirty families to central Utah, where they founded the town of Fillmore in the county of Millard. Both were named in honor of U.S. President Millard Fillmore. Because of its central location, Fillmore was selected by the territorial legislature as the capital of Utah Territory, and in 1853 a statehouse was begun. The building was never completed, however, and only one legislative session was held there (1855–1856). It became clear that it was simply too far from the population center, and in 1856 Salt Lake City was renamed the capital city.

In January 1851, the newly incorporated city government began to function. Its first officers were appointed by Governor Brigham Young and the legislature to serve until superseded by the first regular election. That came in April, when practically all the appointees, including Mayor Jedediah M. Grant, were publicly elected. The city charter was revised from time to time, with a new charter granted by the territorial legislature in 1860 and revised in 1865. By 1860 the council had become relatively sophisticated, for it had twelve standing committees: municipal laws, ways and means, revision, finances, improvements, unfinished business, claims, elections, police, public works, public grounds, and licenses. The council referred petitions and general matters to the committees, who considered them and reported back their recommendations.

Jedediah M. Grant, First Mayor of Salt Lake City and Member of LDS Church First Presidency. Courtesy, Utah State Historical Society.

Mayor Jedediah M. Grant was one of the most colorful characters in Salt Lake City's history. The seventh of twelve children, he was born in trans-Applachian New York in 1816. He was converted to Mormonism in 1833 and from that time on his life was devoted to missonary work and preaching. It soon became clear that Grant had a flair for forcefulness, as symbolized by the title of his biography, *Mormon Thunder*. His lanky, six-foot frame, deep-set eyes, and square jaw seemed to add authority to his frequent, powerful harangues of both Saint and gentile. Before the death of Joseph Smith, his numerous church activities included presiding over the church in Philadelphia. Later, in October 1844, he became a General Authority of the church with his appointment to the First Council of the Seventy. In 1854 he was chosen as Brigham Young's second counselor in the presidency of the church. Almost from the time of his conversion, a close affinity developed between Grant and Young, and the two men saw eye to eye on many things—especially on the need, in Utah, to maintain the purity of the faith and to improve the faithfulness of the Saints. His impact on the Saints was characterized thusly by his biographer:

> In his mind, the Spirit of God and successful preaching were interconnected . . . . For Grant and many other Mormon leaders, this idea led to a measure of freewheeling exhortation that produced an assurance in preacher and listener alike that God himself sanctioned everything said. Even when on the spikes of a Grant tirade, most Saints therefore accepted his words and in surprising displays of humility emotionally promised to overcome their sins, most of which they were unaware before the second counselor mounted the stand for a fiery sermon.

> Preaching had even more significance in Mormonism than in other frontier religions because of the Saints' conception of their leaders as modern prophets after the Old Testament pattern. . . . Jedediah Grant bathed himself in this belief, making even his pronouncements as mayor of Salt Lake City shouts from Sinai, commandments to Israel from the mouthpiece of God.

It was a foregone conclusion that the interests of the church and the people representing its concerns would dominate city government. Mayor Grant was a General Authority of the church, and President Brigham Young himself attended the opening meeting of the city council. There he outlined many of its responsibilities. They must regulate markets, keep streets clear, and remove nuisances, he told the new city fathers. Then, after some instructions from Attorney General Daniel H. Wells (who replaced Grant in the presidency of the church in 1857 and who became the third mayor in 1866), the clerk read the rules of the city of Nauvoo, which had been prepared by Joseph Smith, as the definition of the dutes of this city council. As in many, if not most, American cities in the nineteenth century, Salt Lake City used party ballots rather than secret ballots, so church leaders, if they wished, could keep tabs on who voted for whom and what. More significantly, throughout the period a church-dominated caucus nominated candidates for public office, and little or no opposition arose to those so nominated. There were no political parties in the city for over twenty years. In effect, it was a one-party political system, but few seemed to mind.

Daniel H. Wells, Mayor of Salt Lake City (1866-1876). Courtesy, Utah State Historical Society.

Actually, the relationship between the church and city government was a very practical thing. One of the first things the new city council did was to divide the city into four political wards—which also became the ecclesiastical wards for the church. Very soon, however, there were nineteen ecclesiastical wards. The council frequently used the wards as convenient units for public activities, and ward bishops thus found themselves carrying out civic as well as ecclesiastical responsibilities.

Brigham Young maintained close surveillance over the city council—it affected, after all, how the very heart of Mormondom would be governed. He attended council meetings from time to time and felt perfectly at liberty in speaking his mind and even using his influence when he felt strongly about something. On June 21, 1867, several members of the council arrived at the meeting place but found no quorum in attendance. Normally under such circumstances they would simply disband and go home, but Brigham Young was also there and wanted to discuss the coming Independence Day celebration. There were people standing around (quite often there were citizen observers at the council meeting), so the governor simply suggested that they form themselves into a citizen's meeting, transact the necessary business, and leave it to the council to ratify the proceedings later. One of his most controversial interventions came during the election of 1868 when the voters elected a popular bishop as a write-in candidate, over the church president's own nominee. Brigham Young objected so strongly that the elected alderman declined the office and a holdover was continued. In one sense, city government was considered an arm of the church, for it had a special task to perform in creating a political setting conducive to the growth of the spiritual Kingdom. At the same time, observes historian Dale Morgan, "it was ridden with such a sense of civic conscience as probably will never be seen in [Salt Lake City] again." That civic conscience expressed itself regularly, as the council dealt with a myriad of plans and problems.

One problem was city finance. The city grew rapidly, but few immigrants had much money. Except for the gold brought in by the gold rush, and the coin minted by the church mint, there was a scarcity of specie, and much of the early economy operated on the basis of trade and barter. This meant, at least at first, that the city treasury had little cash to take care of such necessary items as road, city buildings, and office expense, and law enforcement. Until various businesses were established, they had a relatively thin tax base. Again, the interests and programs of the church went hand in hand with the needs of the city. Much of the early work that in other cities might be paid for through taxes was performed by immigrants and others in church-sponsored public works projects, or as "tithing labor."

The city needed a regular income, however, and in 1850 the council imposed a fifty percent tax on all "spiritous liquors." At the same time, recognizing the pressing needs of a pioneer economy, it exempted from "all and any assessment, or tax whatever," such things as iron, steel, castings, glass, nails, hardware, paint, oils, dyestuffs, all food items, medicines, boots, shoes, and leather. Eventually the city financed itself through property taxes, business licenses, fines, land sales, road taxes (particularly on businesses affected by the roads), liquor taxes, sales of liquor directly by the city, and other general city taxes. The council also allowed city scrip to circulate—evidently a form of deficit spending for services, accepted as legal tender for taxes and other debts owed the city.

As in every other city in America, many people complained about taxes, and some thought they were being dealt with unjustly. In 1858, for example, two city policemen complained to Brigham Young that the city had deducted $300 from their wages for county taxes. The church president appeared before the city council in their behalf, arguing that they were relying on the cash to feed their families, and that people should not be compelled to pay taxes when they did not have the means to do so. In 1859 the city merchants refused to pay the full amount of their taxes in cash. The taxes were really too high, they said, but they would pay part in cash for regular city purposes and the rest in "store pay" (i.e., scrip). The council finally decided that "store pay" would be acceptable for road taxes.

Law enforcement had the potential, at least for a while, of becoming one of the most difficult financial problems. In September 1858, as Johnston's Army and its huge retinue of hangers-on were beginning to make their influence felt, Brigham Young became concerned with growing lawlessness in the city. He took it upon himself to call the council together and propose an increase in the police force to two hundred men. The council immediately passed a bill to that effect, but then Mayor Abraham Smoot raised the natural question: how were they going to pay for such a force? There seemed to be no immediate solution, but the governor replied in typically blunt (though perhaps impractical) fashion that any lawbreaker apprehended should receive a heavy fine. The following month it was clear to the council that there was simply no money to pay the expanded police force but Brigham Young, again somewhat impractically, suggested the use of the road tax. Mayor Smoot kindly reminded him that this could not amount to over $1,200, while the police bill would come to $30,000. At the same time there was

Abraham O. Smoot, Mayor of Salt Lake City (1857-1866). Courtesy, Utah State Historical Society.

$5,000 worth of city scrip in circulation, and the council was seriously considering its devaluation. All Brigham Young could reply was that they should not devalue the scrip but nevertheless they should pay the police as fast as possible.

The city fathers paid regular attention to the kinds of rules needed to ensure peace and order, and in some cases their rules reflected the combination of rural-urban circumstances in the community. In 1854, for example, they prohibited anyone from riding or driving animals on the sidewalks, made offenders liable for damage done to sidewalks or foliage, and levied a five-dollar fine for each offense. In 1858, when Salt Lakers were worried about the impact of Johnston's Army on the life of the city, a policeman was murdered, and the *Deseret News* called for establishing a citizen's posse, if necessary, to reestablish order. While the posse was not established, the council continued to look hard at anything it thought would threaten peace and good order. One such threat was a request for the licensing of a "ten pin alley" (i.e., bowling alley), which the council rejected outright. Prostitution and gambling were also prohibited in the city, and the laws against them became especially pointed after the first army troops arrived.

In the late 1860s the people of Salt Lake City were convinced that serious crime and disorder was on the rise, and two murders in 1866 only seemed to verify the feeling. In April S. Newton Brassfield, a transient freighter, was killed by an unknown assailant after he had induced the plural wife of a Mormon missionary to forsake her husband and marry him. Salt Lakers would hardly be sympathetic with Brassfield, but his murder was nevertheless shocking. Then, in October, Dr. J. King Robinson was decoyed from his home under the pretext of the need for his services, and killed. Again the murderer disappeared. Robinson had been in conflict with the city fathers over property at Warm Springs, in the north part of the city, and many people began to blame the church for both murders. Brigham Young was indignant, and personally added money to the reward being offered for Robinson's killer. The *Deseret News,* meantime, prompted by the murder, lamented that the "class" of people who committed serious crimes was on the increase, and called for the police to step up their efforts to keep violence at a minimum. It also reported, on October 31, that the amount of reward money put up by church leaders and by the city had reached $9,000. Two years later the *News* observed even more violence, including a daring series of robberies. There was a time, it lamented, when citizens did not need to lock their doors and windows, but that time was past. More significantly, it even called upon the men of the city to teach their wives and daughters how use pistols.

54

One complicated issue was liquor control. While wine and other alcoholic beverages were not totally absent from Mormon tables, church leaders warned against their abuse and, in particular, inveighed strongly against drunkeness. At the same time, the sale of liquor was a possible source of city revenue, as seen in the heavy 1850 tax on all "spiritous liquors." In 1851, however, the city council made it illegal to sell or "otherwise dispose of" hard liquors in the city, although beer was permitted, but it appears that the law was not strictly enforced. The following year Councilman Jeter Clinton visited the city brewery and complained to the council that he had discovered swearing, drinking and gambling going on. The city marshal made a similar complaint, saying that the proprietor's attitude was bad and that his establishment was a nuisance. The proprietor, on the other hand, claimed that he was actually performing a public service: he was collecting $4,000 per year from the immigrants and this he spent among the people generally.

The city council soon began to grant licenses to certain establishments to sell liquor as well as beer. In 1852 the going price was fifty dollars per year, payable in advance. But the council also rejected several petitions for such licenses, and in 1853 actually closed the "Deseret House" for distributing liquor freely. In 1855, after considerable discussion on the propriety of an absolute ban on the sale of liquor, discretionary power was granted to the mayor to regulate it. The city fathers did not do away with liquor in the city, but, at least until around 1860, they prevented the spread of bars. In 1861 the French traveler, Jules Remey, noted that in Salt Lake City "no grog-shops or gaming houses are met with."

Interestingly enough, the city apparently decided that one way to deal with the liquor problem was to create a liquor monopoly for itself. The city began to operate a distillery, and when Brigham Young visited the council on June 7, 1863, the mayor told him that this was such a lucrative business that it brought in more revenue than city taxes. In 1866 the council passed an ordinance that absolutely forbade the private manufacture and sale of "any spiritous, vinous, or fermented liquors" within city limits, and also the keeping of gaming houses or brothels. Violators were subject to a fine of $100 or six months in prison, or both, and the city could confiscate and destroy any gaming equipment or liquor it found. The city itself retained, by law, the exclusive right to sell liquor, and provided that the proceeds went into the city treasury. The law still had loopholes, however, for the council continued to discuss petitions for liquor licenses, and in September 1866, had to issue a special order for the closing of the bar at the Salt Lake House. But other bars continued to operate in the city, though in May 1868, the *Deseret News* reported with some satisfaction that even though there had been three bars in town, one had moved to another city and a second had fallen into financial difficulty. "Our citizens enjoy the quiet and peaceful change," the paper quipped. That same month the city began negotiations with William Howard for the purchase of his distillery, at a cost of about $35,000.

Mayor Abraham Smoot's statement to Brigham Young that the distillery was a better source of city revenue than taxes was at least symbolically accurate in suggesting that in various ways liquor licensing and sales provided the bulk of the income for city government by the late 1860s. During the fiscal quarter December 1, 1865 through February 28, 1866, the city collected $20,715.72 in revenue. Of that amount $4,448.40 came from the liquor store, $2,688.77 from the Salt Lake Bar, $4,177.92 from the Billiard Saloon and $233.74 from the distillery. This amounted to well over half the total revenue. City taxes provided $4,144.45, and other licenses, fines, rents, and miscellaneous items provided the rest. To many people it would seem a strange irony indeed that something akin to "sin taxes" should be the mainstay for the government of the "City of the Saints."

The city fathers were absolutely determined to create a beautiful city—almost, it seemed, whether the citizens wanted it or not. They paid careful attention to planning and beautification, and their wide streets, with irrigation ditches running down either side, became a standard item for commentary from travelers. In general, the town was laid out in ten-acre blocks, with streets numbered in each direction from the temple block. East Temple street, which soon became the center of business activity, ran north and south past the east side of Temple Square. It was not long before people began calling it Main Street, and eventually that name stuck. The planners began an early program of planting linden, poplar, and other ornamental trees. Residents were urged to keep their yards clean and neat, and not only to plant vegetable gardens but also to decorate with flowers, shrubs and trees. In spite of the fact the Mormonism was becoming increasingly unpopular in the public press, journalists and other visitors were almost uniformally impressed with the appearance of the Mormon city. According to one traveler as early as 1850, it resembled "a large garden laid out in regular squares." The broad streets, wide sidewalks, and clean water running down both sides of Main Street were all to be observed and talked about by curious passers-by in the years to come.

Emphasis on beautification continued throughout the period . By 1864 several streets were graded and curbed, and several ditches paved. As early as January 1851, the Council appointed supervisors of shade trees. A year later it found that the citizens were lax in keeping their city clean, and had to require them by law to remove from the streets and sidewalks such things as wagons, lumber, wood, boxes, and fencing. It also prohibited them from placing cow yards, privies, and any other "filthy substance" in or near any city stream. By 1855, however, Mayor Grant was still not satisfied, so he donned both his ecclesiastical and his secular hats and issued, through the pages of the *Deseret News,* a thunderous denunciation of all who were not keeping their fences in repair, paying proper attention to their ditches and bridges, setting out shade trees and ornamentals, and keeping their sidewalks clear of trash and debris. If cow pens and pigsties were not kept twenty feet away from the street, and not cleaned every day, he warned, they would be removed forthwith at the expense of the owners. "This may make the drones and sluggards grunt and whine, and perhaps leave the hive; if so there will be more room for the industrious bees to store their honey."

The city tended to grow to the south and southwest, for the Jordon River blocked expansion to the west and the stockyards and sulphur springs discouraged growth to the north. There was expansion, however, onto the benchlands north of the Temple block, which necessitated some modification in the standard block pattern, as well as onto the benchlands to the east. This was a choice area, for culinary water was in ready supply. There a large spot of land was designated as the site for the University of Deseret, and in 1862 the United States government took advantage of the area with the establishment of Fort Douglas.

One interesting project, begun in 1853 but never completed, was the erection of a wall around the city. Partly to demonstrate to other cities the practicality of building such a protection against Indians, and partly as a public works project, the wall was twelve feet high, six feet thick at the bottom, and two and a half feet thick at the top. It was made of mud mixed with grasses, bushes, and "gravel when convenient." It rose rapidly in 1853 and 1854, with various wards providing the labor. "The 18th Ward is progressing rapidly with the city wall," reported the *Deseret News* on November 24, 1854. "What are the other wards [doing] . . . about this pleasant weather? Let spades answer." By 1860, however, the wall was beginning to deteriorate, and only portions of it remained standing in 1869.

At the same time, the city expanded its canal system in order to provide plenty of water for irrigation and culinary purposes, and this became one of the items most frequently commented on by visitors. "Through the city itself flows an unfailing stream of pure, sweet water, which," wrote Captain Howard Stansbury in 1850, "by an ingenious mode of irrigation, is made to traverse each side of every street, whence it is led into every garden spot, spreading life, verdure and beauty over what was heretofore a barren waste." Even *Harper's Weekly,* which, in 1858, published a vicious tirade against the Mormons, commented favorably on the well-thatched, comfortable adobe brick homes as well as the "admirable system of internal water-works. It is a miniature Venice. A stream, which originally flowed through the site covered by the city, has been diverted into a number of channels running through each street. Every resident thus has a never-failing supply of good water at his own door, and is enabled to raise trees and flowers; which, in that climate, could never be grown without this artificial irrigation." It was a city of "magnificent distances," observed Horace Greely in 1859 as he commented on the wide streets and huge city lots.

It also became, to some degree, a city of fine buildings. Many Mormons, including Brigham Young, brought with them a love for fine craftsmanship. Even though the first homes and public buildings were simple structures made from such easily obtained material as adobe, stones, and logs, it was not long before sawmills, kilns, and brickyards dotted the valley and the Mormons began to erect more commodious dwellings, a few luxurious homes, and several substantial, even elegant, public and church buildings. One of the first permanent public buildings was the Council House, located on the southwest corner of Main and South Temple and completed in 1849. Its two-story design with a shallow pitched, hipped roof, reflected architectural features from both the Georgian-Federalist and the Greek Revival styles. It seems to have provided at least part of the inspiration for City Hall, on First South near State Street, which was approved in 1852 but not completed and dedicated until 1866. These two buildings strongly influenced various county court houses throughout the territory. Other Greek Revival buildings included the Social Hall and the Endowment House, both erected in the 1850s. The latter was used for the most sacred Mormon religious ceremonies, awaiting completion of the Salt Lake Temple. Architect for City Hall was William H. Folsom, who had traveled widely in the United States studying architectural style and who also planned several other Salt Lake City buildings. These included the Seventies Hall of Science, the Salt Lake Theatre, the Gardo House and, along with Truman O. Angel, both the Salt Lake Tabernacle (where the Mormons began to hold most of their public meetings in 1867) and the world-famous Salt Lake Temple. The latter, begun in 1853 but not completed until 1893, was an elaborate example of the Gothic Revival style that also appeared in at least a few of Salt Lake City's noteworthy homes owned by some if its elites. One of these homes was Brigham Young's Lion House, designed by Truman O. Angel. Located on Brigham Young's block just east of Temple Square, this unique building contained several apartments and is said to have housed as many as twelve of his families at a time. Its many gables characterized its purpose, and a crouched lion mounted above the front entrance seemed to warn unwelcome curiosity seekers to stay away. Brigham Young also had his official residence, the Beehive House, constructed on this same block.

Another elegant home was the Devereaux House (named for the English estate where its second owner was born). Built in the French Second Empire style, it was designed by William Paul about 1857 and built for William Staines, though in 1867 it was enlarged for its subsequent owner, William Jennings. Noteworthy as Salt Lake City's first

Brigham Young's Estate, 1862. Courtesy, Utah State Historical Society.

Eagle Gate, 1892. Designed originally to mark the entrance to Brigham Young's Estate, it has ever since been a prominent landmark on State Street. It has been redesigned at least twice.

millionaire, Jennings was mayor from 1882 to 1885. He sometimes loaned his mansion to Brigham Young to entertain large groups or special guests. Such appearances of affluence may have been deceiving, however, for certainly no large portion of the population became wealthy.

These early years were also characterized by efforts to regulate the sale of building materials. In December 1851, for instance, the *Deseret News* declared in a column entitled "To The Saints" that "the buying or selling, borrowing or lending, swapping or exchanging of building materials, such as lumber, stone, adobies, timber, glass, nails, paints, &C, without the consent of the superintendent of public works, is not right, and cannot be permitted." Such building material, still relatively scarce, had to be controlled, it seemed, for the benefit of the community, and at that point the community would not stand either for personal profiteering or private decisions that affected the economy of the whole.

This is not to imply that all private enterprise was discouraged—only that in the beginning Mormon leaders felt the need to control economic planning and development in the interest of the church. Very quickly, however, the market system found its roots in the city, as Mormons and gentiles alike nurtured their personal trades and interests. The church continued to urge the development of specific kinds of enterprise, particularly agriculture and local manufacturing (or, as it was called, "home manufacturing").

In an effort to make the whole region self-sufficient, Brigham Young and the church leaders followed a merchantilist policy. They promoted the manufacture of almost everything needed, even including sugar and silk. The Deseret Agricultural and Manufacturing Society, incorporated by the legislature in 1856, led out in attempting to educate the people in the production of a variety of commodities, and even established an experimental garden in Salt Lake City in 1861. Mormon enterprise in the valley was, ideally, a kind of mixed enterprise—based on private ownership and responsibility but planned and regulated to the degree thought necessary to promote the interests of the community. At the same time, the church opposed certain activities, especially mining for precious metals. Brigham Young apparently believed that a search for gold in Utah might too easily divert the Saints from the immediate needs of the Kingdom to the quest for quick wealth. All this helped set the direction of economic activity in the region until non-Mormon influences led to the development of mining as well as church-sponsored cooperative merchandising.

Salt Lake City's commercial activity was, like other towns in Utah, at first largely a barter economy. In spite of the church mint established

Deseret Store and Tithing Office ca. 1868. Currently the site of Hotel Utah. Courtesy, LDS Church Archives.

in 1849 and the flow of gold from California for the next year or so, there was not enough specie to provide an effective circulating medium, at least for a while. Besides, agriculture was still the principal occupation in Utah; this plus the church's system of tithing in kind created a peculiar institution that became an early center of commerce in Salt Lake City and actually dominated many smaller communities for years to come. This was the tithing house, where faithful Saints brought a portion of all their production in produce and livestock as an offering to the church. The tithing house in each community became a trading center, as Saints could barter surplus goods for things they needed, deposit extra goods (i.e., beyond the requirements of their tithing) for scrip that could be exchanged for merchandise or credit. Located in Salt Lake City, the General Tithing Office of the church became a place for gathering and redistributing certain goods from throughout the territory.

It was not long, however, before other forms of merchandising began to appear in Utah's capital city. The irony of Salt Lake City's economic growth and stability was the fact that it came about, in spite of the Mormon emphasis on local self-sufficiency, only with the partial but significant help of the rest of the nation.

Utah, with Salt Lake City as its economic heart and showplace, was really a community within a community. Certainly a distinctive Mormon way of life held sway, as did Mormon political control and economic planning. But the larger American community from which Mormonism sprang still surrounded it, and would not be denied influence. The beginning of that influence was not slow in coming, as gentile freighters and merchants saw just as much value in the Mormon dollar as that of anyone else. Though the Mormon pioneers brought many goods with them in their immigrant companies, regular freighting of goods from the states was left largely to the non-Mormon entrepreneurs who plied the western trade. From at least 1849 on, when the St. Louis firm of Livingston and Kinkead opened a store, these enterprising merchants appeared regularly in Salt Lake City. The following year Holladay and Warner opened a store, as did two Mormon brothers, John and Enoch Reese. Such firms eventually produced fortunes for themselves, for they brought to Salt Lake City goods the Mormons either could not produce as cheaply or could not produce at all.

It was not only the Mormon dollar the merchants were after. Ironically, Salt Lake City, where the Mormons hoped to find relative isolation, was actually located where it would become a major stopping place for California-bound travelers. It was the only major city between the Mississippi and the West Coast, and naturally attracted those who sought to make a profit not only from the settlers but from all the business conducted along the overland trail to California. By 1854 at least twenty-two merchants were doing business in the city that was later dubbed by its boosters "The Crossroads of the West."

The amount brought in from the states was huge. In 1855 Livingston and Kinkead advertized in the *Deseret News* that on August 15 it had a train of forty-six wagons arriving "loaded with a very full and general assortment of new goods." They brought such diverse items as tea, coffee, rice, sugar, tobacco, soap, candles, seasonings of all sorts, hats, shoes, clothes, nails, shot, sheet and bar iron, tin, stoves, and liquor. At the same time all the smaller merchants provided, in the aggregate, even more goods than the few large dealers, and one writer has indicated that during this same year the hauling of merchandise to Utah employed 304 wagons and 3,210 oxen.

Prices were high, for the cost of overland freighting was high (about seventeen and a half cents a pound in 1855), and it was not unusual for western merchants to take a hundred percent markup on many items. But Utahns were willing to pay, for they simply never produced enough either of the necessities or the luxuries to become economically independent. Brigham Young was not happy with the high cost of doing business with gentiles, and in 1857 he established the Brigham Young Express and Carrying Company (popularly known as the YX Company) in the hope that it would receive the overland mail contract, provide a means for immigrants to come to Utah more cheaply, and provide much less expensive consumer goods. In less than a year, however, the company failed, and eventually the firm of Russell, Majors and Wadell dominated much of the Salt Lake freighting, as it did for other western areas.

The same was true with mail service—it was dominated by the same major firms that contracted for other western mail. By June 1858, John Hockaday had a contract to provide a weekly mail service from the Missouri River to Salt Lake City, and George Chorpening had a similar contract between Salt Lake City and California. Utah was becoming part of the national economy as freight lines, mail lines, passenger lines, and, in 1861, the telegraph, linked its economy and communication with the very people its pioneers had tried to escape. The coming of the railroad in 1869 completed at least this phase of the binding process. Main Street became the center of commerce, and Sir Richard Burton's description of the way it looked to him in 1860 leaves one with the impression of a very robust economic community. To quote from his book, *The City of the Saints:*

> Main Street is rapidly becoming crowded. The western block, opposite the hotel, contains about twenty houses of irregular shape and size. The buildings are intended to supply the principal wants of a far-western

Main Street Looking South, Late 1860s. Courtesy, Utah State Historical Society.

Sketch of the Salt Lake Valley looking West from the Illustrated London News, *1858. Courtesy, Utah State Historical Society.*

settlement, as bakery, butchery, and blacksmithery, hardware and crockery, paint and whip warehouse, a 'fashionable tailor' . . , shoe stores, tannery and curriery; the Pantechnicon, on a more pretentious style than its neighbours, kept by Mr. Gilbert Clements, Irishman and orator; dry goods, groceries, liquors, and furniture shops, Walker's agency, and a kind of restaurant for ice-cream . . . ; saddlers, dealers in 'food, flour, and provisions', hats, shoes, clothing, sash laths, shingles, timber, copper, tin, crockery ware, carpenter's tools, and mouse-traps; a watchmaker and repairer, a gunsmith, locksmith, and armourer, soap and candle maker, nail maker, and vendors of 'Yankee notions'.

On the eastern side, where the same articles are sold on a larger scale, live the principle Gentile merchants, Mr. Gilbert and Mr. Nixon, an English saint; Mr. R. Gill, a 'physiological barber'; Mr. Godbe's 'apothecary and drug stores'; Goddard's confectionery; Messrs. Hockaday and Burr, general dealers, who sell everything from a bag of potatoes to a yard of gold lace; and various establishments, Mormon and others. Crossing the street that runs east and west, we pass on the right hand a small block, occupied by Messrs. Dyer & Co. suttlers to a regiment in Arizona, and next to it the stores of Messrs. Hooper and Cronyn, with an ambrotype and daguerrean room behind. The stores, I may remark, are far superior, in all points, to the shops in an English country town that is not a regular watering place. Beyond this lies the adobe house, with its wooden Ionic stoop or piazza (the portico is a favourite here), and well-timbered garden, occupied by Bishop Hunter; and adjoining it the long tenement inhabited by the several relics of Mayor Jedediah M. Grant. Further still, and facing the Prophets' Block, is the larger adobe house belonging to Gen. Wells and his family. Opposite, or on the western side, is the well-known store of Livingston, Bell, and Co., and beyond it the establishment, now belonging to the nine widows and the son of the murdered apostle Parley P. Pratt. Still looking west-wards, the Globe bakery and restaurant, and a shaving saloon, lead to the 'Mountaineer Office', a conspicuous building, forty-five feet square, two storied, on a foundation of cut stone stuccoed red to resemble sandstone, and provided with a small green-balconied belvidere. The cost was $20,000. It was formerly the Council House, and was used for church purposes. When purchased by the Territory the Public Library was established in the northern part; the office of the 'Deseret News' on the first story, and that of the 'Mountaineer' on the ground floor.

If the entrepreneurs of the larger American community thus influenced the economy of Salt Lake City, certain political developments helped weave the expanding web of economic dependency even tighter. One was the so-called "Utah War." This bloodless conflict began when certain federal officials, particularly Judge W. W. Drummond of the territorial supreme court, wrote letters to American president James Buchanan accusing the Mormons of a variety of un-American and illegal activities. Eventually Buchanan became convinced that the Mormons bore watching, and that Brigham Young must be replaced as governor of the Territory of Utah. The president should have investigated the charges more thoroughly but instead, and without notifying Governor Young, he sent an army of 2,500 men to occupy the territory and assist the new governor, Alfred Cumming of Georgia, in establishing control.

While Brigham Young may have known earlier, he announced the approach of the army on July 24, 1857, while attending a celebration in Big Cottonwood Canyon commemorating the tenth anniversary of the arrival of the Mormons in the Salt Lake Valley. Angered, and without reliable information as to the purpose of the Utah Expedition, Young considered the approaching army a hostile force and declared martial law in Utah. In a comic-opera series of events, Mormon guerrillas harrassed and delayed the oncoming troops until they were forced to spend the winter of 1857-1858 in the bitter cold of the partially destroyed Fort Bridger, Wyoming.

Early in February, however, Thomas L. Kane, a longtime and influential friend of the Mormons, arrived in Salt Lake City as an emissary from the president. He persuaded Governor Young to allow the new governor to enter the city and be officially installed.

The Mormons also agreed later that the army could enter Utah peacefully the following year, but only if it would not stop in Salt Lake City. This had a direct and dramatic effect on the city. Still distrustful of the army, the Saints held to a decision made in March that all the residents of Utah's northern settlements, including Salt Lake City, would move south, where they would be out of the way in case of treachery and where they could prepare themselves, if necessary, for a prolonged season of conflict. In April and May they went, leaving behind only enough men to tend the crops and set fire to the straw-filled homes if the army should stop. As if expecting the worst, and showing their total disdain for those whom they considered invaders, the Mormons hid all the stone already cut for the Salt Lake Temple, and covered the partially completed foundation so that the building site appeared to be nothing more than a plowed field. They carried with them grain, machinery, equipment, and all the church records. On June 26 the army passed through an almost totally deserted Salt Lake City, and the only Mormons remaining were ready to set torch to it if the troops should stop. That night the army camped on the banks of the Jordon River, west of the city, and not long after that established a permanent post, Camp Floyd, in Cedar Valley thirty miles to the southwest. In July the saints returned to Salt Lake City, with Brigham Young leading the way.

The army, commanded by General Albert Sidney Johnston, remained at Camp Floyd until, in 1861, it was recalled because of the American Civil War. But its economic and social impact on Salt Lake City provided a taste of the growing bittersweet influence of outside forces. On the negative side, so far as the Mormons were concerned, were the so-called "blessings" of civilization introduced by the soldiers and camp followers who could hardly stay away from Salt Lake City. Prostitution flourished in the City of the Saints as women of the streets plied their trade. In addition, liquor flowed more freely than ever before, and Main Street was soon nicknamed "Whiskey Street."

Economically, however, the occupation proved a windfall for the Mormon economy, and hence the economy of Salt Lake City. The troops paid hard money for whatever trade goods and agricultural items the Mormons could supply. Further, in a process similar to the impact of the 1849 gold rush, the sale of surplus army property provided many things at very reasonable, even bargain, prices to the Mormons—especially in 1861 when the evacuation of the troops led to what has been called the largest government surplus sale held in America up to that point. Nearly two-fifths of all the property, including iron, tools, equipment, livestock, and food, was purchased in the name of Brigham Young and turned over to Salt Lake City's Department of Public Works. William Clayton probably reflected the attitude of many people when, in a letter written in July 1861, he reported the end of "the great Buchanan Utah Expedition, costing the Government millions, and accomplishing nothing, except making many of the Saints comparatively rich, and improving the circumstances of most of the people of Utah."

Not all church leaders agreed, however, that this economic windfall was such a boon. Some were still attempting to promote home industry, and saw the army windfall as another step toward undermining their independence. Complained Apostle George A. Smith in a sermon six years later: "I have heard men say, 'What a blessing it was to the people of Utah when that army came, it made them so rich.' How did it make us rich? You got their old iron, and that put a stop to the manufacture of iron here; you got the rags they brought here to sell, and that put a stop to our home manufactures; hence I do not think that, financially, our condition was much improved. . . as it turned out it educated us into the idea that we must buy what we needed from abroad."

The impact of the Utah War on Salt Lake City was real, but the impact of the Civil War was more visible and long-lasting. After Johnston's Army left, Utahns hoped for no more "occupation" troops, and they were delighted when, in 1862, they received a commission from President Abraham Lincoln to guard the overland mail and telegraph line along the southern Wyoming route. Their service was short-lived, however, for in October Colonel Patrick Edward Connor arrived in Salt Lake City at the head of 750 troops of the Third California Volunteers and this military detachment took over the guard duty. The Mormons were dismayed, for again their loyalty as well as their ability seemed cast in doubt, and it appeared that the troops were there not only to guard the mail route but also to keep an eye on them. Connor seemed to confirm this suspicion when, instead of taking his troops south as Johnston had done, he built a military post, Camp Douglas, on the east bench of Salt Lake City where he could overlook the heartland of Mormonism.

As more troops arrived, the impact of this new military force was not unlike that of Johnston's Army. Social conflict with the Mormons was inevitable, and Mormon leaders were dismayed when any of their followers seemed to associate too readily with this intrusive element that seemed to threaten their values and life style. Economically, trade with the military helped stimulate Salt Lake City's economy, as it had done previously. It has been estimated that contracts for supplying food, clothing, and fuel came to $150,000 annually, much of which went to Mormon contractors. Edward Tullidge, one of the city's early publishers and the first to write a history of the city, observed that Mormon entrepreneurs, in particular, prospered from such trade when, in 1864, the firm of Hooper and Eldridge brought in goods costing in the East over $150,000 plus $80,000 freight, and William Jennings bought for his business a train of goods worth $250,000,.including freight. The following year he purchased a half million dollars worth of goods in the East, which cost another $250,000 to haul. Other Mormon firms also prospered, as did such non-Mormon firms as Walker Brothers and Auerbachs. The latter came to Salt Lake City in 1864 after Frederick Auerbach, who, along with his brothers, had previously operated stores in California and Nevada mining towns, obtained Brigham Young's help in securing property for a new venture on Main Street. Several other new outlets also appeared on Main Street, such as William Jennings's stone structure (transformed from one to three stories in the 1880s) known as Eagle Emporium, Walker Brothers new store, an imposing building erected by W. S. Godbe, and a store built by the Woodmansee brothers.

Equally important in the long run were Connor's plans to upset Mormon political hegemony by introducing a new element into the economy: mining. At Camp Douglas he published a newspaper, the *Union Vedette*, that not only criticized Mormon society but also promoted mining in Utah, much to the consternation of Brigham Young. Connor's troops were encouraged to prospect for precious metals, particularly in the Oquirrh Mountains west of the Salt Lake Valley. The *Deseret News*, on the other hand, did all it could to dispel rumors that gold was in the hills. Both gold and silver were discovered, however, and in 1864 a mild mining boom began. Connor dreamed of a new gold rush to Utah that would bring in enough gentiles to counteract Mormon influence at the ballot box. The dream was unrealistic, but at least the "Father of Utah Mining," as he has been called, changed the course of Utah's economy. Mining not only increased the money supply, thus stimulating trade, but it also contributed to the establishment of the first bonafide banks in Salt Lake City, most of which were dominated by non-Mormons. The first banks were established by freighting and merchandising firms, to serve the mining companies in the area, and in 1866 the Miners' National Bank of Salt Lake City was founded, under a federal charter. Connor's plan to destroy the political influence of the Mormons through mining did not succeed, but at least it strengthened the economic influence of the gentiles and, in the long run, contributed to the apostasy of a number of influential Mormons who disagreed with Brigham Young's continued and dogged opposition to mining development.

There were other economic influences at work that, in combination with those already mentioned, would soon cause the Mormons to attempt to reassert control over the economy of Salt Lake City and the rest of Utah. Mines were opening in nearby Idaho, Montana, and Nevada, and Utah traders enthusiastically began to mine the miners by selling Utah foodstuffs to them at the fabulously high prices they were willing to pay. Church leaders feared the possibility that the rapid export of food would create dangerous shortages in Utah at the very time they were bringing in more and more immigrants. In addition, national greenbacks were circulating in Utah, and their fluctuating values were highly unsettling in the agricultural market. Complained the *Deseret News* on July 13, 1864, the greenbacks had begun "to seriously effect [sic.] the equilibrium of trade in Utah, and prices are jostled from the staid scale of years past into a fitful up and down, constantly changing, very high and ever higher rate, to keep even pace, if possible, with the value of 'greenbacks' as quoted in Wall Street."

One answer to these problems was price control, and Salt Lake City became the center for a new round of economic regulation in the later 1860s. As early as 1862 church leaders met with Salt Lake City bishops and proposed that all trade with Camp Douglas and "outside" merchants be conducted through specially appointed committees. The bishops approved and so did their congregations. In this case minimum prices were set, and farmers from throughout the territory channeled their goods through the General Tithing Office in Salt Lake City. It appears that local prices were raised sufficiently at least to discourage some of the precious foodstuffs from being exported to the mines. Then, in 1864, church leaders called for a price convention to meet in Salt Lake City on August 8. Some 120 delegates from throughout the territory met there, and the Presiding Bishop of the Church was elected president. The convention set uniform prices on a long list of foodstuffs with flour, the most important item, priced at $12.00 per hundred: twice its usual price. Even freighting costs were controlled. The results, as viewed by the Mormons, were satisfactory, for they established prices at what they believed to be reasonable levels, prevented the depletion of surpluses, and actually stimulated more production. In April and October 1865, and April 1866 similar price conventions were held in Salt Lake City, in connection with the general conferences of the church. In 1866, however, church leaders changed tactics and promoted the organization of the Utah Produce Company, a joint-stock company supervised by the First Presidency of the church but supported by the private investment of prominent Mormon businessmen and merchants. Effective price control was nearing its end, however, and the Utah Produce Company quickly disappeared as the transcontinental railroad entered Utah in 1868-1869.

These experiments in economic regulation may have been satisfactory to most Mormons, but certain non-Mormon businessmen began to feel, and with some reason, that church policy might well hurt them. Brigham Young constantly maintained that he had nothing against gentile merchants who were fair and honest, and, indeed, he had even helped some of them get established in Salt Lake City. But he also believed that many of them intended to hurt the Mormons, and were taking advantage of them dishonestly. Connor's activites in instituting mining in Utah, anti-Mormon legislation passed by Congress in 1862, and continuing criticism of Mormon social and political customs (particularly polygamy) from gentiles in Utah all fed his distrust of those outside the Mormon faith. This, together with Brigham Young's concern that the Mormons become self-sufficient and learn to trade with each other as much as possible, led to a boycott of gentile merchants in Salt Lake City in 1865 and 1866. The mercants were irate, and on December 20, 1866, several of them joined together in addressing a letter to the church leader criticizing him for his continuing advice to the Saints that they not frequent non-Mormon establishments. At the same time, the merchants offered to leave the territory if the Mormons would pay all outstanding accounts and buy out all the goods they had on hand plus all their homes and property at cash value, less twenty-five percent. President Young sent a stinging reply, for he saw through what he believed to be simply another scheme to get rich at the expense of the Saints. "If you could make such sales as you propose," he scolded, "you would make more money than any merchants have ever done in this country, and we, as merchants, would like to find purchasers upon the same basis." Besides, he told them again, they might go or stay as they pleased. The Mormons were not opposed to them because they were non-Mormon; they were only opposed to those who acted dishonestly and were "avowed enemies of this community."

Out of all this came, at last, a more permanent and workable plan for Mormon economic cooperation against the gentiles. In the General Conference of October 1868, a new boycott was announced. This was quickly followed by the organization of Zion's Cooperative Mercantile Institution (ZCMI), a producer's cooperative. Again, what happened in Salt Lake City affected all the other Mormon settlements in the territory. ZCMI was a joint-stock company, controlled by the church, and the stock sold widely throughout Utah. Prominent Mormon entrepreneurs, however, were among its major initial investors: William Jennings subscribed $200,000, the firm of Eldridge and Clawson put in $75,000, N. S. Ransohoff & Co. subscribed another $75,000, and Henry W. Lawrence put in $30,000. According to plan, it became the parent company for a chain of hundreds of other stores, many of them formerly privately-owned by Mormon merchants, who cooperatively purchased goods through it and allowed it to maintain control over their prices. Obviously such purchasing power gave it a great advantage in the market, and with the renewed boycott against the gentiles (not fully successful but, at least, effective) ZCMI became an almost overnight financial success. Its parent store became a permanent fixture in Salt Lake City—rivaling or exceeding its most prominent gentile competitors.

In spite of these efforts, the larger American community gradually imposed itself upon and influenced the Mormon economic community in Salt Lake City. The final turning point in the path toward nearly complete economic integration was the coming of the transcontinental railroad. In this case church leaders and the city fathers did not resist but, in fact, welcomed the railroad as a boon to the economy as well as to the other interests of the Kingdom. For one thing, as the Union Pacific and Central Pacific approached Utah territory from opposite directions, Brigham Young was able to get construction contracts from both companies for building the line within the territory. "This contract is viewed by the brethren of understanding as a God-send," wrote the Mormon leader to the church's emigration agent in Liverpool. "There is much indebtedness among the people, and the territory is drained of money, but labor here and coming we have in large amount, and the contract affords the opportunity for turning that labor into money." Brigham Young was able to put hundreds of Mormons to work in 1868 and 1869 and, as in so many other cases, ecclesiastical wards organized the work forces. Even though collecting payments from the Union Pacific ran into serious complications, the railroad became one of those outside influences that was a boon to the Mormon community even before it was completed. Its later benefits were even more imporant, for they included such things as a drastic reduction in the speed and cost of immigration, a boost to permanent employment possibilities, and vastly improved trade opportunities, both within and outside the territory, especially when feeder lines were built both north and south from Ogden and Salt Lake City. It also stimulated coal mining and many other businesses in Utah.

In order for the railroad to serve Salt Lake City and the Mormons best, however, Brigham Young had some defininte ideas about what should happen to it. With the Union Pacific coming down Weber Canyon, he believed that the east-west junction should be at Ogden, where the line could then turn south, go through Salt Lake City, and head for California via the southern tip of the Great Salt Lake. In order to entice the two railroad companies to Ogden, church leaders gave them an offer they could hardly refuse. They persuaded certain landowners to sell them approximately 133 acres of land at $50 per acre, or, in some cases, to donate land, provided it was used for railroad purposes. This land, all in one block on the west side of Ogden, was then offered as a gift to both the Union Pacific and Central Pacific, with the proviso that they locate their depots and shops on it. The amazed company officials grabbed the offer with relish. This resulted in the rise of Ogden as the railroad capital of the region, and the rapid decline of the gentile community of Corinne, northwest of Ogden, which had hoped to play that role.

The more important concern of the Mormon leaders, however, was that the railroad pass through Salt Lake City, and they did everything within their power to bring that about, including mass meetings, petitions to Congress, and pressure on railroad officials. Both companies, however, determined by independent investigation that the northern route around the Salt Lake was best. The only thing left for Salt Lake City was for a separate line to be built from Ogden, and Brigham Young ultimately saw the wisdom of cooperating with the Union Pacific in this.

It was an important day for Utah when, on May 10, 1869, the rails were joined at Promontory Summit. But it was a more important day for the citizens of Salt Lake City when, on January 10, 1870, the last spike was driven on that part of the Utah Central Railroad that connected them with Ogden and, through the transcontinental, to the rest of the world. The Utah Central was wholly owned by local investors—mostly prominent Mormons from Salt Lake City. Approximately 15,000 people turned out for the ceremony, Brigham Young drove the last spike, and both spike and hammer bore the inscription "Holiness to the Lord." Symbolically, this represented the significance of 1869-1870 as a turning point in Salt Lake City's history. The Mormons could still speak proudly of the economic independence and self-reliance that had allowed them to build the Utah Central, but at the same time they were tying themselves to the rest of the nation in the belief that the economic benefits would be mutually advantageous. It was not long before freight and passenger depots as well as other facilities were in place and at least two trains a day were puffing their way between Utah's two largest cities.

The railroad brought potential problems as well as ultimate benefits for both Salt Lake City and the Mormons as it brought the last vestiges of their isolation to an immediate and irreversible end. The economic benefits were clear, and the impact on immigration was profound. With respect to other interests of the Kingdom, however, Mormon leaders had some fears. The coming of the railroad was inevitable, and, in a way, their welcoming it with open arms was a kind of defense mechanism against possible problems. They were concerned with the rapid influx of gentile workers, whose different life styles, they feared, could undermine the conservative ideals of the Mormon community. Brigham Young's monopoly on the construction contracts, however, largely took care of this. But it did not prevent the railroad from helping to attract more gentiles to Utah, from contributing to the promotion of mining for precious metals, and from lowering the costs of imported manufactured goods, thus actually undermining the effort to promote home industry. Because of the railroad, Salt Lake City would not only have better contact with the world beyond, but also become more dependent on it. Even the spiritual values of the Great Basin Kingdom would seem threatened by the widening worldly contacts symbolized by the puffing iron horse.

Salt Lake City saw a number of newspapers appear in this period. The *Deseret News* was first issued in June 1850, and became the nearest thing to an official church organ. It printed items of both local and national import, published church-related announcements, and editorialized in behalf of the church on all issues that concerned Mormon leaders. Originally published bimonthly, it became a weekly paper in 1853 and a daily in 1867.

Beginning in the late 1850s, Kirk Anderson began to publish the *Valley Tan* at Camp Floyd, and his paper became the first local challenge to the *News* as well as the first Utah press to comment critically on the social and religious practice of the Mormons. But the *News* chose to ignore the *Tan*, and the upstart Camp Floyd paper lasted only eighteen months. The anti-Mormonism of the *Tan*, however, actually fostered the founding of a second Salt Lake City paper, the *Mountaineer*. Not a church-owned paper, the *Mountaineer* nevertheless spoke out defensively while the *News* remained silent on the *Tan's* specific anti-Mormon challenges. The next city paper was the *Union Vedette*. Published by Charles H. Hempstead at Camp Douglas, it became Utah's first daily. It, too, editorialized against Mormon policy, and again the *News* was disdainfully silent—practically ignoring it. The obvious pro-Mormon foil to the *Vedette*, however, was T.B.H. Stenhouse's *Salt Lake Telegraph*. After the *Vedette* expired in 1867 the *Daily Reporter* started up, was printed on the same press, took the same attitude, and was ignored by the *News* in the same manner. Other short-lived experiments in publishing included the *Peep O'Day*, an erstwhile literary magazine published by E. L. T. Harrison and Edward Tullidge, and the *Utah Magazine*, founded by the same two men with the backing of a prosperous Mormon merchant, William S. Godbe. The latter was replaced in 1870 by the *Mormon Tribune*, which changed its name to the *Salt Lake Tribune* the following year and became an avowedly anti-Mormon rival to the church-owned *Deseret News*. Again the *News* practically ignored its rival, but, on June 5, 1870, Mormon publishers inaugurated the Salt Lake City *Herald*. Later the *News* itself became more outspoken, and in the pages of these papers the modern reader can trace all the major concerns of the Mormons as well as the rapidly growing opposition to Mormon domination.

The social and cultural life of Salt Lake City, like everything else, was influenced heavily by the church but also affected by outside forces. Some of it was peculiar to Mormonism, while much of what Salt Lakers did reflected their desire also to import and make their own whatever was "of good report or praiseworthy" from the rest of the world.

In general, life in Salt Lake City centered around the family, and here the Mormon women dominated. Not so different from the way it was in other American communities, the mother was usually responsible for whatever education—both secular and religious—the youngsters received at home. While her husband clerked, labored, farmed, hauled wood, or provided a livelihood in other ways, the mother cooked, made and mended clothes, did all the household chores, beautified the house and yards, tended the garden, and taught her children how to help her. A few husbands may have exercised a kind of patriarchal despotism, and in one instance Brigham Young complained of "scores of men in this congregation who have driven their children from them by using the iron rod." But there is also evidence that many, if not most, fathers were no more authoritarian than others in America, and often less so. "Do not be so stern and rigid in your family government as to render yourselves an object of fear and dread," Apostle Orson Pratt warned parents in 1854. ". . . Mercy and love should be the great moving principle interweaving itself in all your family administration."

But there were also differences between some Mormon homes and those in other parts of the nation. For one thing, Mormon families seemed to have more children—as many as thirteen were not uncommon. For another thing, women sometimes played a more prominent role in family leadership. A few fathers were absent for long periods of time, serving on proselyting missions for periods varying from several months to three, even four, years. Others were absent because they were visiting additional families. As discussed below, some men had more than one wife, and this complicated the family pattern in certain peculiar but most interesting ways.

At the same time, the life of a woman in Salt Lake City was not always tied to the traditional duties of hearth and home. Many women played important roles in the community, especially in this early period, as school teachers, midwives, telegraph operators, and employees in various business enterprises. Midwives were even "called" and "set apart" (i.e., given special priesthood blessings in connection with their "callings"). Later Brigham Young recognized the need for more professional training and encouraged Mormon women to study medicine in eastern universities. Many did so, including some with families, and by the end of the century Salt Lake City and other parts of Utah benefited from several female medical doctors. In 1869, moreover, just two decades after the founding of the city, Brigham Young was delighted with the fact that the University of Deseret offered classes that could prepare girls to be "bookkeepers, accountants, clerks, cashiers, tellers, payers, telegraphic operators, reporters, and fill other branches of employment suited to their sex." It was not long before a number of women were running their own stores and co-ops.

Some women were especially visible as leaders in the community. One was Eliza R. Snow, who was variously called "poetess, prophetess, priestess, and presidentess" by those who knew and revered her. Well educated, highly literate, intellectually curious, and a prolific writer, she ultimately published nine volumes of poetry and other writings as well as many other separate pieces. Though her poetry is not considered great by modern standards—critics found it maudlin and superficial—it helped endear her to the people of Utah and is still important for, as her modern biographer has commented, it tells, "better than do many prose accounts, the history of a faith in the building and a nation in the making. In her verses can be found the whole sweep of the Mormon story." One of her hymns, "O My Father," expresses some of Mormonism's most imporant theological concepts and is still a favorite among the Saints.

But Eliza was significant far beyond her poetry. Baptized into the Mormon church in 1835, she moved to Kirtland, Ohio, lived in the home of Joseph and Emma Smith, and ran a school for sixty-five children. Totally devoted to every aspect of the Mormon gospel, she became one of Joseph Smith's polygamous wives in 1842. After Joseph's death, she married Brigham Young, also as a plural wife. Already she was one of the leading intellectual and administrative leaders among Mormon women, having served as secretary of the highly important Women's Relief Society while Emma Smith was its president. She was also a spiritual leader among the women, serving as recorder in the Nauvoo temple and conducting the sacred temple ordinances for the women both in Nauvoo and in the Endowment House in Salt Lake City. Because of this involvement, she was even called High Priestess, and she often pronounced blessings upon the women that went far beyond the scope of the temple ceremonies themselves. In Salt Lake City she was sought after to bless the sick, even annointing them with consecrated oil—a practice now reserved to male priesthood holders in the church. When other women began to conduct similar ministrations it was Eliza who taught the proper procedures and determined the qualifications for those who could perform them. This practice, as Maureen Ursenbach Beecher has observed, "promoted by Eliza R. Snow, following the approval of

Eliza R. Snow, Early Utah Women's Leader and President of the LDS Church's Relief Society. Courtesy, Brigham Young University.

Joseph Smith, continued well into this century, and perpetuated the name of Eliza R. Snow as a priestess to the women of the church."

In 1855 Brigham Young called upon Eliza to help revitalize the Relief Society organization in various Salt Lake City ecclesiastical wards. In 1866 she was instructed to set up relief societies throughout the church, and in 1867 she became president of the church-wide Relief Society organization. Hence the title Presidentess was unofficially attached to her name. Though a supporter of the male priesthood leadership of the church, she was also a highly independent spirit and quickly "learned to circumvent the snags with which bureaucracy can trip the meeker souls among us." In 1870 she was also assigned to lead out in forming Retrenchment associations—a reform movement concerned with improving the practical, economic, and cultural skills and interests of the young women. Though not an innovator, she has been characterized as "a paragon of administrative skill and a dynamo of executive energy." She led in setting up the Children's Primary Association, became a leading nineteenth-century Mormon feminist and supporter of women's suffrage, and was responsible for the success of the *Women's Exponent*, a Mormon feminist publication. She was also an avid defender of polygamy, and when a mass meeting of five to six thousand women was held in Salt Lake City in January, 1870 to protest proposed federal anti-polygamy legislation, Eliza gave one of the most stirring arguments of the day in favor of Mormondom's most peculiar institution. She saw it not as servitude or vassalage, but as a divinely ordained partnership. In the long run, she probably had more influence on the cultural tone of Salt Lake City than any other person of her time.

To most Americans, the wholehearted acceptance of polygamy by Eliza and other women of her abilities seemed incongruous. Images of male dictatorship and female bondage spread readily through a reform-minded American public, and in 1856 the Republican party platform even linked it to Southern slavery by calling for the elimination of the "twin relics of barbarism," slavery and polygamy. Introduced into Mormon doctrine by Joseph Smith, it was considered part of the latter-day restoration of all aspects of the ancient gospel. It found scriptural support particularly in the Old Testament and in modern Mormon revelation. Joseph Smith, however, practiced it secretly, and taught it only to his closest associates in Nauvoo. It was not announced publicly until Orson Pratt was assigned that task at a special conference in Salt Lake City in August 1852. At that same conference a corps of missionaries was called to go out to the world not only to preach the traditional Mormon gospel but to defend polygamy as well. From that time on, along with church political and economic control in Utah Territory, this practice became the basis for renewed anti-Mormon activities nationwide and a major stumbling block in Utah's quest for statehood.

All the General Authorities of the Church, as well as most bishops, were polygamists—it was necessary, after all, that the leaders set the example of what was considered fundamental church doctrine and sacred principle. Most leading church families, therefore, consisted of more than one household. In some cases the wives lived in separate houses, while in others they lived under the same roof—often with surprising ease. Most other Mormons accepted the idea in principle, although only about 25 percent of the married men had more than one wife, and the overwhelming majority of these, 66.3 percent, took only one extra wife. Only a few, such as Brigham Young, married numerous wives, but it was on the basis of imagined widespread abuses in such relationships that much of the anti-Mormon propaganda spread throughout a curious and gullible nation.

There is abundant evidence that many plural marriages worked well—especially when the two wives were sisters, cousins, or good friends, as frequently happened. Children often grew up to revere their mother's "sister wife" as a close aunt, and there is evidence that young women raised in polygamous households were much more willing—even, in some cases, eager—than their mothers were to accept that marriage system for themselves. Further, being a plural wife was sometimes an advantage so far as status in the community was concerned, for it meant association with some of the most influential people. Religiously, it was considered an essential step toward the highest degree of eternal exaltation, and this even resulted in some first wives actively encouraging reluctant husbands to take new partners. For most women, it appears, acceptance of "the principle" was considered a virtuous and honorable act, and one that could give them a sense of pride and importance within the community.

This is not to say, however, that plural marriage did not produce problems. One was economic, for most polygamists were not highly affluent and their wives and children were called upon to produce a substantial part of their own livelihood. This became especially true in the 1880s, when husbands often fled the territory or went in hiding on the "Mormon underground" in order to avoid federal prosecution and prison terms. But even without such prosecution, some husbands were so preoccupied with church and other duties that they hardly had time for one family, let alone several. Polygamy could also lead to certain emotional problems, as young plural wives found that they did not share the fullness of their husbands' affections. In spite of whatever valiant efforts both the husband and the first wife made to treat a new wife equally, the mere existence of another wife introduced a whole new source of strain into the marriage relationship. Romantic love was not necessarily the prime reason for most plural marriages, and this made a difference right from the beginning. In addition, the second wife often found it necessary to treat the first with at least some degree of deference—and in some cases that deference was demanded. The first wife, on the other hand, was suddenly faced with the reality that her relationship with her husband was no longer exclusive, and such an adjustment was not always easy. Jealously was not uncommon, though it sometimes found an outlet not in rages or arguments but in competition between wives in the various household arts.

The measurement of "success" in this, or any other, form of marriage is nebulous, but at least one sociologist has tried. Kimball Young, in his important though somewhat impressionistic study curiously entitled *Isn't One Wife Enough?*, concluded that 53 percent of the plural marriages were highly or reasonably successful, 25 percent were in the moderate to doubtful category, and 23 percent were clearly unsuccessful. A more recent study has looked at divorce rates among polygamists. A full record of such divorces will probably never be uncovered, but at least the study has demonstrated that official attitudes toward divorce in this period were quite lenient, and that many plural marriages were rather unstable. Brigham Young himself had at least one divorce, and during his presidency he granted 1,645 others. The evidence suggests that most, if not all, of these certificates of divorce were issued to polygamists, and in one unusual case a man was divorced from three wives on the same day and a fourth within five weeks. Such problems, nevertheless, had negligible impact on the Mormons' commitment to a system they believed divinely inspired, and the small number of people who practiced polygamy in Salt Lake City were significant beyond their numbers.

Beyond the family, the most important social and cultural unit was the Mormon ward. The people of the several wards looked to their bishops to lead in everything, including the establishment of schools and the supervision of all public affairs within ward boundaries. Though Sunday preaching services were held in the bowery and, later, in the tabernacle, the bishops also held worship services in their wards and they preached to the people on everything from their spiritual salvation to the problems of irrigation. Bishops were responsible for the temporal salvation of their flocks, which meant collecting tithes and taking care of the poor. An indication of their success is seen in the Salt Lake City thirteenth ward in 1857, where over half the family heads paid a full ten percent tithing, and another third paid at least a part tithing. This varied from ward to ward, however, and the thirteenth ward had one of the best records in the city. The bishops also collected contributions to the missionary fund, building funds, the Perpetual Emigration Fund, the Women's Relief Society, and even road and school taxes levied by the city. On the first Thursday afternoon of each month, ward members were asked to fast and, in the afternoon, attend a "fast meeting" where they would bear testimony and also donate fast offerings for the poor. Usually, especially in the early years, the tithes and offerings were paid in kind. As all this might suggest, for many citizens of Salt Lake City the church, with the bishop as its symbol, dominated—even consumed—almost every facet of their lives.

Also imporant in the lives of many Salt Lakers were various social and cultural developments—some sponsored by the church and others coming about independently. Church leaders, for example, promoted a number of cultural and intellectual societies, all designed to stimulate appreciation for the arts, literature, science, and the life of the mind in general. As early as 1850 and 1851 the citizens were being treated to lectures on astronomy and phonography (i.e., shorthand).

A number of interesting but short-lived societies sprang up in the year 1855. The Universal Scientific Society, with Apostle Wilford Woodruff as president, included history and religion in its discussions and attracted many of the town's most prominent citizens. The Deseret Theological Association, which met in the Seventies Hall, organized itself under the assumption that the "Science of Theology embraces a knowledge of all intelligence," and considered a wide range of subjects. The Horticultural Society promoted knowledge of agriculture, and later evolved into the Deseret Agricultural and Manufacturing Society.

That same year Apostle Lorenzo Snow organized the Polysophical Society—one of the most famous of all these pioneer groups. As its name implied, the society attempted to cultivate a taste for all kinds of literature and sponsored lectures on a wide variety of subjects. For many, each meeting of the society was a spiritual experience, and it became so popular that it had to move from Lorenzo Snow's home to the Seventies Hall, and later to the Social Hall. Even then it continued to grow until the meetings were divided and, under the auspices of a managing committee, were soon held throughout the city in various ward and school houses. Some of the society's most illustrious members, such as Eliza R. Snow, produced original essays, poetry, and other literary productions for these meetings, and within a year the society seemed to promise a renaissance of literary appreciation among the citizens of Salt Lake City.

Unfortunately, in 1856 the Polysophical Society fell victim to the excesses of a zealous reform movement known in history as the "Mormon Reformation." Dismayed by what he perceived as worldiness taking root among the Saints, the fiery Jedediah M. Grant (still mayor of the city and a member of the church's First Presidency) began stumping the territory with all the enthusiasm of the most colorful hellfire and damnation revivalists. Calling the Saints to repentance, enjoining them to forsake the evils of the world, he and other reformation preachers created a sensation and caused many Saints to take stock of themselves and seek renewal through rebaptism and a recommitment to forsake the ways of the world.

On Sunday, September 20, Grant and other authorities were at the Bowery in Salt Lake City. Thundered the great preacher of the reformation: "If the arrows of the Almighty ought to be thrown at you we want to do it, and make you feel and realize that we mean you." And throw the arrows he did, with deadly aim. Some among them, he said, "get drunk and wallow in the mire and filth, and yet they call themselves Saints, and seem to glory in their conduct . . . . They are the old hardened sinners, and are almost—if not altogether—past improvement, and are full of hell, and my prayer is that God's indignation may rest upon them, and that He will curse them from the crown of their heads to the soles of their feet . . . . I am speaking to you in the name of Israel's God, and you need to be baptized and washed clean from your sins, from your backslidings, from your apostasies, from your filthiness, from your lying, from your swearing, from your lusts, and from everything that is evil before the god of Israel." These and stronger statements caused many a Saint to tremble, and Salt Lakers by the hundreds searched their souls for sin but also felt the spirit of rejuvination once they followed Grant's advice and dedicated themselves to reform. But the Polysophical Society also came under his scrutiny, and it failed to pass muster. Never an intellectual in spirit, and undoubtedly suspicious of anything that seemed to distract the Saints from paying constant attention to what he considered the essentials of spiritual salvation, Grant called the society "a stink in his nostrils," and, much to the dismay of its supporters, it was finally merged with the Deseret Theological Class.

Aside from whatever intellectual stimulation came from such societies, Salt Lakers were also treated to a variety of public lectures, particularly under the auspices of the Seventies Quorum. Beginning in the early 1850s, when a committee was selected to choose lyceum speakers for each Wednesday evening, they heard local as well as visiting orators expound on such diverse topics as Bible history, the history of France, education, physiology, astronomy, photography, and home manufacturing. Sometimes the addresses were published in full in the *Deseret News*.

Formal education was also important to the citizens of Utah and Salt Lake City, though economics and other constraints made it difficult for a time to establish an effective system of public schools. The earliest schools were conducted either as private enterprises or under the auspices of the Mormon wards. In 1850 a series of common schools began in Salt Lake City, and plans were being laid for building schoolhouses in every ward. Also that year a "parent school" was established, designed to qualify those who would teach in ward and district schools. Orson Spencer and W. W. Phelps were in charge, and Orson Pratt taught subjects such as astronomy and mathematics. When the third term began in the fall of 1851 there were nearly 100 people in attendance, paying five dollars each (half in advance) for the training.

In 1851 the territorial legislature passed the first public school law, and the following year Great Salt Lake County was divided into thirty-two school districts. Since the school districts generally corresponded to ward boundaries, the bishops in each district were responsible for conducting elections for trustees. Teachers were poorly and irregularly paid, however, and often had to take their pay in produce. Such poor conditions led many of the most competent teachers to continue their own private schools, such as three schools announced in 1852. S. M. Blair began a German class. Eli B. Kelsey began a school in "Governor Young's school room" that included all the common subjects related to reading, writing, and arithmetic as well as philosophy and chemistry. Both day and night classes were held, but evening school students were each required to furnish their own lights. Orson Pratt also announced an evening school, costing $15 per quarter, where he would teach science and mathematics. Such private instruction was announced frequently in Salt Lake City, and other teachers included Orson Hyde, who taught grammar classes, and Zerubbabel Snow, who taught arithmetic, grammar, and geography.

In 1860 Richard Burton commended the efforts of the Mormons at education. He was especially impressed with some of their learned men and the numerous languages that could be learned, but he was not impressed with the general quality of education when compared with what he had seen in Paris and London. Recognizing the need to train the young men in the practical skills of farming and mechanics, he nevertheless chided Salt Lakers for their apparent attempt to "rear a swarm of healthy working bees. The social hive has as yet no room for drones, bookworms, and gentlemen." There was no difficulty, however, he said in obtaining a "mediocrity of knowledge between learning and ignorance."

There were also attempts at higher education, and as early as 1850 the legislature chartered the University of Deseret, forerunner of the University of Utah. Efforts to establish a permanent program were abortive, however, until regular classes began in 1867 and a systematic college curriculum was established in 1869 under the leadership of John R. Park.

The life of the mind was enhanced by a small public library, originally funded by the United States Congress. It appropriated five thousand dollars for a building in 1851, and fifteen hundred for the first books, which were obtained by John M. Bernhisel and arrived in February 1852. By 1860 the library contained about a thousand volumes, and the librarian opened it every Thursday for loaning out books. Reference works, travel books, popular histories, and novels made up the bulk of the collection.

Salt Lake City did not ignore the arts, and particularly the theatre. In 1850 the Deseret Dramatic Association, originally called the Musical and Dramatic Association, was formed. The association put on several plays a year and Brigham Young was one of its greatest advocates. "The people must have amusement as well as religion," he reportedly declared. The association's activities declined during the Utah War but, after the dedication of the magnificent Salt Lake Theatre in 1862, it flourished again and produced many of the prominent plays that were popular throughout the country. The actors came largely from local talent, though often visiting national stars were also there to perform. In 1864, for example, George Pauncefort of London became the first to produce *Hamlet* and *Macbeth* in Salt Lake City, and the citizens seemed to enjoy them both. In 1868 an eastern critic even compared the Salt Lake Theatre favorably with the stage in New York, San Francisco, and London (or so the *Deseret News* reported). After the coming of the railroad in 1869, the Deseret Dramatic Association again declined as more professional stars and traveling troupes found their way to Salt Lake City.

Music and dancing were also important, and such societies as the Deseret Literary and Musical Association and the Deseret Philharmonic Society, both founded in the 1850s, did much to promote concerts and other musical performances. William Pitt's brass band gave concerts regularly in the early days, and eventually a number of instrumental groups as well as choirs began to entertain the citizens of Salt Lake City. In 1861, for example, a Quadrille Band, under the leadership of William Clayton, conducted a ball at the Social Hall and the music received high praise in the *Deseret News*. When Richard Burton visited

Salt Lake City in 1860 he was deeply impressed with the love its citizens showed for dancing. "The Prophet dances, the Apostles dance, the Bishops dance," he wrote. "A professor of this branch of the fine arts would thrive in Zion." He observed, however, that some affairs were fairly expensive, and therefore select in their attendance, for tickets to balls at the Social Hall cost ten dollars for each gentlemen with a lady, and two dollars for each additional lady.

The visual arts did not catch on quite so quickly, but by the end of the 1860s a number of prominent artists made their homes in Salt Lake City. C.C.A. Christensen, who arrived in 1857, made himself famous by touring the state displaying a series of huge paintings depicting Mormon history, and giving accompanying lectures. Danie Weggeland arrived in 1862 and began working with Christensen on scenery for the Salt Lake Theatre. He also did other landscape work, and was eventually commissioned to paint scenes for Mormon temples. He became one of Utah's prominent art teachers. Other prominent Salt Lake City artists included George M. Ottinger, Alfred Lambourne, and John Hafen. In 1863 a number of artists formed the Deseret Academy of the Arts, designed to promote appreciation for all the visual arts as well as to teach classes. Said the *Deseret News* as it enthusiastically endorsed the new venture: "Our circumstances as a people have hitherto constrained our attention mainly to matters of utility and necessity; but everything now indicates that Providence, which established a people in these mountains, and led out the minds of our leaders in plain practical directions, is now shaping our career as a nation towards the day of refinement and polish."

As a distinctive community with the larger American community, and because of its convenient location on the route between East and West, Salt Lake City became the focal point of a great deal of curiosity, interest, and public reporting. The reports were mixed, with most of the criticism levied against the Mormon marriage system and political hegemony. So far as the city itself was concerned, however, by far the majority of travelers were favorably impressed with its appearance and life style. Many of the most glowing descriptions were published in the *Deseret News*, especially during the early years of its history. Said one in 1850: "A more orderly, earnest, industrious, and civil people I have never been amongst . . . and it is incredible how much they have done here in the wilderness in so short a time . . . . I have not met in a citizen a single idler, or any person who looks like a loafer." Richard Burton was impressed, in 1860, with the openness of Mormon society, symbolized to him by the fact that in Salt Lake City he found every anti-Mormon publication, no matter how derogatory. Some people, such as O. E. Babcock in 1857, found the Mormons industrious, but fanatical, and suggested that they still could bear watching by the government. Other people saw a certian elitism in the City of the Saints that they did not like. Most likely there were elements of truth in all these observations, as Salt lake City grew toward becoming one of the major cities in the American West.

First South in 1872, showing the Salt Lake Theatre on the Left. Courtesy, Utah State Historical Society. Photo no. 979.21 P3.

4

Mormons and Gentiles, 1870-1892

Under the stimulus of economic development and the gathering of the Saints to Zion, Salt Lake City grew very rapidly in the late nineteenth century. From an 1870 population of 12,900, the city expanded 68 percent to 20,800 in 1880 and again 116 percent to 44,800 in 1890. An economic boom between 1886 and 1891 doubled real estate values.

While visitors around 1870 commented favorably on Salt Lake's majestic setting in "an oasis in the great American desert," with the Wasatch Mountains thrusting magnificently to the east, some were not so impressed with the residential sections of the city. One described the houses as "a congeries of hovels, struck irregularly along a number of straight, wide, unpaved roads, turned here and there into quags and pools by the wandering, ill-kept gutters." Nevertheless, single-story houses of wooden planks had replaced the adobe cabins of the earlier years. He observed that a few Mormon leaders had built "terrace-like houses . . . for the accommodation of several families." Temple Square seemed plain with its wooden gates and "low, squat, rickety" old tabernacle, and the new oval roofed tabernacle seemed undistinguished to the visitor used to the lavish Victorian architecture already gracing the streets of other cities. Even the public buildings such as the meeting-houses, school houses, the townhall, the university, and the theatre seemed "commonplace."

Visitors also commented on the business district. Running a few hundred yards on Main Street (then called East Temple) south from Temple Square, it boasted two- and three-story buildings and signs advertising wares and services. Grocery stores, milk shops, drapery makers, millinery shops, "silver smith, druggists, confectioners, tinsmiths, turners, toy-shops, bookshops, perfumers," and other sundry businesses lined the street. In warm weather, blinds and awnings, dropped to deflect the heat, exhibited painted advertisements. Visitors could not help but notice also the ubiquitous Zion's Cooperative Mercantile Association signs above shop doors with the motto, "Holiness to the Lord," and its all-seeing eye trained on those below.

Notable by the absence of the Mormon logo were stores of ex-Mormons and Jewish businessmen. The most prominent ex-Mormon establishments were William S. Godbe's drugstore, set on the corner of Main and First South, and the establishment of Joseph R. Walker and his brothers, Samuel S., David F., and Matthew H., collectively known as the Walker Brothers, on the corner of East Temple and Second South. Active in Salt Lake City business from the 1850s, these merchants had broken with Brigham Young when he began the organization of cooperative manufacturing and commerce in the 1860s. The stores of Auerbach Brothers, Siegel Brothers, Kahn Brothers, and Charles Popper represented the Jewish community.

Salt Lake City showed many signs of change. In the initial plan of the founders, eight lots were to have occupied each ten-acre block. By 1870, however, the scarcity and high price of property in the business district brought about the compacting of buildings. In the northeast portion of the city, a subdivision of recent survey, the blocks contained only two and a half acres each and the streets were narrower. This is now the "Avenues" section. A new section in the northern portion of the city, west of what is now capitol hill, exhibited crooked and irregular streets planned, in part, to match the steep slope of the ground. The original grid plan had been modified by the city's prosperity and expansion.

Early in 1870, Main Street also began to take on a new look. In January, the Utah Central had been completed from the Union Pacific-Central Pacific Junction at Ogden to Salt Lake City. Miners had begun pouring into the territory and Salt Lake City boomed under the impetus of commerce spurred by mining development and the newly available transportation. "Shaggy looking, roughly-dressed" sourdough miners had begun to hang around the hotels and street corners to "spit and chew." Many shops on Main Street sported heaps of ore specimens on shelves or window sills. Mining had already expanded to Parley's Park (later Park City), Big and Little Cottonwood Canyons, and Bingham Canyon, ringing Salt Lake City on the east, south, and southwest.

The face of downtown Salt Lake changed during the 1870s as well. In 1873, architects William Folsom and George Romney built a three-

Temple Square, 1882, showing, from left to right, partially completed temple, the Assembly Hall, and the Tabernacle. Courtesy, Utah State Historical Society. Photo no. 979.21 P17.

Salt Lake City Residential Unit, 1890. The Unit could have accommodated two polygamous families. Courtesy, Utah State Historical Society. Photo no. 979.21 40 (17238).

story brick building for Dinwoody Furniture Company on First South between Main and West Temple. Folsom also completed, in 1876, the handsome wrought iron front for ZCMI's main store on Main between South Temple and First South. By 1877, the face of downtown, according to one observer, looked like that "of other large cities." By 1884, the Temple walls had risen to a height of eighty feet, and the Fortress-Gothic building, completed in 1893, was described as a structure "of Cyclopean strength," with walls ranging from sixteen feet thick in the basement to seven feet at the top.

By the mid-1880s, the residential section too had undergone a somewhat belated transformation. In the mid-1870s, observers indicated that outside the business district the city seemed "a picture of self-complacent poverty." Only a few two-story brick houses and some handsomely designed wooden structures had joined the plank cottages. By the mid-1880s, however, rich lawns greeted the visitor's eye, and trees, shrubs, and plants enhanced the scene. The Gardo House, or Amelia Palace, designed by William Folsom and completed in 1881 stood on the south side of South Temple, or Brigham Street, as it was called. It set a standard for later residential construction on that street and in the Avenues section.

Economic activity in and around Salt Lake City expanded rapidly. Only two days after the completion of the Utah Central, the Woodhull Brothers shipped a carload of ore over the railroad, and by late September, they had successfully completed their first run of crude bullion at their smelting works six miles south of the city.

In the meantime, a host of other factories had been established to meet the needs of the population and its expanding economic base. These included two woolen factories with about five hundred spindles each, a large number of flour, saw, and grist mills, tanneries, furniture factories, breweries, and foundaries.

Undoubtedly the largest manufacturing businesses for other than local consumption were those associated with smelting and refining of ores. The 1884 *Gazetteer* for Salt Lake City and Utah listed seven smelters, two mills, and two sampling works in and around Salt Lake City. Most were located to the south in Sandy and what would become Murray. The largest of these, the Germania, which opened in 1872, boasted four shafts and one reverberatory furnace producing lead and silver.

Brigham Young's opposition notwithstanding, mining and mineral products were becoming extremely important to the economies of Utah and Salt Lake City. In 1882, Utah imported approximately $11.4 million worth of goods. These were largely finished products. Nevertheless, the territory enjoyed a favorable balance of trade, with exports of approximately $11.5 million. Of these, $9 million were mineral products, especially silver, lead, copper matte, and gold. Agricultural commodities were a distant second.

Under these conditions, Salt Lake City solidified its position as manufacturing, commercial, and financial center of the territory. The entrance of the Denver and Rio Grande into the city in 1883 and the completion of the Utah Southern Railroad extension to Milford, Frisco, and the Horn Silver mine in 1880 provided important links between the burgeoning Mormon capital and other areas. Feeder lines, generally narrow gauge, connected these railroads with the principal mining district and drew the ores to Salt Lake Valley for processing.

While one tends to think of Ogden as the railroad center of Utah, Salt Lake City was, in fact, the principal destination of persons and products shipped into the territory and the shipping point for most exported goods. In 1882, for instance, ZCMI of Salt Lake City imported fully one-third of all merchandise consumed in the territory. The products of Salt Lake Valley smelters were shipped largely on the Utah Central, with its connections to the Union and the Central Pacific, and on the Denver and Rio Grande Western.

At the center of Salt Lake City's business community were its banking institutions. The *Gazetteer* for 1892-1893 listed seven building and loan associations and fifteen banks. Some were clearly more important than others. Deseret National Bank was the principal Mormon institution. Union National Bank, successor to Walker Brothers Bank, was a major gentile institution. Wells Fargo and Company, under cashier John E. Dooley, represented the principal western branch bank. McCornick and Company, established in 1872 by W. S. McCornick, was the principal private bank, with correspondents in the financial centers of the United States and in London. The principal savings bank was Zion's Savings Bank and Trust, with Wilford Woodruff as President.

Before 1870, Salt Lake City had no organized political parties, in the sense we understand that term today. Politics were nevertheless highly partisan largely because of the antagonism between Mormon and gentile. City officers generally had been orthodox Latter-day Saints, and in many cases high church officials. In 1870, Daniel H. Wells, Second Counselor in the First Presidency, served as mayor. His successors were four prominent Mormon businessmen, Feramorz Little of the Utah Southern Railroad, William Jennings of ZCMI, James Sharp of the Utah Central Railroad, and Francis Armstrong, a contractor, lumberman, and investor. After 1889, conditions changed, and the next two mayors were George M. Scott, a gentile merchant, and Robert N. Baskin, a non-Mormon lawyer.

With the coming of the railroad to Utah in 1869, the subsequent influx of gentiles into the city, and the defection of a group of dissident businessmen to the Godbeite movement, non-Mormons felt strongly that they deserved some representation in city government. On February 9, 1870, the gentiles and ex-Mormons organized political parties concurrently in Corinne, the would-be gentile capital of Utah, and in Salt Lake City. The group in Corinne adopted the name "Liberal party," and the coalition of Godbeites and gentiles in Salt Lake City called themselves the "Independent ticket," to offer an alternative to the regular Mormon slate for the city election to be held February 14, 1870. The two groups joined at Corinne in July 1870 with the organization of the Liberal party. In response, the Latter-day Saints formalized the structure for nominating and electing local officials that had existed from the early 1850s by founding the People's party.

In assessing the role of the Liberal party in Salt Lake City during the ensuing years, it should be emphasized that many of the Godbeites and gentile businessmen did not generally exhibit the rabid anti-Mormonism of most territorial officials. The personal interests of most federal officials lay largely outside the territory, whereas the businessmen had to remain a part of the Mormon community. As Congress considered the anti-Mormon Cullom bill in late March 1870, for instance, Godbeite leaders and a group of conservative gentiles, most of whom had been involved in the Independent party organization a month earlier, held a protest meeting at the Masonic Hall on Main Street. The meeting ended on a conservative tone, without agreeing on any formal action, but William S. Godbe went to Washington to consult with President Ulysses S. Grant and Senator Shelby Cullom on the matter, urging the modification of the bill so it did not attack religious belief and existing family relationships. This same group later protested against the treatment of Brigham Young and other church leaders by Judge James B. McKean. In 1871, Edward Tullidge and Eli Kelsey traded verbal blows with Land Office Receiver George Maxwell and U.S. Commissioner Dennis Toohey after the latter two opened an attack on the Mormon people.

Actually, the basic arguments raised by the Liberals in Salt Lake City elections were derived from the same principles used by the Mormons to argue their right to self-government when they felt put upon by the federal government. Their feelings grew from their positions in the community and the condition of their property. Since one principal source of local revenue at the time was property taxation, these businessmen, who owned some of the most valuable and heavily taxed business property in the city, felt discriminated against since they had little or no voice in city policies. An 1874 study, for instance, showed that gentiles made up about a quarter of the city's population, but paid half the city's budget. They paid more than $46,000 in property taxes and license fees to support a city budget of $110,000. That they had the right to vote meant little to them since, with the Mormon control of politics, they could never hope to elect any candidates sympathetic to their interests.

Salt Lake City, like Rome, served as the seat of both temporal and spiritual governments. Territorial government offices were spread through buildings in the downtown area, with the third district court holding forth in a succession of the larger halls in the area. In 1874, the governor had his office on West Temple between Third and Fourth South. The territorial secretary had an office on First South between Main and First East. The city offices had moved from the Council House to the City Hall. Church offices were located on the north side of South Temple. Brigham Young operated out of his residences in the Beehive and Lion houses, and the church tithing yard was located in the space now occupied by the Hotel Utah, on the northeast corner of Main and South Temple. Also like Rome, this dual capital became the focus of perennial conflict between Caesar's kingdom and God's.

In the attempt of the federal officials to assert their political authority over the people of Utah, a number of conflicts played themselves out in the streets and buildings of Salt Lake City. President Ulysses S. Grant was particularly anxious that the federal officials suppress both plural marriage and religious dictation of political affairs in Utah. Grant himself visited Salt Lake City in October 1875, but in the meantime he appointed, in 1870, a set of federal officials carrying a mandate to change conditions in Utah. The new governor, J. Wilson Shaffer of Illinois, arrived in March 1870. In mid-August, Salt Lake mayor Daniel H. Wells, who also served by legislative appointment as lieutenant general of the Nauvoo Legion (the Utah Territorial Militia), issued orders for a general muster for "drill, inspection and camp duty," to take place before mid-November. On September 15, Shaffer issued two proclamations removing Wells, countermanding his orders, and prohibiting "all musters, drills or gatherings" of militia. Following an exchange of letters, Shaffer died of natural causes, but Wells suspended his orders.

On November 21, 1870, after Shaffer's death, and in apparent defiance of his order, a group of officers in the Salt Lake City Twentieth Ward— the Avenues area—mustered about 300 men from the companies of their regiment to drill. George A. Black, formerly Shaffer's private secretary and then territorial secretary, brought two deputy marshals to the muster. On the representation of Secretary Black, Territorial Justice Cyrus M. Hawley issued a warrant for the arrest of eight of the officers.

After a preliminary hearing, Hawley ordered the officers either to post bond or face incarceration at Fort Douglas pending the outcome of hearings before the third district grand jury. Since the predominately Mormon grand jury refused to indict, the officers were released.

These proceedings were merely the opening shots of a contest of wills between federal officials and their supporters and the citizens of Salt Lake City which continued for several years. In June 1871, the city council appointed a committee consisting of Mormons and conservative gentiles to plan a Fourth of July celebration. At the same time, the gentiles of the city and some of the Godbeites appointed Governor George L. Woods and George R. Maxwell to plan the Fourth of July celebration. The two committees conducted some negotiations in an attempt to promote a joint celebration, but they were unable to agree and Mayor Wells declined to appoint Woods and Maxwell to the city's committee.

Furthermore, Wells called for several militia units to participate in the celebration. Since this seemed to defy Shaffer's order, Secretary Black, acting in Woods's absence, issued a proclamation prohibiting the militia from participating, and called upon the troops at Fort Douglas to enforce his order.

As a result, two celebrations took place. One, held in the Tabernacle, included the Mormon population and a few gentiles, and another, held at the Godbeite's Liberal Institute on Second East between First and Second South, hosted the bulk of the smaller non-Mormon population.

Scene on Second South in Salt Lake City, 1871. May have been taken at the time of Brigham Young's Trial. Courtesy, Utah State Historical Society.

The conflict intensified as Territorial Chief Justice James B. McKean began an attack upon the community leadership. In October 1871, U.S. marshals arrested Brigham Young, Mayor Wells, and Henry W. Lawrence, a prominent Godbeite and polygamist, at their homes on a writ charging them with lewd and lascivious cohabitation and adultery for living with their polygamous wives. Judge McKean admitted Mayor Wells to bail, but refused bail for Young, although he then released him on his own recognizance. Shortly thereafter, McKean secured indictments from a grand jury, empaneled on an open venire in defiance of territorial law, against Wells and Young charging them with the murder of Richard Yates during the Utah War. These charges had rested on the allegations of William H. Hickman, who had confessed to Yates's murder, but who alleged that the others had planned the deed. Wells spent a night in jail at Fort Douglas and the next day was admitted to $50,000 bail so he could carry out his duties as mayor. McKean placed Brigham Young under house arrest. The indictments were thrown out after the Supreme Court decision in the Englebrecht case.

A number of the issues between Judge McKean and the Mormons turned on the attempts of the city to regulate and earn revenue from business within its jurisdiction. In these cases, McKean showed little sympathy with city authorities, largely because the ordinances seemed to bear most heavily on gentiles and to restrict the activities of entrepreneurs. One ordinance, for instance, restricted all grocers and meat markets to a block in the center of the city. McKean ruled that this ordinance was an unreasonable restraint upon legitimate business and an inconvenience to city residents.

Serious conflicts resulted from liquor license fees. Until the growth of the gentile community in Salt Lake, the liquor traffic had been relatively small. In an attempt to control the traffic and obtain revenue, the city had levied inordinately high fees. A retail license cost $750 per month, where at the same time Chicago dealers paid only $56 per year. The city council said the issue was one of morality, but the gentiles found that explanation difficult to accept because the city government engaged in the liquor business itself. After a lower court hearing on the city's attempt to enforce the license fee against druggist William S. Godbe, who sold spirits only for medicinal purposes, the territorial supreme court ruled this an illegitimate exercise of the city's police power.

In July 1872, McKean restrained the city from arresting any liquor dealers, and after some arguments the city agreed to reduce the license fees to $1,200 per year for retailers and $600 for wholesalers, while prohibiting sales between 10 p.m. and 6 a.m. Though not satisfactory to all dealers, McKean found the city within its authority to set those conditions.

Another issue was the regulation of amusements. Alderman and Justice of the Peace Jeter Clinton fined C. W. Kitchen, proprietor of the Clift House Hotel, $100 for refusing to pay a license tax of $1,400 per year levied on all billiard tables. Apparently, the tax had been set at that level on the assumption that billiard games constituted gambling. The levy amounted to nearly twenty times that charged by New York City, and Kitchen argued that he collected no fees from hotel patrons using the tables and allowed no gambling. During the trial, City Attorney E. D. Hoge placed a pool player on the stand in an apparent attempt to show that the players gambled. In particular Hoge badgered the witness over what went on after the game was over. After hedging for some time, the witness finally testified—somewhat embarrassedly—that he had gone to the rest room.

In this case, McKean ruled that though the city had a right to license gambling, it had no right to restrict innocent amusements. If it could license billiards at the Clift House, he said, the city could also license children's ball games. In other cases, however, McKean sustained the city's right to fine or license gambling.

Throughout the period conflicts developed between the citizens of Salt Lake and soldiers stationed at Fort Douglas. Most of the cases involved the breaking of local ordinances by soldiers and alleged police brutality on the part of the city. After a severe confrontation in 1874, in which soldiers from Fort Douglas broke into the city jail to release Thomas Hackett, charged with assault against former Judge Solomon P. McCurdy, the secretary of war intervened and the territorial supreme court ruled that the army might remove soldiers from the city's jurisdiction in cases arising under local police ordinances.

Some conflicts between the federal officials and Salt Lake citizens resulted in violence. In October 1870, a deputy postmaster tried to kill Edward L. Sloan, editor of the *Salt Lake Herald*, after the paper printed an alleged personal insult. The U.S. Third District Court convicted the federal official of assault with intent to commit murder, but then Sloan himself appealed on behalf of the postmaster and he was fined only $100. Abuses came from both sides, as a group of militiamen tried to intimidate Judge McKean in his court in 1873, and in October 1874 a group of armed men attacked George R. Maxwell, then U.S. Marshal, as he tried to serve a summons on Brigham Young to secure his testimony before a federal grand jury.

That the federal officials were somewhat heavyhanded in dealing with the government and citizens of Salt Lake City seems evident from

McKean's decision in a case that arose from the attempt of the city to regulate the liquor traffic. After saloon owner Paul Englebrecht refused to pay the liquor license fee, Alderman Clinton ordered the destruction of his stock of spirits. Englebrecht protested and entered a suit against Clinton in the territorial courts. As in the Young and Wells cases mentioned above, McKean issued an open venire to the U.S. Marshal, who packed the jury with unsympathetic gentiles. Clinton was convicted in McKean's court and ordered to pay $59,063.25. On appeal, however, the U.S. Supreme Court overruled McKean's method of empaneling juries and ordered him to obey the territorial law. The decision nullified grand jury indictments against Wells, Young, and other local officials including Chief of Police Andrew Burt and one of the police officers, B. Y. Hampton, who were charged with murdering Dr. J. King Robinson, who had allegedly tried to jump the city's Warm Springs land claim.

The conflict with Robinson was partly related to the inability of city officials to obtain clear title to the city's land and to provide legal deeds to city lots. Congress passed a special act to allow the mayor to file for Salt Lake City since it fell within school sections of the public land, and since the city encompassed a larger area than that allowed by the general townsite act. Not until June 1872 did Mayor Wells actually receive a patent for land encompassed within the city under a special act of Congress passed for the purpose. Until that time, residents of the city were technically squatters on the public domain.

James McKean also presided over what was undoubtedly the most famous and bizarre divorce proceeding in Utah history. In 1873, Ann Eliza Young—said to be Brigham Young's twenty-seventh wife—sued for divorce. At first referred to the Salt Lake County probate court, the case returned to McKean's Third District Court after passage of the Poland Act removed such jurisdiction from probate courts in 1874. Ann Eliza wanted alimony, which Brigham Young refused to pay on the ground that her previous divorce from James Dee had not been legal and that she was a plural or celestial wife and thus not legally married to Young. The prophet said he was married to Mary Ann Angell. McKean nevertheless ordered Young to pay $500 per month alimony pending the outcome of the suit. The judge pointed out that no matter what sort of marriage he and Ann Eliza had entered, it was legal provided both parties were competent to marry, since Utah had no marriage laws. Young bore the burden of proof to show that Ann Eliza had been married to James Dee or that he was married to Mary Ann Angell.

The ruling posed a problem for the Mormon prophet. Dee and Ann Eliza had been divorced by action of the local probate court and the Poland Act had legitimized previous actions of the court. Young appealed to the territorial supreme court and refused to pay the alimony. On March 11, 1875, McKean ordered the prophet to pay a $25 fine and spend a day in prison for contempt. Young left under escort for the old territorial prison in Sugar House, south of Salt Lake City, where he spent the night. Later the U.S. attorney general ordered the suit dropped on the ground that, as a plural wife, Ann Eliza could never have been legally married to Young and thus was not entitled to alimony.

In both the February 1874 city elections and the August elections for territorial delegate, the Liberal party again put forth candidates. In both cases they were unsuccessful, but in the August elections the polling was marred by violence. Two Salt Lake City policemen and a deputy U.S. marshal were arrested, as was Alderman Clinton, and a mob attacked Mayor Wells and tore his coat to pieces.

Conflict between the Mormons and gentiles continued in Salt Lake during the late 1870s and early 1800s until the passage of the Edmunds Act in 1882 and the appointment of Territorial Chief Justice Charles S. Zane in 1884. The Edmunds Act disfranchised all polygamists and made it easier to prosecute plural marriage by defining unlawful cohabitation as well as polygamy. Under Zane's regime, the territorial penitentiary filled with "cohabs," and many church leaders hid out on the underground from pursuing U.S. marshals.

Zane's relationship with Salt Lake City officials, however, differed from McKean's. Interested in upholding the law, he dispensed even-handed justice to Mormon and gentile alike. He allowed the widest possible latitude to the city in establishing and enforcing local police regulations, while punishing lawbreakers. In 1885, at the height of the Mormon-gentile conflict, a group of city police officers, led by Brigham Y. Hampton, hired prostitutes—Hampton called them detectives—to offer their services to and report on federal officials. One of the prostitutes testified that Hampton offered $300 if she were able to compromise the territorial governor. Zane's court, in a decision sustained by the territorial supreme court, convicted Hampton of conspiracy.

Beyond these problems, the political development of most important immediate impact for Salt Lake City and for Utah as a whole was the adoption of woman suffrage in Utah, and its exercise in the Salt Lake City election of February 1870. This important reform seems to have derived from three motives. Representative George W. Julian of Indiana originally proposed woman suffrage for Utah territory in 1869, as a means of undermining the authority of the Mormon hierarchy by granting the vote to women who were presumably oppressed by Utah's polygamic theocracy. At the same time, it has been argued that Mormon leaders embraced the proposal because they hoped to strengthen their hold on the territory through the votes of sympathetic women. But the Mormon leaders also favored woman suffrage because of their belief in the rightness of the proposal as an analogue to women's participating in voting within the church, and their relative autonomy in the governance of organizations such as the Relief Society. In any case, Mormon leaders helped to push the measure through the territorial legislature in advance of congressional action and as one of the first such laws in Western America.

Approval of the woman suffrage bill allowed women to vote in Salt Lake City in the February 1870 election. While few availed themselves of the opportunity in that first election, some, including Seraph Young, a niece of Brigham Young and a teacher at the University of Deseret, did, and statements by LDS women leaders indicated hearty approval of the progressive reform. Their vote had little impact, but its symbolic significance was high.

As the anti-Mormon crusade continued in the 1800s, Congress passed two severe laws designed to aid the prosecution of polygamy in Utah; the Edmunds Act of 1882 and the Edmunds-Tucker Act of 1887. The Edmunds-Tucker Act disfranchised Utah's female population, until statehood. This, together with the loss of the approximately fifteen percent of the voters who had been disfranchised by the passage of the Edmunds Act in 1882, led to the possibility that the Liberal party might win in future elections in centers like Salt Lake City, which had a relatively even number of adult gentile and non-polygamous Mormon males. Apparently seeing the handwriting on the wall, in 1888 the People's party leaders departed from their previous policy of offering only a straight Mormon ticket to voters and agreed to open several places on the city council to four conservative gentiles. Those chosen were businessmen William S. McCornick as one of the five alderman, and John E. Dooly., M. B. Sowles, and Boliver Roberts as three of the nine councilors. The Citizen's Ticket, as it was called, successfully carried the field against the remainder of the Liberal party by a majority of better than two to one.

In August 1889, the Liberals succeeded in electing four members to the territorial legislature from Salt Lake City. Even though they had won by rather slim majorities, the Liberals anticipated a victory in the January 1890 city elections. Preparation for the election was almost reminiscent of slavery and anti-slavery forces trying to get votes in the Kansas statehood battles of the 1850s. Both the People's and the Liberal parties colonized voters in Salt Lake City and both tried to qualify through naturalization as many of their immigrant supporters as possible. After a hearing before Federal Judge Thomas J. Anderson, including testimony that questioned the loyalty of the Latter-day Saints, the court ruled that Mormons might not be admitted to citizenship.

The election campaign typified the tactics of the period. Both parties organized marching clubs, conducted torchlight parades, and held large bonfire rallies. The Liberal party nominated George M. Scott, a hardware merchant and twenty-year resident of the city. The People's party ran Spencer Clawson, a prominent Mormon businessman. The Liberal party carried the day in all but three city council races in the city's fourth municipal ward. Even in those cases, the election officials, all gentiles appointed by the Utah Commission established under the Edmunds Act, issued certificates to the Liberal party candidates. On appeal, Judge Zane sustained the position of the People's party, but the completion of the appeals process took eighteen months and left a full slate of Liberal party councilmen in power until two months before the 1892 election.

Attempting to deal with the problems created by the rapid growth of Salt Lake City and the failure of previous People's party administrations to meet the need for urban services, Liberal party officials embarked on a wide range of municipal improvements and opened the city to various types of business enterprise. The attempts to grade and pave the city's streets, and improve the city's sewer and water facilities, however, led to a 300 percent increase in city taxes and great dissatis-faction on the part of both Mormons and gentiles. In addition, nine new gambling halls and thirty-one brothels opened in the city during the first year of the Liberal party administration. The new government could hardly get along either with Mormons or other religious people that way.

These changes led to a reform movement in the city, and both Mormons and gentiles supported a citizen's ticket headed by Robert N. Baskin, a gentile attorney who had come to Utah in 1865 and who until the early 1890s had been a leading anti-Mormon. Elected mayor in February 1892 and again in November 1893 (the legislature had changed the election day to November), Baskin succeeded in satisfying both Mormons and gentiles of his fairness. By then, political conditions in Salt Lake City had changed considerably. In 1891, the Mormons had disbanded the People's party and had moved into the Republican and Democratic parties. Most gentiles left the Liberal party, and in 1893 it was officially disbanded as well.

By the late 1870s active leadership of the Salt Lake City community had passed from the hands of members of the LDS church's hierarchy to a group of businessmen and entrepreneurs. Born generally outside Utah territory, they were often immigrants from England and Canada. Some of them were Latter-day Saints, but many were lapsed Mormons

William Jennings, Prominent Mormon Businessman, Mayor of Salt Lake City (1882-1884), and owner of the Devereaux House and Eagle Emporium.

or excommunicants who were nevertheless friendly with the Latter-day Saint people. Their principal business activities were in the fields of merchandising, railroading, banking, and mining. Many of the wealthy and influential had investments in all four fields.

A look at a few such community leaders will help typify the rest. Perhaps the best example from the Mormon community was William Jennings, generally said to have been Utah's first millionaire. Born in Yardley near Birmingham, England, September 13, 1823, William grew up in the home of a well-to-do butcher. Showing an early flair for business, he came to the United States to seek his fortune. Non-Mormon at first, he married Jane Walker, a Mormon emigrant, and after coming to Salt Lake City he joined the LDS church and married Priscilla Paul as a plural wife.

After his arrival in Salt Lake City, he again entered the meat business. From there, he expanded into tanning and into leatherwork with the hides from the cattle he butchered. In 1860, he opened a dry goods business, and thereafter expanded into merchandising, becoming a supplier for the overland mail, for Fort Douglas, and for mines in Montana. In 1864, he built the Eagle Emporium on Main Street, which served as the basis for Zion's Cooperative Mercantile Institution, in which Jennings was a shareholder, superintendent, and vice-president. His investments expanded to include banking (The Deseret National), smelting (Germania Smelter), and railroading (Utah Central and Utah Southern). In 1882, he became mayor of Salt Lake City, a position he soon lost because of the enforcement of the Edmunds Act.

Jennings is perhaps best known for his business acumen. In 1861, he entered a contract with the overland mail company to supply 75,000 bushels of grain. Jennings entered a performance bond to supply the grain, but the mail company began buying in the Utah market in competition with him to purchase grain itself. This forced Jennings to buy in a competitive market for a high price and fill the contract at a lower one. Since the amount of grain called for was approximately the entire output of Utah territory in 1861, Jennings was left in an untenable position. Seeing that he could not possibly win under this situation, he forfeited the performance bond, then continued buying until he had cornered the territorial grain market. Now the mail company was left with two alternatives: it could purchase grain from towns on the Missouri River or Pacific Coast and ship it to Utah, or purchase from Jennings at his price. It chose the latter alternative and Jennings made a substantial profit on the deal.

Associated with Jennings in a number of businesses were several other important men. They included William H. Hooper, who in addition to his business career in the Deseret National Bank and in merchandising, served as territorial delegate to Congress from 1859–1873; Horace S. Eldredge, who was associated with Jennings in ZCMI, and who himself was involved in business with Hooper and with Hiram B. Clawson; Brigham Young, with whom Jennings was associated in railroading, banking, and ZCMI; and Lewis S. Hills, who eventually became president of the Deseret National Bank.

On the lapsed Mormon side were the Walker brothers: Samuel Sharpe, David Frederick, Matthew Henry, and especially Joseph R. Born August 29, 1836 in Yeadon, Yorkshire, England, Joseph R. Walker was the second eldest of the four Utah businessmen. Associated with William Jennings and William Nixon in business in Carson Valley, Nevada shortly before the Utah War, Walker returned to Salt Lake City after the war broke out. He and his brothers engaged in business there and at Camp Floyd, and after the closing of the camp they purchased part of the war surplus and expanded their Salt Lake City business.

In 1870, Joseph became extensively involved in mining and milling. In the Ophir district, for instance, he opened a fifteen-stamp crushing and amalgamation mill in May 1871. He also invested in the Germania Smelter south of Salt Lake. He was involved for some time in the Emma Mine in Little Cottonwood Canyon and, in fact, he and his brothers purchased part of the original claim. The other portion was eventually promoted in Great Britain by a number of prominent American and British investors, including Senator William M. Stewart of Nevada and U.S. Minister to England, Robert C. Schenck, and became an international *cause célèbre* when British investors lost their shirts on the scheme. Walker also invested in mines in Butte, Montana, in Idaho and Nevada, and in various districts in Utah including Bingham, Park City, and American Fork Canyon. Proceeds from the merchandising and mining ventures formed the basis for the Walker Brothers Bank and the Union National Bank.

Most importantly, he and his brothers served as a bridge between the gentile and Mormon communities. When Judge James B. McKean threw Brigham Young into jail, the Walkers together with Patrick E. Connor and several other conservative gentiles protested what seemed to them excessively harsh treatment of the aged prophet. Moreover, their business connections bridged the two communities.

Also important in the banking business was William S. McCornick. Born near Picton, Ontario, Canada, the son of George and Mary Vance McCornick, he came to Utah in 1871 after engaging in merchandising in the gold fields of California and the silver mining region of Nevada. In 1873 he established the private banking house of McCornick and

William S. McCornick, Prominent Non-Morman Banker, Founder of the Commercial Club, and City Councilman. Courtesy, Utah State Historical Society.

Company which, by the 1890s, held a larger volume of deposits than any of the national banks in Salt Lake City and was reputed to be the largest private bank between the Missouri River and the Pacific Coast. McCornick's business interests also involved investment in mines, especially in Park City and in railroading. Chosen by the Mormons for the city council on the Citizen's Ticket, McCornick enjoyed a long and prosperous career in Salt Lake City.

Perhaps the most important indication of change in the character of the leadership of Salt Lake City was the organization of the Salt Lake Chamber of Commerce and Board of Trade in April 1887. Organized to promote trade, establish home industries, and attract capital and population, it began as an association of both Mormons and gentiles. Governor Caleb West served as chairman of the organizing meeting and Heber J. Grant, a young Mormon businessman and member of the LDS Council of the Twelve, and Patrick H. Lannan, principal owner and publisher of the anti-Mormon *Salt Lake Tribune,* both signed the articles of incorporation. William S. McCornick served as the chamber's first president. A list of the membership of the chamber's standing committees published in 1892 reveals a broad integration of the city's business community. The finance committee, for instance, included William S. McCornick, John E. Dooly, James R. Walker, Henry W. Lawrence, James Sharp, and Heber M. Wells, representing the gentile, apostate, and Mormon communities.

A published list of business and professional clubs indicates a broad range of interests by 1892. Included among them were the venerated Alta Club, a businessmen's social organization, the American Society of Irrigation Engineers, and three medical societies.

Foreign-born businessmen like the Walker Brothers, Jennings, and McCornick represented quite accurately the substance of the population of Salt Lake in the late nineteenth century. Nearly 69 percent of the heads of households in Salt Lake County in 1870 were foreign born, approximately fifty-six percent of them from English-speaking countries. Thus, the average family in Salt Lake would consist of foreign-born parents and their children. An examination of the names in the various *Gazetteers* from the nineteenth century shows a predominance of Anglo-Saxon and Celtic surnames, with a smaller number of Scandinavians, central European Jews, and a few Italians.

By the 1870s Salt Lake had been thoroughly integrated into the relatively unequal national pattern of wealth holding. Nearly 45 percent of the population owned less than $1.00 in total wealth, and 45.7 percent held all wealth in excess of $2,000 per household. Income statistics are not available, but would undoubtedly reveal a somewhat different pattern, since national studies show greater income than wealth-holding equality. Nevertheless, Salt Lake City was clearly not an equalitarian society by 1870.

Perhaps because of this relative inequality, as well as the good times of the 1880s, labor organization moved ahead rapidly. The Knights of Labor attempted to penetrate Salt Lake City, but were largely unsuccessful because of their vigorous anti-Mormon stance. More successful, however, were the locals which would eventaully make up the American Federation of Labor. In fact, the *Gazetteer* of 1892 lists twenty-five union locals and the Utah Federated Trades and Labor Council in Salt Lake City. The unions represented a broad range of occupations from the Amalgamated Association of Carpenters and Joiners to the Tailor's union. In 1892, they were powerful enough in Salt Lake City to secure city council approval of a city ordinance limiting the hours of work to eight, but the mayor vetoed the proposal.

As unionism developed, so did a movement within the church that had the potential of mitigating inequality. These were the United Orders, begun in part to buffer the rapid change caused by the railroad and mining and in part to promote equality in the Mormon community. In Salt Lake City, however, instead of inaugurating full-scale community ownership as was done in many of the smaller towns, the church instigated a different system. It was designed to set up self-sufficient industries rather than to promote social and economic equality like the United Order in towns such as Orderville, where everything was owned in common, or in St. George, where the community controlled substantial resources.

On April 29, 1874, Brigham Young initiated the movement for urban United Orders in the Salt Lake City Twentieth Ward, in the Avenues section. During the summer of 1874, each of the city wards completed an organization on paper. The goal was regional self-sufficiency, and ward members were usually asked to provide capital for inaugurating a single enterprise. In fact, the orders fell far short of that rather limited goal. The Eighth Ward operated a hat factory, the Eleventh Ward opened a tailor's shop, the Nineteenth Ward opened a soap factory, and the Twentieth Ward operated a boot and shoe shop, but most never produced anything.

Several special types of United Orders, also of limited scope, were organized in the city as well. In May 1874, the Central United Order of Zion, a businessman's United Order, was set up in Salt Lake City under the direction of Brigham Young, his counselors, and the Apostles. In addition, a Tailor's United Order and a Tanner's United Order were organized. What of substance these orders did is not known.

106

Like most cities during the period, Salt Lake City experienced new development in urban services, facilities, and utilities. The police department was small, consisting of only eight men and a number of volunteers in 1880, but the city was relatively free of crime as compared with other cities of similar size. A volunteer fire department, headed by John D. T. McAllister as Chief Engineer, reorganized in March 1871, and consisted of six companies. Two of the companies were outfitted with steam-pumping engines, three with hand-operated pumpers, and one with buckets, hooks, and ladders. By 1890, Salt Lake City boasted a regular fire department of nine full-time and forty part-time firefighters. This was the second stage in development through which most western cities passed.

The city also moved ahead in providing various public utilities. Daniel H. Wells, Thomas W. Ellerbeck, James Jack, and others incorporated the Salt Lake City Gas Company in 1872 to furnish the town with gas manufactured from coal. Unable to make the system pay, the incorporators mortgaged the company to Brigham Young, as trustee for the LDS church. Held in trust by the LDS church, the company was confiscated by the federal government in the late 1880s when it took over most church property under the Edmunds-Tucker Act. Eventually the system became a private concern.

Entrepreneurs in the city also moved rapidly to install electric lights and a street railway. Already in 1880, the city had Bush system electric lights on Main Street, and these were extended to other areas. Other cities of similar size were still using or in some cases just beginning to install gas lights.

Begun in 1872, the mule-powered street railway system boasted 14 miles of track, 21 cars, and a 10-cent fare by 1889. Also inaugurated by Mayor Daniel H. Wells, like the gas system, the street railway ran into financial difficulty, and Brigham Young, acting for the LDS church, bailed it out. After a settlement with the government receiver appointed under the Edmunds-Tucker Act, the property was sold to Francis Armstrong, then Salt Lake City mayor and a prominent Mormon capitalist.

Armstrong was not long in enjoying a monopoly over street transportation. In 1889, just a year after the successful inauguration of the first electric street railway in Richmond, Virginia, the Salt Lake Rapid Transit Company began an electric line in Salt Lake City. A third line, the Fort Douglas Rapid Transit System, organized in 1890, was acquired by the Salt Lake Rapid Transit Company before it began operation.

In addition to the development of urban lighting and transportation, the city moved quite vigorously to develop a water supply, though not

Salt Lake Street Construction ca. 1890s. Excavating for subgrade on Second South. Courtesy, Utah State Historical Society.

a distribution or sewer system. As early as 1871 residents complained about the insufficiency of the distribution system, which consisted of open ditches channeling water from City Creek along the sides of the various streets. The city had no sewer system and a report in 1880 indicated no immediate plans to construct any. In this it was like Austin, Galveston, Lawrence, and Topeka. Most private houses were served with privies, but the water supply was often polluted in spite of municipal ordinances requiring property owners to keep the channels clean. In 1890, the city reported only 5 miles of sewer pipe along 275 miles of streets.

By 1880, the volume of water from City Creek proved inadequate for the city's growing population, and citizens experienced periodic shortages. Under the farsighted leadership of Mayor Feramorz Little, and after approval of a referendum by the city's population, the city incurred a debt of $250,000. On the basis of the bond, the city completed a canal by 1884 from the Jordon River to convey water from Utah Lake into southern Salt Lake County. In 1888, on the basis of water acquired through the canal, the city negotiated the first of a series of exchange agreements by which it obtained the rights to water from Emigration Canyon and Parley's Canyon in return for the Utah Lake water which was made available to farmers south of Salt Lake City.

Beyond this, by 1884, the city had developed an enclosed water system with some underground mains. The system consisted of settling tanks a short distance up City Creek Canyon from which the water was fed into mains extending underground for approximately thirteen miles in the city. In general, however, this supply fed into hydrants used for firefighting.

By 1890, the system was still quite inadequate. An article in *Salt Lake Sanitarian* of 1887 warned of the danger from typhoid fever from well and stream water in the city. These were still in use, partly from lack of a protected water system and partly from a shortage of water, since the city had constructed no conveyance to divert the Emigration and Parley's Canyon water into the existing pipes.

Salt Lake, like most western cities, moved quite slowly with street paving. Some, like Kansas City, Missouri, Lawrence, Kansas, and Los Angeles, had paved a few miles with broken stone. Salt Lake City, like most of the others including Denver, Omaha, Lincoln, and Houston, had no paving in 1880. The census report in 1890 showed an average expenditure of only $30,000 per year for construction and repairs of the dirt streets over the preceding ten years. A major problem in this regard was technological; even in cities like Portland, where the government tried to pave some streets with broken stones in a bituminous matrix, the attempt was unsuccessful because the asphalt tended to melt on hot days. Moreover, the streets of Salt Lake City, Stockton, and Kansas City were rated among the dirtiest in the West, since they were seldom cleaned.

The slow development of street, water, and sewer improvement led to pressure for rapid expenditure for such improvements during the liberal party's Scott administration in 1890. Reports on the water system by A. F. Doremus, M. J. Mack, and C. L. Stevenson that year indicated the system's inadequacy. Petitions for street, sewer, and water improvements poured into Scott's office and the tax increase necessary to meet these needs together with decisions on improvements upset some people. This in turn produced a backlash and pressure for lower taxes in the Baskin administration which followed.

The lack of adequate water, sewer, and street systems in Salt Lake City by 1890 had been accompanied by poor planning for urban health. Not until June 1890, after the Scott administration took office, did the city create a board of health. At that time, a commissioner was hired at a salary of $125 per month. This made Salt Lake City one of the last major cities in the West (Lawrence, Kansas being the other) to provide a health department.

These and other problems caused considerable difficulty, and one of the worst was not really solved until urban heating changed from wood and coal to natural gas after World War II. As early as the 1870s, air pollution had begun to menace the city. Smoke from the railroad and smelters damaged farm crops, and these coupled with soft coal smoke generated by home and business heating made city air extremely unhealthful. Not until 1891 did the city pass an anti-smoke ordinance designed to face the problem of incomplete combustion of soft coal. Even this ordinance was neither wholly satisfactory nor completely enforceable.

Nevertheless, while the health of Salt Lake City citizens was less than optimum by present standards, it was not inferior to that of other contemporary cities. In 1882, for instance, the *Bulletin* of the National Board of Health showed that of 177 cities surveyed in the United States, 60 had a lower mortality rate and 116 a higher one than Salt Lake City. The death rate stood at 16.3 per 1000 compared with 20 for San Francisco, 30 for Los Angeles, and 36.2 for Minneapolis. The situation was essentially similar for mortality of children under five. In Salt Lake City the rate stood at 3.1 per 1000 while 61 cities had a lower rate and 115 a higher one.

By the 1870s, charitable organizations had begun to provide hospital care for some citizens. St. Mark's Hospital, operated by the Episcopalians, was the first hospital for physical illnesses established in the city. Located first in a converted residence at Fourth South and Fifth East Streets, it opened in 1874 as a miner's hospital. Supported by the deduction of $1 per month from the wages of miners, it was available largely for the care of miners with lead poisoning. In 1883, it treated 800 patients.

The second hospital, Holy Cross, was opened in 1875 and operated by the Roman Catholic church's Order of the Holy Cross. Also basically a miner's hospital for the treatment of lead poisoning, it was sustained largely through payroll deductions and contributions. It was located on Fifth East between South Temple and First South.

In 1882, after the Holy Cross Hospital vacated its premises for a new building further to the east, the Latter-day Saints opened the city's first general hospital in the building Holy Cross formerly occupied. Founded by the Relief Society, the Deseret Hospital was administered by Ellen B. Ferguson as Resident Surgeon, and later by Martha Hughes Cannon. A number of women doctors, among them Romania B. Pratt, Ellis R. Shipp, and E. S. Barney, served as visiting physicians. The hospital had a capacity of thirty to forty patients, but treated an average of sixteen. It was a subscription hospital to which members of the association paid $1 per year. In addition, the Relief Society, the Young Ladies and Young Men's Mutual Improvement associations, and private donors contributed to its operation.

Salt Lake City was also the site of a number of other benevolent institutions. The Salt Lake County Almshouse in 1890, for instance, housed forty-four paupers, seventy percent of whom were foreign born. The Young Ladies' Aid Society, a nonsectarian association to help young women moving to the city, is another example. In 1872, the territorial hospital for those with mental diseases was located in Salt Lake City near where the This is the Place Monument is now situated. Financed by the city, it was under the supervision of Seymour B. Young. Young bought the hospital in 1876, and he operated it as a private facility until the territory established a mental hospital in Provo in 1885. There was also an Orphan's Home and Day Nursery, operated by the ladies principally from Protestant churches, and it provided shelter and care for orphans and a day nursery for children of working mothers.

The Industrial Christian Home, located on Fifth East between First and Second South, was chartered by Congress as a refuge for wives and children trying to escape polygamy. Operated by the Industrial Christian Home Association, the home was never successful, and was eventually turned over to the Interior Department and used as an office building for territorial officials before its sale as a private club.

In addition, some church-related benevolent associations were organized. In 1883, for instance, Feramorz Little erected a home for the benefit of the worthy poor of the Thirteenth Ward, which encompassed the area between South Temple and Third South and Main Street and Third East. The building, constructed behind the ward meetinghouse, was dedicated in September.

Students attending school in Salt Lake City in the late nineteenth century had essentially two choices: Mormon-dominated public schools or Protestant-or Catholic-related private schools. The public school system was divided into districts that corresponded with the city's LDS wards. Financed in part by property taxes and in part by tuition, the schools often taught Mormon doctrine in addition to secular subjects. The schools were generally one-teacher establishments, and in 1889, an average of only seventy-two students attended each school. The Twentieth Ward school under Karl G. Maeser, W. H. Rager's Seminary in the Thirteenth Ward, and the Social Hall Graded School under Mary E. Cook, were reported to be among the best. Salaries for teachers tended to be quite low. In 1884 they averaged $46.80 per month for men and $28.31 for women.

The movement for fully tax-supported public education, or "free schools," came quite slowly and was accompanied by pressure from the gentile community for nonsectarian education. The territorial legislature in 1872 considered but did not act on petitions for a free school law. In April 1873, the residents of the Seventh Ward school district, located between Main and Third West and Third and Sixth South, urged the adoption of free schools. In spite of Brigham Young's opposition to the movement, sentiment continued to grow. As early as 1874, some of the districts in Salt Lake City established free schools by taxation of the residents. Finally, in 1890, the legislature provided for free tax-supported elementary education.

The controversy over sectarian religious instruction in the schools reached its peak during the mid-1800s and, at times, even reached the courts. In 1884, for instance, the residents of the Seventh Ward voted to increase their tax assessment to build a new school. Gentiles objected to the school and brought the case to the Third District Court, Charles S. Zane presiding. Though contradictory evidence was presented, Judge Zane ruled that the preponderance of evidence demonstrated that the school was a legally valid project in the district. He found that sectarian doctrines were taught in some schools, but heard no evidence that this was the case in the Seventh Ward school. He indicated that residents must support such schools since "the social forces affect each member of the social organization, and the causes that make society better benefit us all."

The alternative to these district schools in Salt Lake City was a system of sectarian education established largely by non-Mormon churches. Though supported in part by tuition, in many cases these schools supplied education without charge to children unable to pay the tuition in the predominantly Mormon district schools. Their purpose, at least in part, was to undermine Mormon education and convert Mormon children to "Christianity" as part of the anti-Mormon crusade. The first of these was St. Mark's School, founded by the Episcopal Church in 1867 and operated at first in the basement of St. Mark's Episcopal Church. In 1871 St. Mark's School for Girls was founded. It also admitted boys under twelve years of age. In addition, the Episcopal church opened Rowland Hall, for girls, in 1880.

Several other religious schools opened as well. The Methodist Episcopal church opened the Salt Lake Seminary on Main Street at Third South in September 1870. Temporarily closed, then reopened in 1879, it included primary, intermediate, grammar, academic, college preparatory, art, and music departments. The Congregational church's New West Educational Commission operated schools in Salt Lake City as well. Two were the Plymouth and the Pilgrim elementary schools. In addition, the Congregationalists founded Salt Lake Academy in 1873. In 1881, the Congregationalists erected Hammond Hall on Third South and Third East.

The Catholic church also operated schools in Salt Lake City. St. Mary's Academy, opened in September 1875, offered education both to boarders and day pupils under the Sisters of the Congregation of the Holy Cross. By 1876, average attendance was reported at 100. By 1881, it was reported that poor Catholic children "scattered in isolated places in the mountains and over the desert wastes," received "the benefit of a good Catholic education" at St. Mary's. The Catholics also operated St. Joseph's School, designed for boys under twelve years of age. It enjoyed an average attendance of about 40 in 1876, most of whom were non-Catholics.

For a time several schools were operated that seem to have had no religious affiliation. In December 1871, it was announced that Professor C. F. W. Bergmer would open a gymnasium for children. In September 1880, the Salt Lake Kindergarten and Graded School opened. It had an attendance of 50 in 1882, but it seems not to have endured.

In addition to these schools, two institutions of higher learning grew in Salt Lake City during the period. In 1875, the Presbyterian church established the Salt Lake Collegiate Institute designed to provide a college preparatory course. Enrolling 142 pupils the first year, by 1883 it boasted an enrollment of 245. In 1887, the institute commenced a collegiate program, under the name Sheldon Jackson College. Between 1891 and 1904, the Collegiate Institute dropped all grades below high school because of its inability to compete with free public schools. In 1902, the name of the institution was changed to Westminster College. Principal financial support came from Presbyterian churches throughout the eastern United States who responded to appeals for funds to help make inroads into the Mormon community.

Most important for the future development of education in Utah was the revitalization of the University of Deseret—later the University of Utah. During the 1860s, Salt Lake City had been the home of two commercial colleges. One, the Morgan Commercial College sponsored by John Morgan, had been quite successful; in 1872 it boasted an enrollment of 689 students. It declined after 1875 when the largely moribund University of Deseret improved its commercial offerings. In 1869, John R. Park, a medical doctor who had left the profession for teaching in South Willow Creek (now Draper) was hired as principal of the newly revitalized "university." Other distinguished faculty members included Karl G. Maeser, a German immigrant who was largely responsible for the Twentieth Ward School, perhaps the best of the many district schools in the city, and who later became the guiding light of Brigham Young Academy in Provo. Another was Joseph L. Rawlins, later a lawyer and United States senator. David O. Calder headed the commercial department, and Louis F. Moench, who taught in Calder's department, was later instrumental in the development of the Weber Stake Academy in Ogden. George Careless provided instruction in music, and Dan Weggeland, the father of Utah painting, instructed in drawing. Mary Elizabeth Cook and Ida Ione Cook, well-trained profressional teachers who operated the Social Hall School in Salt Lake City, taught academic and primary courses in educational methodology.

After struggling through one year, the university suspended operations, then reopened in 1872. Occupying the Council House in the corner of South Temple and Main Street, it moved to Union Square, the site of West High School in 1876, where after considerable difficulty a campus was constructed. Part of that difficulty came from Governor Eli H. Murray vetoing acts appropriating funds for operating the university and for building construction in 1882, 1884, and 1886. Since the vetoes of territorial governors were absolute, construction and operation of the university continued only under private subscription.

In handing down his vetoes, Murray gave three reasons. First, he said the appropriations would incur a deficit, since insufficient revenue would be available to meet the proposed appropriation. Second, he alleged, sectarian doctrines were taught in the university. Third, he said that the territorial organic act vested him with authority to appoint the university's regents, whereas the legislature had been in the habit of appointing them by joint vote of both houses.

Murray was essentially right on the first and third points, though the members of the legislature and prominent citizens of Salt Lake City disagreed with his views. On the second point, however, he was quite wrong. Although John R. Park, a majority of the members of the faculty, and virtually all the regents were Latter-day Saints, all agreed with George Q. Cannon that the university must be "non-sectarian in its character and conducted in such manner as to avoid giving a bias in the pupils' mind in favor of any particular form of religion."

In 1870, Salt Lake City supported three major newspapers. The *Deseret News* generally supported the decisions and opposed the critics of the prominent Mormons who governed Salt Lake City. After the inauguration of the Liberal government in 1890, it became a severe critic of Mayor Scott and his administration. Editors of the *Deseret News* were all prominent Mormons, including George Q. Cannon of the church's First Presidency (1867–1873 and 1877–1879), David O. Calder (1873–1877), and Charles W. Penrose (1880–1892).

In 1870, William S. Godbe, Elias L. T. Harrison, Eli B. Kelsey, and Edward W. Tullidge launched the *Mormon* (afterward *Salt Lake*) *Tribune*, as the organ of the Godbeite movement. In policy it was mildly critical of the local and church leadership. In 1873, however, the owner-ship of the paper changed as Fred Lockley, George F. Prescott, and A. M. Hamilton bought out the founders. The city council, infuriated by a *Tribune* account of a council meeting, ejected the newspaper's reporter from a meeting, and adopted a motion closing the chamber to the newspaper's representatives. Thereafter, the paper conducted a no-holds-barred campaign against the city administration. In 1883, Lockley associates sold out to Patrick H. Lannan and C. C. Goodwin, and while the paper continued to press the fight against Mormon domination, "the voice was not so shrill." As conditions changed in the early 1890s, the newspaper shifted its position to promote Mormon-gentile cooperation and Goodwin became a strong supporter of accommodation and eventual statehood.

The *Deseret News,* though vigorous in its defense of the church, was somewhat reserved in its attacks on anti-Mormons. This was not the case with the *Salt Lake Herald.* Founded in 1870 with Edward L. Sloan as editor, John T. Caine as associate editor, and William C. Dunbar as business manager, the paper became a vigorous supporter of the Salt Lake City government and the LDS church and answered in kind the intemperate and sometimes vicious attacks of the *Salt Lake Tribune* and the anti-Mormon gentiles, whom it labeled a "ring" or a conspiracy to defraud the people of Utah.

By 1890, the city also supported several foreign language newspapers. Several of them failed after only a few issues, but the *Salt Lake City Beobachter,* a German language newspaper, began publication in August 1890 and continued into the twentieth century. Others included the *Utah Posten* (Norwegian) and the *Bikuben* (Danish). These were sponsored by the LDS community and served to provide information both secular and religious to new immigrants.

The city also served as home of several newspapers and periodicals for special interest groups. One, the *Utah Mining Gazette,* eventually merged with the *Salt Lake Tribune.* The *Juvenile Instructor,* edited by George Q. Cannon, served the interests of the Latter-day Saints' Deseret Sunday School Union. The *Women's Exponent,* edited by Louisa Lula Greene Richards, provided stories and political, social and religious information for the large community of Mormon women. In 1889, Susa Young Gates began publication of the *Young Women's Journal,* a magazine for teen-age and young adult Latter-day Saint women, contain-ing stories, religious articles, and general interest pieces.

In 1890 it was reported that 17,500 people out of a population of 44,842 or thirty-nine percent of the population, belonged to some church. Most, of course, were Latter-day Saints, who had twenty-five wards in

Salt Lake City, an increase of five since 1870. Membership in the other major churches ranged in 1890 from a high of 1,350 Catholics to a low of 24 Lutherans. One hundred citizens professed membership in the Jewish congregation. In 1892, the city supported thirty-two church edifices, the majority of which were Mormon. The Methodists, however, had five churches, including one African Methodist Episcopal Church. The Baptists, Catholics, Congregationalists, and Presbyterians each had two churches, the Episcopalians and Lutherans had three each, and the Christian Scientists had one church in the city.

There were also a number of Christian charitable, educational, and cultural societies in the city. These included the Salt Lake County Bible Society, the Salt Lake Sunday School Association, the Utah Christian Endeavor Union, and the YMCA. By far the largest associations were Latter-day Saint. These included the Relief Society, a charitable, educational, and cultural association for women; the Young Ladies Mutual Improvement Association, providing the same services for young women; the Young Men's Mutual Improvement Association, an educational and charitable association for men; and the Primary Association, providing religious instruction for young children.

Such a range of charitable organizations coupled with a large number of lodges and secret societies indicates a rather wide range of interests in the city. By 1892, for instance, the city boasted organizations such as the Ancient Order of Foresters of America and the Ancient Order of United Workmen. There were also patriotic organizations, such as two posts and two ladies' auxiliaries of the Grand Army of the Republic and four camps of the Patriotic Sons of America. The Knights of Pythias boasted seven lodges, the Masons had eleven, and the Independent Order of Odd Fellows eight. Even the Red Men and the Sons of St. George boasted one lodge each. The broad range of lodges, charitable associations, and churches constituted a part of the popular culture of Salt Lake City and indicated the arrival of a true urban environment with the possibility of a large number of subcultures based on a wide range of interests.

By 1892, the city also sported a broad range of special interest clubs. The Salt Lake Rowing Club, founded in 1888, and the Salt Lake Sportsman Club, founded in the same year, are examples. The Tonic Sol Fa Society, founded in 1891, the Salt Lake Dramatic Association, the Salt Lake Fencing Club, and the Harmony Dancing Club catered to specific avocational and cultural interests. In fact, by 1892, the city boasted fifteen bands and three choral groups all organized since 1887. In 1890, the University Club had nearly fifty members, all college graduates from colleges and universities throughout the United States.

Numerous literary societies including the Chautauqua Literary and Scientific Circle offered their programs to members and the public.

The immigrant groups in Salt Lake City tried to maintain the cultures of the countries from which they had come. As early as 1878, the Scandinavians boasted a fine choir. In 1891, the Scandinavian Dramatic Club toured the southern part of the territory. The German Concordia Singing Society provided concerts as early as 1871. By the 1890s, the city boasted a German Turnverein with physical exercises and gymnastics.

Both the Latter-day Saint and gentile subcultures sponsored various literary organizations. The Liberal Institute, established by the Godbeites, provided space for Chautauqua meetings, lectures, and religious services for non-Mormon churches unable to construct their own meeting houses. The Latter-day Saints, particularly before the organization of the Young Ladies and Young Men's Mutual Improvement Associations, sponsored such organizations as the Wasatch Literary Association, which during the mid- and late 1870s provided a literary and social outlet for groups of people.

Salt Lake also supported a number of theatrical establishments. The epitome of these was undoubtedly the Salt Lake Theatre, which served both as a stage for prominent national road companies and for the Home Dramatic Company. The Liberal Institute died because of competition from the Walker Opera House, which also provided theatrical, musical, and cultural fare. By 1892, two other popular theatres, the Pavilion and the People's provided somewhat more pedestrian and typical vaudevillian entertainment.

The city also supported a museum with collections of some interest. Opened in 1869 with John W. Young as proprietor, the Deseret Museum housed a potpourri of art, native products, manufactures, ores and minerals, Indian artifacts, Kit Carsons's boat, and examples of native animals, birds, and reptiles. James E. Talmage became curator in 1891, and the museum served as the basis of the LDS church's visitor center museum on Temple Square.

The city also sponsored various types of athletic and leisure time amusements. As early as 1871, the city had several bowling alleys. Guests of the Clift House, and perhaps other hotels, could play billiards. Trobridges and other billiard halls provided a resort for that amusement as well. By the early 1870s, citizens could watch, and bet on, trotter racing at Faust's track.

Perhaps the greatest public interest developed during the 1870s and 1880s in a series of amateur and semiprofessional baseball teams. In the period from 1877 through 1879, the local rivalry was extremely intense as the city boasted two teams, the gentile-dominated "Deseret

Club" and the Mormon "Red Stockings." The Deseret Club was particularly aggressive, at times hiring professional players. Interest was so high that for several games fully a fourth of the city's population came to Washington Square (site of the present City and County Building) to watch the games.

By 1880, conditions had changed in local baseball. The Deserets had become a frankly professional team made up largely of players recruited from outside the city. The public lost interest, and even became hostile to the degree that the city would no longer let the teams use Washington Square for their games. Baseball revived again after 1883, but on the basis of business promotion rather than intensive subcultural support from interested Salt Lake partisans.

By the early 1870s, the city had become large enough to support libraries. The largest and by far most successful was the Masonic Library. It was founded in 1873, and by 1888 it housed 17,850 volumes. Special interests of the Masonic Library included Masonry, geology, mining, farming, and silk and bee culture. In 1833 it served an average of thirty-seven persons per day in its reading room. Other libraries operating by 1892 included the IOOF library with 2,000 volumes, the Pioneer Library with 9,000 volumes, the Territorial Law Library (housed in the Salt Lake City Building) with 4,500 volumes, and the University of Utah Library with 12,000 volumes.

In spite of the ease with which citizens could escape to the nearby mountains, go to Great Salt Lake for bathing, or take the waters at Warm Springs, the desire for pastoral oases in the city led to the creation of parks. The most important of these, Liberty Park, started with the purchase of farm property during the Feramorz Little administration. By 1892, the city had several other parks—Arsenal Block and the Capitol Grounds (the present site of the State Capitol), Calder's Park (west of Seventh East and south of Thirteenth South), the Salt Lake Driving Park (south of Fifth East below Twelfth South), Smoot's Gardens (on Eleventh East and South Boulevard), and Washington Square.

In addition to these generally respectable forms of recreation, the city housed other less desirable resorts. Centered around what is now Regent Street (then called Commercial Street), Franklin Avenue (now Edison Street), and Victoria Alley, a block south of Commercial Street, were houses of prostitution and opium dens. A study in 1880 estimated that Salt Lake City had five houses of prostitution, and estimates in the early 1890s placed the figure near thirty-five. These were subjected to periodic raids by the city police department largely for the purpose of control and raising revenue.

There were at least two Chinese opium dens in the city, and a reporter from the *Deseret News* visited them in August 1883. One, operated by

Chinese Dick, could be reached only after passing down a dark "musty and unwholesome" stairway to an underground apartment. The sides were faced with rough boards and around the room "were large shelves covered with matting, on which the opium smokers engaged in their pernicious practice." The den sported a table for gambling. The reporter also visited the den of Quong Wah Sing, next door, which, like Chinese Dick's was reported to cater to twenty to thirty lodgers each night, "packed away like sardines" in "the foul, fetid, atmosphere that necessarily pervaded these degraded dens."

In some ways, two events of this era are especially significant not only intrinsically, but also for what they reveal about the culture of Salt Lake City. The first was the debate on August 12, 1870 between Orson Pratt, a member of the Council of the Twelve of the LDS church, and Methodist minister John P. Newman, chaplain of the U.S. Senate, on the question of whether the Bible sanctioned polygamy. The second was the murder of Salt Lake City chief of police and well-liked Mormon bishop Andrew H. Burt and the subsequent lynching of his murderer, a black named Sam Joe Harvey, on August 25, 1883.

The Pratt-Newman debate is probably best known. Edward L. Sloan, then editor of the *Salt Lake Daily Telegraph*, suggested editorially that Newman come to Salt Lake City to discuss the subject of polygamy. Arriving in town without previous arrangement, the Reverend Dr. Newman promptly wrote Brigham Young accepting what he assumed to be a challenge. Young demurred on the ground that he had issued no such challenge, but offered the pulpit of the tabernacle to Newman. After an exchange of correspondence, Young agreed to send Orson Pratt or John Taylor to debate.

The debate reveals much about the community. In the first place, there was a general tendency on the part of the gentiles to assume that Brigham Young controlled everything that went on there and thus to believe that a suggestion from the newspaper editor was equivalent to the transmission of an order from his church president. Brigham Young's consternation at Newman's interpretation is understandable since he recognized that the LDS community, especially in Salt Lake City, was quite diffuse, and that while Mormons held most important positions in the city and territory, he did not dictate each set of events—not even the dictator in a totalitarian society could do that.

Second, the debate demonstrated the sophistication of some in the city. Orson Pratt reportedly accounted himself well in the interchange. A careful, if biased, student, he had a good grasp of the culture of Biblical peoples and was able to express himself with eloquence. Edward Tullidge, at the time estranged from the Latter-day Saints, thought Pratt had the better of the exchange.

Third, the debate symbolized the division within the community. Pratt represented the Latter-day Saint faction which made up the majority in the city. Newman stood for the nationally more numerous Protestants who perceived the Mormons to be barbarian, un-Christian, and ignorant slaves of Brigham Young. Many Protestant educational efforts in Salt Lake and elsewhere were aimed at converting the Latter-day Saints to enlightenment and Christian civilization. Salt Lake City thus exhibited two cultural groups with some overlapping interests, but a broad range of incompatibility and antagonism.

The Harvey-Burt episode is perhaps less well known. Harvey, an unemployed black, came to Salt Lake City on August 25, 1883. After panhandling somewhat belligerently through the city, he got into an argument with Frances Grice, another black, at the latter's restaurant on South Main. Grice offered Harvey a job, which the vagrant angrily declined, and after threatening Grice, he purchased a rifle with what was apparently stolen money. After learning of the incident through a telephone call, Andrew Burt tried to arrest Harvey, who shot and killed him. Harvey was taken into custody and beaten by the police officers, then turned over to a howling mob estimated at 2,000, who hanged him in a nearby stable. Unsatisfied with the results, a second mob cut the body down and dragged the corpse through the alley and along State Street. Sickened by the events, one prominent citizen, William H. Sells, tried unsuccessfully to stop the mob, which threatened him with lynching for his efforts. Outraged by the sight of the mutilated corpse, Mayor William Jennings, accompanied by the U.S. Marshal E. A. Ireland, succeeded by sheer force of will in extricating the body from the mob. On August 28, a griefstricken city laid Andrew Burt to rest after a funeral in the tabernacle.

These events say much about Salt Lake City. They suggest that for some things the citizens of the city, or at least one group drawn principally from the lower-middle and lower classes, were able to overcome the Mormon-gentile division and act together in a common cause. Beyond this, the city was divided into at least three groups along economic and social rather than religious lines. Mayor Jennings, a businessman of wealth and station, and William Sells, a lumber dealer, were obviously of a different temperament and outlook than either the lynch mob made up of lower-middle class and lower class citizens or the vagrants, like Harvey, living on the edge of the law. That Harvey was black made his situation even more precarious both among Mormons and gentiles. Here too, class differences transcended religious lines.

Even in this incident, however, the division between Mormon and gentile came to the surface. A journalistic war between the *Deseret*

Dectective Paul Cephas Howell, who served on the Police Force for more than twenty years. Courtesy, Utah State Historical Society, Peoples of Utah Collection.

Orson Pratt, LDS apostle, and the Church's representative in the Pratt-Newman debate in 1870. Courtesy, LDS Church Archives.

News, the *Herald* and the *Salt Lake Tribune* ensued in which the *Tribune* intimated that the Church was somehow responsible and that the incident was an example of the ineffective administration the Mormon majority had provided for the city. Replying in kind, the *Deseret News* charged the *Tribune* with sustaining the city's lawless element, a charge which the *Salt Lake Herald* echoed.

In fact, the journalistic postmortem which ensued also reveals much about the temper of the city at the time. All three newspapers and John Taylor, who delivered Burt's eulogy, deplored the mob violence. Nevertheless, the *Tribune* helped to frustrate any attempt to achieve justice by cloaking its call for an investigation in anti-Mormon rhetoric, and the *Deseret News* and *Herald*, while deploring vigilantism as a breach of the rule of law, argued that Harvey deserved death as a matter of justice.

By 1892, Salt Lake had passed the village stage to become what was for the time a modern city. It had moved most rapidly to provide those services for which an apparent, though at times unrealized profit, seemed possible. Thus, electric, gas, transportation, and telephone service came more rapidly to Salt Lake than to other contemporary cities. On the other hand, the city lagged behind in providing water, sewage, paving, and health services. The result was a pent-up pressure which caused considerable local conflict when released during the Scott administration of 1890–1892, when the citizens had to pay the bill for the People's party's unwillingness to provide such utilities.

By the early 1890s as well, the city had reached a critical mass of population, and virtually anyone could fit into some subcultural group. For most Latter-day Saints, their lives revolved around their ward. Nevertheless, those interested in business, music, drama, literature, sports, or even gambling could find a group well suited to their liking within the city. For a time, at least, politics had been removed from the religious realm, and Mormons and gentiles could work together to see their common economic, political, and social interests realized through the political process.

Salt Lake City ca. 1910 Looking North from Third South. Courtesy, Utah State Historical Society.

5

The Americanization of Salt Lake City, 1893-1911

People often become inured to existing conditions and reluctant to accept change. They are sometimes dubious about the motives and programs of those who work to bring about change until it becomes apparent that the changes will be to their advantage. This conservatism was evident in a number of ways in Salt Lake City in the period between 1893 and 1911. Some members of the Liberal party were reluctant to drop that affiliation because they mistrusted the motives of the Latter-day Saints until it became clear that Mormons had really divided into two parties and that they could not win elections in opposition to the Republicans and Democrats. Later, after the organization of the American party, Republicans and Democrats were dubious about supporting fusion tickets in Salt Lake even though the division into three parties left the upstart third party in control of the city government for six years.

The 1893 city election brought out this conservative tendency in the *Salt Lake Tribune*. In 1893, Robert N. Baskin bolted the Liberal party to run for reelection as mayor on a citizen's reform ticket. The *Salt Lake Tribune*, for years the organ of the Liberal party, expressed dismay at this situation, and while it had supported Baskin's candidacy on the Liberal party ticket in 1891, it refused to do so in 1893 when he ran on the citizen's ticket. Baskin nevertheless won the election.

In 1895, Utah elected the first group of officials to the new state government, and the major political parties engaged in a hard-fought battle for control of city government. Republican James J. Glendinning, a local businessman, had been associated with former Liberal party mayor George Scott. Francis Armstrong, former mayor and prominent businessman, received the Democratic party's nod, and Elijah Sells, formerly Republican territorial secretary, ran as a Populist. While the Populists constituted a basically agrarian party in the South and Midwest, in the Mountain West they formed largely an urban coalition. Glendinning won by about fifty-three percent of the popular vote in the Republican landslide of the first statehood election. The city council, however, was almost evenly divided with eight Republicans and seven Democrats.

Glendinning moved in an extremly partisan fashion to remove certain employees held over from the Baskin administration. He replaced Chief of Police Arthur Pratt with Samuel Paul, and secured the enactment of an ordinance abolishing the office of Inspector of Provisions, relieving James G. McAllister of that position. This was very serious since the inspector certified the purity of food and drinks sold in the city. By the second year of Glendinning's administration, this partisanship had fueled an open rupture between the mayor and the council, and a number of the less partisan Republican members sided with the Democrats in disputes with the mayor over the salaries and positions of the police captain and the mayor's clerk.

By 1897, this partisanship had fouled the water for the major parties. To a number of prominent Salt Lake City citizens it seemed to undermine the necessary efficiency and effectiveness of city administration. Some of them caucused, therefore, and nominated a "Citizen's Reform Ticket," headed by businessman John Clark, a nominal Democrat who was also a member of the Salt Lake Stake High Council. The slate for councilmen and other officers consisted of Mormons and gentiles from both political parties. Repudiating Glendinning, the Republicans nominated Abraham F. Doremus, a civil engineer, and the Democrats selected William H. Dale, a banker. The Populists nominated Henry W. Lawrence, a prominent businessman and former Godbeite, and the Socialist Labor party nominated Richard A. Hasbrouck, a physician and former Populist. Clark won the election with fewer than 100 votes over Dale and pulling less than a third of the popular vote, Doremus and Lawrence ran far behind, and Hasbrouck barely exceeded 100 votes. Despite Clark's narrow margin, this temporary victory for nonpartisanship revived the spirit of Baskin's second election, and anticipated the final banishment of party labels in 1911. It also reflected a trend toward "non-partisanship" seen in many British and American cities of the time.

In 1899 the Citizen's ticket withdrew and the next two mayors were Republican businessman Ezra Thompson, and Democratic businessman and former city treasurer Richard P. Morris. With Thompson and Morris, Salt Lake City had its first Utah-born mayors. Their immediate predecessors, Glendinning and Clark, had been born in the British Isles, and Baskin came from Ohio.

During the administration of Robert Baskin, Salt Lake experienced all the pains of the nationwide depression of the early 1890s. Mining, commerce, and transportation, the mainstays of the city's economy, suffered considerably. Between 1891 and 1893, railroad construction, which had sparked a boom in the 1880s, slowed to a halt, the production of silver dropped 33 percent, copper production declined 48 percent, and salt production dropped 92 percent. Estimates placed unemployment in Salt Lake City at 4,347 in a labor force of 9,000, or 48 percent in the spring of 1894. Though some observers doubted the accuracy of the figure, all conceded that unemployment was "dangerously high."

Attempts to alleviate the distress caused by these economic problems came from a number of sources. The LDS church responded in a variety of ways. It encouraged those who could to leave the city and move to country settlements, or, alternatively, after the Spanish-American War began, to enlist in the service. It also urged missionaries to discourage migration to Utah. LDS wards in Salt Lake City secured unused land for the unemployed to grow vegetables, and they sent groups to outlying farms to glean wheat, fruit, and potatoes. Church members were encouraged to fast one day a month and turn the uneaten food over to their bishop to support the needy. A report at the Salt Lake Stake conference in March 1894 indicated that more than 1,600 persons relied upon the church for support, which came from fast offering, tithing, and from the Relief Society. Mormons were further encouraged to patronize home industries to provide employment for local members.

These, however, were only temporary expedients that did little more than redistribute the poverty. More basic measures included the financing of several new and expanded businesses designed to provide goods and services for the community and to employ those without work. Following a calculated policy of deficit financing, the church, under President Wilford Woodruff, promoted a number of businesses around Salt Lake City. Especially important for the city were the development of the Inland Crystal Salt Lake Company, the Intermountain Salt Works, Saltair resort, and the Salt Lake and Los Angeles Railroad (later called the Salt Lake, Garfield, and Western).

Beyond these LDS activities, various other organizations undertook measures to try to ameliorate the impact of the depression. One of the most active was the Populist party, which began an organization in Utah. Populism in Utah had its principal success in Salt Lake City and Ogden.

Mainstreet About 1900. Courtesy, Utah State Historical Society.

After inaugurating a territorial organization, centered in Salt Lake City in the fall of 1893, the Populists began to respond to economic distress. Between 1893 and 1895, they organized a lending library, a board of labor, an employment office, and worker clubs which pressed Salt Lake City government with only minimal success for municipal public works projects. In March 1895, Populists also led a group of demonstrators who demanded work. The party promoted its program through the pages of the *Intermountain Advocate*, a newspaper published in Salt Lake and edited by Warren Foster, a Kansas newspaperman who came to Utah in 1894.

The Populists continued to operate in Utah at least nominally, but their fusion with the Democratic party in 1896 was both the high point of their strength in Utah and the beginning of their decline. Henry Lawrence, as candidate for mayor in 1897, secured the largest number of Populist votes in a Salt Lake City election—he had just over 1,000, but even this was only a fraction of the total vote. Lawrence called for an increase in taxation on vacant property, humane treatment of vagrants and prisoners, and increased public works for the unemployed and for prisoners. The Populists ran William S. Godbe for mayor in 1899. He received only 184 votes, or 1.2 percent of the total. Relatively good times had returned, and pressure for the sort of reforms the Populists demanded no longer drew significant support.

The expansion of railroad construction and mining paced the return of prosperity to Salt Lake City after 1897. Senator Thomas Kearns of Utah, Senator William A. Clark of Montana, R.C. Kerens of Missouri, future Senator Reed Smoot, banker William S. McCornick, and others organized the Los Angeles and Salt Lake Railroad Company in November 1900. Later incorporated into Edward H. Harriman's Union Pacific system, the road reached southern California in 1905. In November 1909, the Western Pacific completed construction between Salt Lake City and San Francisco. The completion of the interurban Salt Lake and Ogden Railway, owned by Simon Bamberger, between Salt Lake and Ogden in 1910 improved transportation. So also did the Salt Lake and Utah Railroad (nicknamed the Orem Line after its founder Walter C. Orem), which was extended to Payson in 1916. Both the Union Pacific and the Denver and Rio Grande built impressive depots on Salt Lake's west side, which provided a sense of stability to that portion of the city.

Undoubtedly the most significant development in the economic growth of Salt Lake City was the expansion of mining. Despite the closing of the Ontario Mine in 1897, Park City mines served as the source of the fortunes of a number of entrepreneurs who made Salt Lake their home.

In 1883 John J. Daly organized the Daly Mining Company, first of several of his Park City operations. Others included the Daly-West and the Daly-Judge Company, incorporated in 1901. David Keith went to Park City first as a pumpman in 1883. Later serving as foreman of the Ontario mine, he met Thomas Kearns. With Kearns, John Judge, Albion Emery, and Windsor Rice, Keith secured a lease on the Mayflower property and the Silver King. In 1892 they organized the Silver King Company and in 1907 they incorporated the Silver King Coalition Mines Company, both of which proved enormously successful.

Similar development at Bingham helped Salt Lake City to grow as well. Precious metal mining had begun earlier at Bingham, but in 1896 Samuel Newhouse and Thomas Weir organized the Highland Boy Gold Mining Company and a group of British investors established the Utah Consolidated Gold Mines, Ltd. to provide capital. Newhouse and Weir found extensive copper deposits, and in 1899 sold a controlling interest to Standard Oil Company officials William Rockefeller and Henry H. Rogers. In the meantime, Newhouse and Weir formed the Boston Consolidated Copper and Gold Mining Company, Ltd. on adjacent claims. They headed Boston Consolidated until its absorption by the Utah Copper Company in 1910.

Organized in 1903 by Daniel C. Jackling, Charles M. MacNeill, and Spencer Penrose, the Utah Copper Company secured financial support from the Guggenheim interests. In 1906 they initiated open cut operations in Bingham Canyon on the low grade porphry ores. By 1912, Utah Copper employed 4,500 men in the mine and 1,200 in its large smelter.

Other mining districts produced wealth that flowed to Salt Lake as well. Gold mining operations took place concurrently under John and George H. Dern at Mercur, and mining in the Tintic district also expanded during the first decade of the twentieth century.

Other businesses in and around Salt Lake City contributed to its growth as well. It is estimated that by 1907 the forty-four largest businesses in the city had an average payroll of $17 million per year. The Inland Crystal Salt Company developed a virtual monopoly of salt production for the intermountain market. Salt Lake City was also headquarters of the Utah-Idaho Sugar Company. Organized first as the Utah Sugar Company in 1891, it was reorganized through a merger with the Idaho Sugar Company to form the Utah-Idaho Sugar Company. Utah Fuel Company, with extensive coal mining operations in Carbon County, had its headquarters in Salt Lake City as well.

Residential and business construction in Salt Lake City slowed between 1893 and 1898. The major exception was the Salt Lake City and County building on Washington Square in 1894. This building, designed by Henry Monheim, George W. Bird, and Willis T. Proudfoot, is perhaps the finest example of Richardson Romanesque architecture in the state. All these buildings had been started before the depression. Nevertheless, between the 1890s and 1915, expenditure of the new wealth transformed the face of downtown Salt Lake City into the early twentieth century urban visage it was to wear until quite recently.

In designing buildings for downtown Salt Lake City, architects did not adhere slavishly to any particular style. The Dooly Building, designed by Louis Sullivan in 1894, was the first of several Sullivanesque buildings. Others included the McCornick Building designed by Mendelsohn and Fisher of Omaha, and the McIntyre building designed in 1909 by Richard Kletting. A number of neoclassical buildings included the Federal Building, the nearby Salt Lake Stock Exchange, and the Park Building at the University of Utah. The latter two buildings were designed by Lewis T. Cannon and John Fetzer.

Buildings in Salt Lake were constructed in various popular architectural modes. A number of buildings were built in the Renaissance Revival style. These include Frederick Albert Hale's Alta Club, erected on South Temple in 1897. The Commercial Club Building on Exchange Place designed by Walter E. Ware and Albert Owen Treganza represents the Italian palazzo style. Richard K. A. Kletting, perhaps Salt Lake City's best known early twentieth-century architect, designed a series of four brick and stone buildings in 1901 and 1902 for the University of Utah. Additional Kletting structures included Saltair, the Kearns Building (1910), and the state capitol building completed in 1916. A reinforced concrete frame structure draped with granite, the state capitol was inspired by Maryland's statehouse and the United States Capitol building.

Many downtown buildings were designed in the then-popular commercial style. These included Kletting's Deseret News Building (1902) on the northern boundary of the central business district. The southern end of the district was marked by the Judge Building (1906) and the twin Boston and Newhouse buildings (1910) flanking Exchange Place and Main Street.

The Mormon church also contributed substantially to the changing face of Salt Lake City. In 1910 it completed the new Bishop's Building on the block immediately east of the Salt Lake Temple, as well as a new recreational facility, Deseret Gymnasium. The handsome five-story Church Office Building, a granite, neoclassical structure completed in 1917, was located at 47 East South Temple and seemed to be a symbol of the church's twentieth-century prosperity and of its increasing acceptance in the world. To make room for these and other structures, the church razed the prominent old Deseret Store and other nineteenth-cen-

South Temple and Main Street, July 1909. From Left to Right: Almost Completed LDS Church Bishop's Building, Excavation for Hotel Utah, and Framework for the Deseret Gymnasium. Courtesy, Utah State Historical Society.

tury structures relating to the Presiding Bishop's office. In addition, modern architectural design was introduced into Latter-day Saint meetinghouses. Largely the work of Harold W. Burton and Hyrum C. Pope, who were influenced heavily by the prairie-style architecture of Frank Lloyd Wright, many new chapels provided a noticeable contrast to the early mixture of Gothic and classical design.

Such rapid change in the face of the city did not long go unnoticed. Special editions of the *Salt Lake Tribune* in January 1905, touted as a "business proclamation," linked the changes with mining, the progress of the railroad, and other industries in and around the city. In December 1909, the *Deseret News* published accounts of more than sixty buildings of importance "finished and commenced" in the city that year, including the Newhouse Hotel, the Hotel Utah, the Newhouse and Boston buildings, the D and R. G. W. Depot, the Kearns building, and the New Street Car Barns on Seventh East (now Trolley Square).

The construction of these new buildings heralded the arrival of a new urban elite, which did not displace the earlier groups but took its place alongside those that had arisen in the 1870s. The elite of the 1850s had represented the LDS church leaders. That of the 1870s had founded their fortunes on commerce and banking, but the new elite, while often holding investments in commerce, transportation, and finance, owed their principal wealth to mining.

In addition to commercial structures, the new generation of elites constructed homes that became personal monuments. A great many located along South Temple, or Brigham Street, as it was familiarly known, and a number bear mentioning. Samuel Newhouse, born in New York City in 1854 to Russian-Jewish immigrants, studied law; then, after engaging in an unsuccessful practice in Pennsylvania, he moved to Colorado where he met and married Ida Stingley. After activity in Leadville, Cripple Creek, and Denver, he invested in the Highland Boy property at Bingham and in mines near Frisco in Beaver County. After purchasing the property at 165 East South Temple, he remodeled the home into a colonial mansion, which together with residences in London, Paris, and Long Island, served for his noted entertaining.

Enos A. Wall also began his mining ventures in Colorado. Then, after investing in Montana and northern Idaho, he turned to Utah. His investments included mines in Silver Reef, Little Cottonwood, Ophir, Mercur, and Bingham. He also served as chairman of the Salt Lake City Board of Public Works. In 1904, he purchased a two-story adobe home originally built in 1880 by Bishop James Sharp and hired Richard Kletting to transform it into a Renaissance villa. There he once hosted President Theodore Roosevelt.

Another member of the former Colorado crowd was Daniel C. Jackling. Born in Missouri and orphaned at an early age, Jackling worked his way through the Missouri School of Mines and moved to Cripple Creek. Associated at first with Joseph R. DeLamar, he invested with and then became disaffected from Enos Wall at Bingham. One of the organizers of the Utah Copper Company, he successfully initiated the low grade copper operations in Utah and achieved a degree of wealth and a life style which led to a reputation as a reprobate and to a subsequent separation from his wife. Living first in a home designed by Walter E. Ware for William A. Sherman, he moved in 1911 to a suite on the upper floors of the Hotel Utah in 1911. In 1915, he moved to San Francisco.

Best known of the Brigham Street elites was Thomas Kearns, who, like David Keith and John Daly, made his fortune at Park City. Socially and politically prominent in Utah, he had been born in Canada to immigrant parents and grew up on a Nebraska farm. His wife, Jennie Judge, oversaw the construction of their home, now the governor's mansion on South Temple, which was built in the French Renaissance style.

Kearns served as a member of the state constitutional convention, as U.S. senator from Utah, and was owner of the *Salt Lake Tribune*.

Representative of the social side of this new elite was Susanna Egeria Bransford Emery Holmes, often called Utah's Silver Queen, who purchased the Amelia Palace or Gardo House Brigham Young had constructed for his wife Amelia Folsom. Mrs. Holmes became the arbiter of Salt Lake's high society, offering previews in her home of coming attractions of the Salt Lake Theatre and other entertainments to elite congregations of 200 to 300 guests.

Though most of the new elite owed their wealth to mining, some, like James E. Cosgriff, amassed fortunes from other fields of business. Cosgriff moved to Salt Lake City from Wyoming in 1905, where he invested heavily in the wool-growing industry. In 1910, he founded the Continental Bank and Trust Company, which moved rapidly into the front ranks of Salt Lake City's financial community. In 1913, he purchased the Thomas Weir home on South Temple, a classically styled building of yellow sandstone.

Increasingly, Salt Lake's business elites combined with outside financial interests to link many of the businesses in and around Salt Lake City to national monopolistic corporations, which began to dominate American economic life in the twentieth century. Edward H. Harriman's Union Pacific Company absorbed the Salt Lake, Los Angeles, and San Pedro Railroad Company and the Salt Lake City Street Railway. The Utah-Idaho Sugar Company came under the domination of Henry Havemeyer's American Sugar Refining Company. Utah Copper Company became part of Kennecott Copper Corporation. Utah Fuel Company, a subsidiary of Denver and Rio Grande Western, monopolized the coal market until the monopoly was broken during World War I. Even the local ice business was dominated by an oligopoly of two companies that charged what many considered extortionate prices for blocks of ice cut from local ponds during the winter or, after 1900, manufactured in newly constructed refrigeration plants.

On occasion, the old elites and the new interlocked through familial, club, and business connections. Thomas Weir, for instance, became a vice-president of Walker Brothers Bank. Thomas Kearns joined with Reed Smoot and William S. McCornick to invest in railroads. Heber J. Grant and Thomas Kearns rubbed shoulders at the Commercial Club. John Henry Smith, John Dern, Daniel C. Jackling, and Anthon H. Lund all served on the Capitol Commission.

At the other end of the economic spectrum, a new group of immigrants also came to the city, joining two minority groups that had been there earlier. The Chinese had arrived with the railroad, moved into service and commercial occupations, and centered their community in the Eleventh Ward, particularly around Plum Alley which ran between Main and State Streets between First and Second South. Blacks had been in Salt Lake City from its beginning and tended to live in the Eighth Ward, which was located between Third and Sixth South and Main Street and Third East. New additions to the black community included incoming railroad workers and members of the Twenty-fourth Infantry which arrived at Fort Douglas in October 1896. Most black soldiers left during the Spanish-American War, but in 1899 some of the black Ninth Cavalry was stationed at Fort Douglas.

Other newcomers arrived from Southern and Eastern Europe, the Middle East, and Japan, and most came after 1900. For them, the dividing line between their ghettos and the rest of the city became West Temple on the east and First South on the north. The Japanese community centered on a two-block area between West Temple and Third West along First South Street. Syrians congregated near Third South and Fifth West. Italians, who had begun to come to Utah somewhat earlier than the other immigrants, tended to spread out over the west side, generally near the railroads. The Greeks located on West Second South between Fourth and Sixth West. These areas were the most poverty stricken parts of Salt Lake City.

Each of these ghetto-like communities developed its own institutions. The blacks sponsored newspapers like the *Broad Axe* and the *Utah Plain Dealer*. Greek newspapers included *To Fos* and *O Evzone*. The Japanese published the *Rocky Mountain Times* and later the *Utah Nippo*. Businesses catered to ethnic needs as Greek coffee houses and Asiatic specialty shops offered food, drink, and entertainment familiar to the immigrants. Agents like Leonidas G. Skliris and Edward D. Hashimoto furnished railroads and mining companies with laborers, and their fees were drawn from the workers' wages.

In general, these new immigrants came to Utah in search of jobs. In many cases, they developed a labor consciousness, and tried to bargain for better working conditions and higher wages. The last wave of this early twentieth-century migration—the Mexicans—came after 1912 to break the strike of Greeks and Italians at Bingham Canyon. Like their predecessors, many moved to Salt Lake City seeking work. They, too, found homes on the city's west side.

In part because of the efforts to replicate their culture and in part because of the attitudes of Americans of Northern European extraction, these people paid a considerable psychic and personal cost for their immigration to the United States. Italians were referred to by such derogatory names as "dagos." A headline in a 1907 issue of the *Salt*

Lake Tribune editorialized: "Vicious Dago Scoundrel Murders Inoffensive Railroad Employee." A master's thesis completed at the University of Utah in 1915 indicated the prevailing attitude toward Greeks and Italians. Averring that the Greeks and Italians "are perhaps the most careless and shiftless people found," the author went on to say that they found comfort only in smoking and drinking and that their standard of living "is lower than of any other nationality." Moreover, she asserted they "seem to have no initiative or resources of their own." "They lack," the author opined, "a fighting and persevering spirit that might lead them to a better life."

From his office on West Second South, Leonidas G. Skliris, "The Czar of the Greeks," preyed on his own people by providing jobs at a fee. Born in Sparta, Skliris imported workers from Greece or sent agents to recruit them at the nearby railroad stations to work in various occupations—principally on the railroads and in mines in Utah. Skliris could supply strikebreakers on demand for companies in the American West. New immigrants, looking for work and generally not oriented to conditions in the community, agreed to pay him a $20 initial fee (a month's wages for many) and $1 per month. As part of the agreement, Skliris expected them to trade only at businesses operated by his friends.

Trying to keep their cultures together, they replicated the institutions and customs of their old countries. The Greeks built Holy Trinity Church, a small one-domed brick building on Fourth South between Third and Fourth West. Dedicated on October 29, 1905, it served Greeks, Serbians, Albanians, and Russians. Priests in their traditional robes, pectoral crosses, and cylindrical hats administered the sacraments and settled disputes. At the coffee houses they drank *ouzo* or *mastiha*, watched puppet shows, or listened to songs from the war against the Turks.

Although the largest percentage of foreign born in Salt Lake City continued to come from northwestern Europe and Canada, the number arriving from other areas after 1890 is significant. The Japanese population jumped from none in 1890 to 345 in 1910. The black population increased from 218 in 1890 to 737 in 1910. Italians numbered 379 in 1910, up from 100 in 1890. Greeks boasted 621 in 1910, an increase from virtually none in 1890. The Chinese population, on the other hand, decreased from 266 in 1890 to 193 in 1910.

By comparison, however, immigrants from northwestern Europe and Canada far outnumbered those from other areas and continued to dominate Salt Lake City's foreign-born population. Of those living in the city in 1910, 5,934 came from England, and another 2,261 from other parts of the British Isles. Germany was home to 2,102 immigrants, Sweden to 2,278, and Denmark to 1,554.

Leonidas Skliris, Greek Labor Agent. Courtesy, Utah State Historical Society.

As the economy of Salt Lake City changed, and with the continued importance of the immigrant community, the labor movement also underwent significant changes. During the depression of the 1890s, in spite of the vigor with which organizations like the Populist party moved to alleviate suffering, severe economic conditions, the competition for jobs, and the Mormon-gentile division virtually destroyed the movement. Between 1900 and 1920, however, organized labor was revitalized, and by 1920 it exhibited the characteristics typical of craft unionism.

Salt Lake City workers led out in the organization of Utah labor. Largely responsible for its revival was Robert G. Sleater, a Salt Lake typographer who became president of the Utah Federation of Labor in 1896. By 1899, labor was strong enough in Salt Lake City to reorganize the Building Trades Council, similar to the Building Trades Congress which had dissolved under depression conditions in 1894. By that time most unions were affiliated with the Utah Federation of Labor, which, despite its name, was rather more a Salt Lake City central than a statewide organization. Between 1901 and 1904, unions, particularly the building trades, were generally successful in organizing and securing settlements of disputes over wages and working conditions based on negotiations of their demands with employers.

As might be expected, management organized as well to meet what it perceived as a threat to the control of their businesses. In 1903 a Citizen's Alliance of Salt Lake employers formed to combat unionism. Pressure of the Citizen's Alliance increased, but it was generally not successful until after World War I.

Another component of the labor force in Salt Lake City deserves mention. There is a tendency to think of the Utah family in the period before World War II as consisting of a father who worked outside the home, a mother who worked in the home, and children who attended school. This was not always the case. In fact, particularly in urban areas like Salt Lake City, during the 1890s and the first decade of the twentieth century, significant numbers of women worked outside the home. Many worked as milliners, dressmakers, and lodging housekeepers. A number entered trades, and others worked at jobs in domestic service, laundries, or as seamstresses. Some entered professions, especially nursing and teaching, where women outnumbered men, and medicine, where women constituted a significant component of the Salt Lake City community.

Somewhat typical of employed women in Salt Lake City were Lois and Josie Ellen Maxfield. Reared on a homestead in Big Cottonwood Canyon, they were recruited for work by the Utah Independent Telephone Company, a short-lived competitor of the Bell System. One left to become a cashier at Lyric Theatre, and after the telephone company

Martha Hughes Cannon, prominent physician, state senator, and progressive politician. Courtesy, Utah State Historical Society.

folded, both of them became saleswomen at a local department store. They remained in this position until they married in 1919.

Less typical, perhaps, was Martha Hughes Cannon. Born at Llandudno, Wales, she came as an infant with her convert parents to Salt Lake City. She set type for the *Deseret News* for a time and in 1876 enrolled in the medical department of the University of Deseret (now University of Utah). In 1878, with the blessing of church president John Taylor, she left for the University of Michigan where she completed her medical degree in 1880. She received further education at the University of Pennsylvania.

On her return to Salt Lake City, she entered private practice, then became a resident physician at the Deseret Hospital. There, she met Angus M. Cannon, who was a member of the hospital board, and she married him as a plural wife in October 1884.

She later established a school for nurses, reared a family, became involved in the woman's movement, and promoted the public health movement. In 1898, she spoke at the fiftieth anniversary commemoration in Washington, D.C. of the Seneca Falls declaration of women's rights. In 1897 and again in 1899, she was elected to the Utah State Senate as a Democrat, reportedly the first woman state senator in the United States. In the first election, she ran in a field of candidates that included her husband, a Republican. Her major interests included legislation to protect the health of women and girls, education for the deaf and blind, and the creation of a state board of health. After creation of the state board of health, she was appointed a member.

While economic development, new buildings, and the immigrant community assumed more long-range importance in Salt Lake City's development, political affairs caught more contemporary public attention. Between 1905 and 1912, control of Salt Lake City's government passed to a coalition of anti-Mormon ministers, businessmen, and professional people organized as the American party. Coincidentally, the movement for nonpartisan civic government intensified until in 1911 it became more urgent than the anti-Mormon sentiment, and resulted in the establishment of a commission system which lasted until 1980.

Precipitating the anti-Mormon movement was the 1904 testimony of LDS church president Joseph F. Smith before the Senate Committee on Privileges and Elections in the case of Senator Reed Smoot. Smoot, a Mormon apostle, had been elected in 1903, but the Senate tried to expel him. Hearings on the motion to expel centered on church influence in Utah politics, society, and economy, and on polygamy. Smith testified that he was knowingly breaking the law by living with plural wives married before the 1890 Woodruff Manifesto, which had ostensibly

*Emmeline B. Wells, LDS Women's and Political
Leader. Courtesy, Brigham Young University.*

brought an end to the practice. Further testimony revealed that the
church continued its heavy involvement in politics and business in Utah
and surrounding territories. This became the catalyst for organizing the
anti-Mormon American party.

At first cool toward Thomas Kearns, who with David Keith had
purchased the *Salt Lake Tribune*, the American party organizers
swallowed their pride and joined forces with Kearns in September 1904.
In the meantime, Kearns had lost a battle with Smoot for control of the
Republican party and committed political suicide by openly opposing
the church and Smoot.

After its formal organization in September, the party ran a slate of
candidates for state office. All were defeated, but the election returns
showed that the party already controlled about twenty percent of the
popular vote in the metropolitan Salt Lake area. A special election for
the Salt Lake City school board in December 1904 further confirmed
this strength when the Americans elected Joseph Oberndorfer from the
fifth municipal ward by a narrow plurality.

As a result of the showing in the 1904 elections, the American party
seemed confident as the 1905 Salt Lake City elections neared. It chose
former mayor Ezra Thompson as its mayoral candidate to oppose Democratic mayor Richard P. Morris for reelection and William J. Lynch,
the Republican candidate who had served as chief of police under both
Thompson and Morris. The issues in the election were LDS church

interference in politics and the policy of the Morris administration in securing water for the city from Little Cottonwood Canyon under an agreement which seemed to benefit the Utah Power and Light Company and indirectly the LDS church.

In the ensuing election, the American party elected the mayor and six of the councilmen. Two of the Republican holdovers professed sympathy with the American party and the anti-Mormons thus seemed to have a narrow majority.

It appeared at first that Mayor Thompson would offer himself as a candidate for reelection in 1907, but a series of events led to his resignation in August of that year. In September 1906, two Scottish visitors to Salt Lake City joined in a poker game in a rooming house on West Second South. Bilked of $10,000 by bunco artists, they opened a trail which seemed to lead to Chief of Police George A. Sheets and Chief of Detectives George Raleigh, both of whom resigned. On August 2, 1907, two days after Sheets's resignation, Thompson also submitted his resignation, assigning ill health as the reason. Nevertheless, Sheets's resignation may have had something to do with Thompson's, since the mayor had strongly supported the police chief. Raleigh's resignation came on August 8 while he was under indictment for conspiracy in the case. Appointed to replace Thompson was John S. Bransford, a Democrat who, like Thompson, had earned a sizeable fortune from mining. He had been associated with Kearns and Keith in the Silver King Coalition.

In spite of the scandal, the American party again proved victorious in the 1907 city elections. A group of businessmen tried to put together a fusion ticket for mayor, but that proved unsuccessful partly because prominent church leaders refused to become involved for fear of fueling charges of ecclesiastical interference in politics. Several fusion candidates for council, nevertheless, ran, and two of them won. The Democrats nominated former Mayor Morris, and the Republicans chose Dr. Charles G. Plummer, a local physician. Extremely popular, recognized as a man of ability, and not subjected to charges of anti-Mormonism from the *Deseret News* or the *Salt Lake Herald*, Bransford carried the election with 48.4 percent of the popular vote.

By 1909 the movement for non-partisan urban government in Salt Lake City and other Utah cities had reached a peak. Similar movements had developed throughout the United States and in England since the 1890s. The relationship between the early twentieth-century movement in Salt Lake and the nonpartisan movements which led to the election of Robert Baskin and John Clark in the 1890s is not clear, but in March 1906, a group of civic leaders organized a civic improvement league

Mayor John S. Bransford, American Party Leader. Courtesy, Utah State Historical Society.

in Salt Lake City. Announcements of the organization pointed explicitly to the similar civic leagues in other cities throughout the United States.

The opening meeting was both nonpartisan and nonsectarian. The ten speakers at the meeting included Republican Susa Young Gates, Democrat William H. King, Episcopal Bishop Franklin S. Spalding, former federal judge Orlando W. Powers, and others. Chosen as president of the league was Frank B. Stephens, who had been city attorney during the Morris administration. Second vice-president was Mrs. W. W. Riter, active in the LDS church's Relief Society. Mrs. Simon Bamberger, wife of the prominent Jewish business and civic leader served as treasurer. Enos A. Wall the mining magnate served as first vice-president, and other prominent citizens served on the board of directors.

The league continued as decidedly nonpartisan and nonsectarian. In 1908, W. Mont Ferry, who had been a strong American party supporter, was president, and, as in the past, the league represented both political parties, various segments of the LDS and gentile communities and various interest groups. Its principal support came rather more from the business and professional interests of the city than from other identifiable factions.

The league moved rapidly to promote its programs, emphasizing economy and efficiency. In April, they announced support for macadam rather than asphalt for roads and improvements in the city's sewer

Second South, Looking West from Main Street, May 22, 1907. Courtesy, Utah State Historical Society.

system. In May, it called for consolidation of the city and county governments and reduction of the city council to five members. In September, it urged the reorganization of city government along the commission plan which had been instituted with such good results in Galveston, Texas, Des Moines, Iowa, and Washington, D.C. Those cities were already realizing savings in urban expenses and better definition of administrative responsibilities. A committee from the league drafted a bill to institute commission government in Salt Lake City. In March 1907, Senator George Sutherland endorsed the proposal, arguing that it would prevent manipulation of elections in small districts and provide better administration in municipal affairs. Though the bill failed to pass in the 1907 legislature, the league continued to promote it.

In 1909, the legislature unanimously passed two complimentary commission government bills. Governor William Spry pocket vetoed them, arguing that the bills would be unconstitutional and objecting to the direct democratic features of the bills, including recall of public officials. He was also opposed to the power granted to regulate utilities in the cities.

Undaunted by these setbacks, members of the Civic League organized a Citizen's party movement in September 1909, in anticipation of the upcoming election. Led by Republican businessman Nephi L. Morris, Democratic attorney Frank B. Stephens and others, it called for an end to the inefficiency and scandals of the American party administration. In addition to the gambling scandals, City Engineer Louis C. Kelsey had made a mistake which cost the city more than $100,000 and was charged with accepting kickbacks on contracts. The Citizen's party also addressed the prohibition question, arguing for more strict enforcement.

Receiving the strong support of the *Deseret News*, the Citizen's party called upon the Republican, Democratic, and Socialist parties to join them. Apostle-Senator Reed Smoot, the "Federal Bunch" Republican machine, and many of their supporters within the LDS hierarchy refused to support the movement. Nevertheless the American party organ attributed the citizen's movement to church influence.

After the organization of the Citizen's party, speculation abounded on the possible candidates of the various parties. Rumors circulated that the American party might dump Mayor Bransford, and representatives of Democratic, Citizen's, and Republican parties approached him about running as their candidate. The American party, however, supported Bransford, and the other parties searched elsewhere. The Democratic party nominated William R. Wallace, president of Ridge and Valley Mining Company, and the Citizen's party supported him. The Republicans nominated James D. Murdoch, president of Utah Lime, Coal and Junk Company. The Socialists nomiated Homer P. Burt, an electrician.

145

During the campaign, President William Howard Taft visited Utah, and the Federal Bunch kept him closely in tow, slighting Mayor Bransford.

Charges and countercharges abounded during the campaign. The other parties made much of their opposition to an experiment in regulated prostitution which the American party, with Bransford's support, had inaugurated in December 1908. They also cited the alleged graft and corruption associated with the office of City Engineer. The engineer eventually resigned his position. Both the American and anti-American parties seem to have imported ineligible voters into the city.

After the hard-fought campaign, Bransford won handily. He received 1,000 votes over the combined totals of Murdoch and Burt. The new council was overwhelmingly American.

By 1911, the situation in Salt Lake City had changed considerably from that in 1903. Thomas Kearns had pulled back from active involvement in politics. A lawsuit early in 1911 revealed that the pro-American party policy of the *Tribune* and *Telegram* had cost the papers dearly in legal and business advertising, and several local businessmen had come out in opposition to the negativism of the papers.

Increasingly the business and professional community opted for the Civic Improvement League's promise of efficient and effective government. The Civic Improvement League had been the prime mover in the press for commission government in Salt Lake, but it had received the strong endorsement of the Salt Lake Commercial Club. Beyond this, prominent members of the American party, including W. Mont Ferry and even Mayor Bransford, had been active in the Improvement League's campaign for commission government. In addition, the movement had the overwhelming support of the state conference of mayors, most of whom were unaffected by the American party's efforts. In the 1911 legislature a new commission government bill, stripped of the referendum, recall, and initiative provisions that conservative governor William Spry found objectionable, passed and was signed into law.

While the *Tribune* and a number of American party members charged that the movement was largely a church-sponsored ploy to neutralize the anti-Mormon element, the situation was really more complex than that. In fact, the movement for commission government was part of a general attitude in the progressive era of promoting efficient, effective, economical, and more businesslike administration. Each of the members of the new five-man council were to become managers of city departments under their jurisdiction. In theory, partisanship was to be removed from the electoral process and each candidate was to run for office on his managerial ability rather than his partisan support.

146

Furthermore, cracks had appeared in the American party organization which boded ill for its future success. In an attempt to promote economical adminstration, Bransford had refused to increase the city's mill levy and thus alienated many in the party who relied on city contracts and jobs for their support. A "love feast," promoted by the party's American Club in late April 1911, attracted only half the expected number, Mayor Bransford and other supporters were conspicuous by their absence, and comments by Thomas Weir and councilman J. W. McKinney indicated dissatisfaction with regulated prostitution. Perhaps the crowning blow was the defection from the American party in the late summer and early fall of Protestant clergymen like the Reverend William M. Paden, who had been instrumental in formulating the protest against Reed Smoot in 1903.

In spite of the nonpartisan spirit in which elections under the commission form were to have been held, the 1911 election was rife with party spirit. In part, this was a result of the transition from the extreme partisanship of the previous years to the nonpartisan commission form which was to obtain afterward. In part it can be seen as the death throes of the previous division of political parties on religious lines.

One thing that bears emphasis in connection with the adoption of commission government is that it was certainly not a shift in the locus of power in the city. All of the major candidates represented portions of the city's business community that had controlled city government since the beginning. The American party renominated Bransford for mayor, who under the commission system would become the chairman of the five-man city council. Other American party nominees were Charles Read, an estate manager, George A. Whitaker, a cigar manufacturer, Charles H. Reed, a superintendent at the *Salt Lake Telegram*, and hotel owner Sam B. Porter. Emergent in the election was a "businessman's ticket" made up of two Republicans, two Democrats, and a Socialist. Samuel C. Park, the mayoral nominee, was a prominent Salt Lake City jeweler, former Mayor Richard P. Morris owned a coal company, Socialist Henry Lawrence had extensive investments in real estate and mining, William H. Korns owned a warehouse company, and George D. Keyser was general manager of an investment company and vice-president of a warehouse company.

Several other candidates entered the field. The Republican organization put forward a "Good Government Ticket" which a few insurgent Americans supported. Elmer O. Leatherwood, a Salt Lake attorney, headed the ticket. Other mayoral candidates included socialist Welcome F. Ramsay, and former mayor and state supreme court justice Robert N. Baskin.

The primary election on October 25 led to the elimination of all except the "businessman's" and American party tickets led by Park and Bransford. The major issues in the campaign were the continuation of vice in the city, alleged corruption on the part of the American party administration, and charges of church influence in politics. The primary vote demonstrated the vulnerability of the American party, since Bransford received only about a third of his 1909 vote and achieved a plurality of only about 500 over Park.

During the succeeding campaign, evidence of changing conditions in Salt Lake City was clearly evident. David C. Dunbar, formerly Bransford's campaign manager, announced his defection from the American party, commenting that it was absurd to assume that gentiles like Park and Lawrence were tools of the Mormon church. The *Tribune* continued to harp on the charge of ecclesiastical influence, but it rang increasingly hollow. In the election, Park and the businessman's ticket carried the city by an impressive plurality.

While the 1911 election represented the final defeat of political parties based on religious lines, it also marked the official acceptance of the philosophy of nonpartisan businesslike government in the city. Thereafter, whatever issues might surface in the campaigns, party affiliation was generally not as important as other considerations. More often, efficiency, economy, and personality became the major issues between candidates.

During the American party administration, a number of important social and economic issues arose in the city, some of which the administration addressed and others it was unable or unwilling to confront. Perhaps the most important was the movement for regulated prostitution.

In general, prostitution was confined to Commercial Street, Franklin Avenue, and Victoria Alley, with a few houses on Main Street. By the first decade of the twentieth century, however, sex for sale had begun to spread to South Temple and State Streets and it appeared to many people to have become an intolerable nuisance.

Police could control but not supress the practice. In the mid-1890s, officers conducted monthly raids on brothels, fined the madams $50 and the prostitutes $8.50 per month, gave the women physical examinations, and allowed them to return. By 1908, the American party administration had worked out an extralegal system of registration, under which each madam turned in a list of her "girls," and each was expected to pay a fine of $10 per prostitute per month.

Public attitudes tended to polarize. By the turn of the twentieth century vigorous opposition to prostitution arose in Salt Lake City as in many other American cities. At the same time, in Salt Lake City as elsewhere some sentiment for regulated vice existed.

Trading on that sentiment, Chief of Police Thomas D. Pitt recommended in 1907 that the city move the red light district from Commercial Street and establish a regulated vice district elsewhere. Mayor Bransford accepted Pitt's recommendation, as did several American party councilmen including Lewis D. Martin, and Martin E. Mulvey, who owned a saloon on Commercial Street. Pitt subsequently changed his views, but Bransford and the others did not.

In the spring of 1908, Bransford and Mulvey, with the approval of the council, approached Mrs. Dora B. Topham, who was doing business as a madam in Ogden under the name Belle London. With their support, she formed the Citizen's Investment Company to open a regulated vice district between 500 and 600 West and running north and south between 100 and 200 South. The district seemed ideal since it was virtually surrounded by railroad tracks and located in the middle of the emergent Greek town. Beyond this, Bransford owned property across from the entrance on Second South.

Almost immediately, the city divided in a bitter controversy over the district. The American party's *Tribune* and *Telegram* supported what became known as the stockade, while the Mormon *Deseret News*, the Republican *Intermountain Republican*, and the Democratic *Salt Lake Herald* opposed it. The Salt Lake County sheriff conducted periodic raids on the district. Protestant ministers spoke vigorously against it, and the Latter-day Saint leadership allowed comment in the *News, Republican*, and *Herald* to reflect their opposition.

The controversy continued until, on September 28, 1911, shortly after the primary election, London announced that the stockade would be closed and the property sold. The Salt Lake Women's League organized the Womens' Rescue Station to help the prostitutes find work as maids and domestic servants, but their efforts proved generally unsuccessful. Most of the prostitutes left the city or relocated elsewhere in the downtown area and continued to ply their trade. Many returned to Commercial Street which remained the city's red light district until the late 1930s.

Other vices concerned the people of Salt Lake City as well. In 1905, as the American party fought its campaign for control of the city government, the *Salt Lake Tribune* presented evidence that gambling in the city had been subjected to regulation much like that of prostitution. Publishing lists of gambling halls, the paper charged that the police did little except to bring in the owners of gambling establishments once a month to fine them $299. The shift in adminstrations did not help to eliminate gambling, however, because evidence presented in the *Deseret News* implied that gambling still flourished in at least a dozen places in the city.

A third vice problem—use of alcohol—also received some consideration in the city during the period. During the 1890s, the *Tribune* devoted considerable space in its columns to allegations that, contrary to LDS propaganda, liquor sales had soared in Salt Lake City long before the gentile population reached a significant size.

By the turn of the twentieth century, sentiment for prohibition, especially among Evangelical Protestant churches in Utah and elsewhere, had reached a high pitch. By 1906, the LDS church was moving toward a policy of requiring abstinance from liquor for full fellowship, and several members of the church's hierarchy, especially Elder Heber J. Grant of the Council of the Twelve, favored statewide prohibition. In December, 1907, the Reverend Dr. George W. Young of Louisville, Kentucky, assistant general superintendent of the Anti-Saloon League of America, came to organize a chapter of the league in Salt Lake City. Heber J. Grant became an officer of the Utah organization and the Reverend Dr. Louis S. Fuller, superintendent of the league for Utah and Idaho, worked with Grant, Protestant ministers in Salt Lake City, and others to try to achieve statewide prohibition.

After the campaign for prohibition began, Salt Lake sentiment divided into a number of groups. Republicans sympathetic to Reed Smoot and Joseph F. Smith generally opposed statewide prohibition, professing to favor local option. A group of reform Republicans led by Nephi L. Morris, with a power base in the Salt Lake Civic Improvement League, favored prohibition. The *Salt Lake Tribune* and the American party were generally opposed to it. Local Evangelical Protestants generally favored prohibition, as did a number of Democrats led by Heber J. Grant.

The focus of the prohibition fight shifted to the state legislature in 1909 and 1911. In 1909, the legislature passed a local option bill by an overwhelming majority, but Republican governor William Spry, pocket vetoed it. Carl A. Badger, another of Smoot's supporters, introduced a similar bill in the 1911 legislature, which Spry signed. In the local option referendum in Salt Lake City, however, prohibition was defeated, and Salt Lake City did not go dry until after 1917 when the legislature adopted general statewide prohibition.

A question closely associated with the prohibition movement was Sunday closing. In 1900, the city passed a Sunday closing law under pressure from the Retail Clerks' Union and various religious associations. The ordinance applied generally to all businesses except those catering to transients. It was poorly enforced, however, and in March 1906, Councilman Rulon S. Wells introduced a proposal to prohibit the opening of theaters on Sunday for anything other than sacred concerts. The American party majority rejected the proposal on the grounds of infringement on individual liberty. Proponents tried, unsuccessfully, to secure the passage of a Sunday closing law in the legislature.

In addition to these questions a number of other problems came before the public. They generally fell into the categories of civic services and physical health. One of the most important was the impact of air pollution caused by the increased use of coal for home heating and the growing number of smelters in Salt Lake Valley. In August 1905, the Salt Lake County Horticultural Society reported on harmful effects of smelter smoke on plant life. Newspaper reports in September 1906 indicated that smelter smoke had damaged the foliage of Liberty Park and surrounding residential areas. By that time farmers south of the city had petitioned the federal district court for a permanent injunction against the smelters. The major problem stemmed from sulphur-laden gas which combined with rain to form sulphuric acid. In November 1906 a federal judge granted the injunction and prohibited the smelters from processing ores with a sulphur content in excess of ten percent. In spite of the injunction, urban air pollution continued to plague Salt Lake City and it was never really effectively addressed until the introduction of natural gas for heating, the closing and removal of some of the smelters, and the introduction of air pollution control equipment on the others.

Another problem faced by the people of the city was the introduction of adulterants in purchased food. Perhaps the most prevalent example was the use of formaldehyde to prevent the spoiling of milk. The elimination of the office of Inspector of Provisions by the Glendinning administration retarded a solution to the problem, but even the reintroduction of the office did not correct it. In some cases, dairymen without licenses, usually with small operations and trying to undercut the competition, would engage in the practice. By 1900, the city was again regularly inspecting milk samples and instituting suits against those found selling adulterated products. The situation was never satisfactory, however, until the state began regular food and agricultural inspection and issued licenses to those establishments found in compliance with pure food laws. At the forefront of the campaign to enforce the health laws was the Utah Health League, led by prominent Salt Lake City citizens such as Nephi L. Morris, Heber J. Grant, and John S. Bransford.

Another health problem which Salt Lake citizens faced until well into the twentieth century was recurrent smallpox epidemics. The city board of health reported 442 cases of smallpox resulting in one death in 1900.

As a result of the epidemic, the State Board of Health issued a proclamation, supported by the School Districts of Salt Lake County and the Salt Lake City Board of Health, requiring all children attending school after January 1, 1901 to be vaccinated. Almost immediately a Utah-Anti-Compulsory Vaccination League was organized with Thomas Hull, a member of Reed Smoot's Federal Bunch, at its head. Under pressure from anti-vaccination groups, the state legislature passed a law over Governor Heber M. Wells's veto prohibiting compulsory vaccination and thus subjecting Salt Lake City children to continued exposure to smallpox until the general acceptance of vaccination in the 1920s.

In the promotion of various efforts as civic improvement, as well as those to retain the status quo, a number of voluntary organizations were quite in evidence. Even clubs that might usually be thought of as social, such as the Women's Literary Club, worked for the improvement of medical facilities for schoolchildren in the city. There was seldom a reform proposed in the city that some voluntary organization failed to work for or against. In this regard, Salt Lake City was like other cities in the United States; in the 1830s Alexis de Tocqueville noted the reforming nature of American society and commented on how different it was from Europe, where most reforms were promoted by governmental agencies or the aristocracy.

The city faced a number of problems in providing services for a rapidly expanding urban population. Expansion came in essentially two ways. In the first place, city lots were subdivided into smaller units which allowed a greater density of population. This eliminated any remaining vestiges of farming in the city together with a number of the large kitchen garden plots characteristic of the nineteenth century. Secondly, as the streetcar system expanded, it became possible for the city to annex areas that were once considered suburbs, but that today would be perceived as easily within the city.

The best examples are perhaps those upper middle class subdivisions in the northeast portion of the city. Between 1888 and 1902, nine subdivisions were platted in the Avenues section. A representative example was Darlington Place, encompassing the area between N and S Streets and First and Third Avenues, and named for its promoter Elmer E. Darling. The subdivision could be incorporated in the city during the pre-auto age largely because the streetcar companies built electric lines on First and Third Streets. In 1909, the city incorporated Federal Heights west and north of the newly created University of Utah campus. Other subdivisions included the Gilmer Park and Ivy League Streets, also west of the University of Utah. By 1910, part of Sugar House had been incorporated, and in fact, the 1910 city directory listed four pages of subdivisions which had been added to the city, many as streetcar suburbs.

Streetcar companies themselves underwent considerable reorganization during the period, largely as part of the general movement toward monopoly characteristic of the nation's business community in general. By 1890, all mule lines had been replaced with electricity, and two companies, Salt Lake City Railroad Company and the Salt Lake Rapid Transit Company, competed to extend their service into various areas. Since the companies operated under franchises granted by the city, citizens took grievances over service to the mayor and council. In 1900, for instance, numerous complaints came to the council that the cars were overcrowded during the evening rush hour, between 5:00 and 7:00 P.M. After a hearing, the city ordered the companies to provide better service or subject themselves to a suit to compel action. In 1900, the two lines were consolidated into a single company, the Utah Light and Railway Company, which effectively eliminated competition in public transportation from the city.

As U. L. and R. continued to operate, the city reconsidered the original franchise in 1905. The company still had forty-one years on its original contract, but it proposed the extension of the franchise for another fifty years. A large number of protestors met in the Grand Theatre despite bad weather and darkened streets. The *Tribune* and gentile leaders in the city were particularly opposed to the extension, since the LDS church owned a large block of the company's stock. The company proposed a franchise with no restrictions, while many on the city council wanted a forfeiture clause, and some wanted to consider a proposal from Samuel Newhouse for an alternative franchise. In early August 1905, after many proposals and counter proposals, the city accepted a somewhat modified franchise agreement by a vote of seven to six, with one gentile siding with six Mormons to approve the franchise.

The movement toward monopoly was further strengthened in October 1906, when Edward H. Harriman, owner of the Union Pacific Railroad Company, and a group of New York investors purchased a controlling interest in the Utah Light and Railway stock. Though the board of directors consisted of prominent local businessmen, they were largely fronts for the Harriman interests.

Part of the reason for the willingness of the city to grant such a favorable franchise to the Utah Light and Railway Company was the company's control of rights to water in Big Cottonwood Canyon, one of its major points for generating electricity. The city had obtained the right to water in Utah Lake in the early 1890s, but the shallow grade between the lake and the city made the water largely unusable without

153

the addition of expensive pumping equipment. The other alternative was trading Utah Lake water for Big Cottonwood water owned by farmers and certain companies. As a result of exchange agreements, the city obtained rights to approximately fifty percent of the primary flow of Big Cottonwood Creek for culinary purposes.

The city was also served by a single gas company. In March 1895, it was reported that the company, Utah Gas & Coke, had completed laying gas pipes under Main Street and on March 8 they were charged. Gas and electric rates were regulated by the city in the absence of any statewide regulation. In 1907, a controversy between the gas monopoly and the Utah Light and Railway Company erupted when the city proposed to return to gas lights on Salt Lake City streets. The electric company protested, arguing that it had an exclusive franchise to provide street lighting. Eventually the streets continued to be lighted by electricity.

With water and sewer service provided by the city and transportation, electric, and gas service provided by private franchises, virtually the only unmonopolized service during the first decade of the twentieth century was the telephone company. Citizens of Salt Lake City had a choice between two companies, Rocky Mountain Bell and Utah Independent. A survey of the city directory of 1910, however, indicates that Bell had outstripped the independent in securing subscribers within the city. By 1913, Utah Independent had left the field to its larger competitor.

As the level of service for some public utilities improved, others deteriorated. The Civic Improvement League had urged the city to use macadamized stone rather than asphalt for paving city streets, largely because of the stone's economy and alleged durability. Both Morris's Democratic and Thompson's American administration agreed and moved ahead quite rapidly in paving. Unfortunately, the improvements were made without adequate testing by the city engineer's office. By 1907, reports indicated that the street were deteriorating rapidly and becoming more mud than pavement. Various groups pointed fingers, but no one seemed willing to take the blame for the costly error.

The other civic improvement that elicited considerable controversy was the paving of sidewalks within the city boundaries outside the downtown area. In 1907, the city council passed an ordinance authorizing the paving of sidewalks in an area as far east as Thirteenth East and as far south as Ninth South. Some wondered how the city would pay for it, but in 1908 the city let contracts for $203,000 worth of sidewalk improvements, about a quarter of which would be paid for by general revenues, and three-fourths from assessments on improved property.

The one improvement that most greeted with favor was the burying of utility lines and their consequent removal from the city streets. As the streetcar lines were electrified in the late 1880s, the telephone companies and their subscribers complained about the induction-caused disturbances on the lines. The extension of streetcar lines coupled with increasing traffic in the downtown area and its increasingly modern attractive buildings led to the decision to place transmission lines in conduits under the streets. Begun in 1901, the project was hastened in 1908 as the two telephone companies, Utah Light and Railway and the Western Union Telegraph Company, replaced the existing jungle of poles and lines.

In addition to these utilitarian improvements, private citizens and the government of Salt Lake City moved explicitly to join the "City Beautiful" movement then current in American cities. In 1900, the city planted trees in Liberty and Pioneer parks and on Washington Square around the City and County Building. Walks and drives on Liberty Park, the showplace of Salt Lake open spaces, were improved and a set of large iron gates was placed on the north entrance. A playground for children was added in place of a deer park, the occupants of which were moved to a new location.

Largely because of pressures brought to bear by the Civic Improvement League, the Salt Lake City council explicitly recognized the importance of parks for citizens of the city. In January 1908, the city established a park board, which was to have "wide and comprehensive" powers to make Salt Lake into a "City Beautiful." In December 1909, citizens founded a Parks and Playgrounds Association with members drawn largely from the upper-middle class leaders of the city. The association was part of a national movement designed to provide playgrounds and parks for children. By that time, ninety cities in the United States boasted such associations.

In 1898, the city added a public library to the private, state, and university libraries already existing. Shortly thereafter, it purchased land near the corner of State and South Temple streets, and a new building was completed in September 1905 with a donation of $120,000 from John Q. Packard. Formally opened on October 27, the new library contained more than 31,500 volumes. The building housed three reading rooms, a lecture room, and a children's reading room.

Changes also took place in the two major public protection agencies in the city. Increasingly, the city professionalized its police department. In 1888, department personnel began to appear in uniform on the street. In 1903, the city constructed a new jail to replace the justly criticized and inadequate previous facility. But such changes were accompanied by a number of problems rivaling the B. Y. Hampton episode of the 1880s. In 1900, Chief of Police Thomas H. Hilton was subjected to a suit by parents of three young girls arrested on suspicion of moral terpitude who were apparently strip searched and examined by a physician. The suit was subsequently dropped, but not before considerable controversy had developed. Numerous allegations of complicity with bunco artists were leveled against Chief of Police George Sheets during his tenure in 1906 and 1907, until his resignation after the gambling incident mentioned above. A subsequent trial acquitted him, but the scandal undoubtedly hurt the image of the department.

In 1883, after thirty years as a volunteer department, the Salt Lake City Fire Department was reorganized on a professional basis, and while it made significant strides during the next two and a half decades, citizens were certainly not adequately protected by 1910. In 1890, the city placed an electric fire alarm system into operation, and in 1910, it had approximately seventy-five boxes, mostly in the downtown area. The department had six engine houses at the time. Improvement of the facilities seemed to come as crisis demanded. In May and June 1890, for instance, after a disastrous fire at Henry Dinwoodey's furniture store where approximately $120,000 worth of property was destroyed, a call went out for fire plugs in the downtown area, and department chief W. A. Stanton asked for the construction of a new firehouse and the purchase of more hoses for the department. Similar extensive improvements came after fires in the Scott-Auerbach Building and the Progress Building, both on Main Street. In the latter case, inadequate water pressure hindered the fire fighters. At the time the firetrucks acquired adequate pressure only by closure of city water mains outside the downtown area and the use of a steam pumper truck. Under questioning, the city engineer complained that the water system consisted of pipes that were too small, and that the city's reservoir capacity was inadequate.

At the same time, the city began to consider and gradually to adopt ordinances providing for electrical inspections at new building sites. Nevertheless, in December 1909, the National Board of Fire Underwriters reported unfavorably on Salt Lake City's fire protection. The underwriters found the department understaffed and lacking in proper equipment. The downtown area was particularly lacking in adequate protection, electrical facilities had often been haphazardly installed, and more seriously, the city generally did not enforce, "modern methods of fire prevention in construction and equipment."

In addition to dealing with these physical problems, citizens of Salt Lake City provided a combination of voluntary and public assistance for the disadvantaged and indigent. Such associations as the Orphans' Home and Day Nursery continued to operate with both private and public funds. Newer organizations like the Kearns St. Ann's Orphanage,

156

established largely owing to the philanthropy of Jennie Judge Kearns, provided assistance. The Mutual Improvement Association, the Relief Society, and the Primary Association provided help for the various people as did the YMCA, YWCA, and a free kindergarten. In 1905, the city completed the construction of a juvenile detention home in part because of the urging of the city's juvenile court judge.

No surer evidence exists, however, that Salt Lake City had grown larger and that any narrowly defined unitary community which might have existed in the mid-nineteenth century had broken down than the controversy raised by one of the philanthropic organizations. In 1900, protests arose among the residents of Eighth East and First South over a rescue home for wayward girls operated in their neighborhood by a group of Protestant women. The women and their supporters tried to find a satisfactory place for the home near one of the streetcar lines and yet distant from objecting neighbors. Attempts were made to place it in both the Perkins and Lincoln Park subdivisions, but they proved unsuccessful, and the effort was apparently abandoned. At least the home does not appear in the 1903 city directory.

To supplement the already existing St. Mark's and Holy Cross hospitals and to replace the Deseret Hospital which closed its doors in 1894, the LDS church opened Dr. Grove's LDS Hospital in 1905. Established through a $25,000 donation from the estate of Dr. William S. Groves, $10,000 from the Salt Lake City Fifteenth Ward, and $145,000 from the LDS church, it was built on Eighth Avenue between C and D streets.

As Salt Lake City grew and flourished and as the population diversified, religious edifices were constructed to meet the needs of new communicants of the various denominations. The largest number of new buildings were Latter-day Saint wards, but the most lavish and expensive constructed during the first decade of the twentieth century was undoubtedly the Roman Catholic Cathedral of the Madeleine on South Temple, dedicated in 1909.

Salt Lake City was still the Mormon capital, and it continued to carry that image to the world. The church itself did everything it could to enhance it. Early in the century it had opened an information bureau on Temple Square, and by the late 1920s two hundred thousand visitors annually flocked to see the Mormon headquarters. At the same time, Progressive Era muckraking brought new public attacks on Mormonism, as the church was charged with continuing efforts to dominate the political and economic life of the region and with the secret continuation of plural marriage. In response, between 1905 and 1913 Elder B. H. Roberts of the church's First Council of the Seventy published a series

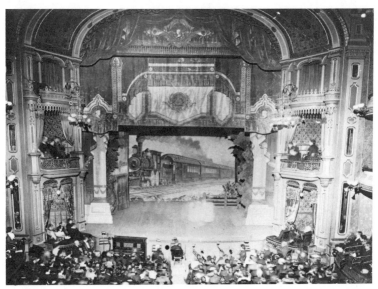

Interior, Salt Lake Theatre about 1900. Courtesy, LDS Church Archives.

of historical articles in the national magazine *Americana*. Designed to counter the anti-Mormon image, they later became the basis for his six-volume *Comprehensive History of the Church*.

The citizens of Salt Lake City were also offered a broad range of popular and formal cultural events and resorts. A cursory examination of the *Salt Lake Tribune* for March and April 1900 reveals the wide range of possibilities. Women's clubs included a number of literary clubs and even "The Club of Mineral Painters." On March 9, it was announced that the YMCA had organized a fencing club to meet each Thursday evening. On April 9, the *Tribune* reported that the Salt Lake Sketch Club would be organized by those interested in promoting art and artistic feelings. On April 10, it was announced that thirty-two new members had joined the Utah Humane Society and that the society was preparing to secure the services of an agent to represent it in the prosecution of those charged with cruelty to animals. On April 21, James E. Talmage presented a lecture entitled "In the Land of the Czar," based on a recent visit to Russia. On April 22, the paper announced a golf tournament at the Country Club on its grounds on Eleventh East.

A broad range of other sports, amusements, and cultural events were also offered. In 1903, the Utah Baseball League was established with teams in Ogden, Murray, Salt Lake City, and Fort Douglas. When it was learned that the Fort Douglas team would be unable to field an adequate team, in the face of opposition from Murray, an agreement was reached to allow a team of blacks called the Occidentals to play in the league. In 1909, it was reported that crowds of 3,500 were not unusual at Sunday baseball games, and that weekday games averaged slightly under 1,000. Nevertheless, attendance was insufficient to support the teams, so the league folded.

Other amusements also seemed to attract citizens. Bicycle races at the Salt Palace attracted between 300 and 400 fans in the summer of 1909. In the fall of 1908, the Utah State Fair attracted approximately 123,000 people, a record for fair attendance at Salt Lake City up to that time. The 1909 annual encampment of the Grand Army of the Republic, a patriotic organization of Civil War Veterans, brought 15,000 to Salt Lake City for parades, meetings, and festivities.

Salt Lake citizens could reach other places of amusement by streetcar, interurban, or railroad. Perhaps the most famous was Saltair. Opened first in June 1893 at a cost of $250,000, it was financed in large part by the LDS church. The resort, located on the south shore of Great Salt Lake, offered band concerts, operas, and dances. It was a constant money loser, and the church sold a controlling interest to a consortium of Latter-day Saint businessmen in 1906. Nevertheless, Saltair reported 5,000 visitors on July 4, 1909. Wandamere, a resort located between Thirteen and Fourteenth South and Fifth and Seventh East reported 10,000 visitors on July 24 of the same year. Also within commuting distance of Salt Lake City was the Lagoon resort, operated near Farmington by the Bamberger interests and accessible on the interurban.

These amusements should not be seen from a Pollyanna perspective. In 1909, for instance, the records of the juvenile courts of Salt Lake City revealed that a number of young girls reached the state industrial school at Ogden after a trip to Saltair at which they became intoxicated. In July 1910, the Saltair management ejected a black from the resort solely because of his race. The man entered suit against the resort but the judge awarded him only the quarter he had paid for admission.

By 1911, Salt Lake City had undergone a transition that had transformed it into what appeared to be a generally typical American city. The differences between it and other cities are often attributed to the Mormon-gentile conflict, but such inter-religious conflict was common elsewhere as well. Carl Harris, for instance, found serious disagreements between pietistic and liturgical groups in Birmingham, and Richard Jensen and Paul Kleppner found such conflict to be at the basis of the political controversies of the midwest. In this regard, Salt Lake City's religio-cultural divisions may not have been as unique as residents and recent commentators have been wont to believe.

*Pavillion at Saltair Resort, completed in 1893. Courtesy, LDS Church
Archives.*

Moreover, economic and political patterns were similar to those in
other parts of the nation. Salt Lake's economy had been integrated with
regional and national markets. Following the national progressive pattern, the city had shifted its administration to the commission form of
city government. Most urban services with the exception of water and
sewer were provided by private companies under civic franchises. The
Civic Improvement League and other voluntary organizations were generally patterned after similar organizations in other cities. Scandals in
the police department and inadequate fire protection were not unusual
during the period. As did most other cities, Salt Lake experienced an
influx of immigrants from southern and eastern Europe who joined the
already numerous group from northeastern Europe and Canada. Gentiles

as well as Mormons often treated these new immigrants with discrimination and contempt. Like other major cities in the Mountain West, Salt Lake City owed its growth to commerce and mining. In short, Salt Lake had become an American city as well as a Mormon-gentile city by 1911 and its future growth and problems would generally be along lines shared with other cities.

Main Street ca. 1920. Courtesy, Utah State Historical Society.

——6——

Progressive City, 1912-1930

B y the 1890s, many people in the United States had become increasingly anxious about the results of industrialization, commercialization, and urban development. This concern led to a sentiment for reform which historians have generally called "progressivism." In part a movement for efficiency and thus for organizational or structural reform, such as adopting more businesslike methods in governmental agencies, progressivism also led some to favor social reform designed to make the capitalist system more humane and to provide opportunity and dignity to those least able to help themselves. On the national level this led to laws dealing with such matters as pure food and drugs, railroad regulation, and conservation of natural resources. The states adopted mine safety, utility regulation, and workman's compensation. In the cities the progressive movement sought such reforms as improved public health, better public utilities, and more effective urban government. Salt Lake City was well known nationally for its adoption of more effective government. The period from 1912 to 1930 was characterized by many progressive reforms, but it also saw many tensions between forces of reform and those of particular interests.

The election of November 1911 had three important effects on the political life of Salt Lake City: it broke the back of the anti-Mormon American party; it minimized the degree to which partisan religious and political preference were qualifications for office-holding; and the city joined the increasing number of American municipalities adopting the commission form of government. Though often referred to as the Galveston plan—named after Galveston, Texas where commission government was inaugurated in 1901—the system in Salt Lake was more like that of Des Moines, Iowa, which inaugurated its commission in 1908.

A committee from the Civic Improvement League had completed a study of Des Moines, and the plan drafted on the basis of their report provided for five commissioners elected at large and serving as full-time administrators. The mayor was first among equals. His authority derived from his position as a member and chairman of the council. Mayorial duties were largely ceremonial.

Under Salt Lake's new government, the council as a body exercised legislative authority over city affairs, and, in addition, each councilman had responsibility for the departments under his jurisdiction. Henry W. Lawrence supervised Public Affairs and Finance. Lawrence administered the city attorney's office, tax collection, the cemetery, and the municipal baths. William H. Korns as water supply and waterworks commissioner administered the city's water and sewage systems. Mayor Samuel C. Park became commissioner of public safety, responsible for the police, fire, and health departments, and the regulation of weights and measures. Richard P. Morris assumed control of the Department of Streets and Public Improvements, which supervised the construction, maintenance, and cleaning of the city's streets. George D. Keyser became director of the Department of Parks and Public Property, which oversaw building inspection, public buildings, parks, city beautification, and recreation.

While most city employees came under the supervision of one commissioner, there were some exceptions. The city auditor and judges were elected separately and were independent of the commission. The public library fell under the jurisdiction of the entire commission.

Given the rancor engendered by the pro- and anti-American party factions and the desire for effective and economical government in the city, it was perhaps inevitable that the new commission would remove a number of old employees in order to make room for its own people. Some rather non-controversial appointees like Superintendent of Parks Nicholas Byhower, Cemetery Sexton J.E. Wiscomb, and Sanitary Inspector J. E. Flynn were retained on the city staff. Most who stayed were employees with obvious professional skills such as City Attorney J. J. Dininny; Health Commissioner Dr. S. G. Paul; and City Chemist Herman Harms.

The two most important new appointments were the heads of the police and fire department. Brigham F. Grant, halfbrother of LDS apostle Heber J. Grant, took the police department helm. He had been active in the Civic Improvement League and highly critical of what he perceived to be the loose administration of vice laws. William H. Bywater, who had reportedly made an extensive study of fire fighting methodology, became fire chief.

Grant moved rapidly against vice and other crime. Regarded as a man expert in the detection of crime, largely because of his efforts to ferret out vice-law breakers, Grant tried to clear the city of gambling, especially slot machines and bookmaking. He also tried to eliminate drug dealers, especially in opium, and red light districts, and to enforce liquor regulations and Sunday closing. In addition, he zeroed in on crimes against persons and property, like the bunco schemes of previous years. Attempts such as that of one drug dealer to bribe and extort favors by placing pressure on Grant's family were unsuccessful.

Grant's programs had some unanticipated results. By mid-January 1912, newspaper reports indicated that jails were overcrowded with prostitutes. Grant tried, with some success, to solve this problem by offering the prostitutes the alternative of leaving town. Drug busts filled the city jail's drug ward, and a city council tour revealed pathetic sights such as two addicts pleading for money, tobacco, and drugs. One inmate went so far as to threaten suicide, and another made an unsuccessful attempt by slashing his wrists.

Grant's annual report in 1914 indicated that overall, crime in Salt Lake City had decreased over the two years of his tenure. He cited the elimination of various types of gambling, decline in property thefts, and the absence of bunco schemes. He averred that no open brothels continued to exist, though he admitted that prostitution continued in connection with saloons.

Some of Grant's campaigns generated considerable controversy. A city ordinance, for instance, prohibited the serving of beer in a saloon apart from meals. A number of establishments tried to observe the letter of the law by offering potato chips as "a meal." Grant refused to accept this as anything more than a ruse. This angered saloon keepers and they tried to have him dismissed.

Grant encountered some powerful opposition. For instance, he appointed Hugh L. Glenn as head of a "purity squad" to enforce liquor and other vice laws. By early 1914, however, sufficient opposition to Glenn's activities had developed in the city's business community that the "purity squad" leader was forced into early retirement. Grant was understandably upset over these efforts to thwart his programs.

Grant's efforts clearly divided the community. The LDS Liberty Stake Betterment League lauded his administration in a petition to the city council supporting the enforcement of laws regulating saloons and dance halls. The Methodist Church Home Missionary Society passed a resolution endorsing action of the city commission in prohibiting all unnecessary buying on Sunday. On the other hand, Stephen L. Richards, a local attorney and LDS leader associated with betterment groups, thought the laws ought to be equitably enforced. Charles S. Varian, formerly United States attorney and a leading gentile Republican, thought that only liquor sales ought to be interdicted on the Sabbath. The *Salt Lake Tribune* editorialized against the city's Sunday closing ordinance, and Simon Bamberger, a local businessman and civic leader, representative of the Jewish community, thought that the ordinance would hurt business.

In apparent support of Grant's campaign, *The Progressive,* official organ of the state's Progressive party, in January 1913 complained of the liquor interests, breweries, horse racing, gambling, and bucket shops, arguing that "to please sacred cows the news of the day is suppressed. Editorial opinion is warped. The people are kept in ignorance of the truth."

Grant's insistence on strict enforcement of vice laws met opposition from some members of the business community. One of his opponents, W. Mont Ferry, manager of estate and mining properties, was elected mayor in 1915. Ferry had been both a Civic Improvement League member and American party supporter. This election, coupled with a controversy over the use of Mayor Park's contingency fund and the police secret service fund to enforce the vice laws darkened the last year of Grant's administration. After Ferry's inauguration, the commission forced Grant out of office. A temporary replacement, C. W. Shores, left shortly thereafter and the commission chose J. Parley White, the State Bank Examiner, in his stead.

In spite of Grant's removal, it appeared at first that the Park administration's good relations with the betterment league, now known as the Civic Betterment Union, would continue under Ferry. In May 1917 the Union, through its secretary Irvin I. Lowrey, a salesman for the Rio Grande Lumber Company, wrote to Chief White commending the police for the "good results you have obtained in bringing about law enforcement."

Still, the issues would not subside. Rather, they intensified as Mayor Ferry, the chief of police, and a majority of the city council opposed the Betterment Union's anti-vice campaign. Ferry's attitude on vice was closer to that of the American party, with its regulated vice district, than to the Betterment Union. Newspaper reports indicated that Union members found it impossible to meet with the chief about their concerns. The city administration denied this, and on June 20, 1917, the Union's executive committee sent a letter to Ferry asking for a meeting, which was held on Monday, June 25.

The meeting aired Betterment Union attitudes about what was perceived to be lax enforcement of vice laws. Elwood Lane, president of the Union, and most of the executive committee urged the police depart-

*William Montague Ferry, American Party Leader, and Mayor 1916-1920.
Courtesy, Utah State Historical Society.*

ment "to make immediate and continuous effort to rid the community of women of ill-repute." On its part the Union pledged to "undertake a constructive work aiming to educate the parents and guardians of the youth here to the danger of allowing their young people, especially young girls, to be on the streets at our places of amusement till late hours." In an apparent attempt to defuse opposition, Mayor Ferry suggested that the city appoint nine members of the Union as special police officers wth full authority to investigate and make arrests. After some prodding, the Union finally submitted the names of six people. Two of them, Francis B. Laney and John Henry Evans, took the oath and secured police badges.

Unfortunately this experiment in civic-police cooperation proved unsuccessful, and on October 15, 1917, Ferry opened a bitter attack on the Union, charging the members with "gross negligence" because they had not presented any evidence of law breaking. He suggested that the Union might have engaged in an "effort to gain cheap notoriety," and implied that they might be "guilty of the very things with which they charged the Police Department, vis: winking at derelictions they were charged with suppressing." Pulling his punches somewhat, Ferry said that his "criticisms" did not "apply to the hundreds of good men and women who are associated in and with this Civic Betterment Union in an earnest desire to do good." In the end, he told the Union to put up or shut up—to supply evidence of unsupressed illegal activity or to stop "these outrageous allegations."

The dispute over the operation of the police department continued into 1918. In early February, Mayor Ferry recommended the reappointment of J. Parley White as chief of police. The Civic Betterment Union protested immediately, and the Salt Lake Ministerial Association asked that the commission appoint the strongest available man for the position. Apparently, White's views reflected all too well the laissez-faire position on vice characterizing the Ferry years. White's reappointment came on a three to two vote.

A series of events which took place in 1919 and 1920 finally led to a resolution of the controversy between the council majority and the Betterment Union. In the 1919 elections, former city auditor E. A. Bock won the mayoral election by a large majority. In the first half of 1920, however, a check of his auditor's accounts revealed a shortage in the special improvement account. When confronted with discrepancy, Bock admitted he had embezzled $10,000 which he had used to buy mining stocks. He paid back the money and resigned in disgrace.

Bock's resignation led the commissioners to appoint C. Clarence Neslen as mayor and Arthur F. Barnes, a groceryman, as commissioner of Public Safety. With that, supporters of the Betterment Union became a majority on the council, since only A. H. Crabbe remained from the old Ferry administration. In addition, Joseph E. Burbidge had already replaced White as chief of police.

In many ways, Clarence Neslen epitomizes the moderate progressive approach of the 1920s in Salt Lake City. Born in Salt Lake City April 17, 1879 to British immigrants, he attended schools in Salt Lake City and the Latter-day Saints College. He entered the business world as an employee of the *Deseret News,* rising to cashier by the end of his fifteen years with the paper. He left to become office manager for the Kimball and Richards Real Estate Company. Elected a city commissioner in November 1917, he assumed the post of the Planning Commission. His wife was Grace Cannon, a daughter of George Q. and Martha Telle Cannon, which made him a half-brother-in-law of City Engineer Sylvester Q. Cannon. A staunch Democrat by political persuasion, he was also interested and active in charitable work for the deaf and blind and the State Humane Society. He also served as president of the Salt Lake Oratorio Society and as bishop of the LDS 20th Ward, which covered part of the Avenues portion of the city.

There was apparently a close relationship between reform elements and the city administration during the 1920s. Neslen continued as mayor until 1928, and Barnes and his successor as public safety commissioner, Theodore T. Burton, seem to have supported the vigorous enforcement of vice laws. While considerable controversy developed over enforcement of statewide prohibition by the Salt Lake County sheriff's office, the city police department came out relatively unscathed. A number of entries in the city council minutes from the period indicate that Chief Burbidge relied quite heavily on the power the city council had to deny business licenses as a means of punishing those violating prohibition and gambling laws, rather than on the more sensationalistic and controversial raids, conducted sporadically by the county sheriff.

If the police department was a center of controversy during both the Park and Ferry administrations, the fire department seemed just the opposite. Under Chief William H. Bywater, fire administration had become both more economical and more efficient. Even though fire insurance rates had increased during the American party period, apparently owing to the ineffectiveness of the city in coping with increasing fire danger, the worst of those problems were reportedly solved by the teens.

By the 1920s, however, a number of problems had developed that led to a confrontation between the fire fighters and Chief Bywater. Bywater seems not to have kept up on developments in the field. What passed for adequate knowledge of fire fighting techniques and administration in 1913 seem not to have availed in the mid-1920s. In addition, city building codes seem to have been laxly enforced and, more particularly, did not require updating of conditions in previously constructed buildings, leaving many buildings with inadequate fire safety provisions. Beyond this, excessive emphasis on economy left the fire department unable to meet the challenge of fighting unusually severe fires. While it was an unusual situation, in June 1921, the Utah Oil Refining Company in the north section of the city burst into flames. Before the fire could be extinguished, three firemen had been killed and fire fighting equipment from neighboring cities had to be called in. Large, but otherwise routine, fires presented a problem since the department was even unable to provide sufficient equipment to fight general alarm fires. It had, for instance, only sufficient protective helmets and coats for the firemen actually on shift. In the case of a general alarm fire such as one in the downtown Hooper-Eldridge block in 1924, fire fighters were expected to battle the flames without coats and helmets.

Most serious for personnel relations, Bywater—apparently from the old school of public administration—adopted a dictatorial and abusive posture toward the firemen. This, coupled with a shortage of bedclothes in the firehouses, led to a threatened walkout by firemen in March 1925, .and a demand for Bywater's removal.

The city council investigated, and its report came down hard on Bywater, but at the same time undermined the efforts of the firemen to deal with future arbitrary behavior by fire chiefs. It revealed that the chief had used abusive language in dealing with his subordinates—one report called it "vile, insulting, and blasphemous." He had, in addition, "failed to provide sufficient blankets and fire coats for his men," probably because of his efforts to achieve the economy demanded by the council. On the other hand, the council censured the fire fighters for threatening to strike and urged them to disband their union organization.

The results might have been predicted. Chief Bywater notified the city council of his intention to retire, but a large number of firemen resigned in protest over his policies. Then the president of the City Fire Fighters Union No. 81, C. Edson Droubay, announced that the union had been disbanded. Subsequently, a large number of firemen withdrew their resignations and were reinstated. In the meantime, a number of the positions on the department were filled by volunteers. The council appointed Walter S. Knight as fire chief.

In spite of these administrative problems, the city, in collaboration with the state legislature, attempted to rationalize its administration along the lines promoted by Progressives. The Baskin administration of the 1890s had tried to remove political preference from the appoint-

170

ment of policemen and firemen, but the Glendinning administration largely nullified those efforts. No serious attempt was successful again until 1921, when the state legislature passed a civil service law for firemen policemen. Amended in 1925 and 1927, the law provided that all appointments and promotions in the department except the position of chief were to be made by a civil service commission chosen by the city commission for staggered six-year terms. Employees could be removed only for cause, and they had the right to a public hearing to investigate the grounds for their dismissal.

The law was not entirely satisfactory. Since it applied only to subordinates, it could not effectively deal with disputes caused by ineffective administration such as that of Fire Chief Bywater's. In addition, the chief of police and the commissioner of public safety complained at times that the procedure made it difficult to remove an officer for cause even though his work might be inefficient and unsatisfactory.

The progressive desire for effective administration and orderly city growth led also to pressure for zoning regulations in Salt lake. In December 1917, George E. Kessler, an expert on urban planning from St. Louis, visited the city at the invitation of the Civic Planning and Art Commission. The next year, apparently without success, the commission requested an appropriation for a comprehensive plan. Again in 1922, City Engineer Sylvester Q. Cannon, after attending a national conference on city planning in Los Angeles, urged the need for attention to zoning and master planning for the city. He was particularly concerned with the need for a plan for major streets, the elimination of railroad grade crossings, and the compulsory filing of subdivision plats.

Pressure from Salt Lake City and elsewhere eventually led the state government to act. In 1925, the legislature authorized city zoning regulations. The city then set up a zoning commission and a board of adjustments to enforce zoning regulations.

The other progressive reform inaugurated in 1925 was the budget system. In this, Salt Lake followed the federal government and various states and larger American cities. The law designated the city auditor as municipal budget officer. By October 1, each commissioner had to file an estimate of the revenues and expenses of his department. The auditor prepared a tentative budget, which he submitted to the commission by November. The commission was then required to hold public hearings on the budget, present it to the public, and formally adopt it.

In line with the progressive penchant for managerial skill, a shift began to take place in the type of person likely to be elected to city government. In the nineteenth century mayors tended to be entrepreneurs, but by the late teens and twenties there was a tendency for those elected to be drawn from managerial or service occupations. With the increasing emphasis on efficiency and economy, the pressure for the sort of freewheeling energy necessary for an entrepreneur in the age of the robber baron was not the skill necessary for managing a city of the increasing complexity of Salt Lake. Three officials, commissioners Green and Scheid and Mayor Bock, moved from other city employment to the council. Mayors Ferry and Neslen and Commissioner Charles N. Fehr were business managers before their election; Commissioner Burton was a real estate agent, and Commissioner Joseph H. Luke was a salesman. Mayor John F. Bowman, who replaced Neslen in 1928, was an attorney. In fact, only Commissioners Crabbe, Barnes, Harry L. Finch, and Patrick J. Moran owned their own businesses, and their interests were apparently not as diversified as those of a number of the nineteenth-century mayors like Armstrong, Wells, and Jennings.

Commissioners were expected to devote full time to their positions. In the 1850s, Mayor Jedediah M. Grant could spend a great deal of his time in Washington lobbying for the LDS church or on missions in the East. Daniel H. Wells could find time to serve as Lt. General of the Nauvoo Legion, as Second Counselor in the LDS church's First Presidency, and as an entrepreneur in various business ventures. William Jennings and Francis Armstrong could administer diversified business empires. By the 1920s, however, that was impossible. Commissioners were required to oversee the day-to-day operation of their departments in addition to legislating on matters relating to the entire operation of the city.

That these officials came from a different class than early city officials and that they represented the Progressive Era's penchant for efficiency, does not mean that they agreed on the nature of the good society they hoped would result from their administrations. In fact, at least two visions of the ideal city are apparent, best seen in the administrations of Samuel C. Park and W. Mont Ferry. Both were businessmen who favored efficient, economical, and nonpartisan administration, but Park and his supporters in the Civic Betterment Union believed that the administration must establish a moral tone in the community which included the vigorous enforcement of standard personal conduct set by the LDS church and Evangelical Protestants. Ferry's vision, on the other hand, was that of secular efficiency. Opposing crimes against persons and property and favoring efficient government, he downplayed the need for the control of vice, and sought to discredit the opposition by laying the onus of ineffectiveness on the Betterment Union.

Clarence Neslen, on the other hand, represented a sort of middle-of-the-road approach. Recognizing the sentiment for a high moral tone in

Looking East Between A and B Streets on South Temple, 1912. Cathedral of the Madelein in the Background, and Prestigious Homes in the Foreground. Courtesy, Utah State Historical Society.

the community in the age of legal prohibition, his administration tried to control vice by the use of licensing regulations rather than more dramatic raids. On the other hand, the council worked to iron out disputes such as that in the fire department within the framework of cultural attitudes of the 1920s, which in Utah were decidedly anti-union and anti-confrontational. Mayor Bowman's administration continued essentially as Neslen's had.

Outside the question of vice law enforcement, however, all of these administrations were in basic agreement, and policies and programs inaugurated in one generally continued to the next. In fact, in many matters, there was a continuity that reached back into the 1890s. The differences, of course, were in the extreme partisanship of the Glendinning and American party administrations.

As each administration attempted to provide improved urban services and facilities, with emphasis on efficiency and economy, it found itself under the watchful eyes of various civic-minded voluntary associations. Some of these, such as the local improvement leagues, were narrow or single interest organizations. Throughout 1913, for instance, the East Block Improvement League pressed the city for such improvements as lighting, sidewalk extension, and sewer improvements in its area. Similarly, the West Side Improvement League asked the city to focus on the interest of citizens in its section, including regulating gypsy fortune tellers, improving the railroad right-of-way, and providing police and fire protection. The Riverside Improvement League wanted a fire station in the northwestern part of the city. Other local interest leagues included the Southeast Improvement League, the Sugar House Businessmen's League, the Third Ward Civic Improvement Association, and the State Street Improvement Association.

Beyond this, there were a number of associations with city-wide interests. Most noted was the Civic Betterment Union, which concerned itself not only with anti-vice campaigns, but also with a broad range of other matters including parks and playgrounds. During the 1920s it was replaced by the Social Welfare League. Perhaps the oldest continuously operating association principally concerned with civic improvement was the Salt Lake Commercial Club. In 1912 the Club boasted 1,200 members, including the city's most prominent businessmen, Utah's governor William Spry, Mayor Samuel Park, and representatives of most of the important professional firms in the city. Its concerns ranged from the perennial problem of smoke abatement to road improvement, and included rat, fly, and mosquito abatement. The Progressive party also constituted a lobbying organization after 1912.

Women's groups also pressured the city government for civic improvement through a number of voluntary associations. The House Wives League, for instance, secured permission in October 1916 to sell popcorn and candy on Halloween to support the fly abatement program. The interests of the Ladies Literary Club and the Utah Congress of Mothers ranged far—from reading and reviewing novels and supporting family solidarity to questions of urban improvement.

During the mid-1920s, however, certain voluntary associations appeared that signaled an undercurrent of opposition to the Progressive penchant for civic improvement. By 1926, the Utah Taxpayer's Association had begun to lobby almost exclusively for economy. This had been part of the goal of many associations, but in most of them economy had been associated with a distinct and often exclusive desire for urban improvements.

In 1914, for instance, a number of the voluntary associations petitioned the city for the establishment of a public market. Among them were the Utah Congress of Mothers, the Association of City Clubs, and the Ladies Literary Club. The council passed an ordinance establishing a market, appointed J. O. Smith as Market Master, and made arrangements for two locations. The first was on the north side of Pioneer Park on the city's west side, where marketing took place on Tuesdays, Thursdays, and Saturdays. The second location was on the north side of the city and county building on Washington Square.

The continuity with previous administrations is evident from the continuation of the "City Beautiful" movement. In 1912, the Board of Park Commissioners adopted a master plan for beautification of the city through the development of parks and boulevards. Estimated at the time eventually to cost $1.5 million, it was expected to give the city a system of parks, playgrounds, parking spaces, and boulevards second to none in the United States.

Main Street 1916 when the new carbon street lights were first illuminated. This was said to make Main Street the brightest lighted street in the world. Courtesy, Utah State Historical Society.

South Temple Street in the 1920s, showing (left to right) Hotel Utah, New Church Office Building, Lion House, Beehive House, and Eagle Gate. Courtesy, Utah State Historical Society.

The city moved quickly to implement the plan. In November 1913, hoping to lay the groundwork for twenty years' growth that would include "all that goes to remove the objectionable from the public gaze," it created the Civic Planning and Art Commission. Members of the commission included Mayor Park, William H. Bennett, George F. Goodwin, Mrs. A. J. Gorham, Albert Owen Treganza, and J. Leo Fairbanks— two businessmen, an attorney, the president of the state federation of women's clubs, an architect, and an artist. In 1914, Superintendent of Parks Byhower recommended that certain streets in the city be designated boulevards. They included City Creek, Eleventh Avenue, B. Street East through Popperton Addition and Federal Heights, Thirteenth East from South Temple to Twelfth South, and Twelfth South from Thirteenth East to Main Street. This proposal received the endorsement of the Art Commission in May. In the long run, the plan was much easier to implement in the original city than in subdivisions with narrow streets like the Avenues. As a result, a number of broad boulevards with parks in the median are still to be found in Salt Lake.

Other less extensive programs were adopted for city beautification. In 1914, for instance, the city passed an ordinance making property owners responsible for weed patches left on their property. At times, voluntary organizations and private citizens prodded the city to enforce the regulations. In April 1915, motivated by a request from the Burroughs Nature Study Association of Utah, the city designated public parks, grounds, and canyons belonging to the city as "bird sanctuaries sacred to the life and growth of the birds of all species for all time." In 1922, under the leadership of Commissioner Theodore T. Burton, the city conducted a "clean-up campaign" and re-emphasized the need of citizens, prodded by the police department, to maintain the grass strips next to the street free from parked cars or vehicles stopped to unload.

Beautification included the public golf course opened in 1922. Charles W. Nibley, then Presiding Bishop of the LDS church and a prominent business leader, donated land to be named Nibley Park, which the city agreed to maintain as a park and golf course. The area located at 2700 South and 700 East had previously been known as Calder's Park and most recently as Wandamere. At the dedication services presided over by Mayor Neslen, President Heber J. Grant of the LDS church offered the dedicatory prayer, and Nibley said that he believed "that this generation and the generations of men and women yet to come, shall find healthful enjoyment and rare pleasure here in playing that splendid outdoor Scotch game known as golf . . . that thought gives me the highest satisfaction and most genuine pleasure."

Efforts to secure a clean town included an attempt to control or perhaps to rid the city of flies and rats during 1914 and 1915. Clean Town clubs were organized in every school district, and these were in turn subdivided into squads assigned to blocks. Prizes were awarded for bottles of flies. In January 1914, the city authorized $41,000 for rat bounties, and the officials placed the burden on home and business owners to kill and turn in the rats they found. On April 30, the city health commissioner said that the "people are taking a great deal of interest in the extermination of flies and rats and results so far accomplished have undoubtedly been of great benefit to the city."

This same thrust brought about other improvements. New parks were opened and the city constructed the Chapman Branch Library with a $25,000 grant from the Carnegie Corporation. The city also continued to operate Warm Springs Bathhouse in the northwestern part of the city, though by 1923 the neighborhood had begun to deteriorate, and some of the "rough element of that part of the city" congregated at "a hot dog and soft drink stand" near the bath where they reviled the patrons with "vile language and other forms of insults." In 1913, the city even designated certain streets for sleigh riding, though by 1922 coasting had created such a traffic problem on some streets that Governor Charles R. Mabey recommended that the city construct coasting ways away from auto routes.

As part of the movement to improve the health of city dwellers, the city undertook a reorganization of its health program. In January 1912, the departments of dairy and food commission were combined with the city veterinarian's office. At the same time the city's garbage department was separated from the health department and the health department was given exclusive jurisdiction over public health. The city veterinarian was charged with inspecting meat, foods, markets, stores, slaughterhouses, dairies, and other food-handling establishments.

Much of what progressives promoted was the continuation of efforts begun long before progressivism became fashionable. One of these was the expansion of urban lighting. The city council minutes indicate a great demand for street lighting in various portions of the city. Urban lighting was provided by Utah Light and Railway Company, predecessor of Utah Power and Light Company, organized in 1913. As part of the movement for economy, the city negotiated a reduction in the cost of street lighting in January 1914. Pressure for street lighting came from voluntary groups and businesses.

The development of urban water and sewer systems continued on the pattern begun in the nineteenth century. By the second decade of the twentieth century, even with the exchange agreements, the free-flowing mountain streams supplied insufficient water for urban consumption, especially in the late summer. In order to alleviate this problem, between 1915 and 1925 three reservoirs were completed to control the discharge of water into the canyons. These were Twin Lakes Reservoir and Lake Phoebe-Lake Mary Reservoir in Big Cottonwood Canyon and Mountain Dell Reservoir in Parley's Canyon. Initial construction was completed on the three reservoirs in 1917, and Mountain Dell was raised to 98 feet in 1925, which increased its capacity from 955 to 3,514 acre feet.

The driving force behind these improvements was City Engineer Sylvester Q. Cannon. Born in 1877 as a son of George Q. Cannon and Elizabeth Hoagland, he attended Latter-day Saints College and the University of Utah before transferring to Massachusetts Institute of Technology where he received his B.S. in mining engineering in 1899. After serving a mission for the LDS church in the Netherlands and Belgium (1899–1901), he worked for the Office of City Engineer in hydrographic work, and in 1913 he was appointed city engineer. His major accomplishments included planning the city's extensive water collection system, originating the efforts at urban beautification, and working to end air pollution. With the aid of the city's legal department, Cannon succeeded in obtaining a judgment in 1920 which allowed the enlargement of the East Jordan Irrigation Company's canal. With this, the city could fulfill its exchange agreements with companies using water from Big and Little Cottonwood to obtain water. Some have questioned the propriety of these agreements because the city received very little water in return for the obligation to furnish water from its canals to some of the farmers. This was especially true of a number of exchanges made between 1921 and 1931 for users with marginal rights on Big and Little Cottonwood and Mill Creek. In retrospect, however, it seems clear that the agreements were quite farsighted, as part of the area, then outside the city, has since been incorporated into Salt Lake and additional collection and distribution facilities have allowed the use of water rights that might otherwise have been in dispute.

Like so many others in prominent positions in the city, Cannon was involved in several enterprises other than the engineering work. President of the LDS Pioneer Stake for many years, he was also a member of the Chamber of Commerce and the Timpanogos Club, and served as a director of a number of hospitals, the LDS Business College, and the McCune School of Music and Art. In 1925 he left the position as city engineer to become Presiding Bishop of the LDS church, and he ended his career as an assistant to the Quorum of Twelve Apostles.

In the cases of some improvements which had begun before the Progressive Era, changes characteristic of the later period altered the picture. The extension of sewers was a good example. The city moved ahead to connect various residential sections to the sewer—not without considerable difficulty. The sewer farm, a large field into which the effluent was discharged in the northwest portion of the city, was apparently too small to contain the sewage of all the new patrons, and the city had to find alternative outlets. On the one hand, the city faced pressure from voluntary organizations like the East Bench Improvement League which insisted that all property owners bounded by Ninth East, Third South, and Fort Douglas and Ninth South be required to connect with the sewer. On the other hand, the River Side Improvement League protested against the construction of a sewer which would continue to empty into the Jordan River. A bond election held in February 1914 provided money to construct the necessary sewer mains and a pumping station that allowed the sewage to be carried to a discharge pipe at Eighth West and Seventh North, which in turn would lead into a canal emptying in Great Salt Lake.

Even this did not solve the problems, since deterioration in the new system allowed sewage to damage property in Davis County. In 1922, the Utah Hunting and Improvement Club asked that the City "at once turn sewage into the Jordan River and repair its flume to prevent further discharge from the canal into Burnham Slough."

In fact, with the rapidly growing population, the city was continually faced with a myriad of improvement problems on its sewers, water supply, curbs and gutters, and streets, not to mention improvements at the Warm Springs, and Liberty Park. In 1919, the city passed a bond issue to provide money for a broad range of civic improvements including all the above plus such necessities as a storm sewer system, a new fire station, a new fire alarm system, and even a comfort station in the business district.

The city's effort to pave its streets caused no little difficulty because of the opposition of certain special interests. In March 1913, for instance, Governor William Spry made the street railway company and Edward H. Harriman very happy by vetoing a bill which would have allowed more rapid paving. Under the law at the time, not more than three miles of streets could be paved in a year. The change would have allowed Salt Lake more fully to meet the needs of a city of more than 100,000, but it was not passed. Nevertheless, the city moved ahead slowly to pave those streets most in need of improvement.

Increasingly, however, Salt Lake City streets were transformed from thoroughfares for pedestrians, trolleys, and horses into auto roads. Citizens and city officials became concerned with the problems caused by this new form of transportation. In 1913, the city commission received petitions asking for the regulation of motor vehicle speed in the city.

In January 1914, the council set speed at 12 miles per hour in the city core, 15 miles per hour in the residential areas, and 20 miles per hour elsewhere. The city also established noise abatement regulations which required mufflers on autos. By 1928, congestion in the streets had become so bad that the city, at the suggestion of Councilman Theodore T. Burton, changed its previous practice of allowing parallel parking and began to require diagonal parking and stricter enforcement of parking regulations. In addition, special "no parking" signs were removed from the downtown area to assist in clearing the streets of automobiles seeking parking places.

While the city railway company at first resisted the improvement of streets for automobile use, by the late 1920s public trolleys too had taken to the asphalt. Under the direction of Jed. F. Woolley, the Salt Lake Traction Company put pneumatic-tired trolley buses in operation in 1928. Reports indicated that Salt Lake was the first city in the world to do this, and representatives from twenty-six states and thirteen foreign countries came to study the design and operation of the buses. This was followed in 1933 by the introduction—also for the first time anywhere—of rear-engine motor buses. These two innovations were eventually to displace the track-borne trolleys, but the motorbuses added to the growing problem of urban air pollution.

By the mid-teens, air pollution had become extremely severe. An article in *Outlook* magazine indicated that "Salt Lake City has become a fit rival of Pittsburgh, Cincinnati, Chicago, and St. Louis as a smoke-plagued city." The article pointed out that the majority of the citizens were contributing to the smog and that all were imposing "an intolerable burden upon their neighbors."

Pressure for positive action on the problem came from various sources, and the city administration finally had to act. The Ladies Literary Club came frequently before the city council in late 1913 and early 1914, asking for the enforcement of regulations and for the appointment of an inspector to enforce air pollution abatement. The Commercial Club supported this pressure, calling for an investigation of the problem, and the *Progressive* made a number of suggestions. In November 1913, the commissioners visited the Salt Lake Hardware Company to inspect a smokeless boiler which the company had installed.

Numerous proposals were made, including the use of anthracite coal or coke, the use of licensed engineers to run heating plants more efficiently, stiffer prosecution of flagrant violators of current laws, and the establishment of a city-run central heating plant. Finally, in February 1914, the city enacted an ordinance designed to deal with the problem. The law established a bureau of smoke inspection within the Department of Public Safety with a smoke inspector authorized to issue citations for violation of the pollution ordinances.

The ordinance was, unfortunately, poorly enforced and the city was subjected to considerable criticism for its failure. During the winter of 1915–1916, a number of complaints arrived on the mayor's desk. In January 1917, the Civic Planning and Art Commission again pointed out that air pollution damaged property, imperiled health, and dirtied the city.

The city persevered, but found the work of smoke abatement extremely difficult. In 1919, City Engineer Cannon enlisted the assistance of Joseph F. Merrill, Director of the University of Utah School of Mines, and engineers from the U.S. Bureau of Mines to investigate the problem and propose solutions. The Walker Bank offered the city use of its observation tower as a vantage point to see polluting smoke stacks. Mayor Neslen recommended acceptance of the offer and the installation of a telephone to call owners of plants found in violation—a proposal which the council accepted.

In July 1920, the United States Bureau of Mines, the city engineer, and the University of Utah completed their investigation. Osborn Monnett, fuel engineer for the Bureau of Mines, summarized the recommendations and estimated that an expenditure of $15,000 per year for two years, assuming no change in fuel use patterns, "should largely rid the city of the smoke trouble." If, on the other hand, consumption shifted to coke and gas, the problem should be easier to solve.

The city moved—though somewhat less rapidly than might have been hoped—to implement the plan. The city council appointed an advisory committee to oversee the abatement program, and by the fall and winter of 1922, City Engineer Cannon could report considerable progress. The Utah Power and Light Company had begun renovating its downtown generating plant to overcome the smoke problem and the Denver and Rio Grand Western Railroad was building a new boiler plant. The question of railroad locomotive smoke had been taken up with executives of other railroads who promised to cooperate. Investigations and instructions on procedures had progressed well with plants, apartments, railroads, and other businesses. By December, Cannon reported that the few remaining businesses refusing to cooperate would probably require legal action. "The main trouble we are having now," he reported, "is with the railroads and with the residence districts." He recommended proceedings against three businesses.

Such prosecutions were politically problematic, and Commissioner Theodore T. Burton proposed that the Smoke Department inform the city council of intended arrests of offenders. Thus, in January 1923, the council approved prosecution of the owners of the Delphia Apartments and the Empire Hotel.

In July 1924, Cannon reported considerable progress since the inauguration of systematic smoke abatement procedures in January 1921. The "production of smoke from industrial and commercial plants [had] been reduced 93 percent; railroad locomotive smoke [had] been reduced considerably and residence smoke somewhat." In general, the railroads had cooperated, but residential heating remained as the major problem. Over the preceding three years, 300 plants—largely businesses—had remodeled their heating installations. In addition to reduced pollution, the program resulted in a fuel saving of just over $280.00 per plant.

By 1927, the situation had improved to such a degree that some suggested that smoke abatement enforcement be curtailed. The Utah Society of Engineers and the new city engineer, H. C. Jessen, protested. Jessen declared, as Cannon had before him, that improved conditions were the result of business cooperation, but also that the records of the Smoke Abatement Division showed that seventy-five percent of the smoke produced during the 1925–1926 heating season came from residential sources.

While a potential source of respiratory diseases was reduced, the city was also faced with other health hazards. In 1918, during the winter following the end of World War I, an epidemic of Spanish influenza ravaged Salt Lake. In November, the city health commissioner had to hire 100 additional deputies to implement emergency measures for dealing with this extraordinary situation. Even the city cemetery had to hire additional personnel and equipment to bury the larger than average number of dead.

Such epidemics, however, were sporadic. More serious was the continued presence of communicable diseases. With the improvement of water supplies and sewage and garbage disposal, typhoid had largely been eliminated by the 1920s and smallpox had been controlled through more extensive vaccination and improved public health measures. A major problem, however, as late as 1927 was the high incidence of diphtheria. In November the city health commissioner cited figures from the American Medical Association which indicated that Salt Lake City children had experienced an average of more than 220 cases of diphtheria and seventeen deaths in 1925, 1926, and 1927. In comparison with mortality statistics from throughout the world, only Mannheim, Germany and Moscow, Russia had a higher death rate than Salt Lake City. This was particularly serious since the diphtheria antitoxin had been available since 1890 and the Schick test to determine immunity had been available since 1913.

It should be pointed out, however, that public health measures in Utah in general, and Salt Lake City in particular, improved considerably. The LDS church Relief Society, particularly through the efforts of Amy Brown Lyman, its secretary and a member of the state legislature, secured state legislation implementing the Sheppard-Towner Mother and Child Health Act. The Relief Society also worked with other private organizations to improve public health. In 1931, the Utah state health commissioner reported that Utah had made a great reduction in maternal death and infant mortality rates, ranking with five other states as the lowest in the nation.

Perhaps the leading Salt Laker in this effort to improve the health of Utahns was Amy Brown Lyman. Born in Pleasant Grove in 1872, she studied at the Brigham Young Academy (later Brigham Young University), where she later became a teacher. Leaving the BYA, she joined the faculty of the training school at the University of Utah. She married Richard R. Lyman, a professor of civil engineering at the University and later member of the council of Twelve Apostles of the LDS church. Joining the general board of the LDS church's Relief Society in 1911, she served successively as general secretary, counselor to the president, and president.

Particularly interested in public health, social work, and mental health, she worked to promote increased emphasis on these matters in Salt Lake City and Utah. In 1919, she became the first director of the Relief Society Social Services Department. She became active in the national social work movement, and worked tirelessly for improvement of public assistance in Utah and Salt Lake City.

Perhaps the most remarkable aspect of charitable work in Salt Lake City from 1911 through 1930 was the degree of cooperation between Mormons and non-Mormons. Old antagonisms seemed to fade in the background as the two groups often worked together. In February 1912, for instance, the Orphans' Home and Day Nursery, a nonsectarian institution, held its annual benefit entertainment, and the committee consisted of both Mormon and non-Mormon women of prominence.

With some notable exceptions, the Mormon-anti-Mormon conflict subsided during the late teens and 1920s. The demise of the American party and the shift in editorial policy of the *Tribune* under the leadership of Ambrose Noble McKay and John F. Fitzpatrick were partly responsible. So also was Thomas Kearns's retirement from active political life. General concern over the condition of the community replaced the old antagonisms.

There were, however, some flare-ups in Mormon-gentile relations. One dispute arose after the publication by Franklin S. Spalding of *Joseph*

Smith as a Translator, which included charges that the Mormon prophet was a fraud. Excerpts were published in The Utah Survey, the organ of the Episcopal church's Social Service Commission, in 1913. Latter-day Saint church members, friendly non-Mormons, and church officials responded in kind through the pages of the church's *Improvement Era,* and the bickering over the question continued for several years.

Most serious, however, was the development of a powerful political machine during the 1920s. In 1922, George Wilson, the Republican boss of Salt Lake County and Ernest Bamberger, a Republican senatorial hopeful, organized a secret political society known as the Order of Sevens. Wilson, the kingpin of the organization, had been Salt Lake County purchasing agent in the late teens and became state purchasing agent in the early twenties. Charges surfaced that Wilson and others in the Sevens were involved in kickback and protection rackets in Salt Lake City. Whatever the truth of this, it was clear that the Sevens were avowedly anti-Mormon.

The Sevens became increasingly controversial. A secret organization with an elaborate set of rituals, the Sevens were organized through a series of interlocking cells of seven people each, sworn to secrecy and dedicated to the Republican party. In the 1922 Republican senatorial nominating convention, through the Sevens organization and Wilson's patronage connections, Ernest Bamberger succeeded in wresting the Republican senatorial nomination from J. Reuben Clark, Jr., who at the time was serving with the State Department in Washington, D.C. Charges of corrupt politics abounded and a number of Republicans crossed over to vote for William H. King, the incumbent Democratic senator. Both Clark and King were active Latter-day Saints.

Bamberger and some of his supporters announced in May 1923 that they were organizing a "Party of Freedom or League of Liberty" to keep the Mormon church out of politics. The church, they said, had been responsible for Bamberger's defeat in 1922. In August 1923, the group announced the organization of a revived "American party," to oppose church influence in politics, and particularly to oppose the reelection of Mayor C. Clarence Neslen, a Mormon bishop. The group nominated Joseph E. Galigher for mayor and Parley L. Williams and George N. Lawrence for city commissioners. Some of the organizers had been members of the pre-1912 American party.

In fact, the LDS church, various civic betterment associations, and other churches were vitally interested in political affairs. In the fall election of 1922, for instance, the Salt Lake City Social Welfare and Betterment League showed concern over what seemed to be lax enforcement of the prohibition laws by incumbent Democratic County Sheriff John S. Corless and the lack of commitment to enforcement on the part of Republican candidate C. Frank Emery. In spite of opposition from some members of the Council of the Twelve, like Reed Smoot, and other highly placed Mormons, the church's First Presidency each personally supported Benjamin R. Harries's independent candidacy. At the same time, Harries received the official endorsement of the interdenominational Salt Lake Ministerial Association and the nonsectarian Social Welfare League.

Perhaps because of this, the American party did not complain of religious support for Harries. What it did call attention to, however, was the efforts of several LDS Apostles, notably George Albert Smith and Richard R. Lyman, in support of cigarette prohibition during the 1923 state legislative session.

As the 1923 campaign progressed, it became clear that Clarence Neslen was the wrong target for anti-Mormon forces. Only the third Latter-day Saint to serve as mayor since 1890, Neslen had been appointed in 1920 by an overwhelmingly non-Mormon city council to replace the discredited E. A. Bock. While his administration had increased taxes to pay for water, sewer, and street improvements, American party campaigners could cite no example of church influence. On the other hand, Neslen's supporters, many of whom were non-Mormons, pointed out that of 125 employees in the Water Department over which Neslen presided, sixty-five percent were gentiles. Perhaps 69,000 people, or about fifty-six percent of Salt Lake City's population in 1923, were Latter-day Saints, which meant that Mormons were actually under-represented in Neslen's administration. Neslen won handily, and all the American party candidates were soundly defeated. The American party had revived only temporarily.

Politics were further complicated by the presence of the Ku Klux Klan. Organized in Utah in late 1921, the Klan in Salt Lake City bore a close relationship to Utah Masonry, since most known Utah Klan officials were Masons. In addition to its much vaunted opposition to any persons not Anglo-Saxons, native-born Americans, and Protestants, the Klan also proclaimed itself in favor of separation of church and state. In the October 1922 general conference of the LDS church, Charles W. Nibley lashed out at secret organizations, specifically naming the Klan, and urging members not to join them. Significantly, city council candidates Galigher, Lawrence, and Williams were all Masons and it is "virtually certain" that Galigher and Henry C. Allen, the American party campaign manager, were both Klansmen. By 1923, however, the Klan was in disarray in Salt Lake, and while Klansmen successfully revived the Hooded Empire in towns outside the city, its recruitment drive in Utah's capital fell flat. Mormon church president Heber J.

Grant refused to meet with Klan officials, and in the October conference of 1924, George Albert Smith again attacked those who "organize groups and take into their own hands the punishment of those who have differed from them in their ideas of religion or government."

Beyond this, the Klan came under official attack from the city commission. After staging a Washington's Birthday March and Konklave in Salt Lake City in 1925, complete with blazing crosses on Ensign Peak to coincide with the April LDS conference, the Klan suffered a near-fatal blow. On June 15, Commissioner Theodore T. Burton introduced an anti-mask ordinance which passed the commission unanimously.

This, together with a combination of antagonism and apathy, led to the Klan's demise. In the 1925 city elections, charges surfaced that the Klan backed Patrick J. Moran and Berkley Olson for commission posts, but the issue was clouded by handbills circulated through the city indicating Klan support for Moran and Harry L. Finch, an incumbent. Klan leaders denied responsibility and denounced the handbills as a "dirty last-hour" trick, but Finch and Moran won and the Klan suffered a public-relations defeat. This setback was compounded by an attack on Santa Claus in December 1925. At a commission meeting, Finch pointed out that sidewalk Santa Clauses were violating the city's anti-mask ordinance. Santas were ordered to unbeard, but Klansmen again lost points.

The death throes of the Klan in Utah coincided with the decline of the Order of Sevens. The Klan and Sevens became an issue in the 1926 Salt Lake County sheriff's race, and the Sevens surfaced again in the senatorial race of 1928. By 1926, Salt Lakers had had enough of the Klan, and while it continued in name until about 1930, any power it might have had was largely dissipated. The Sevens again succeeded in nominating Ernest Bamberger over J. Reuben Clark to run against Senator William King in 1928, but opposition from within the LDS church to secret oathbound organizations led to the decline of the Sevens and to Bamberger's second defeat.

One extraordinary feature of the Klan in Utah was its close link with causes espoused by the Sevens and thus with Ernest and Clarence Bamberger, who were both Jewish. In this case, politics certainly made strange bedfellows.

Salt Lakers, however, were interested in more than konklaves and politics. Public entertainment was geared to attract increasingly affluent citizens. Vaudeville and motion picutres competed with the Salt Palace and the highbrow Salt Lake Theatre, and more traditional entertainments suffered. Saltair—never a money-making operation—continued to lose heavily until a fire in April 1925 destroyed the pavilion. While it was restored and the resort continued to function until 1958, it never recovered from the lost business and the heavy new capital investment.

Perhaps the greatest casualty of shifting public taste was the Salt Lake Theatre. The LDS church continued to subsidize the theatre heavily until, by 1928, its commitments to education, economic development, and building construction made the continued drain on its resources impossible. On October 20, 1928, the theatre opened for the last time as Ada Dwyer Russell read Amy Lowell's poem, "Lilacs." The second act of *Robin Hood* and the third act of *La Traviata* followed. With that, Salt Lake citizens then razed the institution that had witnessed performances of most of Shakespeare's plays and many other significant dramatic works. In its place appeared an unsightly gas station but, in the late 1940s, the telephone company erected an office building that is perhaps the best example of Art Deco building in Utah.

The 1920s also witnessed the inauguration of radio broadcasting in Salt Lake City and in Utah. On May 6, 1922, KZN opened an era by broadcasting from the roof of the *Deseret News* Building. A speech by LDS church president Heber J. Grant preceded one by Salt Lake mayor C. Clarence Neslen. In June 1924, the *Deseret News* sold its interest to one of the station engineers and the call letters were changed to KFPT. In 1925, the LDS church and the *Salt Lake Tribune* acquired stock in the venture and the call letters were changed again, this time to KSL.

One form of traditional entertainment that did not decline was in the field of music. Perhaps the most important development was the revitalization of the Salt Lake Tabernacle Choir by the appointment of Anthony C. Lund as choir director and Alexander Schreiner as organist. Lund remade the choir into a world-renowned organization, and in addition to its regular public performances and extraordinary tours, the choir inaugurated weekly broadcasts in 1929, which have continued to the present time.

Since Utah became urbanized at approximately the same rate as the United States as a whole, Salt Lake City faced problems similar to those of other American cities. This was reflected, in part, in the parallel development of progressive concerns in Utah's capitol at the same time they were surfacing elsewhere. The city also experienced a decline in child labor as did other cities of the period. In 1928, Arthur Beeley of the University of Utah Sociology Department completed a study entitled *Boys and Girls in Salt Lake City*, which revealed a slight decline in the employment of children under age eighteen since 1920. Most girls were employed in domestic and personal service, while boys tended to work in more diverse occupations, most particularly as deliverymen, domestic and personal service, clerks in stores, and miscellaneous occupations.

Juvenile delinquency, on the other hand, presented an increasingly serious problem. Beeley's study showed that between 1923 and 1928, juvenile court judges handled the cases of 3,783 boys and 490 girls out of court and in addition, brought to trial 769 boys and 206 girls. More than half the boys were convicted of larceny and more than half the girls of "immorality." The median age of male offenders was fourteen and of females fifteen, with offenders ranging as young as age nine.

Economically, Salt Lake City suffered fewer long-range effects from the shocks of the period than did agricultural regions. The outbreak of the First World War in Europe in 1914 slowed the economic expansion that had characterized the previous decade, but shortly thereafter the economy boomed and continued to do so until 1919. Then, depressed markets for agricultural products and minerals hurt Utah until late in 1922, when the economy began to revive again. During the remainder of the decade, until the stock market crash in late 1929, Salt Lake City fared better than other areas. Commerce, transportation, banking, and construction recovered quite rapidly after 1922, while agriculture and mining languished. The lackluster performance in the two latter industries hurt Salt Lake somewhat, but not nearly as much as it did those areas with single industry economies.

As a firmly entrenched regional capital, Salt Lake City's size and importance contributed to his continued growth. In 1911, for instance, half of Utah's manufacturing plants were in Salt Lake. In 1919, Salt Lake Valley boasted the greatest smelting district in North America, treating some 4.43 million tons of ore. The Federal Reserve Bank of San Francisco recognized Salt Lake's regional predominance when, at the urging of Utah and southern Idaho bankers and the Salt Lake clearing house association, it established a branch bank in the capital city, razing another downtown landmark—Brigham Young's Gardo House—in the process. In the 1920s, Salt Lake's commercial predominance brought airmail service and passenger flights to the recently inaugurated airport.

The city continued to expand not only economically and in population, but also in circumference. Expansion, however, was uneven. Westward growth was relatively slow, as was movement up the north bench above the Avenues district. Fort Douglas, the University of Utah, and Mount Olivet Cemetery stood as barriers to further expansion eastward until southern annexations passed the graveyard. Expansion to the south and southeast, however, moved ahead rather rapidly and shifted the population farther away from the old core city toward Sugarhouse, Murray, and Midvale.

In the midst of dealing with the problems of urban services in an expanding city, Salt Lake citizens had to cope with conditions brought on by World War I. In 1916, as the United States inaugurated a preparedness movement, young men were encouraged to attend the four Citizen's

Training camps at Fort Douglas. City departments and private employers were encouraged to release men for the purpose. After the outbreak of the war in April 1917, local citizens established the Salt Lake Army Club where chaperoned Comrade Girls hosted the homesick doughboys. The bar of one of the city's hotels, closed by the state's adoption of prohibition in early 1917, reopened as a service men's club with library, lounges, and pool tables. Citizens were encouraged to raise gardens, and the city commission furnished money for seeds and additional water pipes for the gardens.

Fort Douglas, itself, changed considerably. The Citizen's Training Camp became an Officer's Training Camp. The previous four-week military training program became three months, and city employees were given leave of absence to participate. Fort Douglas also became the home of approximately 300 Germans. Generally referred to as prisoners of war, they were actually interned German nationals unfortunate enough to be residents of the United States in April 1917. Also interned there were socialists, pacifists, and a variety of miscellaneous "radicals," since the United States did not recognize conscientious objection in World War I.

War on the home front had its darker side as well. Throughout the United States various organizations—official and unofficial—conducted campaigns against those who seemed to resist suppression of civil liberties. Eugene Debs and other socialists were thrown in prison and hate campaigns were leveled against ethnic Germans. Spurred by the State Council of Defense, the local council and private voluntary associations pressed for "100 percent Americanism during the War." As in other areas, this often resulted in action that reflected a sort of illogical hysteria. Albert Welti and a group of citizens, for example, pressured the city commission into changing the name of German Avenue to West Kensington. The American Defense Society asked the commission to support its petition urging Congress to enact a law imposing "punishment upon all persons or organizations responsible for pro-German activites or for the publication or public utterances of disloyal statements." Treason was already punishable, but this loosely-worded proposal had great potential for abuse.

The problems with reconversion that followed the war presented even more serious challenges to the city. Unemployment reached ten percent in 1916, subsided during the U.S. participation in the war, then again increased owing to the release of able-bodied men from military service and the closing of war industries. City Engineer Cannon recommended hiring men on public works, and the large bond issue in 1919 was designed in part to provide public work projects for unemployed veterans. Nephi L. Morris, executive secretary of the Soldier's and Sailor's Employment Commission, launched a campaign for each citizen to own his own home in order to stimulate construction. Stung by increasing unemployment, radical citizens led by M. P. Bales, a Salt Lake barber, organized a soldier's, sailor's, and worker's council on the Soviet model, urged increased work for the unemployed, and gained control of the Utah State Federation of Labor. This was not entirely unprecedented, since the Utah Federation of Labor had endorsed the Socialist party in 1911, 1912, and 1913.

If Salt Lake City workers had difficulty after the war, it was only symptomatic of general problems throughout the period. While labor made some gains between 1912 and 1930, the subjective evaluation of many was that conditions were never at an optimum and that early advances were offset by the loss of independence and control over their own lives. This was particularly true during the 1920s in part of the virulent anti-Union campaign of the Utah Associated Industries. By the end of the period, the Utah Federation of Labor was hardly a force to be reckoned with in Utah.

At first, it appeared that blue-collar workers might find a sympathetic ear in Salt Lake. In January 1912, for instance, the city council agreed to pay all water department employees the union scale for a day limited to eight hours. The law was not rigidly enforced, however, for 1913 the Salt Lake Building Trades Council cited several examples of contractors compelling their employees to work nine to ten hours per day.

In the 1920s, the right of workers to make independent decisions about their private associations was even more severely limited by what amounted to an anti-labor combination among certain businessmen and community leaders. In 1918, a group of business and civic leaders organized the Utah Associated Industries. Headquartered in Salt Lake City, the organization set as its goal the promotion of Utah business and the dissolution of union organization by encouraging employers to agree to hire only nonunion workers. Its considerable success drew support from community, business, and religious leaders, and its program damaged the union movement considerably in the state as a whole and in Salt Lake City in particular.

The effort to destroy voluntary labor associations received a boost from the sluggish economy of the 1919–1922 period. In January 1922, the city commission agreed to give preference in hiring to the most needy. City Engineer Cannon, the Council of Unemployed, and the Salt Lake Federation of Labor urged the city again to provide employment. Members of the fire department and other organizations donated money for assistance. Unemployment persisted, however, and competition for jobs undermined union organizational efforts.

190

Even before World War I, Salt Lake City was the scene of violent confrontations between supporters of labor and capital. These can be traced, in part, to the activities of and opposition to the Western Federation of Miners organized at Butte, Montana in 1893 and the Industrial Workers of the World founded at Chicago in 1905.

In particular, organizational efforts of the IWW led to violence. As part of its national organizing campaign, the IWW inaugurated street meetings in Salt Lake. On August 12, 1913, James F. Morgan spoke at the corner of Second South and Commercial Street, in the heart of the saloon and red light district. The IWW and Socialist party wanted to speak at Second South and Main, but the city commission restricted them to the less desirable location. As Morgan mounted the speaker's box, Axel Steele, a former deputy sheriff then in the employ of the Utah Copper Company, led a group of men who pulled Morgan from his perch and beat him. In the ensuing melee, guns were fired and six men were injured. Workers were enraged when, in the end, Morgan was tried but Steele and his cohorts went free. Petitions calling for an investigation came from William M. Knerr, then an active Socialist and later chairman of the State Industrial Commission, and from the Salt Lake Federation of Labor. Instead of ordering an investigation, however, the city commission simply buried the petitions in a file. On the other hand, the commission granted several permits to the Socialist party to hold public meetings on Second South and at Liberty Park.

While this incident caused considerable local uproar, a series of incidents in 1914 and 1915 became an international *cause célèbre*. It began with the murders of Salt Lake grocers John G. and Arling Morrison during a robbery on January 10, 1914. Later that night, a Swedish immigrant calling himself Joe Hill, a member of the IWW and an itinerant poet, sought medical treatment for a gunshot wound. Since Arling Morrison had wounded one of the thieves, an investigation led to Hill's arrest, trial, conviction, and sentencing to execution by firing squad. The IWW accused the Utah Copper Company, the Utah Construction Company, and the LDS church with conspiracy in the case. Though there is no credible evidence linking any of these organizations to the prosecution, Utah Copper Company employees had been active in the anti-IWW campaign.

Hill's conviction resulted from circumstantial evidence, and evidence of an unfair trial led to a campaign to persuade Governor William Spry to commute Hill's sentence to life imprisonment. United States president Woodrow Wilson, leaders of the American Federation of Labor, and representatives of the Swedish government joined hundreds in urging commutation. Spry declined and Hill was executed at the state prison in Sugarhouse on November 19, 1915. The fever pitch of agitation led to the disbarment of Hill's lawyer, O. N. Hilton, and the firing of a University of Utah art teacher, Virginia Snow Stephens, for their support of the commutation effort. Hill's body was cremated and portions of his ashes were sent by the IWW to every state in the Union except Utah. Since his execution, whether rightly or wrongly, Hill has become a symbol of labor resistence to oppression.

One group in Salt Lake City that consistently suffered economic discrimination was women, who made up 51 percent of the population in 1930, up from 48.7 percent in 1910. This trend toward discrimination followed that of the nation as a whole. Salt Lake, together with other school districts in the state, had separate and lower pay scales for women than for men with the same teaching duties. Women were consistently found in the so-called "pink collar" jobs such as teaching, nursing, and stenography. Between 1900 and 1930, the percentage of women physicians and surgeons in Utah had declined from eleven percent to three percent of those practicing. Increasingly, women like Martha Hughes Cannon were relics of the past. The biggest increases in women's employment came among clerks, college professors, semiskilled manufacturing operatives, stenographers, bookkeepers, saleswomen, and teachers.

Ethnic identification among women had a great deal to do with the type of employment they found. Black women tended to be employed at a higher rate than others, probably out of economc necessity. In 1930, a foreign-born white woman was almost twice as likely to be found in manufacturing and mechanical employment as a native-born white woman, an indication of the status of those jobs.

In spite of all the changes which had taken place in Salt Lake by 1930, it was still predominantly a city of native whites of northwestern European origin. In a population of 140,300 only 681 or about .5 percent were blacks and only 18,100 or 12.9 percent were foreign born. The percentage of foreign born in Salt Lake was slightly higher than the 11.6 percent in the nation as a whole, and slightly higher than Denver at 11.4, the only other city in the Mountain West with a population of more than 100,000. On the other hand, Denver had more than 7,000 blacks in 1930, or 2.5 percent of the population. In 1930, 29.9 percent of Salt Lake City's population was of foreign-born parentage compared with 34.8 percent in 1920. This was higher than the percentage in Denver (25.1 in 1930 and 26.1 in 1920).

Those who were foreign born came overwhelmingly from northwestern Europe. In 1930, of those in Salt Lake who were foreign born, nearly a quarter came from England and more than 30 percent from the British Isles. More than 21 percent came from Scandinavia and more than 23 percent from Germany, Switzerland, and the Netherlands. Only 6 percent came from Greece and Italy, and Mexico furnished only 2.7 percent. Approximately the same percentage of Denver's population as Salt Lake City's came from Italy and Greece, largely because the Denver population was more diverse than Salt Lake City's. In 1930, Denver exhibited about twice the percentage of Mexicans in its population as did Salt Lake City, only 18 percent came from the British Isles, and 11 percent came from Russia, a group too small to be enumerated separately in Salt Lake.

Given these conditions, the general prejudice against foreigners from areas other than northern Europe, and the general tendency of northwestern Europeans to share the same prejudices against blacks and southeastern Europeans, it is not at all surprising that discrimination and low status were the lot of most of these people. The nonwhite and southeast European groups tended to be relegated to the western part of the city, and they generally got only the most menial jobs. Exceptions existed, to be sure, particularly in the Jewish community, but for the most part these people were "hewers of wood and drawers of water."

All this was symptomatic of a much broader problem faced by Salt Lake City. By the second decade of the twentieth century, the city had become increasingly a series of subcultures. Some of these were interlocking, and in some cases people belonged to more than one subculture. Mayor Neslen, for instance, belonged to the Commercial, Timpanogos, and Exchange clubs, in addition to the LDS church, which was undoubtedly the largest subcultural group. Characterization of Neslen as a tool of the Mormon church, however, missed the salient point that his connections stretched into powerful socioeconomic organizations to which business and professional men from all religions belonged. Joseph Galigher, American party candidate for mayor in 1923, was an outsider—he belonged to none of Neslen's subcultures.

Other subcultures existed as well, to which men of influence like Neslen would not have belonged. The National Association for the Advancement of Colored People wrestled with problems of segregation symbolized by accommodations at the municipal bath house. Blacks also faced harassment in the use of public transportation facilities, especially by soldiers during World War I, and complained to the city commisson about their treatment. Italian citizens organized fraternal and benevolent organizations like La Societá Cristoforo Columbo, the Figlia D'Italia, and the Italian Mothers Club. Some interaction between the Italian and other ethnic communities developed through organizations like the Knights of Columbus, and lodges like the Elks, Moose, and Eagles, all of whom participated in Italian-promoted Columbus Day parades.

The development of Salt Lake's public school system was not unlike that of other systems in the United States in this era. By 1925, the city had fifty-eight school buildings with 800 rooms and employed 900 teachers. The city boasted seven junior high schools and two high schools. In line with Utah's traditional emphasis on education, Salt Lake City required compulsory school attendance until age eighteen. On occasion this was honored in the breach, as the statistics for child labor indicate, but by the 1920s its observance was generally respected. Public education was supplemented by a number of parochial high schools.

At the pinnacle of Salt Lake City's educational structure stood the University of Utah. During this period, however, the university passed through a serious controversy which demonstrated that the autocracy of fire chiefs could be matched by some school administrators. It erupted in 1915 when President Joseph T. Kingsbury acted in several matters. He banned faculty participation in political campaigns, and fired the chairman of the English Department without faculty consultation. He replaced the department chairman with Osborne J. P. Widtsoe of LDS University in Salt Lake. Kingsbury was a non-Mormon, but charges of Mormon influence abounded. A number of faculty members resigned in protest, and the American Association of University Professors undertook an investigation into conditions at the University. After the dispute settled down, Kingsbury resigned and John A. Widtsoe, formerly president of Utah State University, succeeded him. Instituting a system of faculty governance, Widtsoe succeeded in placing the legacy of autocracy and bitterness behind the university and in establishing a sound foundation for future growth.

In retrospect, the history of Salt Lake City between 1912 and 1930 says much about the Progressive impulse. Like most Progressive experimenters, Salt Lake's citizens launched their reforms in a spirit of optimism. Like most progressive reforms, those that succeeded were largely structural rather than social. Commission government proved, at the time, more efficient and effective than the previous system. Moreover, its nonpartisan character defused and finally undermined efforts to reintroduce the Mormon-gentile conflict as a basis of Salt Lake's political system. The reforms in which the city commission succeeded, however, were largely the result of Progressive pressure for the continuation of efforts begun somewhat earlier. That is, the desires of progressively oriented voluntary organizations reinforced earlier efforts to improve streets, provide adequate water supplies, rid the city of sewage, provide lighting, and improve urban transportation. The one new area of significant improvement was in public health, but even that

Salt Lake City's Finest, 1927. Courtesy, Utah State Historical Society.

lagged behind the successes of other American cities, especially in the high incidence of diphtheria.

The Progressive experiments which proved largely ephemeral were the social reforms. The efforts of Chief of Police Grant and the Park administration to rid the city of prostitution and vice succeeded only for a while and only to a limited extent. This campaign was divisive in the community and the succeeding Ferry administration opted for a secular vision of society which downplayed the moral side of social reform. By contrast, the Neslen administration during the 1920s took a middle-of-the-road approach by trying to satisfy all groups. Certainly Neslen's job was easier, since the state had adopted prohibition and the force of a nationally approved law provided at least moral support for his efforts. But Neslen's efforts were not accompanied by the divisive ballyhoo of the Park years.

The one area of social reform that failed most miserably was in the efforts of working people to achieve some means of protecting themselves in the market place. While the state did establish workmen's compensation and the regulation of conditions of work in hazardous industries, the labor movement, which had been behind the effort to provide services for effective bargaining for improved working conditions, was largely destroyed. The Utah Associated Industries reigned supreme in the 1920s.

In general, the results that Salt Lake City experienced seem to have come about because the business-oriented voluntary groups which supported structural reform and physical improvement of the city were divided on the question of moral reform and quite opposed to the sort of social reforms that would have vested new strength in employees. All citizens could support better water supplies and improved urban transportation, but all did not agree with the nature of the anti-vice campaigns and even fewer could accept the transfer of power from the middle-class to the lower-middle and lower-classes inherent in the potential success of the labor movement.

195

Aerial view of Salt Lake City looking northeast, 1934. Courtesy, Utah State Historical Society.

——— 7 ———

Depression Decade

S alt Lake City's fundamental interrelationship with the world around
it was seldom more clear than during the decade of the Great
Depression. As the giant economic maelstrom swept the country, it
wreaked havoc upon the families of Salt Lake City as much as elsewhere,
and its history only emphasized the Mormon capital's vulnerability to
the caprices of national economics and its dependence upon the larger
American community.

At the same time, Salt Lake City itself continued to dominate in its
intermountain setting. It was the central community for a 185,000 square
mile region of 790,000 people that included Utah, southern Idaho,
eastern Nevada and southwestern Wyoming. Its closest rival was Ogden,
forty miles to the north, but the planning of the early Mormon pioneers
had assured Salt Lake City's dominance. As Chauncey Harris, author
of an important study entitled "Salt Lake City a Regional Capital,"
observed in 1939, it was the capital of a state, the seat of a religious
denomination, a nucleus of commercial and financial enterprises, a
focus of transportation, a leading center in educational activities, and
the largest city in the Intermountain West.

In the 1930s the city's commercial core occupied the same area as
that marked out by the first city planners. The major office buildings,
the large hotels, and the most well known department stores were all
located there, chiefly along Main Street. Also there, and appearing to
dominate, was the headquarters of the Mormon church. The city also
boasted seventy-five hotels with nearly 5,000 rooms and thirty-three
"tourist camps" (i.e., motels) with about 500 rooms. West of the central
business district lay the railway terminals, passenger depots, freight
depots, truck terminals, bus terminals, and warehouses. Farther west

was the Salt Lake City airport. Each of these supported important regional economic activities that contributed to Salt Lake City's primacy. The only outlying business center was Sugarhouse, located at Eleventh East and Twenty-first South streets.

Salt Lake City was a center for the distribution of many products and services. As a regional center for banking and transportation, the city attracted other concerns. In 1930 there were at least 600 wholesale representatives who traveled from Salt Lake City throughout the region distributing everything from chewing gum to vacuum cleaners. About 150 insurance companies maintained offices in the city. It was one of thirty-one key points in the United States for the distribution of motion pictures, and its business district housed central offices for several large land and water companies of Utah and southern Idaho, the Utah-Idaho Sugar Company, two Utah oil refining companies, and numerous mining companies. At the end of the decade Salt Lake City's three daily newspapers (the *Deseret News,* the *Salt Lake Tribune,* and the *Salt Lake Telegram*) circulated throughout the region and, with few exceptions, subscribers in communities outside the city exceeded the number of subscribers to papers printed in other metropolitan areas such as Denver and Boise. Its magazines were also of regional import. The religious magazines put out by the Mormon church circulated in all three areas, as did the *Utah Farmer,* the *National Woolgrower,* three mining magazines, the *Intermountain Retailer,* the *Commercial Index,* and the *Utah Educational Review.* The chief radio station in the region was Salt Lake City's KSL.

Salt Lake City was also a regional religious capital. The Baptist church maintained an area office downtown, and the Salt Lake Diocese of the Roman Catholic church was also headquartered in the city. A variety of religious and cultural activities centered around the impressive Cathedral of the Madeleine, and, beginning in 1927, the Catholics conducted weekly radio broadcasts over KSL. Mormons throughout the area looked to Salt Lake City for guidance, and thousands flocked there every April and October for the semiannual conferences of the church.

Though it was the major industrial center of Utah, Salt Lake City was not a major national manufacturing center, except for primary metals processing. It was, nevertheless, the home of several light industries, such as printing, clothing manufacturing, bakeries, bottling companies, and laundries. Its heavy industries included an oil refinery, machine shops, a cement factory, brickyards, meat packing, mattress factories, and the stockyards north of the city. The minerals industry was also important to the city's economy, with mines and smelters located nearby.

Finally, various governmental functions emphasized the city's regional import. As the capital city of Utah, it was the headquarters for such important agencies as the State Board of Agriculture, the Water Storage Commission, the Industrial Commission, the Public Service Commission, and other state regulatory agencies. Equally significant, it was an important regional center for twenty-two federal agencies, most of which were located in the Federal Building on Fourth South and Main streets. Particularly important was the fact that the federal government owned and managed sixty-nine percent of the land in Utah, and a similar portion in surrounding states. Salt Lake City therefore had regional offices for such agencies as the Bureau of Land Management, the General Land Office, Bureau of Indian Affairs, the Bureau of Reclamation, the Bureau of Agricultural Engineering, the Geological Survey, and many others. It was also the location of several New Deal agencies.

As important as all this was, however, it was not the major story of the 1930s. Just before Christmas 1931, the *Salt Lake Tribune* ran a touching human interest story. Intended to encourage generous Salt Lakers to provide more of their means to help the poor, it is still a simple and moving reminder of the human distress experienced during the Great Depression. It was this theme that dominated the concerns of city government throughout the decade.

It concerned a fifteen-year-old boy named Billy, one of nine children living at home in Murray, whose father had been out of work since May. Billy's older brother and sisters were also trying to find employment, but to no avail. Billy decided that even if there was no work for older members of the family, perhaps during the Christmas season a young boy could find something to do in the stores of Salt Lake City. On several different days he braved the wintry winds and snow to walk the seven miles from his home to the city, but no one gave him work. His only comfort was that he did not have to worry about one older sister, for she was married. This was only one of many examples, reported the *Tribune,* where stark poverty would keep Santa Claus from visiting a local family.

The depression hit harder in Utah than in the nation as a whole. National unemployment rose to twenty-five percent of the work force in the winter of 1932–1933, while Utah's reached thirty-five percent. Utah's banks remained relatively stable, though some failed and the prominent Deseret National Bank closed by the middle of the decade. Many businesses closed, bread lines appeared in Salt Lake City, unemployed miners stalked the streets, retail sales dropped drastically, and evictions and sheriff's sales increased. As John McCormick has written, "Long lines of hungry men, their shoulders hunched against cold winds, edged along sidewalks to get a bowl of broth from private-charity soup kitchens or city-operated transient shelters. Apple sellers abounded on city sidewalks. So did shoeshine boys, ranging in age from teenagers who should have been in school to men past retirement age. An army of new salesmen appeared on Salt Lake streets, peddling everything from large rubber balls to cheap neckties."

As elsewhere, the people of Utah showed signs not only of serious unrest but also of outright antagonism toward both the local and the national governments. Citizens expressed their rancor, in part, by popular efforts to disrupt sheriff's sales, and on February 23, 1933, such an attempt in Salt Lake County held up a sale for hours until fire hoses and tear gas dispersed the protestors. This was followed on March 3 by a mass protest march to the steps of the capitol; something not unprecedented in Utah in those years. During that same year, hundreds of homeless families camped on vacant lots throughout the city. In the fall of 1932 the citizens joined with the rest of the nation in voting overwhelmingly for a change in the national administration, and for the man who warmly promised "a new deal for the American people." Franklin D. Roosevelt was a symbol of hope as much in Salt Lake City as anywhere.

At the same time, even while recognizing the seriousness of the problems, some civic leaders maintained a marvelous optimism throughout the decade. In January 1930, the president of the chamber of commerce, E.O. Howard, praised 1929 as a year of "healthy progress," closing a decade of accomplishment "unparalleled in the history of the state." Looking forward to 1931, Gus P. Backman, secretary of the chamber of commerce, delighted in the fact that thirty organizations had held conventions in the city in 1930, tourists and homeseekers had made 50,000 inquiries, the federal government had completed a new office building and planned a veteran's hospital, $25,000 had been spent in advertising Salt Lake's glories: the list went on. He looked forward to the paving of more major highways, the growth of mining in the region, and continuing improvement in building activities. The Salt Lake Clearing House Association reported that the city's banks had never been in a stronger financial position, and the Salt Lake Real Estate board, predicting a great year, took comfort in the fact that realtors had suffered less than other businessmen since 1929. Even declining prices were heralded, for this brought down the cost of home building and raised the hope of more building starts. In addition, everyone expected important federal expenditures for the improvement of Fort Douglas and federal aid for expanding Salt Lake City's municipal airport, and these things promised to provide both employment and cash for the area.

By the mid-1930s the economy seemed to show signs of recovery, and 1936 was the best year, economically, for the New Deal. Salt Lake City boosters looked forward to that year with gusto as they anticipated a major expansion of the airport, the erection of a civic auditorium, new intra-state highways, mining development, the construction of Deer Creek reservoir, a home building boom, a $10,000 tourist trade, and a continuation of the impressive boosts in payrolls experienced in 1935. But if they were enthusiastic about these possibilities, two years later they were ecstatic as they looked back on recent accomplishments: major construction on Main Street that, they claimed, made it "one of the most beautiful business thoroughfares in America"; industrial expansion and its accompanying major building program; expanded commercial activities, such as the expansion of the Union Pacific bus operations, the new Centre theater, Montgomery Ward coming to town, and several business remodeling projects; and, of course, the large amount of federal money pouring into Utah, particularly through WPA projects but also because of the continuing support of Fort Douglas.

This boosterism was well meant but it hardly reflected the seriousness of the depression in the lives of the ordinary citizens, or their heavy dependence on federal assistance. At the end of the decade, for example, the national government was spending about seven dollars in Utah for every tax dollar sent to Washington. Utah had the distinction of being ninth in the nation in per capita federal spending during the decade.

Clearly, Salt Lake's economy was backward. Even before the depression hit, Utah lagged behind the national average in economic growth and activity, and in 1932 its per capita income of $300 was eighty percent of the national average. In the first three years of the decade per capita income dropped by forty-five percent. In 1930 over 6,000 people looked for work in Salt Lake City. Those who had work found their wages and hours both declining, so that by 1932 the wage level had dropped about one-third and the work week by one-fifth below the pre-depression peak. The food price index in Salt Lake City declined thirty-seven percent by 1933. The economy fluctuated in roughly the same pattern as that of the national economy, but in January 1933, some 12,000 families in Salt Lake County were on some form of relief. Welfare statistics for Utah show that in 1934 it had 206 persons per 1,000 on relief, the fourth highest rate in the United States, and that as late as 1940 there were still 48,000 families receiving direct relief, work relief, or Social Security. Government suffered as well. State income tax receipts dropped dramatically in 1933, reflecting serious drops in personal income. City tax receipts also went down, school budgets were slashed, and several city services were curtailed or eliminated. In 1936,

WPA programs were cut because the city lacked money to meet its share of the costs. An upswing in the economy stimulated a building boom in the first half of 1937, but in the second half the value of new permit requests dropped by nearly fifty percent.

At all levels of government, the first order of business in the 1930s was relief from unemployment. Every county and every major city in the state provided some sort of aid for the jobless, but their resources as well as those of private charity were limited. Only federal aid could fill the void, and in 1932 President Herbert Hoover finally signed an act allowing the Reconstruction Finance Corporation to loan money to states. During the winter of 1932–1933 this money provided sixty-eight percent of the funds spent for relief in Utah. Administered by the Governor's Committee on Emergency Relief, these funds provided at least minimal help for some 29,000 Utah families in December and by March they aided almost a third of the population.

The government of Salt Lake City was under pressure from several directions. In January 1931, the chamber of commerce asked city and county commissioners to recognize officially that unemployment relief was a legitimate function of organized government, and that, as public servants, they must take the initiative in promoting it. A citizen's group known as the Unemployed Council demanded investigation of food wasting by wholesalers, saying that this food should be distributed to the needy. In December, the group called for an increase in relief work and the inauguration of a centralized system of relief.

The city was trying. The mayor's advisory committee on unemployment sought funds everywhere, and the city rushed repairs and improvements on public property to provide as much work as possible. In August 1931, Mayor Bowman announced that the city would rotate work on the water expansion program to employ as many as possible. This was not nearly enough, however, as the advisory committee quickly discovered when it launched an extensive survey of unemployment in the city. City construction contracts included a minimum wage of $3.50 per eight-hour day, a requirement that labor be recruited totally from local sources and through the central bureau established by the city commission, and that all construction materials be Utah products and from Salt Lake City if possible.

Meanwhile, to help cities like Salt Lake, the state road commission announced new employment policies. Preference in highway work would be given to men with families. Contractors would be required to make maximum use of hand labor in order to spread the work as far as possible. No one could work more than eight hours per day. Employers must maintain whatever wage scale was current at the time a contract was awarded and must employ as many local men and teams as possible. Such efforts were piecemeal at best, but at least civic and business leaders recognized the immediate gravity of the problem.

At the same time, the chamber of commerce and Mayor Bowman seemed to share President Hoover's philosophy that the depression was only temporary, that economic recovery was just around the corner, and that governments must try to maintain balanced budgets. The continued optimism expressed by chamber spokesmen and other civic leaders in these early depression years was remarkable, and Mayor Bowman declared that the hard times would soon pass and "merge into a period of unprecedented prosperity."

Everyone recognized, nevertheless, that something more must be done immediately, and the fall and winter of 1931–1932 saw a burst of activity. City and county commissioners began holding joint sessions on relief. The county agreed to provide some $340,000 in work relief and the city agreed to begin a major storm sewer project and to call for a $600,000 bond election to finance it. On October 27 the bond election passed by nearly a two to one majority, and, since the planning had already been done by the city engineer, the first unit of the storm drain was underway within a week. The city also continued its water development program, and at the end of September awarded a $92,800 contract for completion of a conduit from Parley's Canyon.

The city also cooperated with various private groups, and especially the LDS church. In August 1931, Sylvester Q. Cannon, Presiding Bishop of the church, was named vice-chairman of the advisory committee on unemployment, and his office and the Relief Society helped carry out much of the city's relief work. Amy Brown Lyman, a counselor in the Relief Society organization, and Ana D. Palmer were placed in charge of the Relief Society. The city established two warehouses for distributing food and clothing. Emergency foodstuffs were given out from the Growers' Exchange warehouse on South West Temple street, and clothing from a building on East First South. Distribution was made only on orders from the LDS Relief Society or one of the various Community Chest agencies. The food warehouse opened on October 16 and that day disbursed more than a ton of garden produce contributed by members of the Grower's Exchange. The emergency relief committee of the chamber of commerce gathered funds to purchase food staples, and also got the executive secretary of the Salt Lake Council of the Boy Scouts to send his boys out collecting clothing and shoes. On October 30 nearly 1,000 scouts canvassed the county. Even convicts got into the act as inmates at the state prison agreed to do their part by repairing shoes and clothing that had been collected. Various city fraternal organizations

LDS Bishop's Storehouse in Salt Lake City. A Relief Society President picks up a welfare order, 1938. Courtesy, LDS Church Archives.

also joined in the cause. In addition, as the November election approached, John M. Whitaker, head of the central employment bureau, requested that voting registrars perform an extra duty by also registering the unemployed. By this means the city gathered a file that helped the central bureau in providing workmen for contractors engaged in public construction.

During that desperate fall and winter, many of those still working made generous efforts to help. One was a massive benefit performance initiated by the chamber of commerce and held in six Salt Lake City theaters the night before Thanksgiving in 1931. Musicians, other performers, and theater employees all donated their time while the chamber of commerce organized a massive ticket sales program and streetcar drivers donated their labor to get patrons to the theaters. While only 8,000 people actually got into the performances, several thousand more tickets were purchased simply as donations. In all, the chamber raised some $8,000 for the needy.

More significant was the willingness of some people to share their incomes. At the end of November, state employees at the capitol building agreed to donate four percent of their salaries for the next four months, and the Salt Lake Chamber of Commerce sent out letters to all city, county, and school employees, inviting them to follow suit. Many did, and by mid-November teachers in Salt Lake City and Murray agreed to have two percent deducted from their pay for the months of January, February, and March. In addition, beginning in January, many teachers donated their time to conduct special late afternoon classes in an effort to help the city's jobless increase vocational skills. In January, newly elected Mayor Louis Marcus announced that he would give ten percent of his salary to the Community Chest, and other elected officials responded with similar donations for unemployment relief. At the same time, employees of various private companies also voted for small pay reductions in order to help the needy. In January, for example, workers at Utah Gas and Coke Company, Utah Oil Refining Company, Continental Oil Company, and Pike Manufacturing Company all voted for a two percent cut.

The city government, the county government, and the chamber of commerce all appointed voluntary make-work committees that attempted to raise money and find every possible avenue for providing work. On October 15, for example, 100 unemployed persons were used to take the annual school census. The city committee decided that it must use all funds raised for labor only, unless contributors specifically indicated they wanted their money used some other way. The chamber of commerce asked all city and county agencies to rotate employees on a part-time basis, so that they could distribute available funds as equitably as possible.

Through these and other means, the city inaugurated a broad range of projects. Public improvement projects supported by make-work activities included work on the state fair grounds, the University of Utah campus, the state capitol grounds, Hogle Gardens Zoo, and the Bonneville golf course. In addition, by January two work centers established by the women's division of the city make-work committee employed about twenty women to repair clothing and make quilts.

By January the make-work programs had made some 900 assignments, but anticipated funds trickled in too slowly and projects used them up too rapidly. The city committee had collected $13,754.76 and spent $13,103.17. The city had to halt several projects, and on January 6, in his first public address as mayor, Louis Marcus asked the people to respond more generously. Government alone, he said, could not care for the unemployed: the burden rested upon those who had jobs and money. Make-work projects continued only as the city collected more money.

It may seem almost an anomaly that Louis Marcus should head the city government during the early 1930s. It was not unusual that the Mormon-dominated city should elect a non-Mormon: this had happened before and would happen again. But certain church interests openly

Louis Marcus, Businessman and Mayor, 1932-36.

opposed Marcus, yet he won the election. He was a nominal Republican, yet he was elected just the year before Salt Lake residents helped sweep Republicans out of national office, including their own Senator Reed Smoot. Mormon leaders opposed repeal of prohibition, but Marcus helped lead the fight for repeal, and yet retained his popularity. The anomaly was more apparent than real, however, for the actions of the voters only reflected an already well-established tradition of independence in political thought.

Born in Brooklyn in 1880, Marcus migrated to Utah in 1907 to work as a mechanical engineer with a mining company at Pelican Point on Utah Lake. Eventually he came to Salt Lake City, where his attempt to set up an electrical business failed but he soon got work in a movie theater. Perhaps even then the people of Salt Lake City were getting to know him, for during intermissions he would entertain the audience by thumping the piano or singing illustrated songs while someone projected slides onto the screen. It was not long before he went into business for himself again, and eventually Louis Marcus Enterprises owned and operated theaters in Salt Lake City, Ogden, and Provo, Utah, as well as in Boise and Twin Falls, Idaho. He became a director of the Walker Bank and Trust Company as well as the Tract Loan and Trust Company, a member of the board of the Salt Lake Chamber of Commerce, a member of the Alta, Rotary, and Country clubs as well as the Elk's Lodge, and he was a thirty-second degree Mason. He also served in various voluntary civic activities, such as the Community Chest, and in 1930 he cut short a tour to Europe in order to become Director General of the Salt Lake Covered Wagon Day celebration. The following year he decided to run for mayor.

The issues in the election were clear and at first not very controversial. Every candidate for mayor and the city commission promised to bear down heavily on crime, improve the water supply, and find ways and means to relieve unemployment. Law enforcement seemed to outstrip the other issues, however, for city voters were cleanup minded because of recent scandals in the police department, suspicion of corruption in other parts of city government, and what seemed to be a rising crime rate in the city. Marcus and incumbent Mayor John F. Bowman emerged victorious from the primaries, with Marcus emphasizing his business efficiency and Bowman running on his record. Marcus appealed to hard times by promising that he would remember that city money belonged to the taxpayers, not to him, and declaring that he had the ability to get full value from every dollar. Bowman promised to complete the water development program begun under his administration.

The last week before the election, however, saw some unfortunate mudslinging against the challenger. Though Bowman denied responsibility, some of his supporters charged Marcus with having underworld connections, and with courting the underworld vote. Marcus replied that no one could succeed in business with the kind of character being reputed to him, and denied that there was such a thing as the underworld vote. If there was, he goaded, it must have grown and flourished during the Bowman administration. The most serious challenge came when Hugh B.Brown, president of one of the LDS stakes of Salt Lake City, came out publicly, in a large newspaper ad, accusing Marcus of wanting a "wide open" town. Marcus, he charged, favored lax law enforcement, particularly with regard to bootlegging and prostitution, and he called on members of all churches to reject him. Brown provided no evidence for his charges, simply saying that he could not make his information public, but he declared his unnamed sources reliable and called on voters to accept his word that Marcus's election would be a threat to the moral and social welfare of the city. He bore no animosity toward the candidate, he claimed, but he thought Marcus's "mental attitude" would promote laxity.

Neither Bowman's record nor Brown's unsupported accusations impressed the voters. In the largest and most decisive municipal vote yet in city history, Marcus won by an overwhelming majority of 27,720 to 15,726. He was installed as mayor on January 5, 1932.

Mayor Marcus's first concern was the city's relief program. By the end of 1932, some Reconstruction Finance Corporation funds had been made available, but they were not enough and the city commission continued its own relief programs. More surveys were taken, funds collected, and make-work projects undertaken. In order to encourage raising food, the city agreed in May to abate water charges where the residents used the water for gardens, and the county furnished garden seed for those who could not afford their own. This combination of local and federal aid got Salt Lake's unemployed through the winter of 1932–1933.

In 1933, for the first time in American history, the national government took responsibility for direct relief activities and, at the same time, inaugurated a series of far-reaching recovery and reform programs that would forever change its relationship to American cities and states. This was the significance of the Roosevelt administration's New Deal, and Mayor Marcus's activities during the next two years were aptly symbolic of this shift. He spent as much time working with federal programs and federal red tape as he did with locally initiated relief efforts, but the more massive aid eventually provided by federal programs was much greater than the city could ever stimulate on its own. In general, the New Deal was well accepted by the populace of Utah and Salt Lake City, as indicated by their overwhelming support of Franklin D. Roosevelt as well as Democratic congressional candidates in the elections of the 1930s. Certain LDS church authorities and many conservative business leaders opposed some aspects of the New Deal, but the average Utahn seemed to see in it his best hope for personal economic security.

Title II of the National Industrial Recovery Act, hurriedly passed by Congress during the famous "hundred days" of early New Deal legislation, established the Public Works Administration and provided it with a $3.3 billion appropriation for relief. The PWA administrator, Secretary of the Interior Harold L. Ickes, was a completely honest, efficient administrator. But these qualities, together with his quarrelsome nature and his determination not to let the slightest hint of corruption enter either the national or local activities of the PWA, put the feisty Ickes at odds with cities and states throughout the nation as they felt frustrated in their efforts to benefit quickly from federal funds.

Salt Lake City was no exception. The city began its negotiations with the PWA in August, and in October Mayor Marcus went to Washington, D.C. seeking a final agreement. He was jubilant on his return, delighting almost everyone with his announcement that Ickes had earmarked $2.5 million dollars for Salt Lake City, and that nearly $900,000 would be available immediately. The city quickly authorized a $715,000 bond issue as collateral for the government loan, and projected several public works that would provide hundreds of thousands of man-hours in employment. The first large undertaking was the replacement of water mains at a cost of $100,000. By mid-November, however, Marcus and the city commissioners were outraged as endless red tape had produced no federal money at all. Salt Lake City could borrow all the money it wanted on the open market, the mayor complained, yet could not obtain a dollar from Washington, and he accused Ickes of being afraid to approve anything for fear of a possible Senate investigation. Among other things, the PWA required that the city submit its bonds for approval, and spent an exorbitant amount of time going over them. It finally ordered detailed changes even in minutiae such as commas, colons, and conjunctions. Ickes astounded the city council even more when he sent orders to cut the general city budget by $250,000 and increase the budgets of departments that would use the first federal funds by that amount. Disgusted with such budgetary sophistry, Marcus nevertheless told the commissioners that they must go ahead with the new "subterfuges and silly juggling."

In the meantime, President Roosevelt himself became impatient with the snail-like pace of the PWA, and on November 9 created the Civil Works Administration, with Harry L. Hopkins at its head. While Ickes thought everything would work out in the long run, Hopkins had pointed out that people must eat every day. The CWA was authorized to hire workers directly, rather than work through loans to local governments, and within a week it began dispensing aid throughout the nation. Credited with getting the country through the winter, by the time of its demise in July 1934, it had spent over $951 million on 181,000 projects.

Almost immediately Hopkins invited Mayor Marcus back to Washington, along with other officials from Utah and other Western states. Hopkins told the group that the CWA would accept not only new projects, but also projects transferred from the PWA. Ickes, however, who was still Hopkins's superior, announced that the CWA could not build water or sewer projects, and that no city having made such proposals could withdraw them in the hopes of getting money from Hopkins. Marcus was furious, and started a furor when he openly lambasted Ickes by telling how, at Ickes' own solicitation, Salt Lake City combed the town for every available project that might put men to work, came up with seventy-four, and then confronted endless bureaucratic delays and stumbling blocks as it tried to meet the requirements for the $250,000 loan necessary to get started. Almost every important city in the West, others complained, was in the same situation, and many applauded Governor C. Ben Ross of Idaho when he declared that the people of the West had lost confidence in the PWA.

They finally reached a compromise, and Marcus returned from his second trip to Washington with the assurance that through a combination of PWA and CWA funds the city could start various public works projects soon. By November 23 some 2,000 men were at work on CWA make-work projects, though these did not include water projects. The city finally abandoned plans for obtaining PWA money that year, and on December 4 the city fathers ceremoniously burned the engraved PWA certificate that would have represented the $250,000 loan. It borrowed the same amount elsewhere to purchase materials for the CWA projects. Mayor Marcus, meanwhile, took a leave of absence because of ill health, and went to California for recovery. His first year as mayor was not easy.

The National Industrial Recovery Act authorized the National Recovery Administration to draw up codes of fair competition for individual industries, and to specify standards for such things as wages, hours, and prices. The act suspended operation of antitrust laws, in the hope that cooperation rather than competition could stimulate recovery. One of the most controversial parts of the New Deal, the NRA initially received wide popular support but eventually failed to please almost everyone. The United States Supreme Court finally declared it unconstitutional.

In Salt Lake City, most cooperated. The newspapers and the city commission announced its support of the program, as did many statewide groups, and the LDS church adopted NRA codes for its workers in church offices. Gus Backman became state director of the NRA.

But it was not without its dissenters. Several city barbers, for example, opposed it, and at one protest meeting they got into an egg-throwing skirmish with 200 of their colleagues who supported the NRA's blue eagle. Not long after that a Salt Lake City judge anticipated the United States Supreme Court by declaring the barber codes illegal under both the Utah Constitution and the state recovery act. In other court action in December 1933, a Salt Lake City coal dealer had the distinction of receiving the first jail sentence in the United States growing out of NRA code violations, though the judge suspended his sentence on condition that he report every Saturday until it expired. A jury convicted him and another dealer of underselling their competitors in violation of prices fixed by the state administrator. They were not jailed, but were later hauled into court again and charged with contempt of court for continuing to advertise prices below those authorized by the code. The codes became increasingly unpopular, and by June 1935, the *Deseret News* declared that the NRA had failed and that the codes were on their way out. Its prediction was correct.

The city profited from many New Deal activities. It failed in its 1934 bid for Federal Emergency Relief Administration funds to address drought problems, but it received other FERA funds later on, including money in 1935 to eradicate rats and mice. In 1934 it finally began to receive PWA project funds that included, Ickes original policy notwithstanding, money for pipelines and water mains. Many Salt Lakers took advantage of the Home Owner's Loan Association home improvement program, as well as the Federal Housing Administration's help in purchasing new homes. Enthusiastic about the New Deal, Utah Labor especially supported it after the 1935 Wagner Act's assurance of its right to collective bargaining. The Works Progress Administration provided direct relief funds for work on state and local projects and, beginning in 1935, Salt Lake City and Salt Lake County received approval for several WPA make-work projects designed to lift their needy from relief rolls to payrolls. The city reduced the number of projects in 1936, however, when it found its own budget so depleted that it could pay its share of only a few. Until the end of the decade, nevertheless, the city continued to receive WPA funds, including help for Utah's artists,

Salt Lake City Street Cleaning Crew, Preparing for Morning Work, ca 1940.Courtesy, Utah State Historical Society.

writers, and musicians. In October 1938, Salt Lake City became the site of the Surplus Commodities Corporation's eighth food stamp distribution center, designed to aid farmers and other low-income groups as well as businesses generally. By that time approximately 20,000 Salt Lake City residents were eligible to participate in the food stamp program because they had previously received public relief or worked on WPA projects.

Though the WPA and other federal programs provided the essential needs for many of Salt Lake City's poor, their impact was not always very long range. Mayor Marcus and other civic leaders had in mind two major projects that would not only provide immediate relief but also, they believed, have a far-reaching influence on the local economy. These were a new civic auditorium and the expansion of the municipal airport. All through the depression, Marcus and the chamber of commerce made every effort to get federal funds for an auditorium. The potential of Salt Lake City as a tourist attraction and a convention center, they believed, was already great, but would be enhanced immeasurably by an auditorium where conventions and other large public affairs could be held. They never received federal help for the convention center, however, and local funds simply were not forthcoming.

The airport was a different matter. After years of putting it on various work proposals, in October 1936 the city obtained presidential approval for an expansion program that would include three runways, a new administration building, and a drainage system. Funds for labor were provided through the WPA, and on October 31 Utah's governor Henry

H. Blood threw the first shovelful of earth as the long-awaited project was officially launched. Completed in 1938, the expansion made Salt Lake City's airport one of America's finest of the time.

With this and other permanent projects, the New Deal had a welcome effect on the citizens of Utah then, and a long-lasting influence on the Salt Lake area's economy and landscape. Many of the buildings erected by the WPA are still among the city's most familiar structures. These include the Field House, Museum of Natural History, and Carlson Hall on the University of Utah Campus, the Salt Lake City school district administration building at First South and Fourth East, and the Officer's Club at Fort Douglas.

During these trying years the Mormon church brought a new round of national attention to Salt Lake City because of its own response to depression problems. This time the publicity was favorable, and actually helped change the Mormon image in the mind of the general American public.

Many church leaders disapproved of public assistance, especially if it seemed to constitute a dole, and were consequently critical of programs that provided relief without work requirements. "The thought that we should get all we can from the government because everybody else is getting it, is unworthy of us as American citizens," said J. Reuben Clark, a member of the First Presidency. "It will debauch us." Federal work relief programs, on the other hand, received full support. Very early, however, church leaders foresaw the possibility that these might be curtailed, and counseled members to prepare to shoulder their own welfare burdens. They also began, as early as 1933, to plan a comprehensive church relief program. Each stake president was asked to conduct a survey of needs and resources, and they urged stake presidents and bishops to be imaginative in developing enterprises where church members could find employment.

A number of stakes demonstrated impressive initiative, and one of the most prominent of these was Pioneer Stake in Salt Lake City. Under Stake President Harold B. Lee, who was also a city commissioner, it instituted a self-help program that provided food, clothing, wood, bedclothes, and even jobs in private industry for its unemployed. The stake also started make-work projects and set up its own warehouse for collection and distribution of welfare goods.

In April 1936, the church officially announced its Church Security Plan, which was later designated the Welfare Plan. The First Presidency assigned Harold B. Lee to head the new program. Every ward was given the responsibility of organizing welfare activities, including raising crops, finding jobs, training people in new skills, developing make-work projects, and keeping abreast of all the needs of ward members. During the first summer of its operation, nearly 15,000 Mormons were transferred from government welfare rolls to church relief, and jobs were found for over a thousand. The program was not intended to replace what the government was doing, but, rather, to assist in the general emergency and to provide a means for taking care of church members if government programs should be eliminated: it was done in the spirit of cooperation rather than antagonism. Though some journalists greatly exaggerated its effectiveness, it nevertheless was an important part of Salt Lake City's response to the Great Depression.

Though the depression did not seem to create any major change in the nature of Salt Lake City households, or the role of women, there were subtle but perceptible shifts during the decade. In some instances, it appears, the wife became a more visible contributor to the family income, however unsteady it may have been. It was not that employers were any more willing to hire women—on the contrary, if the experience of Salt Lake City was anything like that of the nation's other major cities, employers seemed to prefer hiring men, believing that especially in hard times women should remain at home and leave the scarce jobs for the traditional heads of households. Some cities even passed laws prohibiting the hiring of women as civil servants and, in some cases, fired female teachers when they got married. Fortunately, it appears that none of this happened in Salt Lake City. At the same time, women dropped out of the work force more slowly than men, as industrial laborers, who were mostly male, were laid off faster than store clerks, file clerks, and secretaries, most of whom were women. According to one analysis, in 1931 national unemployment was 18.9 percent among women and 26.1 among men, but by 1938 the comparison was just the opposite—22.1 percent for women and 14.3 percent for men.

Making statistical comparisons is difficult, for categories used in different census reports are not always consistent, and the way scholars analyze them may differ also. But if one compares the employment of women fourteen and over in Salt Lake City at the beginning and the end of the decade, some interesting patterns emerge. In 1930, 26.32 percent were employed, as compared with only 25.85 percent in 1940. A more realistic view of what was happening, however, may be obtained by looking at the women between the ages of eighteen and sixty-four. The fact that Salt Lake had not yet become as industrialized as other major cities might affect the validity of comparing these figures with those from other cities, but in 1930, 30.1 percent of the women in Salt Lake City between those ages were employed. In 1940 30.5 percent were listed as being in the work force, with 91.1 percent of that group regularly employed and another 2.5 percent working on public emergency jobs. The beginning of defense-oriented economic activity was clearly making a difference, but even so the 8.9 percent unemployment among women was probably not bad for the times. By comparison, in 1930, 91.6 percent of the men between eighteen and sixty-four were employed, while in 1940 only 75.6 percent of the total (or, 85.9 percent of the work force) were regularly employed.

At the same time, the nature of women's employment changed slightly, seemingly in step with the national pattern. In 1930 some 9.78 percent of all Salt Lake City's working women were employed in manufacturing, and this dropped to 7.63 in 1940, while the percent working as domestic and personal servants dropped from 26.93 to 19.63 percent. Conversely, those employed as clerks and saleswomen in wholesale and retail trades jumped from 13.3 percent to 27.64, while those working in professional services, particularly teachers and nurses, increased from 18.35 percent to 21.72. Curiously, even though the 1930 census reported 26.81 percent of the employed women working in clerical capacities (bookkeepers, cashiers, etc.,) the 1940 census did not specifically include that category, though it did indicate that 6.17 percent were working in finance, real estate, and insurance firms, and that 5.49 percent were employed in government—mostly state and local. All this suggests that the depression contributed in at least a mild way to broadening the areas in which women might be employed, even if it did not greatly enhance their actual employment possibilities.

Salt Lake City's women were becoming increasingly visible in other ways as well. Beyond welfare work, in which the LDS Relief Society and other women's groups were highly active, women's organizations took an increasingly active role in the affairs of city government. The Women's Safety Council kept up an active dialogue with the city commission over such things as installations of semaphores at certain cross streets, and the proposal to install downtown parking meters. At the end of the decade the Women's Chamber of Commerce was active in promoting smoke abatement. The Salt Lake Council of Women promoted, among other things, various civic improvement programs, as did the Federation of Women's Clubs, and representatives of these groups frequently appeared before the council. But perhaps the most notable woman of the period, in terms of her direct involvement with government, was Reva Beck Bosone, Salt Lake City's first female judge and the first Utah woman to be elected to Congress.

Reva Beck grew up about thirty miles south of Salt Lake City, a dyed-in-the-wool gentile in the almost wholly Mormon town of American Fork. She attended junior college at Salt Lake City's Westminster

College, graduating in 1917, and in 1919 she graduated from the University of California at Berkeley. She taught school, first in American Fork, then Ogden High, where she earned an enviable state-wide reputation as a teacher of oratory and drama. Meanwhile, she found ill fortune in a marriage that lasted only a year. In 1927, after controversy over her innovative teaching, Reva resigned her position and enrolled in the University of Utah law school—one of only two women to enroll that year, and the only one eventually to graduate. She married a fellow law student, Joseph Bosone, and after both were admitted to the Utah bar in 1931, the two set up a firm in her husband's home town, the small mining community of Helper. The following year she was elected, as a Democrat, to the Utah House of Representatives, which occasioned a permanent move for the Bosones to Salt Lake City.

As a legislator at a time when reform was in the air, Reva Beck Bosone was determined to push through a bill that would provide greater protection for women and children in industry. With, as her biographer observes, "her usual passion for succeeding," she studied all precedents, effectively blocked Republican and other conservative opposition and, after her bill passed both houses, was instrumental in helping to persuade the governor to sign it. The result was a Minimum Wage and Hour Law for Women and Children, and the creation of the Women's Division of the Utah State Industrial Commission. (Though she and other women have since changed their minds on the need for special legal protection for women, believing that such things really work against equal rights, at the time such a law was in the forefront of women's concerns across the nation.) She also made history as the first woman floor leader of the majority party and the first woman chairperson of the Sifting Committee.

Reva served two terms in the legislature—the second one after having been elected in 1934 by the voters of Salt Lake County. In the meantime she also ran for the city commission, and lost, and in 1936 she shocked the commissioners by suggesting that they should consider her for the job of assistant city attorney. They talked her out of that, only to learn that she had decided to run for city judge. She was elected in the fall of 1936 and, because of the death of the retiring judge, took her position on December 1, a month ahead of schedule. Assigned to the traffic court, Judge Bosone introduced dramatic, sweeping, and often controversial reforms that not only promoted greater traffic safety in Salt Lake City but also influenced similar programs in other parts of the country. Known for both her sternness and her humanity as a judge, she was also concerned with the treatment of alcoholics. She became well known for her efforts at reform in this area, in cooperation with Alcoholics Anonymous. She tried three times, unsuccessfully, to be elected to the city commission, but she was regularly reelected to the judgeship. After sitting on the bench for twelve years, she was elected to the United States House of Representatives in 1948, where she served two terms.

Minority racial and ethnic groups were not large in number during this period, and they seem to have suffered from prejudice neither more nor less than those in other American cities. At the end of the decade there were 694 blacks, or about 0.5 percent of the population, and only 541 American Indians, Chinese, and Japanese combined. Their general employment patterns seemed to follow those of the rest of the population, though there was considerable evidence of discrimination in housing and other areas. Downtown hotels refused housing even to visiting black artists, such as the famed French singer, Lillian Yvanti. Anti-Semitism, on the other hand, was not strong in Utah, and the Jews in Salt Lake City, at least according to Juanita Brooks, were generally well accepted.

In spite of the depression, Salt Lake City enjoyed a certain degree of economic growth and progress during the decade, and the city government had many other municipal concerns. The successful effort to get the federal government to finance the airport expansion was a symbol of the city's continuing importance as a center of regional political and economic activity. The effort to build a city auditorium, though not successful, was a recognition of Salt Lake's growing prominence as a tourist attraction. The year 1939 was a record year for travel to Salt Lake City by automobile, bus, train, and airline. Approximately 403,000 people visited Temple Square that year, and the ski slopes near Salt Lake City attracted thousands of out-of-state visitors. The chamber of commerce boasted every year of the increasing number of conventions in the city. Population growth brought new pressures on housing, and even in the depression years home building slumped only temporarily. The years 1937, 1938, and 1939 all saw substantial growth over previous years in new building starts, and several new subdivisions were opened up. In 1934 a city planning commission was established with an eye toward more effectively regulating the growth of residential areas.

On a lesser scale, the city examined several other proposals for change. In 1933, after months of debate, the voters rejected a plan for a city-owned-and-operated electric power plant. In 1936 the city examined its downtown parking problem and in September made a trial installation of parking meters. Several citizens, especially the Salt Lake Council of Women, angrily opposed the meters and predicted that the new devices would shunt business away from downtown. The city council ignored the protests, and in January 1937 ordered the meters installed. There were several delays, but by 1940 Salt Lake City had eliminated free parking in the heart of its business district.

The city did not ignore civic improvement during the decade of depression. Its library continued to grow, and even though city fathers were tempted to cut its budget drastically, that temptation was resisted and library patrons enjoyed continuously improving service. Parks and other recreation facilities were not neglected, even though they took a large budget. In 1930 the city boasted twenty-one parks and playgrounds covering 3,230 acres of land, five golf courses, and twenty-four tennis courts, all maintained during the depression. Federal relief funds helped improve several facilities, and the city even acquired some new recreational areas, including the Forestdale golf course.

A somewhat surprising source of public controversy in the 1930s was the zoo, originally located in Liberty Park. By 1931 its buildings were too old for continued use, the animals were being treated badly, and there simply was not enough room. Mr. and Mrs. James A. Hogle donated to the Salt Lake Zoological Society a fine piece of property near the mouth of Emigration Canyon, and the city donated the animals. Money for building the new zoo was raised from many private sources, including the LDS church, which donated $2,000. On Friday, July 31, the new zoological park in Hogle Gardens was formally dedicated, and a giant animal move began immediately. A public outcry came when Princess Alice, Salt Lakers favorite elephant, refused to be moved and the city threatened to get rid of her. The protest succeeded, however, and Alice was eventually relocated.

As the depression deepened, the Society found itself unable to meet expenses and continually appealed to the city for financial support. Mayor Marcus doubted the advisability of keeping the zoo, wondering if there was really enough public interest. When the city of Ogden expressed an interest, negotiations were begun for moving it there. Again the public raised an uproar, and in January 1935, civic clubs and citizens throughout the city were crying "save the zoo." The mayor backed off, but he insisted that zoo officials find a way to operate without an annual deficit. It soon became apparent to everyone that if the zoo were to continue to operate, it must be under the auspices of the city, and before the end of the year it was agreed that the Zoological Society would sell it for a price that represented its outstanding debts. The city then decided to move the animals back to Liberty Park, but after more controversy it also backed away from that proposal. In January 1937, the Hogle Gardens property was deeded to the city, and the zoo's place as a permanent fixture there was assured.

A topic of wider public interest was the projected erection of a pioneer memorial monument at the mouth of Emigration Canyon, not far from Hogle Gardens. Recognizing that the pioneer centennial was coming up in 1947, the state legislature authorized the governor to appoint a pioneer monument committee. In January 1938 he did so, naming Mormon church president Heber J. Grant chairman. The Most Reverend Duane G. Hunt, Bishop of the Salt Lake Diocese of the Roman Catholic church, became vice-chairman. Eventually that monument became one of Salt Lake City's most prominent landmarks.

Next to relief, Salt Lake City's most difficult problem in the 1930s was water. The population increased only slightly, from 140,267 to 149,934, but greater demand for water, already in scant supply, continuing dissatisfaction with exchange agreements, and several years of near-drought conditions made water planning one of the most serious challenges of the times. Average precipitation for the period 1928 to 1940 was below the long-range norms in nine out of the twelve years, and 1931 and 1934 were especially critical. Average stream flow in 1934 was far less than half the normal.

The water supply advisory board, appointed in 1928 at the insistence of Mayor Bowman, provided the first long-range plan for Salt Lake City and anticipated a minimum population of 400,000 people. Its 1929 report recommended further development of local sources as well as tapping several surrounding watersheds, including the proposed Deer Creek reservoir in Provo Canyon. After Utah Lake reached an all-time low in 1930 and the year 1931 became another drought year, the citizens of Salt Lake City were aroused and demanded that something be done.

The 1929 report advised against further development of underground water supplies; the legal basis for drilling wells was questionable (because of their impact on other water users) and the source was difficult to develop. Underground water should only be relied upon for short periods of deficiency and not as part of a long-range development program. Mayor Bowman proposed the construction of a storage dam in Big Cottonwood Canyon, but in May 1930 a bond election roundly defeated his plan. According to a later *Tribune* editorial, this was partly because he had not taken the people into his confidence and was not willing to make certain changes in his proposal. This destroyed their faith in his official report.

That same year the mayor rejected a specific proposal for developing underground water, but at the beginning of 1931, when a water shortage seemed imminent, he was suddenly converted. Acting again on his own initiative, he acquired several options in the artesian basin southwest of the city and then proposed to the city commission a $600,000 development program. His plan constituted almost a *fait accompli*, and an acrimonious public debate began. The mayor's own water advisory committee refused to endorse his project and the chamber of commerce came up with a report that was wholly at variance with his plans. The chamber wanted the city to build a conduit from Little Cottonwood Canyon.

It was clear to everyone, however, that a disaster would follow the failure to arrive at an immediate solution to the problem, and in March the water advisory board recommended a two million dollar bond issue in connection with a development plan that included both underground water and the Little Cottonwood project. The mayor endorsed most of the plan but stubbornly rejected the Little Cottonwood conduit. The *Tribune*, as usual, roundly criticized him, and his fellow commissioners approved the entire proposal. A bond election was set for July 2. The newspapers, nearly all the major civic organizations, and President Heber J. Grant of the LDS church all publicly endorsed the issue, and it passed by a margin of two to one. By that time construction was already underway on the seven-mile pipeline from the artesian basin, and by mid-July water was pouring into the city.

As early as December 1933, it was clear that 1934 would be another drought year, and Water Commissioner George D. Keyser proposed that the city develop even more wells. This time the mayor objected on grounds that the cost would be too high and that the city should not incur more debt. But the situation was critical, and efforts to take better advantage of Utah Lake water, through exchange agreements, were ineffective. The difficulty lay not only in the fact that all Utah's lakes and streams were unusually low, but also with the fact that under its exchange agreements Salt Lake City must provide lake water to farmers at a much higher ratio when streams were low than when they were high. In a normal year the city could take about 11 second feet of water from Big Cottonwood Creek in exchange for 28 second feet of Utah Lake water. On August 7, 1934, however, the creek had a net flow of 11.4 second feet, and the agreements required a 5.4 second foot culinary reserve for the farmers. This meant that the maximum possible amount available to the city was only 6 second feet, no matter how much Utah Lake water it could exchange. But in drought conditions exchange rates were greater, which meant that not even this much was legally available.

In spite of Mayor Marcus's initial objections, early in the year the city commission approved another drilling program, and about twenty new wells eventually provided more water. It was still not enough, however, to ward off rationing during the summer. As city attorney Fisher Harris observed in 1935, Salt Lake City's water system was nothing more than patchwork, for, he said, "nothing has ever been done to improve it until an emergency arose."

One hope for a more comprehensive solution was the Provo River project, first recommended to the United States Bureau of Reclamation in a 1931 report by district engineer E.O. Larson. The Deer Creek division of this project called for construction of a dam in Provo Canyon to store runoff from the Uinta Mountains, and anticipated major participation by Salt Lake City. Eventually the city subscribed for 46,000 acre-feet of water from the Deer Creek Dam.

The Deer Creek project was not without its critics in Salt Lake City. One objection was simply that it would cost too much to build the huge conduit necessary to bring Deer Creek water across the mountains and into Salt Lake City mains. Mayor Marcus saw the long-range need, however, and wisely observed that "I do not want this proposition considered in connection either with the present water needs of Salt Lake City or the present financial depression. We must assume that Salt Lake City is going to be here a long time. Someone must provide for the future.... The city will not stand still. It will grow or languish." It was estimated that the conduit would cost three and a half million dollars, but, the mayor observed, if the city eventually needed seventy-five second feet of water, that cost would not appear so large.

In 1935 the state legislature passed the Metropolitan Water District Act, which paved the way for Salt Lake City to incorporate a water district and participate in the Deer Creek project. The issue of whether a district actually should be created was put to the voters on August 15, but before the vote still more acrimony surfaced. With Mayor Marcus leading the fight, the city council, the newspapers, and the chamber of commerce all urged approval, but an embittered group calling itself the "Property Owners Investigating Committee" did everything possible to defeat it. The district could increase its own indebtedness, the committee observed, thus saddling harassed taxpayers with even heavier burdens. The board of directors, it charged, would degenerate into a band of "political dummies" who were nothing more than tools of the politicians. With an amazing lack of foresight the group also argued that the project was unnecessary because "local sources," such as artesian wells, and more acquisitions from nearby mountain streams could provide ample water.

For a while the two sides sparred with kid gloves, but just before the election the gloves turned to mailed fists. Opponents were irate when information booths, manned by boy scouts, appeared in downtown Salt Lake City. It was improper, charged William Langton, chairman of the property owners committee, for the city to distribute propaganda, and he demanded an explanation from the mayor. The city had an obligation

221

to disseminate all available information, the mayor shot back. Besides, he chided, careful investigation had not demonstrated that there was more than one side to the issue. The voters approved the water district by a slim plurality of only 647 votes.

The city moved quickly, and on September 11 the commissioners set up the new metropolitan water district. Local businessman Herbert S. Auerbach became the first chairman of the board of directors. The commission examined many projects, but the Provo River Project was the most urgent. In 1936 it solicited the help of a Chicago firm that had investigated water needs for several American cities, and the final report, delivered on August 8, confirmed much of what the earlier water advisory board had recommended and again urged participation in the Deer Creek project.

The chief stumbling block was the perennial problem of money. Deer Creek dam was paid for by the federal government, but the cost of building an aqueduct weighed heavily on Salt Lake City. Must the city do it alone, or would the national government agree to finance it? In 1936 George A. Critchlow, a member of the board, began the lobbying by traveling to Washington and urging the project on the commissioner of the Bureau of Reclamation. His work was followed by more pressure from people like Governor Henry H. Blood, Congressman J. Will Robinson, and City Attorney Fisher Harris, and in 1937 Secretary of the Interior Ickes agreed in principal to the idea of federal funding.

That same year the board proposed to city voters that they subscribe to the project and enter into a contract for building the aqueduct. It blanketed the city with newspaper and billboard advertising, pamphlets, speeches, and even advertising at the end of motion pictures. One ad showed Uncle Sam saying "Water for Salt Lake City, it's up to you. I've done my part." The result was an overwhelming victory for the board, and the district entered into a formal contract with the Provo River Water Users Association on December 1.

Specific details on the aqueduct were yet to be worked out and the president still needed to be persuaded to approve federal financing. Fisher Harris went to Washington in May 1938 to begin negotiations. His arrival, fortunately, coincided with passage of a work relief bill that would provide large expenditures for public works. Only projects already approved would be funded, but since the aqueduct was considered part of the Provo River project, President Roosevelt was persuaded, and he approved an initial allotment of $2,500,000. Ultimately, $5,550,000 was advanced for the aqueduct by the federal government, to be repaid in forty annual installments without interest.

The significance of all this cannot be overstated, for it provided Salt Lake City with access to a well-designed, long-term water supply, provided ready financing so that the project could be accomplished quickly, and saved the people of the city $140,000 annually in interest payments. The Deer Creek dam was begun in 1938 and completed in 1941, and the Salt Lake Aqueduct was completed during World War II. By that time, due to the influx of wartime industries, the wisdom of such long-range planning was clearly evident.

As if depression and drought were not enough, the decade of the thirties was tinged also with lawlessness and political scandal. General crime was frequently drawn to the attention of the public, though early in 1931 the federal government reported that Salt Lake City had fewer major crimes in proportion to population than any other large city in the country: one major crime every three days as compared with one per day in other cities of comparable size.

Lawlessness in Salt Lake City in the early 1930s included gambling and the violation of prohibition laws. Several raids were conducted on gambling houses and speakeasies, and Police Chief Joseph Burbidge publicly vowed to stamp them out completely. This could hardly be done, however, when police officers themselves winked at them, and early in 1931 several officers were dismissed for entering speakeasies while off duty and drinking in public. Salt Lakers felt it ironic as they read about some police officers walking easily into illegal bars while off duty, and other officers later breaking down the doors of the same bars in order to conduct raids. Citizens became enraged, and Mayor Bowman as well as others charged the public safety department with laxity in enforcing the law. The *Tribune* used the problem as an occasion to question the commission form of city government which, it charged, simply was not controlling the various departments as it should.

The specter of top-level corruption raised its head in February and March 1931, when the public safety commissioner and the chief of police were implicated in charges of a shakedown among Salt Lake City gamblers. Both denied any knowledge of such activities, but when a report on the thriving prostitution trade appeared near the end of February, Mayor Bowman wanted to fire the police chief and reorganize the anti-vice squad. The commission rejected the mayor's plea, however, after a key secret witness against the chief failed to show up. He was scared off, it was said, because of the discovery of threats against the mayor's life. Without the witness, there simply was not enough evidence to justify the mayor's proposed course of action.

Crime of all sorts increased, and by the end of the year 4,154 crimes had been reported, as compared with 2,777 in 1930. This included 1,397 auto thefts, 18 embezzlements, 14 confidence swindles, 15 aggravated assaults, 3 cases of arson, and 9 murders. All this soon forced changes in the rules of the city civil service with regard to the police and fire departments. The new rules included summary discharge for the use of liquor, annual oral examinations, more rigid physical examinations, more experience before promotion, and reducing both the minimum and the maximum age for entry into either department. Explained the chairman of the civil service commission, the rules were needed because so many changes had occurred since the old rules were adopted in 1921: bootleggers and gangsters had sprung up everywhere and the city was caught in an unparalleled crime wave that was sweeping the country. In October county attorney Matthew Cowley criticized Salt Lake City, and Chief Burbidge in particular, for not cooperating effectively with county law enforcement officials. Burbidge was finally forced to resign, and in January a new police chief, W.L. Payne, took over. He pledged to wage unrelenting war on all vice, and began his administration with a dramatic blow at bailbondsmen who were soliciting business inside police stations and police officers who were acting as go-betweens. All such activities were prohibited, on pain of immediate dismissal of offending officers.

Salt Lake City's crime problem was at least partly related to national prohibition, for the illegal sale of liquor, with the resultant increase in a variety of other crimes, became as serious here as in other parts of the nation. Recognizing the failure of prohibition nationwide, in 1933 the Roosevelt Administration moved to change things by proposing the twenty-first amendment to the Constitution, which would repeal the prohibition amendment. The battle over repeal was as heated in Salt Lake City as any place, for a number of Mormon church leaders came out against it while most civic leaders supported it. Ironically, this was the centennial anniversary of the church's revelation called the "Word of Wisdom," which dictated against the use of strong drinks by faithful church members. "The ground already gained ought not to be surrendered," declared the First Presidency of the church. "Liquor has always been and it will continue to be the intimate ally of crime." Mayor Marcus took the opposite view. "I am for a repeal for reasons ethical, economic, moral, physical and legal," he proclaimed in October 1933. "Ethically because it is a controversial subject that interferes with personal liberty. Economically because it is a direct revenue producer without creating a hardship. Morally because it permits strict control of the traffic to prevent surreptitious use by minors. Physically because it affords relief from consumption of poisonous liquors. Legally because prohibition of any kind should never be included in constitutions which are drawn to give all people equal rights. Finally it will do away with the bootlegger and the racketeer." The mayor was joined in his campaign by the Salt Lake chamber of commerce, the *Salt Lake Tribune*, Utah's delegation to Congress (all Democrats) and the Democratic State Central Committee. In the election held on November 7, Utahns voted overwhelmingly in favor of repealing both the Eighteenth Amendment and the state's prohibition law. It was Utah's ratification that put the repeal amendment in the Constitution.

Marcus and the city commission were not lax in attempting to enforce the new state liquor law, passed in 1934. Hugh B. Brown, Marcus's old political foe, became chairman of the state liquor commission, established to control the sale and distribution of liquor. Marcus cooperated fully in police efforts to raid and put out of business the speakeasies that still operated in the city in 1935.

Mayor Marcus was generally well liked, and as the election of 1935 approached it appeared that he would have no trouble in his bid to be returned to office. In October, however, the legally nonpartisan city elections began to take on a partisan flavor as it became evident that the city's Republican machine was going to support Marcus and that the Democratic party was openly behind his opponent, auto dealer E.B. Erwin. Then, during its final week, the almost lackluster campaign suddenly burst into a political inferno. Political advertisements were published on Saturday, November 2, that accused Marcus as well as the city attorney and the chief of police of entering into a secret agreement with the underworld. Illegal liquor dealers, it was charged, were permitted to operated without restraint on condition that once a month they take a bottle into court and pay a fine. Marcus emphatically denied the charges, but he had little time to do anything about them before the Tuesday election.

The unfortunate ads appeared first over the name of Parnell Black, chairman of the citizen's campaign committee pledged to defeat Marcus. But Black denied all knowledge of, or any belief in, the charges and immediately resigned from the committee. Subsequent ads appeared over the name of Frank Page Stewart. In the end, they accomplished their purpose, even though no connection between Marcus and the underworld was ever demonstrated. The victim of political foul play, Salt Lake's most capable mayor of the decade lost by a vote of 20,414 to 19,297. But the fates would have expected it, for since the establishment of the city council form of government in 1912, no Salt Lake City mayor had been elected to office twice.

The new mayor, E.B. Erwin, got off to a poor start with his colleagues on the city commission, and this unfortunate beginning seemed to symbolize what was in store throughout his term. Looking with a hungry eye at their first patronage opportunity in years, the Democrats were anxious to have Erwin head the finance department. But Commissioner-elect William Murdoch, also a Democrat, wanted the same position. Both men were equally unexcited about the other option, the public safety department, and even before the new city government met in January the issue caused a serious split in the ranks of city Democrats. Ironically, it was up to the three Republican holdovers on the commission to decide between the newly elected Democrats, and in their first meeting they gave the nod to Murdoch.

Dismayed, Erwin took the public safety position under protest but promised that he would make the department fully efficient. His relationship with the commission went from bad to worse, however. His idea of running the public safety department efficiently was to appoint an office manager. He got commission approval and then gave the position, along with almost dictatorial power, to J.S. Early. The mayor took practically no personal interest at all in the inner workings of the department. His next fight with his fellow commissioners came when he took enough interest to want to fire police chief Payne and replace him with Harry L. Finch. That did not sit well with anyone. Payne was popular with the people, and the commissioners supported him. On the other hand, Finch was a nominal Republican, so Democrats were unhappy with Erwin's apparent spoiling of the spoils system. Payne himself finally came to Erwin's rescue by resigning, and Finch was appointed. The mayor had won a skirmish, but it was an empty victory that only turned to disaster two years later.

The mayor came up with another idea that looked promising at first but had disappointing results: the appointment of an advisory council consisting of representatives from various civic organizations. The council would be concerned largely with the public safety department, but would also affect all aspects of city government. Gus P. Backman was named chairman, but within four months he resigned, and the mayor dissolved the entire committee. There was no public explanation, but there were indications that Backman's letter of resignation contained criticism of the mayor's policies and that the other advisors had been asked for virtually no advice. A promising plan had failed for lack of follow-through.

The mayor continued at odds with the rest of the commission. He was particularly dissatisfied with the practice of assigning each member of the commission management of one department, for he believed that the commission as a whole should take an active interest in all phases of city government. In this he was actually highlighting one of the weaknesses of the commission form of government, for this practice tended to divide the interests of the commissioners. Erwin was trying to get more supervision of all phases of government, for under this system he had no more power than any other commissioner.

Erwin said he wanted to promote more efficient, effective government, but instead a new scandal reared its head right under his administrative nose. On January 21, 1938, just two years after the mayor took office, Fisher Harris presented to the city commissioner a list of illegal establishments that had been making payoffs to police officers. These included three lotteries, two dice games, seven poker games, three bookmakers, sixteen houses of prostitution, and various private clubs such as the Past Time Club, the Western Social Club, and the Horse Show Card Club. "I have found also," he said, "that with rare exceptions no illegal activity in Salt Lake City is exempt from the payment of a tribute; that those I have mentioned, with a few exceptions, pay each month a previously agreed upon amount for the privilege of operation during the month."

Harris had the names of all those receiving payoffs, and both the police chief and the mayor were implicated. The evidence showed that Erwin and Finch regularly took bribes from operators of houses of ill fame as well as from gambling houses, allowing them to flourish in the city. They did not actually collect the money themselves but, rather, used go-betweens, including local attorney R.O. Pierce. The plan was apparently conceived by Erwin who, according to the Utah Supreme Court's opinion after the case was appealed, planned from the beginning "to get 'his' while he had a chance, and with this in mind he chose the chief of police." Certain citizens' committees and women's clubs complained that vice was being conducted openly in the city, and this led Harris to begin his intensive and far-reaching probe.

In the same meeting in which Harris presented his charges, the commission voted 3–1, with Erwin dissenting, to remove police chief Finch. Erwin complained that nothing had been proved against his appointee, but by then he was so at odds with the rest of the commission on almost all important matters that his voice had little influence.

O.B. Record, who was part of the vice clean-up campaign seven years earlier, was appointed acting chief, and immediately began raiding the houses of ill fame and other illegal establishments. Commissioners Keyser, Murdoch, and Goggin ordered him to report to the whole commission instead of to the mayor alone. The following Sunday, January 30, Mayor Erwin left for a ten-day rest in California, and on February

6 he announced his resignation. "I do not envy the future public safety commissioner," he wrote to the commission, "and I trust that you will consider my repeated suggestions concerning the assignment of city departments, particularly the making of the entire commission responsible for everything."

The mayor's concept of weaknesses in the commission form of government may have been accurate, but that did not keep him from being sent to jail for his part in one of the most serious scandals in the history of Salt Lake City. On June 8, 1938, he and several others were indicted by a grand jury. At their first trial, Erwin and Pearce were acquitted of felony charges, but in a later trial, presided over by Judge Oscar W. McConkie, they and Finch were convicted of misdemeanors. On May 6, 1939, Erwin and Finch were sentenced to a year in the county jail, and Pearce was sentenced to six months. Appeal proceedings took nearly three years, but on December 11, 1941, the Supreme Court upheld the convictions, and on March 24, 1942 it denied a petition for rehearing. Erwin finally entered the county jail on April 2, and on December 19, after eight and a half months, the parole board terminated his sentence. He soon returned to Los Angeles.

After Erwin's resignation, Commissioner William Murdoch was named acting mayor, but on February 19 the city commission appointed John M. Wallace, vice-president of Walker Bank and Trust Company, to fill Erwin's unexpired term. This was only after a new controversy broke out in which city judge Reva Beck Basone was a prominent contender for the job. Various women's groups and political and labor organizations supported Judge Bosone and were angered, especially since it was known that Wallace did not even want the job. On the day Wallace was officially appointed, the president of the Utah Federation of Labor presented petitions which, it was said, represented 10,000 citizens in behalf of Bosone. "Judge Bosone is not the champion of any group or clique," the petition read. "She does not fear the political graveyard that is the job of commissioner of public safety. We feel our candidate is more qualified than anyone who has been or will be considered." Several prominent Salt Lake men and women were at the official session of the city commission that began at 10:00 A.M., but they were unable to persuade the city fathers who, after hearing their fill of accusations and complaints, made Wallace's appointment official.

As might be expected, the new mayor was immediately handed the public safety department as his administrative responsibility. One of his first acts was to appoint William C. Webb, a retired army officer, as police chief. He also got the other commissioners to agree that they would all carry mutual responsibility for that department, at least until the problems were straightened out. In the meantime, the revitalized police force continued its war on crime and seemed to satisfy the public that at last the battle was accomplishing something.

Wallace was content with a half-term as mayor, and even though he got along well with the commission and had public pressure on him to stand for election, in November 1939, the voters turned to the lustre of Salt Lake City's world-famous race car driver, Ab Jenkins, and by a slim fifty-one vote majority over Herbert A. Snow elected him mayor. In a curious way, the election of a world figure to serve the city in the 1940s was symbolic of the world influences that would begin to dominate Salt Lake City as the nation raced toward involvement in the affairs of Europe and, eventually, in a second world war.

Main Street looking south in 1940s. Courtesy, Utah State Historical Society.

—— 8 ——

War and Prosperity, 1941–1945

As the 1930s drew to a close, Americans looked with increasing fearfulness at the war clouds of Europe and Asia. Many, if not most, Utahns shared America's general isolationist sentiment, believing that it was in the nation's interest to maintain strict neutrality, though their sympathy was clearly with Britain, France, and the other nations being crushed by the Nazi juggernaut. When war finally came to America, Salt Lake City's interests quickly turned to wartime needs, and to playing its role in the new national crisis. "As of last Monday morning," Mayor Ab Jenkins told the city commission four days after Pearl Harbor, "this body became the war government of Salt Lake City. Last Saturday at noon, we were a city government concerned with problems of normal city operation. This condition no longer exists." That assessment was not quite accurate, for Mayor Jenkins's own administration, both before and after hostilities began, was racked with political squabbles that had little to do with events outside the city. For the most part, however, the demands of wartime became the major concerns of Salt Lake City and its government.

The years 1939 to 1942 were transition years, as New Deal spending phased out and defense spending phased in. In 1938 Utah still had a much higher percentage of its workers on New Deal agency payrolls than the national average, but these programs were declining. Salt Lake City did not have enough money to pay its proportionate share of all the WPA projects the government was willing to sponsor, though funded projects in 1941 included sewers, repairs of curbs and guttering, road repairs, and autumn tree trimming. By the time the program was liquidated in February 1943, it had performed a million dollars worth of work on the campus of the University of Utah, including considerable building construction and repair as well as the operation of a nursery school for children between the ages of two and five. In addition to these and scores of smaller projects, it had also built 100 miles of city sewers and contributed the major share of the airport expansion project. The Utah WPA administrator was slightly critical of Salt Lake City, however, for he believed that a great deal more could have been accomplished, and more people taken off unemployment rolls, if it had been willing to sponsor more projects. In spite of everything done there, Salt Lake City received less aid in proportion to its size than most communities in the state.

The New Deal was a lifesaver for Utah and Salt Lake City, but by no means did it bring about full economic recovery. Only defense-related spending of the wartime years did that. In 1942 the war created some 12,000 new jobs in Salt Lake City, and total employment in Utah during the war years jumped by fifty-five percent. From 1941 through 1943, defense spending created 49,500 new jobs in Utah. Though many were filled by longtime residents, the new jobs also attracted newcomers, and by mid-1943 nearly 40,000 people had streamed into Salt Lake City alone. In addition, between 50,000 and 60,000 military personnel were stationed in Utah at the height of the war, many of them in and around Salt Lake City. All this had a permanent economic impact as Utah remained a key defense area even after the war, with some 14,000 defense-related jobs continuing. Employment and income both went up during the war, not only in terms of dollars but also with respect to the national average. In 1940, Utah's per capita income was 81.8 percent of the average, and in 1943 it was 102.7 percent. From the beginning of the New Deal, Utah's economic health (including that of its capital city) was tied to the willingness of the national government to provide the elixir of federal spending, and World War II only enhanced that willingness.

Salt Lake City benefited from defense spending largely as a result of its strategic location. It was the natural focus for a multitude of regional economic activities, as observed in previous chapters. Its inland location, sheltered by the Rocky Mountains, together with its railroads, highways, population, and an adequate water supply, made it an equally natural location for key military installations and defense industries. Early in 1942 the Army's Ninth Corps Area Service Command moved from the Presidio of San Francisco to Fort Douglas, making that military base a western states headquarters. It also became an examination, induction, and separation center. Kearns Army Air Base, built twenty miles south-west of Salt Lake City, provided basic training for more than 90,000 airmen between August 1942 and October 1943. These, plus eight other military bases and an army hospital in Utah, contributed directly to the economy of Salt Lake City and to the number of servicemen who became part of its human scenery.

As early as 1939, under prodding from President Franklin D. Roosevelt, the United States began organizing its industrial production for defense purposes. Tax incentives for building defense plants, pressure on automobile manufacturers to begin converting to military production, federal allocation of certain raw materials: these and other government pressures put the United States fairly well on the road toward a defense-related economy by 1941. That year the state of Utah established a Department of Publicity and Industrial Development, and charged it with the responsibility of attracting defense-related industries to the state. Its lobbyists succeeded well, and between 1939 and 1947 the number of manufacturing establishments in Utah rose from 549 to 772. Nearly all of Utah's industrial expansion was financed by the national government, and the state's key role in defense planning is illustrated by the fact that the $311 million in federal funds allocated to Utah amounted to thirty-eight percent of the total authorized for all the mountain states.

In Salt Lake City, the Remington Small Arms Plant, begun late in 1941, became one of Utah's major defense plants. It operated until late 1943, employing 10,000 people at its peak. The Utah Oil Refinery stepped up its gasoline production, especially after a government-financed $20 million expansion program was completed in 1944, and in 1945 it set a world's record of forty gallons of 100-octane aviation gasoline produced from 100 gallons of crude oil. Other defense industries included the Eitel McCullough Radio Tube Plant, a huge low-grade aluminum ore mill, and a tungsten treatment plant. Nearby, the American Smelting and Refining Company, the International Smelting and Refining Company, and Kennecott Copper Corporation all spent huge sums on expansion and provided thousands of jobs for people in and around Salt Lake City. All this, together with the numerous defense installations in surrounding counties, greatly stimulated the city's housing and construction industries, as well as all other aspects of its economic life.

The effects of the war were felt on every hand. In 1940 the United States government inaugurated the first peacetime draft in American history, and suddenly Salt Lake City families saw hundreds of their young men join the 1.2 million draftees who were inducted for a year of military service. Before many of them were home, America had entered a shooting war, and the army extended their year to the duration. The city commission did its part to show support for city employees by passing an ordinance on March 28, 1941, guaranteeing the restoration of their jobs when they returned. Although this action did not absolutely bind future administrations, the year 1945 saw many city employees returning from the armed forces and being reinstated in their former jobs.

The city fathers were not so understanding with employees who left to find more lucrative work in war industries. In 1942 the fire department, in particular, was suffering from such losses, and the city council refused to grant leaves of absence to those who left for jobs with better pay. It did, however, provide pay raises during the war, but many firemen discovered that even this did not provide an adequate living, and they continued to be tempted by better paying industrial jobs. It was the classic dilemma of higher wages now as opposed to guaranteed work later. In May 1944, the city council addressed this problem by allowing firemen to work twelve hours a day and asking some of them to return to work on their normal days off. They hoped the extra pay, plus pay raises in June, would meet the firemen's needs and at the same time provide adequate protection for the city.

This was only one aspect of the labor shortage caused by the war. In spite of the rapid inflow of job-seekers, a number of firms in Salt Lake City found themselves lowering age and physical requirements, hiring more women, and cutting employment corners. Women found themselves driving trucks, taxis, and buses, loading ammunition, doing sheet metal work, and engaging in a variety of other jobs not normally, in those days, considered women's work. They also gave much-needed volunteer service to hospitals, the Red Cross, and the United Service Organization (a national program for providing hospitality and entertainment for servicemen). Many a high school and junior high school student who would have found no work a few years earlier found himself contributing to the family income by working after school and on weekends in Salt Lake City business establishments. Some construction projects were critical, and when labor shortages slowed the expansion of the Utah Oil Refinery, the national war Production Board halted work on part of Utah County's Geneva Steel plant in order to provide labor for the top-priority job in Salt Lake City. At times the city also witnessed recruiting parades organized to obtain defense plant workers.

City government and civic organizations tried to anticipate the coming problems, but, treading in unfamiliar territory, the city council did not always agree on how to deal with them. In almost laughable proceedings in January 1942, the council practically came to blows as it considered the question of loyalty tests for city employees. There was no serious question with respect to current workers, but Mayor Jenkins proposed that all current and future employees be required to fill out a new questionnaire, prepared by his office, that included questions relating to loyalty. In the end, the council decided that all new employees must fill out the questionnaire, but the inconsistencies inherent in the council form of government were demonstrated when it became apparent that only the employees of departments headed by Jenkins and councilmen Fred Tedesco and Oscar W. McConkie would be required to fill them out, that those under John B. Matheson would be given their option, and that George D. Keyser would not even mention it to his employees.

In September 1941, the chamber of commerce named twenty-six standing committees to concern themselves with various aspects of the new defense-oriented society. In November the city council met with the county Civilian Defense Council in an effort to stimulate public interest in the defense program, and in December the city organized its own defense committee. Gus P. Backman, in attendance at this organizational meeting representing governor Herbert B. Maw, proposed that the committee use existing organizations to work out the civil defense program. One possibility, he suggested, was the "block teachers" program of the LDS church. The defense committee was also charged with preparing for the influx of servicemen into the city, establishing hospitality centers, and leasing buildings for other necessary activities. A few months later a Citizens Defense Corps was organized, which continued where the old defense committee left off in providing instructional and training programs. The community responded excellently, it was reported in June 1942. The city also began early cooperation with the airport in improving its security provisions.

The city government encouraged Salt Lakers in all the patriotic duties of Americans during wartime. It pushed the purchase of war bonds and stamps, for example, and it encouraged conservation and salvaging of critical materials. It even provided city trucks to pick up tin cans at schools and take them to detinning plants, and in order to conserve gasoline, tires, and automobiles by eliminating unnecessary stops, it discontinued the operation of traffic signals at certain intersections outside the center of town.

Citizens of Salt Lake City experienced the same wartime shortages as the rest of the nation, and adjusted their lives accordingly. The few shoes and stockings available came in limited colors, and women's nylons disappeared altogether. Housewives saved fat and newspapers, and sent them to school with their children where a government salvage operation picked them up. Because of gasoline and tire rationing, many Salt Lakers stored their cars in garages for most of the duration, others drove only infrequently, and many rode city trolleys twice as much as they ever had before. Food, particularly sugar, meat, and coffee, was rationed and often disappeared completely from the shelves. Such ordinary things as paper bags also disappeared. No distant conflict, the war was present for everyone as the people of Salt Lake lived with scarcity, purchased government bonds, sent boys to fight, and reordered their lives in a dozen different ways.

Salt Lake City schools, along with those of the rest of Utah, also contributed to the war effort. In his biennial report for 1942, State Superintendent of Schools Charles H. Skidmore observed that since Utah was a "critical war area," several Wasatch Front school districts would face unusual problems in providing enough teachers and adequate facilities for the people who were pouring into the state. The state was already planning sixteen WPA Child Protection centers for taking care of preschool children of mothers engaged in war work.

At the same time, a farm labor crisis provided a unique opportunity for high school students. Educators, farmers, and food processors held meetings throughout the state, and it was decided that each school district should arrange its own program of cooperation with agricultural interests as well as cooperate in the salvage drive. The results were impressive. In 1944, the 20,000 Utah students who assisted in crop production accounted for some 60 percent of the farm labor placement in the state. School children of all ages participated in scrap drives by scavenging in their own homes as well as going from door to door, and by the end of 1944 they had collected 61,400,000 pounds of scrap metal and 820,000 pounds of paper, accounting respectively for 22 and 35 percent of all the collections in the state. All Utah schools sold war bonds and stamps, and thus many students not only learned something about financing a war but also found themselves later cashing in on the savings encouraged by the war. Skidmore called the students a "third front army" in the national war effort.

Salt Lake City schools also provided other services. In 1942, for example, they began offering a special defense curriculum to qualified high school students. If he could graduate by taking only a half day of regular classes, a student could spend the other half day in classwork that would train him in such defense-related skills as machinist, mechanic's helper, sheet metal work, and plumbing. In addition, the University of Utah became a specialized training center for young men in the army carefully selected to receive training as specialists in various technical fields essential to the army's activities.

Other social patterns in the war years were probably to be expected, and in each case the statistics clearly followed national trends. The rate of violent crimes, except murder, and crimes against property increased, partly because so many young people remained unsupervised and families were dislocated. Juvenile delinquency, especially among children ages eleven through thirteen, climbed. Social workers attributed this largely to absent parents and easy money. The divorce rate in Salt Lake County went up from 25.3 per one hundred marriages before the war to 31.7 during the war. Desertions also showed an increase, while the traditional standards of sexual morality seemed to decline. At the same time, special services for children increased, and scouting, in particular, seemed to boom. The number of scout troops actually quadrupled during a six-year period, and the LDS church was given great credit for the leadership it provided in that area. General interest in religion also increased during the war, as all churches reported improved attendance and activity.

War also struck a blow at the heart of one of society's most important institutions: the family. Probably reflecting national trends, sociological data gathered after the war demonstrated its specific effects in Salt Lake City. The housing shortage sometimes caused "doubling up" of familes, and this congestion, more than either substandard or inadequate housing, had negative effects. The sense of identification with the primary family as well as respect for the rights of others tended to suffer. Beyond this the data varied, but there was evidence that the absence of both parents from the home, as many mothers took wartime jobs, weakened some family ties, though this undoubtedly depended more upon the quality rather than the quantity of time parents spent with their children. Families also suffered from emotional problems, the impact of wartime deaths, and lower moral standards. Counseling agencies reported that the most frequent problems coming to their attention were those related to personal emotional health, whereas before the war they were related to education. Second on the list was family relationships, as contrasted with economic and financial problems before the war.

At the same time, the impact of the war on family life was not all negative. There was evidence that, in many cases, it actually strengthened family ties, possibly because busy or absent parents were motivated to take special pains in this direction. A general upswing in religious interest seemed to promote increased spiritual values, at least for some groups, in spite of the corresponding rise in delinquency and youthful immorality. For some, the war provided financial benefits and opportunities, along with a higher standard of living. It also stimulated interest in public affairs as well as cooperation within the community. Various wartime youth programs even helped develop leadership abilities. And certainly the war promoted interest in foreign countries, increased various kinds of knowledge, and stimulated in many people a greater appreciation for democracy. Taking all this into consideration, the Utah Preparatory Commission concluded in its 1948 report to the International Congress on Mental Health that in developing sound peacetime mental hygiene programs, "we must try to find the 'moral equivalent of war.'"

Probably more than any event up to that time, the war seemed to have a long-range impact on the activities of Utah women. In 1940 one in four of those over fourteen was a wage earner, but a decade later this ratio had changed to one in three. During the war some 24,000 Utah women who had not previously worked outside their homes, and many of whom had children, began to fill jobs vacated by the men who had gone into military service. Nearly thirty percent of them became skilled mechanics in war industries, while others found work in various aspects of transportation, wholesale and retail trade, and as unskilled workers. Unlike the situation at the end of World War I, this time many were able to hold their jobs, or were replaced by other women, and the trend toward increasing employment opportunity for women continued.

Beyond that, many women were still vitally interested in social services, and the war enhanced those opportunities greatly. They named the centers established to help new families find homes, hosted servicemen at the USO, and trained as volunteers in all aspects of civil defense.

Amy Brown Lyman, whose career of social service reached its peak during the war, was still one of Salt Lake City's most prominent women. Her husband, a professor of engineering at the University of Utah, was responsible for devising the street numbering system now used in Salt Lake City and throughout the state of Utah. It was while he was working on his Ph.D. degree at the University of Chicago that Amy got acquainted with the famous Hull House and other Chicago charities, and that began her lifelong fascination with and commitment to, as she put it, "helping raise human life to its highest level."

On January 1, 1940, Mrs. Lyman became president of the Relief Society, and she held that position for over five years. Beginning to

Amy Brown Lyman, State Legislator, Relief Society Leader, and Humanitarian. Courtesy, Brigham Young University.

fail a little in health, she nevertheless led out in some important wartime activities. To assist in the war effort, the women of the Relief Society contributed sewing, knitting, food, and nursing care. They sponsored Red Cross first aid courses, promoted savings bonds, created special lessons for Relief Society meetings relating to wartime problems, and cooperated with the church as well as other charitable groups in Salt Lake City on various welfare programs. In spite of great personal tragedies that came to her in this period, Amy Brown Lyman was one of the wartime pillars of strength, not just for Salt Lake City's Mormon women but for others as well.

Salt Lake City's ethnic minorites remained a very small portion of the total population during the war, though the number of blacks and Japanese increased more significantly than others. The black population jumped from about 700 in 1940 to 2,500 at the end of the war, as defense-related jobs attracted black workers, but in the next five years it declined again to about 1,130. The Japanese population in 1940 was 359, as compared with 1,721 in 1950. The Chinese community went from 102 to 173, and, according to the census figures, the American Indian population dropped from 40 to 30 in that period. Although there were few examples of open ethnic conflict, general discriminatory attitudes toward blacks continued during the war and discrimination against them in housing, jobs, and public accommodations did not generally abate.

The most obvious opportunity for ethnic conflict came with the intensification of anti-Japanese emotionalism. Many Utahns seemed to share the national hysteria, brought on by Pearl Harbor, that fed the belief that anyone of Japanese ancestry might well be an enemy. The city's Japanese-American community was painfully aware that such feelings could exist, and the day after Pearl Harbor Dr. Jun Kurumada, a local dentist and chairman of the Japanese-American Citizen's League, called a hurried meeting at which they discussed their circumstances. He also assured the FBI of complete cooperation in stamping out any possible subversive activity among local Japanese, and urged employers to give them a chance to prove their loyalty. "America's fight is our fight," the Japanese-Americans proclaimed at the meeting, and they appealed to their fellow citizens to apply their sense of fairness and recognize their loyalty.

The potential for tension was obvious, and both Japanese and other Americans were somewhat bewildered as they tried to figure out how best to confront each other. A Japanese professor of anatomy at the University of Utah, Dr. Edward Ichiro Hashimoto, helped his class solve the problem beautifully. As he walked in the day after Pearl Harbor, he was met by a profound silence. "What are you fellows staring at?" he asked the students. "I'm Irish. I was home in Dublin at the time!" The students were delighted, the atmosphere relaxed, and because he could draw human figures with either hand Dr. Hashimoto was known from then on as the "Ambidextrous Irishman."

In spite of such overtures and accommodations, Salt Lake City succumbed to the national mood. In the aftermath of December 7, city officials warned foreign-born Japanese, especially, to "remain at home during the next few days and nights." Signs declaring "No Japs Wanted Here" appeared in hotels and restaurants, employers fired Japanese workers, and school children were harassed by their former playmates. Though it appears cruel and needless with the benefit of hindsight, such treatment is nevertheless explainable in terms of the sudden nationalism that spread across the country overnight, and the feeling that if Pearl Harbor could be attacked so suddenly there could be subversive elements anywhere. The Japanese were the principal targets of immediate precautionary measures or, in some cases, illogical emotional reaction. An immediate movement arose to keep more Japanese ancestry from buying or leasing land in Utah. The Salt Lake chamber of commerce, with the support of the Salt Lake Federation of Labor, tried to stop any more Japanese-Americans from operating businesses in the city. Chamber representatives argued that without such a restriction more Japanese would be attracted to the city and this would only create problems of law and order. At the same time, the people of Utah seemed to support the decision of the federal government to relocate 8,000 Japanese from the West Coast in the hastily constructed relocation camp of Topaz, near Delta, Utah. Some from Salt Lake City were also relocated there. Ironically, Japanese-Americans were allowed to join the American military forces, and many of them fought heroically in Europe. The names of eighteen Japanese-Americans killed in the war are inscribed on the Nisei War Monument in Salt Lake City. Actually, anti-Japanese sentiment in Salt Lake City was not as bad as that in some other American cities, and possibly for that reason the national headquarters of the Japanese-American Citizen's League was located there during the war.

The migration to centers of defense employment was bound to create a housing shortage. Officials in some areas anticipated it while those in others did not. Salt Lake City's wartime housing activity was part of a gigantic national program that began as early as June 1940, when Congress authorized the War and Navy departments and the United States Housing Authority to provide homes for defense workers. Eventually, in February 1942, several government agencies were brought together by executive order to form the National Housing Agency, which supervised most defense housing and allocation of building materials during the war. By the end of 1944 NHA had programmed housing in 1,281 localities. The federal government and private enterprise worked together in carrying the financial burden.

In Utah, planning began in July 1941, when the state defense coordinator, Gus P. Backman, and representatives from Salt Lake City, Ogden, Provo, Clearfield, and Layton met with Louis E. Scarborough, assistant regional coordinator for defense housing. Scarborough reviewed the critical situation but indicated that the national government did not want to take over the housing problem unless the state itself was unable to handle it. In August the State Defense Council organized a housing committee that immediately began a detailed survey. Potentially critical needs were identified, especially in the vicinity of Ogden, but there was some resistance to public housing on the part of local financial and real estate interests. They softpedaled the extent of the emergency, warned against overbuilding that might glut the housing market after the emergency, and were optimistic that private enterprise could provide enough housing to meet the real emergency after all available empty rooms were taken up. At a state planning meeting on August 21, for example, Richard F. Harding, secretary of Salt Lake City's Real Estate Board, declared that the use of hotels, apartments, tourist courts, and rooms in private homes could take care of the immediate problem in the state capital. Even though 3,500 defense workers were expected shortly, he believed that only about one-third would bring families and thus require homes. Even a WPA survey in November suggested that no emergency existed in Salt Lake City, though military commanders in the area publically warned against that attitude. Soon enough, however, the failure of its planners to recognize the potentially critical situation caught Salt Lake City short.

In January, 1942 they began to take a second look. The Army Ninth Corps Area moved to Salt Lake City that month, and on the first Sunday of the month city and county officials found themselves spending the full day placing 150 families in temporary quarters. By the end of the day practically all available housing had disappeared. The problem for the Ninth Corps became so serious that it moved sixty trailers into the city and parked them on vacant grounds next to the University of Utah stadium. Army employees occupied these temporary quarters until adequate facilities were completed at Fort Douglas. The 3,500 potential war workers now loomed larger in the eyes of the city fathers, and in February they began searching for a twenty-five-acre parcel of land suitable for a federal housing project. In April they selected a site on the west side of the city, and Glendale Gardens, as it was called, was soon underway. Similar to Ogden's Grandview Acres, the frame, multifamily units were quickly and cheaply constructed, but were also comfortable and met the emergency needs of many families very well.

Private enterprise also moved quickly to try to fill the void. In just four months, April through July, contractors completed Ambassador Gardens. Its ten brick buildings, more solidly constructed than the federal project, contained thirty-eight compact apartments. The same year Douglas Arms Corporation put up a housing project with thirty-six units. But the flow of incoming workers continued, and in July Salt Lake's Home Registration Bureau processed between 150 and 200 applicants daily. In 1943 the Federal Housing Administration authorized private contractors to erect a 1,000-family project in Salt Lake County and south Davis County. The first thirty-two units, located in the southeast section of Salt Lake City, were begun in August. In spite of all this, workers on the Utah Oil Refining Company's new aviation gasoline plant remained homeless, and in August the city council authorized installation of a federal trailer park and agreed to connect it with city water and sewer lines. Dubbed Aviation Village, the park was finished in January 1944, and consisted of 150 trailers that housed 500 tenants. More relief for war workers came in October 1943, when the War Production Board and the National Housing Agency authorized them to build their own homes.

Private enterprise also tried to meet the shortage by remodeling existing housing, and just as the government released critical construction material for new housing it also cooperated in this effort. The War Production Board authorized 1,034 units for conversion to rental apartments in Salt Lake City, and the government agreed to lend as much as $100 per room for these conversions.

As might be expected, however, private citizens were not always as cooperative as they might be—not even in friendly Salt Lake City. Even though family housing was the most critical need, some landlords, assured that they would have little difficulty renting their houses and apartments, refused families with children. In November, 1943, about 250 families were on the housing registration lists in the Salt Lake area. Many had found temporary shelter in substandard housing for the summer, but as winter approached they urgently sought better quarters. Still some landlords would not allow children on their premises. Even some native Salt Lake City women whose husbands were overseas were forced to care for their children in hotel rooms.

All of Utah's major defense housing projects built by the government were completed in the early months of 1944, but shortages continued. In August of that year, for example, Salt Lake City's housing center received 600 calls for homes, but only 200 vacancies were available.

Neither did the crisis abate after the war, as hundreds of returning servicemen found difficulty locating homes. Frequently they occupied the same units used previously by defense workers, and in 1948 Salt Lake City initiated its own public housing project, Airbase Village, for their benefit.

Beyond the war, city government had other problems to deal with. One was the black pall of smoke that still hung over the valley, in spite of the abatement program begun in 1921. This unsightly and unhealthy shroud came from various sources: railroad traffic, coal-burning industrial plants, and the fact that nearly seventy percent of the homes having central heating used coal in their furnaces, and eighty-seven percent of those without central heating also burned coal. In the minds of many citizens the problem was becoming worse rather than better.

The commissioners began working on a new abatement program, and on March 7, 1941 they held a special hearing. Present were representatives of various civic and business organizations: the Utah Coal Operators' Association, the Women's Chamber of Commerce, The Utah Conservation and Research Foundation, the Denver and Rio Grande Railroad, The Industrial Committee of the Associated Women's organization, city judge Reva Beck Bosone, and many other interested groups and citizens. Commissioner John B. Matheson candidly admitted that lack of funds had made it impossible for the city to continue the old abatement program. In spite of a variety of ideas and disagreements, everyone seemed at least to agree that the best answer was the use of smokeless fuel (i.e., specially processed coal that produced a minimum of smoke) and the proper mechanical equipment for feeding furnaces. Several people were impressed with reports that St. Louis, Missouri had eliminated sixty-six percent of its smoke without working a hardship on anyone. The coal industry declared that it had a smokeless fuel available, and that it was willing and able to work with coal users on the proper selection, installation, and use of new equipment. Several people felt that the city should install a processing plant in order to assure adequate smokeless fuel, but the city commissioners pointed to the budget as the prohibitive factor.

In March the city outlined a complicated new anti-smoke program that was soon implemented by various laws and regulations. It restricted the production of smoke by railroads and industries, required all new heating plants to be equipped with mechanical firing devices or to use smokeless fuel, and prohibited the burning of leaves and trash in the city. Two examining boards were established, one to investigate the qualifications of journeyman installers of heating equipment, and the other to examine operating engineers and firemen in steam pressure

243

plants. The D&RG, meanwhile, spent $100,000 in the development of a new process for firing "cold engines" so that less smoke was produced, and also began to use diesel switch engines in the Salt Lake City yards. In the long run, it appears, the program was only moderately successful, as the clouds from residential heating continued to hover over the city until most homes were converted to natural gas. At the same time, automobile, truck, and industrial pollution increased over the next several years, and, like so many other American cities, Salt Lake still visibly suffers from this by-product of modernization.

Politically, the early 1940s were raucous, discordant years on the city council as Mayor Jenkins frequently exchanged blows publicly with one or more of the other commissioners. Some issues seemed almost inconsequential, others had far-reaching implications for public policy, but whenever the acrimony renewed itself, the council seemed almost like a comic opera.

One quarrel concerned Mayor Jenkins's proposal, in March 1941, that the city appoint an independent expert to study the general operations and efficiency of city government. It was important, the mayor believed, to have the study finished before the 1942 budget hearings, and he wanted authorization to spend $5,000 for it. The proposal sounded like a good idea to the members of the chamber of commerce, and they publicly congratulated the mayor, but the commissioners dragged their feet because they did not want to put up the funds from the existing budget. Finally, near the end of April, they authorized the survey but told the mayor he would have to raise the money himself, from private contributions. The *Tribune*, a strong supporter of Jenkins' plan, castigated the commission for the kind of "official apathy" that could result in such a "reactionary disappointment." To require the mayor to raise his own funds for such an important project was not only undignified, but it reflected a smugness and self-satisfaction that made the commissioners seem wholly indifferent. The mayor was nevertheless determined to have his survey, and began trying to collect the money, but after considerable public pressure the other commissioners backed down. They agreed to fund the survey at a cost not to exceed $2,500, and each agreed to provide $600 from his own departmental budget.

The Public Administration Service of Chicago was hired to do the survey. Its report, made public on December 1, was a serious indictment of the commission form of city government, though its charges had been heard before from other critics. The five department heads, it observed, continually competed with each other for authorizations and appropriations, and exhibited no unified interest or control over all municipal functions. It suggested several changes in procedure, but the

*"Ab" Jenkins, Internationally known Race Driver and Mayor 1940-44.
Courtesy, Utah State Historical Society.*

245

main proposal was that the city adopt a new form of government: either the city manager system or the "strong mayor" and council system. Either of these would bring greater efficiency and economy.

The mayor attempted to reorganize the public safety department according to some of the suggestions, but, possibly because of the preoccupation with the war after December 7, nothing was done to implement the whole proposal. In February, however, the mayor took on the entire commission, after an argument over checking parking meters and tagging traffic law violators. All of them, he said, should resign, for they failed to comprehend the law setting up the present form of government. Rather, each seemed to think that he had been "elected, ordained, or especially created to devote his time and ability to efforts for securing funds and favors for the department assigned to him, regardless of the general welfare." Again the *Tribune* supported the mayor, pointing to the rivalries that seemed never to end, but not until 1980 would Salt Lake City change its system.

The public bickering between Jenkins and his fellow commissioners sometimes became very personal. In January 1942, he had a row with Finance Commissioner Oscar W. McConkie. In a debate that went on for days, Jenkins charged that there was waste in purchasing policies, and that McConkie did not consult with the city auditor in preparing his budget. McConkie denied the waste, claiming that he had investigated the mayor's accusations with regard to a radio purchase and found them in error, and declared that he had carefully consulted with the city auditor on every item in the budget. He also got in his own licks against the mayor by accusing him of an "un-American" attitude for stirring up strife, and commented that this was only an aid to Hitler. In April the mayor leveled another blast at McConkie by accusing him of trying to secure the release of a member of the city attorney's staff so that a Democrat could be appointed. McConkie replied that he would never vote for such a thing, let alone propose or plan it, whereupon the mayor jauntily proposed that the FBI be invited to bring in its lie detector to see who was telling the truth. Disgusted, McConkie simply said that he had no inclination to engage in such petty political propaganda. Even the young, well-liked commissioner Fred Tedesco crossed swords with the mayor. In a city council flare-up on October 9, 1942, Tedesco called the mayor "juvenile" for certain criticisms of the city auditor. Jenkins replied in kind by calling Tedesco a "boy scout." Commissioner George D. Keysor had to shout to make a motion for adjournment. The next year, in December, the mayor accused Tedesco of coercing his parks department employees into having two percent deducted from their salaries and put into a special political fund. He was no doubt chagrined when, on December 29, over 140 men and women, practically every employee in the parks department, crowded the city chambers in a show of support for Tedesco and denied that they had ever been coerced into paying anything. Jenkins, who was not at that meeting, later reiterated his charges, but nothing ever came of them.

The public eventually grew tired of the continuing series of colorful, quarrelsome meetings of the city council. The council itself had become the community "problem child," the *Tribune* editorialized on June 22, 1942, because of its wrangling, personal politics, and woeful lack of clear-cut policies. Instead of acting as a governing unit, it charged, the members of the council seemed to have the idea that their body was a "hydra-headed monster which has five mouths to feed but no collective responsibility." The mayor eventually seemed to see the handwriting on the wall, and on February 10, 1943, nine months before the coming election, he called for a truce. Asking for an end to "tempestuous business sessions," he promised no longer to publicize matters of concern and said that he saw the need for an end to public quarrels.

His effort to calm down, however, did not help Jenkins break the political hex that seemed to follow incumbent mayors and public safety commissioners. Earl J. Glade, a newcomer to politics, defeated him by a vote of 19,153 to 16,869. The change, commented the *Tribune*, marked the end of a "tumultuous but interesting interlude in municipal government," and an administration that had been "exasperating to some, laudable to others, but never dull."

Though the new mayor was a novice at politics, he was not new to public life. Born in Ogden in 1885, he served an LDS mission in Germany, graduated from Brigham Young University, and took advanced training at the University of Chicago. He served for a short time on the faculty of BYU and for twelve years on the business school faculty of the University of Utah. For twenty years he was a radio promoter and executive, and he helped finance and build radio station KZN, which eventually became KSL. He was also affiliated with KLO in Ogden. Before he was elected mayor, he had served as president of the Salt Lake City Chamber of Commerce, the Rotary Club, and the Bonneville Knife and Fork Club; as a regent of the University of Utah; president of the United War fund of Utah; and as a member or sponsor of numerous other committees and organizations. A specialist in public relations, he seemed admirably suited to guide Salt Lake City through the remainder of the war and into the problems of the postwar years.

The immediacy of wartime problems did not keep some people in Salt Lake City from considering postwar planning. As early as 1941 the city council talked with the WPA about providing jobs when defense

Earl J. Glade, Early Manager of KSL radio, businessman, and Mayor 1945-56. Courtesy, Utah State Historical Society.

employment tapered off. In October 1942, Salt Lake City became one of only a few cities in the country to which the National Resources Planning Board sent consultants to help out with postwar planning. The national board justified the service on the basis of the city's central location, which had resulted in unusual development of war industries with resulting problems in housing, labor, and transportation. In July 1943, the city council published a fifty-year planning report, compiled by the city zoning engineer with the help of the national organization. Emphasizing the need for a massive "housecleaning" designed to prevent serious economic and social dislocation after the war, it dealt with such major issues as land acquisition and use, housing redevelopment, improvement of blighted areas, building up the city's west side, new parkways, new railroad and bus facilities, a civic auditorium, and more water development, sewage systems, and storm drains. The report was not specifically followed through, but at least Mayor Glade and the city council, as well as other civic groups, continued to discuss the future and tried to anticipate the adjustments that might be needed when the nation entered a new era of peace.

Main Street Looking North, 1958. Courtesy, Utah State Historical Society.

9

Growth and Stagnation, 1946–1960

With the end of World War II, Salt Lake City residents faced the immediate problem of reconversion from war to peacetime. Without the benefit of war-related industry, the city could no longer rely upon the federal government to finance its growth. Recognizing this, business and civic leaders worked together to promote economic expansion. Although the business community continued to grow between 1945 and 1949 and somewhat more slowly between 1950 and 1960, the city's population began to show the same symptoms experienced by other urban areas in the United States. It grew only four percent as increasing numbers of city residents sought homes in the country. Nevertheless, many commuted to jobs in the city, the business interests of the city continued to multiply, and Salt Lake further entrenched itself as the commercial, financial, and industrial center of the Mountain West.

Some of the economic changes following the war resulted from the conversion of wartime facilities to peacetime uses. In 1948, most of the land occupied by the Fort Douglas military reservation became part of the University of Utah campus. By 1949, the Remington Arms Plant became the Salt Lake Industrial Center under the control of a syndicate headed by John M. Wallace and Leland S. Swaner. They paid only $1.7 million for the $20 million facility, but by 1949 Wallace and Swaner had spent an additional $75,000 surfacing streets and making other improvements. Served by both the Union Pacific and Denver and Rio Grande, it proved an ideal location for light industrial and commercial firms.

Private businesses made similar purchases of other plants. In August 1947, the Utah Oil Refining Company, a subsidiary of Standard Oil of

Indiana (AMOCO), paid $4.1 million for the $15.9 million oil refinery it had operated during the war. In March of the same year, the Utah State Road Commission purchased the Eitel McCullough radio tube plant into which the federal government had poured $759,000 in capital. The federal government sold all of these plants at a fraction of their original cost, and the purchasers either converted them to some other purpose or continued in their original use.

In some cases, former government plants served as the nucleus for continued industrial or commercial expansion. Utah Oil Company, for instance, spent $10 million on an expansion program. Moreover, continued exploration for oil in the Intermountain West, coupled with Salt Lake's advantageous location and existing facilities, brought new refineries to the city. Between 1948 and 1950, for example, Standard Oil of California (Chevron) spent $34 million to construct pipelines from Pasco, Washington and Rangely, Colorado to a refinery that it built north of Salt Lake City. During 1950, Phillips Petroleum, Co. constructed a refinery in north Salt Lake. Later, the nationally prominent Northwest Energy Company, one of the most important pipeline companies in the United States, would locate in Salt Lake City.

The federal government also added some facilities in Salt Lake. Shortly after the war, for instance, it constructed a Veterans Administration hospital at a cost of $8 million.

Private companies added still more economic growth, and by 1950, Salt Lake City stood within a twenty-five mile radius of 573 manufacturing plants. Within a thirty-mile radius was located what *Business Week* called "the nation's greatest concentration of nonferrous mining, milling, smelting, and refining." Moreover, Kennecott Copper Company's mine at Bingham produced thirty percent of the nation's copper, was its leading producer of molybdenum, and as a by-product of its operation poured gold, silver, and other metals onto the market.

The emergence of a steel industry in Utah following World War II aided the economic expansion of Salt Lake City. The United States Steel Company's Geneva Plant at Orem, forty miles south of Salt Lake City, reopened, and by late 1947 it had attracted a number of steel fabricating plants to Utah. United States Steel had purchased the $200 million plant at a fraction of its cost from the federal government. In Salt Lake, the Chicago Bridge and Iron Company established a plant at Fourth West and Thirteenth South to make storage tanks from steel produced at Geneva.

Economists and business observers expected purchasing power deferred by wartime shortages to provide an impetus to the economy during the immediate post-war period. Commercial activity proved these predictions correct. Department store sales during the week of December 28, 1946, increased 79 percent over the corresponding period a year previously. On September 2 and 3, 1947, the city administration and the chamber of commerce declared the first million dollar sales days since World War II. The success continued, since 1949 proved more profitable than any previous year, lengthening a string of twelve years of unbroken expansion dating from before the war.

In laying out goals for post-war expansion, Gus P. Backman, of the Salt Lake chamber of commerce, placed increased tourism high on the list. Promotion did increase tourism, but perhaps more important was the 1947 centennial of Utah's settlement. Sports events slated for the year included the NCAA track and field championships at the University of Utah, the national downhill and slalom ski championships, and the U.S. clay court tennis championships. More than a million people visited Temple Square during the year, and 500,000 attended the state fair. In the arts, centennial concerts in the Mormon Tabernacle featured prominent American vocalists, the centennial commission sponsored an art exhibit featuring the best of American painting, and a musical, "Promised Valley," composed by Crawford Gates, celebrated the Mormon entry into Salt Lake Valley.

Perhaps the most lasting feature of the centennial celebration was the dedication of the "This Is the Place Monument." Situated at the mouth of Emigration Canyon, the monument celebrates Utah's explorers, pioneers, and early builders. The state commissioned Mahonri M. Young, Brigham Young's grandson, who had earned a well-deserved national reputation for his artistic achievement, to sculpt the monument. President George Albert Smith of the LDS church dedicated the monument before an audience of 50,000 who came to memorialize the state's founders and to honor a nationally famous artist.

The only achievement of 1947 that might rival the dedication of the "This Is the Place" monument was the appointment of Maurice Abravanel, a native of Greece and a much sought-after conductor, as music director and conductor of the Utah Symphony. Begun in 1936 as the Utah Music Project, the symphony gave its first concert in 1940 at the University of Utah's Kingsbury Hall. Abravanel's vision spread much wider than a local audience in Salt Lake City, however, as he proposed to take the symphony and fine classical music to all the people of Utah, and to make the Utah Symphony into one of the premier musical organizations of the United States. Under Abravanel's direction, the symphony succeeded on both counts by presenting concerts in Utah's rural towns and in the great concert halls of the world.

The rapid influx of people during the war, coupled with the shortage of building materials and labor, left the city with a considerable housing shortage. Gordon Weggeland, Federal Housing Administration Director for Utah, estimated in January 1946 that Salt Lake City had a 6,000 unit housing deficit. With this in mind, Mayor Earl J. Glade appointed a committee headed by Melvin L. Dye, president of First Federal Savings and Loan, to coordinate priorities for meeting housing needs. Shortly thereafter, Mayor Glade expressed the hope that realtors could place ten new homes on the market each day. The same month, Arch G. Webb, executive secretary of the Utah chapter of the National Association of Home Builders, announced plans for the construction of 1,000 low-budget homes for veterans. Designed to rent for $30 to $40 per month, the homes could also be purchased with guaranteed loans. As a result of these activities, the value of building permits in 1946 nearly tripled those of 1944, and real estate sales exceeded the 1945 volume by forty-eight percent.

By the early 1950s, Salt Lake builders had met the housing deficit, and citizens faced a new problem of urban "dry rot." As developers constructed new housing units, they paid little attention to the city's central core. Many people searching for homes moved from the inner city to the newer sites in the city's fringe areas or in the suburbs, leaving the central city in stagnation. An editorial in the *Salt Lake Tribune* in November 1951 emphasized that Salt Lake's problem was not as serious as similar difficulties in cities like Boston, Chicago, or Cleveland, but the paper called for intensive urban planning to deal with the threat before it became insurmountable.

Unfortunately, between the end of World War II and 1960, Salt Lake City's business community did virtually nothing to improve the downtown area. The major exception was the First Security Bank building constructed at Fourth South and Main. It was, however, "the first major structure added to the Salt Lake City skyline in twenty-eight years," and further construction did not follow rapidly upon its heels. Nor were many buildings in the city's core renovated during the period. In September 1949, the city considered demolishing the old city hall at 120 East First South. A lovely Greek Revival structure like the Salt Lake Theatre, it had fallen into disuse and had been condemned in 1943. The county commission recommended a joint renovation project, but the commission refused to use public money to restore and maintain the building. They considered razing the structure, but protests from the Sons of the Utah Pioneers led them to recede from that position for the time being. In the 1960s, however, the building was demolished to provide space for new construction.

Given the backlog of capital improvements created by the war, the city had to construct sewers, roads, curbs, gutters, and water lines. The principal need was a new storm sewer system, which the city began in 1946. In general, local taxpayers financed the improvements, since the city administration under Mayors Earl J. Glade and Adiel F. Stewart shied away from accepting federal grants. The post-depression and post-war economy, they believed, could flourish without them.

Perhaps the most important long-range success was the improvement of the city's water supply and system. In 1953, largely through the efforts of Commissioner Grant Burbidge, the city began the construction of its first water treatment plants. It installed the first facilities on City Creek, in Big Cottonwood Canyon, and in Parley's Canyon. The latter plant was completed after 1959 when Burbidge left office. Beyond this, the city covered or replaced all the reservoirs to make them more sanitary. Two new concrete reservoirs built on the east bench were designed to blend in with the landscape. Moreover, the city extended water lines in order to meet the needs of "clean" industries like Litton and Sperry. To reimburse the city for water facilities for new subdivisions, the commission required developers to pay the cost of extending water and sewer lines from existing locations. The developers, however, got their money back from homeowners who hooked up to the new lines.

Burbidge reorganized the water department by hiring new employees, retraining those already in office to operate the new system, and installing new equipment. Relying upon the expertise of Grant Borg of the University of Utah's Engineering Department, he inaugurated classes to train waterworks employees in the operation of the modern system. New meters allowed the department to determine the condition and needs of the system without making trips to physically inspect the reservoirs and other facilities. He had radios installed in all water department cars so emergency crews could be sent by a dispatcher at headquarters to deal with immediate problems.

Moreover, Burbidge strove to improve the city's water and insure an adequate supply for the future. Following city policy, he purchased the culinary water stock of new subdivisions carved from farm land, and installed water systems to furnish their needs. In addition, the city continued to hold rights to deep wells that, drawing upon the Salt Lake Valley aquifer, provided additional water during the heavy demand of summer months. It was also during Burbidge's administration that the aqueduct from Deer Creek was completed, as were feeder lines designed to conduct Deer Creek water to the city's north bench and industrial sections.

Through these policies, the city acquired rights to a great deal more water than its residents could possibly use. Since the Salt Lakers had paid for the water rights and the delivery system, the commission felt quite justified in selling water to other cities and unincorporated areas at one and a half times the amount it charged local users. In a number of cases, earnings of the water department went to pay for other city needs.

Another major improvement of city facilities was the construction of a new air terminal. Begun in the late 1950s, it was designed to serve the city's needs until the early 1970s, when, the commission realized, the airport would need additional expansion to meet growing needs. A tax on aviation fuel used by the airlines, basic charges levied on the flights, and a federal grant of about $1 million paid the cost of construction.

Other important changes were implemented under Parks commissioners Fred Tedesco and L.C. Romney. Tedesco, a former professional football player, worked particularly on the development of the Hogle Zoo in the mouth of Emigration Canyon and expanded the city's parks and golf courses. Romney developed the Rose Park golf course in the northwest part of the city both for recreation and to provide a buffer between residential and industrial districts in that part of the city. In addition, he began the development of the Parley's Canyon golf course, which brought him into conflict with Mayor J. Bracken Lee in the early 1960s. Both Tedesco and Romney worked to develop Little League baseball, tennis courts, and professional baseball in the city. Tedesco also served as the prime mover in the construction of Derks field, which became the home of a succession of minor league baseball teams in the Pioneer League and later in the Pacific Coast League.

Most importantly, Romney, in cooperation with the city and county commission, conceived the idea of creating a permanent barrier between the largely industrial section in the western part of the city and the primarily residential area further to the east. Recognizing that the interstate highway system conceived by the Eisenhower administration would bisect the valley in some way, they decided it could serve a dual purpose. In inaugurating the system, the state decided to construct the interstate through the more expensive urban areas first and leave the less expensive rural highways to the last. In planning for the highway through Salt Lake Valley, the city and county commissioners agreed to open a green belt about two thousand feed wide, extending the full length of the valley, through which the interstate could be built and which would serve as a physical barrier between the two sections of Salt Lake City. That goal was not completely achieved, however; many homes remained on the west side, and the residents of this section still constitute a significant portion of the city's population.

Freeway construction was only part of a larger problem of public transportation which the city had to address. As the war ended and restrictions on the sale of gasoline, tires, and automobiles were lifted, the streets soon filled with more cars than ever before. Moreover, increased affluence allowed families who had never previously owned cars to purchase them, and many bought two or more. Traffic accidents increased in 1946 as automobile use in Salt Lake City rose fifty-two percent above the 1945 level.

The rise in use of automobiles corresponded in Salt Lake City, as nationally, with a decline in public transit. Between 1945 and 1960, mass transit ridership dropped nationally from 19 billion to 7.4 billion passengers. In Salt Lake City, ridership dropped from 33 million passengers in 1946 to 12 million in 1960, a decline of nearly sixty-four percent. During the same period, Salt Lake City Lines decreased its service by about one-third, from 6.2 million to 4 million miles per year, and the company raised its rates. Salt Lake City Lines was a privately franchised company, organized in 1944 after an antitrust suit forced Utah Power and Light Company to sell Utah Light and Traction Company, a wholly owned subsidiary. By 1960 the bus company, under pressure of declining earnings, allowed equipment and service to deteriorate and hired drivers it could secure at low wage levels. By 1960, the average bus in the fleet was fourteen years old and the newest more than three years old.

Service continued to deteriorate until 1968, when the city signed an agreement with Union Street and Railway Company to guarantee continued operation. At the same time, the city agreed to provide a $210,000 subsidy over a two-year study period. The company agreed to acquire Salt Lake City Line's rights and, in addition, to give the city government an option to purchase the bus line after two years and operate it as a public transit system. In the meantime, the city lobbied with the legislature to secure authority for urban areas to form transit districts to meet local needs. In 1969 the legislature passed a bill approving the change, and the cities of Salt Lake, Murray, Midvale, South Salt Lake, and Sandy agreed to establish the Utah Transit Authority to operate a public system. In 1970, Salt Lake, Davis, and Weber counties joined UTA. In the meantime, Salt Lake City acquired Union's rolling stock, partly with the help of an urban mass transit grant from the U.S. Department of Transporation. In 1974, the state legislature approved funding of mass transit systems through an optional quarter-cent per dollar sales tax increase, which the voters in Salt Lake approved.

It had almost become a tradition for the city police department to have its problems and, not surprisingly, in the post-war era they often had to do with vice. On the night of April 11, 1949, two officers from the city's anti-vice unit, disguised as sailors, arrested five persons: two men for bootlegging liquor, one man for pimping for prostitutes, and a woman for "vagrancy." After learning about the arrests, Mayor Glade expressed shock at this use of subterfuge, and Scott M. Matheson, then United States District Attorney for Utah, declared that the unauthorized use of armed services uniforms "is a violation of federal laws." Public Safety Commissioner L.C. Romney said the police department did not consult with him about the action, and officers of Utah veterans organizations registered a protest against the illegal use of the uniforms.

In response to the protest, Captain Golden Haight, who supervised the anti-vice unit, said that the action had been taken at the request of military authorities. Venereal disease had become an increasing problem in the city, in part because of post-war apathy, and navy security officers had requested police assistance in controlling its spread among military personnel. Matheson agreed not to prosecute because of the intent of the officers, and the *Salt Lake Tribune* praised the officers "for ingenuity and imagination while hoping that the next time they can successfully use other means of artifice."

Vice often seemed to be a matter of contention in the city. In December 1949, the Salt Lake County LDS Stakes' law observance and enforcement committee released a nine-page document charging twenty-three taverns in Salt Lake City, Salt Lake County, and Davis County with permitting gambling or selling beer and cigarettes to minors. Mayor Glade called a special meeting of the city commission for Friday, December 9 to "get to the roots" of the matter. After an inquiry, the commissioners voiced confidence in the police department. They essentially sidestepped the allegations by concluding that the city had too many beer dispensaries and that some taverns were inadequately lighted. They resolved to take steps to overcome the problems, whatever they might be.

Problems with the police department continued. Often, they resulted as much from a loss of public confidence as from positive signs of corruption or other deficiencies. In some cases, they were attributed to inefficiency in the department and in its management at the commission level. On October 20, 1951 the *Deseret News* published an open letter to Mayor Glade in response to a "continuous series of sexual attacks [numbering nearly 200 since early June] on Salt Lake City women and girls" and "youthful hoodlumism," which seemed rampant in the city. The letter called upon Glade and others in the commission to provide funding to adequately staff the police department and pay its officers to "carry out the desperately necessary duties of their job."

The next day, Glade reported a program he hoped would "check the rising tide of hoodlumism in Salt Lake City." While the plan included a thorough exploration of the issue with the commission and with heads of the police department, it did not include the promise of additional funding for improved service. Mayor Glade seemed to have sensed that, while most citizens of Salt Lake said they wanted better police protection, most were unwilling, at the time, to pay the cost in higher taxes needed to provide it.

Under Mayor Adiel Stewart, however, the city tried with notable success to improve the professional competence of the police department. In 1955, the city commissioned a study of the department by a New York consulting firm which found "low morale, inefficiency, lack of manpower, inadequate technical equipment and loss of public confidence." Little seems to have been done with the study during the remaining months of Glade's administration, but after seeking the advice of FBI director J. Edgar Hoover, Stewart recommended that the city hire W. Cleon Skousen, who after sixteen years as an FBI agent had left to accept a position as director of public services and assistant professor of speech at Brigham Young University. Taking a leave of absence from BYU, Skousen was given a free hand in reorganizing the department.

Reports indicated that while Skousen had some problems, he succeeded in modernizing the department and creating what *Time* magazine called "a model police force." In 1958, the *Tribune* became upset because Skousen opposed its publication of a report of an investigation of a narcotics ring at the Utah State Prison. At the same time an editorial in the *Deseret News* praised Skousen's administration for fighting narcotics and for vice enforcement.

Such things as improvements in the water system, development of recreation facilities, and professionalizing the police department cost money. As a result, the city's budget increased over the period. In 1940, it stood at $3.4 million, by 1948 it had grown to $6.6 million, and in 1961 it stood at $14.5 million.

Salt Lake City faced other problems in this era, some of them caused by Mother Nature. Early in 1952 a rapidly melting snowpack, together with the city's failure to provide adequate water control facilities, resulted in some of the most serious flooding in its history. Water filled Mountain Dell Reservoir, Emigration Canyon creek, and City Creek, then deluged streets in the eastern section of town, filled the storm sewers, and poured down Thirteenth South to the Jordan River. There, the water caused additional problems since the river channel had not been cleared of obstructions. The flood cost the city more than a million dollars, though efficient work by city crews saved an additional $5 to $10 million in property damage.

Perennial controversies erupted over the mill levy and over methods of taxation in the city. Grocers, for instance, objected in 1947 to a one-fifth of one percent tax on retail sales. Some citizens raised concerns about the rates charged for residential and industrial water, and the city administration lobbied for larger shares of certain state tax revenues, such as the state liquor and highway taxes. In 1951 the city considered then rejected a proposal to inaugurate a city income tax, and the proper use of sales tax revenue presented a constant problem.

Between 1953 and 1955, Mayor Glade and Utah governor J. Bracken Lee engaged in a running feud over the city's budget. In December 1953, Lee criticized Glade for extravagance in replacing a judge who resigned, in spite of the law which required Glade to do so. Lee also complained at the shortage of funds for libraries and other services while city employees received salary increases. In 1955 Lee vetoed a bill allowing a special four mill levy to finance construction of water purification and sewer treatment facilities. The legislature overrode the veto, but in the meantime Glade had accused Lee of breaking faith with the people of Salt Lake City.

Throughout the 1950s, the city administration found itself under pressure from at least two sets of middle-class critics. On the one hand were those who insisted upon a higher level of services, especially in public safety, and greater expenditures for capital improvements. On the other were those who believed the policies of the commission were extravagant.

In spite of these competing pressures, the city operated under a very tight budget and managed to maintain a relatively high level of fiscal integrity, though it failed to satisfy either faction completely. The city had sunk heavily into debt in the 1930s, but during the Marcus administration the commission had established a debt retirement schedule which it continued to maintain through the mid-1950s. In 1949, for instance, the city's net debt stood at $5.98 per resident, which was the lowest of the West's twelve major cities with populations over 100,000. At the same time, its tax burden stood at $17.06, fourth from the bottom of the same list of cities. By the late 1950s, however, the city was in the throes of an argument over the budget. Critics charged that the commissioners were running in the red, but city officials claimed the budget was in balance and they could meet current operating expenses. Nevertheless, the budget became an issue in the 1959 election. On balance, it seems probable that the city was actually in relatively good financial shape, but was unable to meet its capital needs. Salt Lake carried a Triple A bond rating throughout the period.

Despite all the controversies over the city's budget after overcoming the disclocations of the immediate post-war period, the people of Salt Lake City lived quite well. An article in *Business Week* in 1950 indicated that the life style of the majority of the people was satisfactory, if generally quite conservative. Liquor did not flow as freely in Salt Lake as in many other cities, and family values predominated. Even though per capita income stood below that of the United States and the Mountain West, sixty-nine percent of the people owned their own homes and children had a good chance of going to college.

Moreover, the college education they could receive in Salt Lake City became increasingly competitive with the best available in other parts of the country. As early as 1948, the University of Utah's medical school, for instance, had begun to receive national recognition, in spite of the fact that it had been established only in 1944.

Thus, Salt Lakers enjoyed a relatively satisfactory life style in spite of lower than average per capita income. This was due in part to the fact that while the birth rate was higher among Salt Lake's Mormon majority than among other groups in the nation, these same Latter-day Saints insisted that a good proportion of their income go for education and cultural amenities.

Large families and long lives seemed a significant feature of Salt Lake Mormons. In 1947, the post-war high point, the birth rate among Latter-day Saints in Salt Lake City actually reached 38 per 1,000 population which was more than 11 points higher than the national average. By 1950 the rate among Salt Lake Mormons had declined to 35.3, which was equal to the 1910 rate, but was still significantly above the national level. Moreover, the Latter-day Saint death rate in the city stood a point below the national rate, and was substantially lower than the death rate for Salt Lake City gentiles, which was slightly higher than the national average.

Over the long run, these patterns posed less of a problem for Salt Lake City than for other areas of the country since the religious composition of Salt Lake began to change in the post-war period. During the 1930s, Mormons and gentiles had left the city in approximately equal numbers. It is estimated that nearly 3,000 Mormons and the same number of gentiles moved out during the decade. During the period from 1940 to 1949, an estimated 1,200 Mormons moved out, while nearly 4,500 gentiles moved in. During the 1950s, both groups migrated out of the city, but the Mormons left at a significantly higher rate (19,300 vs. 12,200). The city's population increased by only 7,000 during the decade and natural increase made up most of the growth. Thus, while Latter-day Saints in Salt Lake City experienced a higher birth rate, a higher percentage of non-Mormon familes remained in the city than did their Latter-day Saint neighbors. As a result, Salt Lake City became less Mormon than the average of the state as a whole, and the higher Mormon birth rate posed less of a burden to city taxpayers than it might otherwise have. than it might otherwise have.

By the early 1950s, the impact of television and changing reading habits had brought the city's daily newspapers into a precarious condition. In 1949, Salt Lake City businessmen inaugurated two television stations: KDYL and KSL. In 1947, the *Tribune* stood in first place in circulation, with more than 28,600 subscriptions, the *Telegram*, the *Tribune's* evening counterpart, stood second with 20,000 and the *Deseret News* followed with 12,500. As television drew more people to the tube instead of the printed word, a furious battle for subscriptions followed, and when the dust had cleared in 1952, all three papers were in serious financial difficulty. Both the *News* and the *Telegram* were losing money and were kept alive only by the largess of the LDS church and the *Tribune*. To control some of the bloodletting, the *News* agreed to purchase the *Telegram*, leaving the city with only one afternoon paper.

That solved only part of the problem, since under the existing arrangement both papers had to maintain separate printing plants. The two papers addressed this difficulty on August 12, 1952 by the organization of the Newspaper Agency Corporation. The agreement provided for joint business, production, and distribution operations with separate publishers, owners, and editorial policy. Although the Justice Department considered instituting an anti-trust suit against the corporation, federal attorneys dropped the matter after documents demonstrated the economic necessity for the reorganization. Under this arrangement, the two newspapers prospered, offering two independent editorial voices to the people of the Intermountain West. In a sense, the agreement signaled the formal end to an era which had in fact long since ceased to have relevance for any but a few fanatical anti-Mormons and embattled Mormon zealots.

This is not to say that social problems did not exist in Salt Lake City. Perhaps the most serious lay in discrimination against blacks. A Utah anti-miscegenation law interdicted marriage between blacks and whites from 1898 until its repeal in 1963. Laws, local ordinances, and "gentlemen's agreements" restricted the access of blacks to public accommodations. During the 1940s and 1950s, nationally famous entertainers like Marian Anderson, Harry Belafonte, and Ella Fitzgerald were either refused accommodations at the Hotel Utah, or allowed to stay there only under unusual restrictions. Lagoon Amusement Park and Rainbow Rendezvous dance hall refused admission to blacks until Robert E. Freed integrated the resorts in the late 1940s. In 1948, the Youth Council of the Salt Lake Chapter of the National Association for the Advancement of Colored People (NAACP) protested against the refusal of the management at the city and county building lunch counter to serve blacks. The city commission agreed at that time to require the counter to serve anyone not personally objectionable, presumably by reason of demeanor rather than race.

Perhaps the greatest difficulties resulted from attitudes which the majority of whites in Salt Lake shared with other Caucasians throughout the nation. In 1939, Sheldon Brewster, a local realtor, presented to the city commission a petition with a thousand signatures asking that it pass an ordinance restricting blacks to one residential area. In a sense, the petition called for the formal creation of a black ghetto in the city, but the council ignored it. Brewster also tried to get blacks voluntarily to agree to sell their homes and live in one location, but he likewise failed in that effort. In response to Brewster's machinations, blacks marched to the state capitol building in protest. Real estate companies, on the other hand, circumvented the movement for integration by inserting restrictive covenants into contracts prohibiting sale to "any person not of the Caucasian race." Such covenants were ruled illegal in 1948.

While Salt Lake whites shared the attitudes of others throughout the United States, many justified their racial prejudice by reference to the religious practices of the dominant Mormon church. Since Brigham Young's time, the LDS church, while admitting blacks to membership, had denied them the right to hold the priesthood. This practice, and with it any religious basis for discrimination, was ended in 1978 when President Spencer W. Kimball of the LDS church announced a revelation opening the priesthood to all worthy men. In the meantime, court decisions and federal and state legislation had removed the legal basis for racial discrimination in Salt Lake City.

In many ways, the politics of city government were the least important developments of the post-war years. While many problems arose, Mayor Earl J. Glade really dominated the news to the exclusion of other members of the commission and other city political figures. At the same time, however, the real power in the city lay not in the commission but with the extra-political triumvirate of Gus P. Backman of the chamber of commerce, David O. McKay, president of the Church of Jesus Christ of Latter-day Saints, and John F. Fitzpatrick, publisher of the *Salt Lake Tribune*.

Gustave P. "Gus" Backman was born in Salt Lake City in 1891. After working in the family business, G.H. Backman and Sons, abstractors and attorney, he moved to ZCMI where he became manager. In 1930, he resigned to become secretary—later executive secretary—of the Salt Lake chamber of commerce. Backman took what in the 1930s was a rather moribund organization that had grown out of the former

John F. Fitzpatrick, Long- *Gus P. Backman, Long-* *David O. McKay, Presi-*
time Editor of the Salt *time Executive Secretary* *dent of the Church of*
Lake Tribune, and promi- *of the Salt Lake Chamber* *Jesus Christ of Latter-*
nent Civic Leader. Cour- *of Commerce.* *day Saints and Promi-*
tesy, Utah State Historical *nent Civic Leader.*
Society.

Salt Lake Commercial Club, and made it into an enormously powerful force in Salt Lake City. At the same time, he became an influential figure in Salt Lake and Utah affairs, serving on a great number of public bodies during the 1930s and 1940s. It was Backman, an inactive Mormon, who served as the public face of the triumvirate, and who represented the business community. After the three discussed matters, Backman would often represent their united concerns to members of the city commission. The city fathers and many others in the city recognized and appreciated this relationship because it served as a means of reconciling various interests in the community.

Second in this informal group was David O. McKay, prophet, seer, and revelator, and president of the Mormon church. Born in 1893 at Huntsville, he served a mission for the LDS church, graduated from the University of Utah, and served as president of the Weber Stake Academy (later Weber State College) in Ogden prior to his call as an Apostle in 1906. Sustained as Second Counselor to Heber J. Grant in 1934, he served in the same position under George Albert Smith before himself ascending to the presidency of the church in 1951. He was also active in community affairs in Salt Lake City and Utah during the 1930s and 1940s.

The third member of the triumvirate was John F. Fitzpatrick. Born in Pottsville, Pennsylvania in 1887, he grew up in Burlington, Iowa, where his father, a railroad engineer, had moved after being blacklisted for union activity. After working in railroading for some time, Fitzpatrick took a position as secretary to Thomas Kearns. Publisher of the *Tribune* from 1924 until his death in 1960, Fitzpatrick represented the Catholic and thus the gentile community in the triumvirate. Significantly then, the triumvirate consisted of a Mormon, an inactive Mormon, and a gentile.

During the years of heated battle between the *Tribune* and the LDS church, Ambrose N. McKay (no relation), general manager of the *Tribune*, exempted David O. McKay and Anthony W. Ivins from his paper's attacks on the church's leadership. Fitzpatrick continued the warm relationship, but he was never close to the Mormon leader until he was appointed to the executive committee of the Utah Centennial Commission, of which McKay was chairman, and which planned the 1947 centennial observance. The two of them began meeting with Backman on Tuesday mornings to discuss commission business, and after 1947 continued with the discussion of community and business affairs.

Representative of the chamber of commerce, and as such a lobbyist of sorts, Backman could approach members of the city commission in what the three perceived as the interest of the community. In some cases, members of the commission consulted, through Backman, with others of the triumvirate. Beyond this, McKay and Fitzpatrick controlled the editorial policy of the two major dailies in the state and represented the two principal religious groups as well.

The major problem in dealing with the activities of this triumvirate is in getting specific information on its activities. For that reason, this study has dealt principally with the surface manifestations of its leadership by considering the activities of the commission, policies relating to economic and social matters, and political campaigns between various commission and mayoral candidates. Interviews with former city officials and printed sources indicate that the three consulted together frequently and that city officials consulted with them on matters of importance. It should not be thought, however, that all this means that the LDS church controlled the city. It indicates, rather, considerable power and a high degree of amiable cooperation on the part of conservative religious, social, and business groups in the city.

Dominating the news during the period was the city's only three-term mayor, Earl J. Glade. Apparently learning from previous mayors, Glade shunned the public safety commissioner's post and opted instead for finance and public relations. These were logical positions for the former businessman and radio official, and Glade made a good record and presented an impressive public image. A fine public speaker, recognized for his integrity, honesty, and good administrative ability, he led the fight with the legislature for more adequate financing of urban needs through a larger share of the liquor and road funds.

After remaining rather closemouthed about his future plans, Glade ran again for mayor in 1947. Ab Jenkins, whom Glade had defeated in 1943, entered the race once more. Jenkins charged Glade with extravagant increases in the city's budget, then called for additional urban improvements such as a viaduct to the west side and a new civic center. Glade's personal magnetism seems to have carried the day, and he won the election by a greater margin than in 1943 (24,400 to 17,400).

In the other 1947 commission races, incumbents L.C. Romney and David A. Affleck were also reelected. Elmer G. Thomas, a retired army colonel, attacked Romney, who had served as public safety commissioner, charging him with being soft on vice and calling for exclusive use of public parking meter revenue for police services. Newell Knight, an inspector in the city waterworks department, called for a reduction in taxes by putting business regulation into practice. He also insisted upon improvements in the water department. David Affleck, who had made a good record there through expansion of water facilities, had little trouble in defeating Knight. It is perhaps an indication of the undesirability of the public safety position that before running for reelection Romney moved to the parks department seat after the incumbent Fred Tedesco retired from the council.

In the 1949 commission race, incumbent Ben E. Lingenfelter, who had been appointed to the commission on Tedesco's retirement, ran for reelection. Three other candidates ran, including Joe L. Christensen, a former junior high school teacher and coach and director of the Salt Lake County Recreation Department. Lingenfelter had been an athlete at Drake University and assistant football coach at the University of Utah. Neither had much difficulty in defeating William W. Horne or Mrs. C.L. Jack. Newspaper reports indicated a lackluster campaign with no real issues.

Even though city elections were still theoretically nonpartisan, both the major political parties took an active interest in them. When David Affleck died in office, for instance, the commissioner chose Grant Burbidge to replace him, in part because he represented the Republican party as Affleck did. Romney, a Democrat, received the active support of the Democratic party. Glade, an active Democrat with considerable independent support, got help from both parties.

All accounts of the 1951 election indicate that interest had reached a low ebb. Glade ran unopposed for reelection as mayor and Burbidge and Romney with their strong backing and position as incumbents had little trouble defeating Wendell L. Cottrell and Louis E. Holley. Charges of hoodlumism and youth crime were thrown about, but since Romney and Burbidge held the parks and water seats, such allegations had little effect.

By 1955, Mayor Glade had nearly completed an unprecedented three terms in office and seemed to many virtually unbeatable. He was quite popular, and knowledgeable political analysts saw him as an easy winner. He had maintained good relationships with the LDS church, the chamber of commerce, and the *Tribune*. Neither political party wanted to oppose him.

Nevertheless, he had some liabilities. The city had failed to meet some of its capital needs. In 1952 flood revealed the lack of an active watershed control program and inadequate storm drains due to budgetary pressures. In spite of his charisma, Glade found it difficult to conduct an active political campaign. While he spoke very well, he seemed to feel it beneath his dignity to contact people and ask them to vote for him. Moreover, city budgetary pressures led him to alienate city employees. Late in his third term city employees came before the commission asking for higher wages, but instead of sympathizing with them and pleading city poverty, or playing the conciliator, Glade confronted a representative of the fire department with the comment that he did not look underfed and then told him if he didn't "like working for the city, why don't you find employment elsewhere."

Glade and his supporters took reelection for granted, but Adiel Stewart, then serving as a county commissioner, organized an effective campaign to replace the three-term incumbent. Faulting Glade on his failure to set up an adequate capital improvements budget, and pointing to the lack of business expansion during the 1950s, Stewart surprised most political observers by defeating Glade at the polls. Commissioners Burbidge and Romney had little trouble securing reelection.

Stewart exhibited a much different political style than Glade. A man of strongly held views, he was much more confrontational. Less interested in public relations than good management, Stewart often expressed himself off the cuff in public and in commission meetings. Because of his interest in capital improvements, he pressed for the construction of a convention center and, of course, he was largely responsible for hiring Cleon Skousen and modernizing the police department. His penchant for effective and efficient administration eventually led him to retire as mayor after one term. In August 1959, Stewart announced that he could not "in good conscience run" again "under the commission form of government." By then he had become convinced that modernization of city government required a change in the system. In spite of his stated views, he did file for reelection, but was swamped in the primary.

Stewart was not the first to raise questions about the adequacy of the commission form of government. Since the economic difficulties of the 1930s and the Jenkins's survey of 1941, many citizens had wondered about the efficiency of the system. In late September 1955, scarcely more than a month before the election, a committee consisting of Burtram A. Weight, executive vice-president of the Salt Lake Real Estate Board; Fullmer H. Latter, secretary-treasurer of the Teamsters local; Esther Landa of the League of Women Voters; J.D. Williams, professor of political science at the University of Utah; and David S. Turner, a labor organizer for the the Sheet Metal Workers, came with a petition asking that the city commission place the question of changing the form of government on the ballot. The proposal had been drafted initially by Williams and M. Walker Wallace, a professional city planner and marketing consultant. At the time, the commission refused to submit the proposal since a majority thought the electorate would not have time to study the issue.

The question of changing the form of government, called "home rule" by its supporters, arose for essentially two reasons. First, proponents argued the ineffectiveness of the commission form of government. They pointed to problems in the city's civil service system, the haphazard budget-making process, the failure of the city to plan for necessary capital improvements, and ineffective police services.

Secondly, those who prepared the petition sought to challenge the city's current power structure. Realizing that actual political power rested with the Backman, McKay, Fitzpatrick triumvirate, they argued that the commission seemed to address problems raised by the business community, property owners, and supporters of strict personal morality. Labor seemed unrepresented in the town, as did other interest groups such as women and those concerned with urban planning.

Nevertheless, those supporting the change realized that they stood little chance of success without support of the business community, especially those prominent in the chamber of commerce, since Gus Backman had opposed the initial proposal. In addition, the proponents had to convince many in the city that theirs was not simply another proposal for a city manager system, and that what they really wanted was efficient government—probably through a strong mayor-council system. As a result of effective lobbying, the chamber finally endorsed the home rule proposal and, much to the chagrin of early labor supports, Joseph Rosenblatt, a prominent industrialist, became chairman of the home rule committee.

With this expanded base, the proponents asked the city commission in August 1957 to place the proposal on the November ballot. After considering the matter for some time, the commission again denied the request, and the supporters had to mount a last-minute petition drive to get the matter before the voters.

Opposition formed quite rapidly. The city's Apartment House Association, led by Paul Roberts, opposed home rule because they feared a city manager system and urban renewal would follow. Various conservative groups followed. City employees feared the loss of their jobs. Labor, which at first supported the proposal, wound up in opposition, fearing the loss of its already diminished power. Perhaps the most significant opposition developed within the leadership of the Salt Lake County Democratic party organization. Out of power in Salt Lake County since 1948, the Democrats apparently feared a loss of influence in Salt Lake City. Public relations consultant Jennings Phillips mounted an effective opposition, aimed at the Domocratic and labor constituency.

Supporters had a much thinner organization. Leaders in the Republican party and businessmen principally concerned with efficient government seem to have made up the largest block. Progressive forces interested in urban planning and participatory democracy, including people like Walker Wallace and J.D. Williams and groups like the League of Women Voters, provided the remaining active support.

Opponents of home rule feared a change to the city manager system, but ironically this was no real option. In addition to voting on home rule itself, voters chose members of the commission that, if the proposal passed, would prepare the new charter. Of those candidates for the charter commission who expressed themselves, most favored a strong mayor-council system and most of the rest wanted a modification of the existing commission form.

Home rule proponents really had no issue or incident which engendered strong public support for their cause. The League of Women Voters talked about the American tradition of home rule, and advertisements emphasized the need for capital expenditures for a fire station and sewage treatment, the problem of the city's debt, and the divided executive responsibility inherent in the commission system. None of these points seemed convincing.

Opponents capitalized on the absence of a strong feeling against the commission system. In spite of the contention of the home rule proponents, the city carried a Triple A credit rating. The commission had kept the city solvent and had staved off inordinantly large tax increases, and opponents emphasized that the city already had home rule since commission members were responsible to Salt Lake voters. To most voters the home rule proponents seemed confused, and what's more, they had demonstrated no need for a change.

On November 5, 1957 the voters soundly defeated the home rule proposal while electing an absolute majority favoring home rule to the now superfluous charter commission. The proposal carried among upper

*LaVern Watts Parmely,
Former LDS Primary Pres-
ident and civic leader.
Courtesy, Brigham Young
University.*

*Belle S. Spafford, Former
LDS Relief Society Presi-
dent and national women's
leader. Courtesy, Deseret
News.*

income groups in the city's east side, but lost soundly in the lower and lower-middle income groups. The conclusions of one home rule proponent that the change would come when the LDS church, the Salt Lake *Tribune*, and the chamber of commerce favored it, flies in the face of the lineup in the 1957 vote. In fact, the LDS church maintained a sort of quiet support, and both the *Tribune* and the chamber of commerce endorsed home rule.

It seems probable that the majority of lower-and middle-class citizens believed the commission system served them well. More concerned about jobs and tax rates than about a new fire station or a sewage treatment plant, they identified with the existing commission rather than with the coalition of upper-middle and upper-class progressives and businessmen who pushed for change. In the absence of a major scandal, such an alteration of governmental structure seemed unlikely to appeal to these voters.

The home rule election reveals something also about the nature both of participatory democracy and influence politics. Given any considerable support, it is possible to get an initiative on the ballot. After it gets there, however, proponents need a groundswell of public indignation to secure its adoption against the natural tendency of people who are moderately well off to fear that change may work against their interests. Beyond this, a powerful triumvirate like the Backman, McKay, Fitzpatrick group will find it easier to influence elected representatives in the commission or city departments than individual voters, especially in the absence of a *cause célèbre*.

In retrospect, the late 1940s and 1950s seem to have constituted a transition period for Salt Lake City. Citizens had not yet reached a consensus on the future direction of the city. Unwilling to commit themselves to the sort of capital expansion either in the business community or the public sector required to make the city into a first-rate attraction for new business, or to meet their own needs, Salt Lakers marked time. Suspicious of change, they seemed unwilling either to take the drastic measures characteristic of the Lee administration or inaugurate the progressive management seen during the Garn and Wilson years. Though the city began losing population during the 1950s, no one seemed to know what to do to deal with the problem. Perhaps the ironic results of the 1957 home rule election characterize the era best: while vetoing the creation of a home rule commission, voters elected a majority to that commission in favor of home rule.

LDS Church complex, downtown Salt Lake City. Prominently seen are: the Tabernacle, the Salt Lake Temple, Hotel Utah (beehive tower on top), Old Church Office Building, the New Church Administration Building (completed 1972). In the background is the Church-owned Deseret Gymnasium. In the foreground is the Kennecott Copper Company Building. Courtesy, Utah State Historical Society.

272

10

The Changing Face of a Mature City, 1960–1983

The administration of Mayors Glade and Stewart constituted a transitional period from stagnation to growth as government and the people adjusted to the new world emerging after World War II. During the twenty years after 1960, many expectations of the immediate post-war period became reality, as the city witnessed enormous changes in its economy, society, and appearance. The effort to reform the structure of city government succeeded, and new business brought not only continued prosperity but also a change from defense industry to service and highly technological enterprises. City planning became more effective than it had been for generations as new buildings, modern architectural style, and urban redevelopment changed the face of the central city. At the same time, the people of the city adopted a new awareness of the rich cultural heritage they bore, and they preserved beautiful and culturally significant buildings, often in the face of powerful resistance. These and other accomplishments reflected the industry and civic pride of Salt Lakers, and helped make it an attractive place for new business and new people.

Like other cities, Salt Lake also continued to experience problems of urban sprawl as many people and businesses moved to the suburbs, leaving a decaying inner city. This, in fact, became one of the chief challenges for the new generation during the 1970s and 1980s. As the suburbs increasingly became bedroom communities for people employed in the city, such things as transportation, coordination with the county on government services, and effective planning for urban renewal presented new problems to community leaders.

At the same time, some things did not change. Political controversy did not abate, vice did not disappear, colorful and effective civic leaders continued to emerge, economic problems continued, and in the city's west side, pockets of poverty remained. Moreover, the Mormon church remained a dominant force, both in the consciousness of Salt Lake residents and in the national public image. The Tabernacle Choir still broadcast weekly from "The Crossroads of the West," and Temple Square, with its new tourist center featuring automated displays and messages, was still the most frequently visited site in Utah, attracting millions of people annually.

The election of 1959 brought to the mayor's chair of Salt Lake City perhaps the only authentic political maverick Utah has produced. Ultra-conservative, politically independent, economy-minded, and feisty, J. Bracken Lee had formerly served as mayor of Price, governor of Utah, and candidate for the United States Senate. These characteristics made him perhaps the city's most colorful mayor. Lee received a majority of the vote in the primary and outpolled Bruce Jenkins to win handily in the general election in November. Lee won by fifty-four percent of the popular vote in spite of Jenkins' endorsement by a citizen's group and prominent Republicans and Democrats.

J. Bracken Lee, Mayor of Salt Lake City, Governor of Utah, and Political Maverick.

During the campaign, both candidates quite candidly discussed their perception of the future of the city and the role of government. The issues they addressed clearly reflected the problems and controversies of earlier years. Jenkins promised to work for a change to the mayor-council form of government, while Lee favored continuation of the commission form under the leadership of "someone who has a hand on the rudder and who is responsible to the people." Jenkins thought an increase in local sales taxes might be necessary to build needed capital improvements. Lee promised he would approve no new taxes. He called for a referendum on a proposed bond issue for such improvements as a civic auditorium, sewage treatment plant, and sewer line. The bonds, he said, could be retired from available revenues without new taxes. Lee's strategy of talking in generalities, adroitly avoiding commitments on specific issues, and calling for economy seem to have been effective. His blunt manner and his uncompromising attitude toward economy appealed most to the lower-middle and middle classes in Salt Lake City.

Lee moved immediately to try to implement several economic reforms. He tried, at first unsuccessfully, to unseat Commissioner Theodore I. Geurts as finance commissioner; he also tried to place public safety under the entire commission rather than under a single commissioner. He failed there too, and the commission appointed him as public safety commissioner. He secured approval for a number of economy measures, including abolition of the post of city public relations director, placing a moritorium on salary increases of $100 per month previously granted to city employees, and opposing the use of sales tax revenues for routine rather than capital expenditures. He recommended the release of nearly 240 city employees of more than sixty-five years of age. Through these and other measures he expected to save the city more than $1 million per year. He also opposed completing the golf course in Parley's Canyon, which he characterized as a facility designed for a privileged group rather than for the "general welfare of the people."

Lee's economy measures did not succeed completely and did not sit well with all in the city government. Though exact figures are in dispute, the city government continued to run a deficit in its regular budget during 1960. Conrad B. Harrison, appointed to the commission in place of Geurts in June, argued the need to increase salaries in the police department and suggested that the city borrow money from the presumably separate capital improvements budget to balance the regular city budget. A transfer of $350,000 left the city with a surplus of $259,000 in 1960. Lee opposed the salary increases and thought the borrowing unwise, but the other commissioners overrode him.

Still, the budgetary conditions were not satisfactory. The city had achieved a balanced budget through what the *Salt Lake Tribune* called a "financial yo-yo game." Eventually, it had to repay the capital improvements budget for the amount borrowed.

It was clear that Salt Lake City needed some basic fiscal reform. Though it still carried a Triple A bond rating, the necessity for borrowing from the capital improvements fund to balance the budget did not augur well for the future, and the city did not seem to have good control over its income and expenditures.

Help came from Fred M. Oliver, of the accounting firm of Haskins and Sells. The 1925 revision of city budget procedures had become outdated by the 1950s and Oliver, working for the Utah Municipal League and with the assistance of attorney A.M. Fergo, drafted an act revising the budget procedures for Utah cities. Passed by the legislature in 1961, the Uniform Municipal Fiscal Procedures Act prohibited expenditures in excess of appropriations and established orderly procedures for financing capital improvements.

In spite of Lee's opposition—he hated "consultants" and "experts"—the commission voted to hire Oliver as a fiscal consultant to prepare the 1961 budget. The budget was extremely tight, and the city was forced in 1961 to borrow money from the capital improvements account again to purchase a fleet of police cars. In the long run, however, the new budget procedures, Lee's penchant for economy, and the financial acumen of Fred Oliver put the city back in the black.

Lee's economy drive alone would not have been enough. Lee tended to shoot from the hip, but as Conrad Harrison indicated, the city had to plan its long-range budgetary needs, not simply rely on quick fixes. Fred Oliver, in cooperation with City Treasurer Louis E. Holley, provided the fiscal and administrative framework to gain control of the city budget.

Harrison found the new procedures particularly helpful in the water department, which he supervised. A new accounting system allowed the city to place the department on a cash basis. The water system was expected to pay its own way, but not to supply funds for the capital improvements budget.

The other reform proposed by Fred Oliver, and one that helped the city considerably, was the change in the city's fiscal year. Previously, it had run from January 1 through December 31, but Oliver proposed a change to July 1 through June 30. Lee and Commissioner Herbert Smart opposed this proposal because of the expense of changing over, but Harrison and the other commissioners approved because of the long-term savings promised by the reform. Previously, the city had to borrow money on tax anticipation notes from January through November because the bulk of property tax revenues came in shortly before November 30. The change in fiscal year made such borrowing necessary only from July through November. The new program began in 1961.

With the city on a sound financial footing, it was possible to move ahead with needed capital improvements. In August 1961, the Advisory Committee on City Planning and Capital Improvements, which the Stewart administration had set up, made several far-reaching proposals. Included in the $19.5 million total were such items as new sewage disposal facilities, a Metropolitan Hall of Justice to be built in cooperation with the county, a trunk sewer line on Redwood Road in the western portion of the city, a public library, and a storm sewer system.

Controversy erupted over the proposal to construct a combination civic auditorium convention center and arts complex to be named the Salt Palace. For nearly the entire century, and especially since the organization of the chamber of commerce, city boosters had been trying to generate funds for a civic auditorium. Lee absolutely opposed the project. Commissioner Harrison, on the other hand, formerly a newspaper man, had written a series of articles in the *Deseret News* in March 1961, favoring the center. Some controversy developed between Salt Lake City and South Salt Lake over the location of the facility, since

Salt Lake City Skyline 1970, looking east. Courtesy, Deseret News.

South Salt Lake wanted it on Thirty-third South. The parties finally agreed to locate it somewhere in the downtown area, which was then deteriorating, where it could form the core of a long-range urban improvement program. The key factor in the decision was the donation of land for the complex by the LDS church.

Lee's opposition stemmed from his penchant for economy. Voters approved a bond issue for demolition of existing buildings and for construction on the downtown site, but Lee called it a burden on taxpayers and helped sponsor a petition for a referendum on the project. The petition drive failed, in part because citizens learned that the city and county had already put $3 million into the project, which would have been wasted.

Lee and his supporters expressed further displeasure after the county opened construction bids. The architect had estimated a cost of $12.6 million, but the lowest bid was $16.9 million, which did not include an estimated $4.8 million for clearing the site. Since this exceeded the bond limit, the county commissioners agreed to eliminate the proposed concert hall and to build only the sports and exposition complex at a cost of $11.7 million. The county signed the contract in March 1967, and two years of construction followed.

In the end the Salt Palace was an important turning point in city history. Much of the surrounding area was soon rehabilitated or scheduled for refurbishing. It attracted major new restaurant, shopping, and hotel facilities in the vicinity. Further change and development came with the completion, in 1984, of the first phase of the Triad Center, north and west of the site. In addition, professional basketball and hockey teams were headquartered at the Salt Palace, and the Symphony Hall, added in 1979, became the home of the world-renowned Utah Symphony Orchestra. It also attracted numerous major conventions and became an economic boon to the city.

Another issue which surfaced during the Lee administration was urban planning and renewal. The need was suggested by what was happening to the city's population. Between 1950 and 1960, Salt Lake City's population grew only four percent, from 182,000 to 189,000. After 1960, the population actually declined. By 1980, it was down to 163,000, a drop of nearly fourteen percent in two decades. At the same time, the number of housing units in the city increased as smaller and older families remained in and moved into the city and young families with large numbers of children chose to locate beyond Twenty-first South in the rapidly growing communities of southern Salt Lake County or north of the Davis County border in Bountiful or Farmington. The city retained a proportionately higher percentage of minorities and people below the poverty line.

The decline in the city's population together with the apparent deterioration of the city's west side led to pressure for revitalization of the core city. In the early 1960s, a number of people began to argue for urban renewal. The movement included constructing more pleasant housing, and building newer commercial structures in the city's core area. Proponents of urban renewal said that Salt Lake City could avoid the national trend to urban sprawl if the core city were made more pleasant. In addition, they said, property owners should be encouraged to refurbish their buildings and landscape their property.

By 1965 a majority of the city commission and most representatives of the business community favored urban renewal under federal grants, but Lee and others opposed the idea and forced a referendum on the issue. Commissioners agreed that if voters approved the organization of a redevelopment agency, they would appoint themselves as the agents. Certain small businessmen led by motel owner Sheldon Brewster and druggist J. McKinnon Smith, and supported by Lee, mounted a successful campaign in which they linked their opposition to urban renewal to the dominant Latter-day Saint idea of personal liberty and to the loss of the "God-given, inalienable right to own property." This was coupled with a scare campaign aimed at big government's use of eminent domain. The referendum lost by a six to one margin.

Though the economic condition of Salt Lake City in the early 1960s was certainly not optimum, neither was it entirely bleak. By 1965, presaging changes to come, a number of buildings had recently been constructed or were being planned. The Metropolitan Hall of Justice complex east of Washington Square, built between 1963 and 1966, was an example of the "New Formalist" school of architecture, as were a number of other structures. This style is characterized by freestanding blocks with symmetrical elevations and flat projecting roofs. In 1962, the work on a new state office building and plaza north of the state capitol building had been completed, as had a new addition to Holy Cross Hospital and $4 million worth of improvements at the Salt Lake City Airport. The eighteen-story Kennecott Copper Building was planned for the corner of South Temple and Main Street, and plans were already laid for the construction on the twenty-eight-story LDS church office building on North Temple, though that building was not completed until 1973. The University of Utah Medical Center was under construction east of the University of Utah Campus. The Salt Lake Public Library was completed in 1964.

The absence of a master plan for revitalization presented a major problem. Without such a plan, decisions on the integration of architecture, landscaping, and traffic patterns could not be made.

In the meantime, Mayor Lee's position was one of adamant opposition to urban planning. It could only end up, he believed, with unwarranted regulation of private firms and individuals, which he considered extremely loathsome. For Lee, the use of planning consultants was as basic an issue of personal liberty as was freedom from taxation and the use of federal redevelopment funds.

By 1972, a report to the newly inaugurated mayor E.J. "Jake" Garn indicated that Salt Lake had changed from a planned community to a metropolis of blighted neighborhoods. The report listed three major reasons for the problem. First, "past complacency about physical blight" had focused insufficient attention on maintaining facilities and enforcing housing and municipal codes. Second, most citizens simply denied that the problem existed. Third, while the LDS church had done much to help in decision-making in the community, it was reluctant to take the lead in the urban improvement movement for fear of being accused of interfering in the affairs of the community.

Beyond the issue of urban planning, Lee's attitude toward law enforcement seemed archaic. It is perhaps best exemplified in his feud with Chief of Police W. Cleon Skousen, whom Lee eventually fired. The basis of the dispute seems to have rested on two propositions. First was Lee's penchant for economy and Skousen's belief that though the police department could stand some cutbacks, the $300,000 reduction proposed by Lee in 1960 was far in excess of the reasonable budget cuts. In addition, Lee proposed to step on what Skousen perceived to be his prerogative as an expert in law enforcement in determining how the cuts should be allocated. Skousen predicted that the cuts would force the firing of thirty to forty patrolmen. Lee thought most of the adverse impact could be alleviated by firing Skousen's three assistant chiefs.

Beyond the differences over the budget, the two contrasted sharply in their law enforcement philosophies. Some of the differences appeared in the race between Lee and Bruce Jenkins for mayor. Jenkins charged that Lee would prove as soft on prostitution and vice as he had while mayor of Price. After he became mayor, differences between Skousen and Lee appeared. The police chief favored lie detector tests for department personnel, which Lee considered an invasion of privacy. Skousen favored activity in national and international police organizations, which Lee believed to be a waste of money.

Unable to achieve a satisfactory resolution of the differences, Lee dropped a bombshell on the commission by proposing Skousen's dismissal on March 21, 1960. Although there had been no prior consultation, commissioners Guerts and J.K. Pierce supported Lee because they believed he should have control over his own departments.

Skousen, who had been unaware of the commission proceedings, learned of his dismissal late in the afternoon from Harold Schindler, a *Salt Lake Tribune* reporter. He attributed the firing to differences in law enforcement philosophy. The problems, he thought at the time, could be worked out, but he did not appeal the decision.

On balance, Skousen's handling of the department had undoubtedly been salutary. The *Salt Lake Tribune*, which had criticized Skousen in 1958 over his handling of the investigation of a narcotics ring at the Utah State Prison, now complimented the chief on the efficiency with which he ran the department. He had entered an understaffed department wracked with low morale and inadequate technical and public support and had made it into a model of efficiency. Although the city's police force at 1.4 officers per 1,000 population was below the national average of 1.8 and the recommended standard of 2.0, rates of violent crimes were below the national average. Crimes against property, however, were above the national figure, but these trends were true of Utah as a whole.

As might be expected, reaction to Skousen's firing was immediate and indignant. The *Deseret News* staff prepared a scathing editorial condemning Lee, though Henry D. Moyle, First Counselor in the LDS church's First Presidency and supervisor of the *News*, ordered it killed. Lee and his wife were subjected to abuse both in person and on the telephone. Lee insisted that the church leadership supported him, but Skousen reported that he was told that Lee's role of "friendly gentile" was the reason for refusing to intervene. The church, he said, feared public censure for involving itself in political activities if it attacked Lee. Whatever the truth, it is clear that most Salt Lakers thought Skousen a successful police chief and greeted the abrupt dismissal with dismay.

There is no question that the two differed in their attitudes toward vice. Skousen supported a self-policing system for tavern and nightclub owners through an owners association, designed to maintain order and morality in the clubs without direct police involvement. Lee thought the system too dictatorial since pressure was applied to join the association, and the police department supported the association pressure for members to conform to guidelines. Lee thought striptease shows and gambling in moderation were all right—he participated in them with pleasure. Skousen favored strict enforcement of the law against those vices, which he considered immoral.

Lee seemed to remain soft on vice even after he dismissed Skousen. In 1967 he complained that Chief of Police Dewey Fillis and Public Safety Commissioner James L. Barker spent far too much time searching for vice. Nevertheless, public health officials charged that Salt Lake

City had shifted from a situation in which vice, particularly prostitution, was controlled to one in which the district around West Second South was infested with it. Venereal disease had risen 100 percent during the first half of 1967 and homosexual prostitution had become significant.

Nevertheless, Lee was not entirely consistent since on occasion he publicly called for stronger regulation of prostitution. A quirk in Utah's legal system compounded the problem of regulating street walkers. Since the state had enacted laws governing sexual offenses, the state supreme court ruled that the city might not pass ordinances on the subject. This disconcerted city officials, since state codes prohibited brothels, but did not regulate street walkers. At Lee's and Barker's suggestion, the city began to attack the problem by a loose interpretation of vagrancy laws. While Lee apparently saw little wrong with that kind of vice, Commissioner Barker later said he consistently upheld the laws when violations came to his attention.

The city used two other enforcement strategies. First, the licenses of businesses found catering to prostitution came under attack. Since a license was a privilege granted by the city rather than a right held by a business, evidence from the police department of a pattern of support for prostitutes was sufficient to bring a business license into question and, after a hearing, the city could revoke it. These hearings often made good newspaper copy. In one rather heated hearing, for instance, Lee openly attacked the attorney for Jeff's Grocery Store at 511 West Second South as belonging to a profession with "a license to steal." At the same hearing a woman charged that the mayor abetted prostitution by personally taking payoffs. Lee denied the charge, and it was never substantiated.

The second method used to combat prostitution was apparently the brainchild of Commissioner Barker. Barker decided that the city could control it by attacking the demand side as well as the supply side of the trade. In order to accomplish this, he began in 1971 to use undercover police women as decoys. Lee opposed the system, but acquiesced in it since he did not want to be thought "soft on sin."

The system proved at least moderately successful and achieved some notoriety in 1976 when it contributed to the defeat of an incumbent Utah congressman. After a Democratic party rally in 1976, Alan T. Howe was arrested for allegedly soliciting sex for hire from a police decoy in the West Second South district. Claiming at first that he had been framed by political opponents, Howe resisted pressure from supporters to withdraw from the election in favor of Utah Education Association leader Daryl McCarty. Since he had been certified as the Democratic party candidate, he could not be replaced, and a virtually unknown Republican candidate, Dan Marriott, soundly defeated him and McCarty, who ran as an independent. Howe was subsequently convicted.

Lee ran twice more for mayor. In 1963, his opponent was Sheldon Brewster, who had led the fights for a black ghetto and against urban renewal. Lee defeated the businessman by a margin of nearly two to one. In 1967, D. James Cannon, formerly Utah Travel Council Director and administrator of a private industrial development group, ran against him. Cannon, a moderate Republican, attacked Lee's negativism with a campaign emphasizing the need to improve employee morale and for urban development to make Salt Lake into the business and cultural center of the West. Lee won by slightly less than 300 votes out of more than 51,000 cast in the election. His strongest support came from the lower-middle-class sections of the cty.

By 1971, Lee had been mayor for three terms. He realized that much of his philosophy had become outdated and that people in the city demanded more of the urban administration than he was prepared to give. In spite of a *Salt Lake Tribune* poll which showed a rating of excellent or good from sixty percent of the city's voters, Lee recognized that a seventy-two-year-old man in a city with a mood that had shifted to favor revitalization could probably not be reelected. He bowed out gracefully, and in January 1972 Democratic governor Calvin Rampton sponsored a testimonial dinner at the Hotel Utah.

Lee handpicked as his successor Jake Garn, a former insurance sales-man and at the time a member of the city commission. Garn overwhelmed Commissioner Conrad Harrison with more than 24,000 votes.

Lee also supported Jennings Phillips, Jr., a former newspaperman and city treasurer since 1961, in his bid for finance commissioner. Phillips received more than 31,700 votes in an overwhelming victory.

E.J. "Jake" Garn. Mayor of Salt Lake City and United States Senator. Courtesy, Senator Garn.

In many ways, the Garn administration can be seen as an important phase in the transition from an early-twentieth-century system. During the first decades, the city had to cope with problems of rapid urban growth characteristic of the Progressive Era. By the late twentieth century the city had become concerned with problems caused by the pressure of an urban environment demanding a high level of services and faced with declining inner city population. Although Garn inherited a balanced budget and better budgetary control than before, he also faced a number of problems common to other American cities. Much more open to innovation and change than Lee, Garn sought solutions to the city's problems through a wider range of options than the former mayor had been willing to accept. He had decided to seek the mayor's position because he believed the city was not effectively meeting problems of urban decay, the need for capital improvements, control of drug abuse, and abatement of pollution. City government, he thought, needed modernization, and most particularly, the city and the county must deal with overlapping jurisdictions and the taxation of city residents for services provided only in the unincorporated areas.

With a much more pragmatic attitude than Lee had exhibited, Garn was prepared to accept innovations. As conservative as Lee in his desire for balanced budgets, Garn was much more progressive in his willingness to accept a wide range of solutions for urban problems. He generally opposed the use of federal grants for anything but capital improvements, but he was willing to accept Comprehensive Employment Training Act (CETA) money to provide jobs for the unemployed. Most importantly, he believed that he could learn from the experience of others and that he must work closely with other cities and with the county in solving Salt Lake's problems.

He moved in two ways to try to promote cooperation on the one hand and to protect Salt Lake's prerogatives on the other. He favored consolidation of city and county government, but when that proved impossible he supported the next best alternative, that of consolidating city and county services where possible. One of the most important innovations in that area was the consolidation of the city and county health departments, something that had been proposed but rejected in the 1940s. He wanted to push for combining the fire departments, sharing sewer lines, and cooperating in the maintenance of the city and county building, but these changes were not politically possible at the time. He also favored cooperation with the Council of Governments of Salt Lake County to solve common problems. Salt Lake City's concerns, he realized, did not stop at Twenty-first South.

In the absence of agreements to consolidate services, Garn favored vigorous action on the part of the city to make certain that residents did not pay for county services they did not receive. Salt Lake citizens paid for their own fire and police services, for instance, and there was no reason why they should also pay taxes to support similar services provided for county residents. This problem was solved in part by the creation of special taxing districts within the county to pay for urban services provided to county citizens, thus reducing county taxes paid by city dwellers. Theoretically, the county should have provided only the services of sheriff, the courts, the county attorney, and county records. In fact, they did do much more, and some county commissioners believe they are providing far too many urban services today.

Garn also linked Salt Lake with other cities in the United States by joining the National League of Cities, a step Lee opposed. He quickly became a leader in the league, serving as second vice-president and first vice-president. Through this organization, he sought to confer with other mayors to see how they had solved problems similar to those in Salt Lake and to offer suggestions on the solution of common problems. The organization also served as a lobbying group to get the message of the nation's large cities to Congress and the president.

By working together, the cities were able to pool their resources and save money in the solution of problems. During the time Garn was first vice-president of the National League of Cities, Congress proposed a change in the Fair Labor Standards Act that would have forced the cities to put all employees on a forty-hour week and to pay time and a half or compensatory time during the week following the overtime. Implementation of such rules would have cost Salt Lake City an estimated million dollars per year. Firemen, for instance, would have had to work a forty hour week rather than the customary twenty-four hours on and twenty-four hours off shift. Parks department crews accrued a great deal of overtime in the summer, when care of golf courses was necessary. Customarily, the city had given them time and a half off during the winter when they were not needed. On the other hand, the city was able to balance out the work of streets department employees, consisting of road repairs in the summer and snow removal in the winter. The cities, with the support of the national governor's conference headed by Utah governor Calvin L. Rampton, carried the case to the United States Supreme Court and won. Salt Lake paid $5,000 in legal fees to the common defense fund but saved an estimated $1 million per year by the negation of the proposed work rules.

Garn moved to improve the city in ways perhaps too progressive for J. Bracken Lee. The city commission had dragged its feet for a number of years by commissioning studies on the feasibility of expanding the Salt Lake Airport. Facilities at the airport were too limited and a number of major air lines were reluctant to commit themselves to Salt Lake.

As a result, Denver became the principal connection point on most flights from Salt Lake eastward. In the early 1970s travelers could fly to almost anywhere east of Salt Lake as long as they went through Denver. Garn pushed for renovation of the airport, beginning a project that was to continue for years beyond his administration.

Main Street beautification had been started ten years before Garn became mayor, but had not shown adequate progress. Garn felt strongly that the city needed to look to the future, and that meant comprehensive urban planning. He felt that the city must take active charge of its own future, and the mayor had to lead out rather than being afraid of change. As a result, comprehensive plans were laid and beautification of the downtown area was begun during the Garn administration.

The city was clearly in need of a major renewal. A survey indicated that about 9 percent of the city's residences were eligible for redevelopment, 43 percent would require rehabilitation, and 48 percent were sound. A similar situation obtained in nonresidential buildings, with 9 percent eligible for redevelopment, 35 percent in need of rehabilitation, and 56 percent sound. A number of environmental problems had been created by incompatible land development inaugurated before the city's first zoning ordinance in 1927, and the two areas considered most blighted were the central city and the west side of capitol hill.

In view of these difficulties, the city council decided to launch a community improvement program. The city would upgrade houses that could be rehabilitated and tear down those that could not. In an attempt to keep a balanced growth, zoning in some neighborhoods would be changed to reflect the wishes of a majority of citizens. On this basis, in January 1973, the city established the Salt Lake Redevelopment Agency. A five-member board including Mayor Garn had as its goal to condemn and acquire property necessary for the betterment of the city. Federal funds were obtained through the Department of Housing and Urban Development to help finance projects of the agency. This program was augmented in 1974 by the establishment of a bicentennial beautification committee to oversee the beautification of the city for the 1976 bicentennial of the American Revolution.

Garn also struck out to modernize city government and to provide adequate facilities for urban services. The city commission decided that it could maintain water rights without owning the land adjacent to the water. For this reason, it was able to sell some land near Parley's Reservoir, Little Dell Reservoir, and some other areas of the county. As a result, the city came up with more than $600,000 in cash to pay for a new water department shop facility and at the same time put the property on the Salt Lake County tax rolls. In addition, the city received federal revenue sharing funds—$1.8 million in 1972.

At the same time that Garn became mayor, Jennings Phillips, Jr., a former newspaper man and city treasurer, joined the commission as finance commissioner. From that position, he sought to continue improving the city's fiscal well-being. Prior to his term as treasurer, the city had deposited its money in favored banks that paid no interest. As treasurer, Phillips found that the city had been in the practice of paying interest on tax anticipation notes while maintaining balances of nearly two million dollars in various bank accounts. He proposed to deposit money only in interest-bearing accounts. Some of the bankers pressed Mayor Lee to overrule Phillips, but Lee told them that it was the treasurer's policy and that he supported his subordinates. When the banks refused to pay interest, Phillips put the money in treasury bills. The next year, the banks agreed to take the city's money and to pay interest as well. On that basis, the city earned more than six million dollars in Phillips's last year as treasurer. Phillips was, nevertheless, interested in promoting local business, and he resisted the temptation to deposit city funds in eastern banks which paid a slightly higher rate of interest. For a time, he was able also to deposit federal grants at interest until the U.S. Treasury Department decided that it could just as easily earn the interest itself and began issuing letters of credit instead of cash.

The city also wrestled with the problem of finding other sources of revenue in order to improve the operation of city government and upgrade services for Salt Lake citizens. No matter what taxing scheme it tried, however, taxes proved unpopular. Previously the city had enacted a four percent franchise tax on utilities, and Phillips also favored an income tax on people from outside the city who worked in town—a so-called commuter tax. He lost on that issue by a vote of three to two. At the same time it seemed that no one wanted to increase property taxes, even though Salt Lake City had one of the lowest property tax rates of any major city in the United States. This was to be expected, since surveys have shown the property tax to be the most disliked tax, probably because it is paid in a lump sum once a year, and because it falls in part on unproductive property. The commissioners also considered going to the legislature to secure an increase in the sales tax, but they finally decided against that, for they believed it would cause too big a fight and, besides, the money collected would have to be divided with other municipalities. The commission concluded that the best solution was to increase the utility tax from four to six percent. That tax was unpopular both with the public, who had to pay it, and with the utilities who had to collect it, but demands for services made it necessary.

Jake Garn remained as mayor slightly less than three years until his resignation in December 1974 to take a seat in the United States Senate. The council chose Conrad Harrison as interim mayor. Harrison had been reelected regularly to the council after his initial appointment in 1960, and Herman J. Hogensen took Harrison's place on the council. Harrison remained as mayor less than a year, until Ted Wilson defeated him in the fall of 1975, and he essentially continued the programs inaugurated by the commission of which he was a member under Mayor Garn. Wilson considered Harrison an honest, decent man who had served the city well as commissioner and interim mayor.

Elected in November 1975, Ted L. Wilson, formerly a high school teacher, congressional administrative assistant, and county social services director, assumed the role of mayor in January 1976. He was easily reelected in 1979 and 1983. In part, his programs were also continuations of those of the Garn administration, and in part, they were new departures leading the city in new directions.

Like Garn, Wilson favored city-county consolidation. He too believed that the affairs of the city and Salt Lake County were inextricably bound together and that the separate system allowed far too much overlap and duplication of service, often to the detriment of the city. Those favoring consolidation cited double taxation of city residents for services provided in the county. For many in the county, the special service districts set up to provide urban services seemed unwieldy and far too autonomous.

Many citizens opposed consolidation. Some feared that the large organization would be unwieldy and inefficient, and others were alarmed at the possibility of too much centralization. Many residents of unincorporated areas feared that tax increases would result. In the city, some residents feared loss of control of valuable water supplies which belonged to the city and which county residents had to purchase under the existing arrangement. Others feared erosion of the city's large tax base, particularly if the double-taxation issue were satisfactorily resolved.

The outcome was predictable. All the media, most of the city government, professors from the University of Utah, and most community leaders favored consolidation. The 1975 referendum demonstrated that citizens of Salt Lake City generally favored it while the more numerous county residents opposed it. As a result, the proposal lost by thirty-nine to sixty-one percent.

Like Garn, Wilson also favored the strong mayor form of government. Garn had expressed his views on this question as early as 1971 when he called the commission form "archaic and outmoded." At the time, he stated his intention of fighting for the reform, but in the meantime, he indicated that he would play a forceful role as mayor, just as Lee had done. Symbolically, he started out even more aggressively than Lee, by indicating that as mayor he would cast his vote first in commission meeting rather than deferring to the other commissioners, as had traditionally been the case.

This desire for more efficient government received considerable assistance from several malfeasance and competence scandals which turned part of the electorate against the commission form. In May 1960, Commissioner Theodore Geurts was removed from office. Geurts, whose responsibilities included supervision of the cemetery, wanted some sod for a lawn. Someone in his department told him there was plenty at the city cemetery, so employees delivered a truckload to his property. Political enemies found out about the delivery, complained, and forced his removal from office. During the 1973 campaign between James L. Barker and Glen N. Greener, former mayor J. Bracken Lee issued a written endorsement of Greener which he followed with a television advertisement that questioned Barker's competence in managing the fire and police departments and implied that Barker had received more than $16,000 in wages for a "phantom employee." Lee's endorsement undoubtedly contributed to the relatively unknown Greener's election. Barker filed a suit against Lee, but dropped it in favor of an out-of-court settlement. After the election, Lee opined that Barker probably had done nothing wrong himself and that dishonest employees had probably betrayed his trust.

During his early years in office, Wilson and others continued to push for city-county consolidation, and in the fall of 1978 the county held the most recent of these elections. A scandal originating in that election eventually led to a change from the commission form to the strong mayor form of government in Salt Lake City. The Utah legislature, meanwhile, had allowed such change by passing a law allowing cities to choose optional forms of government from a number of different governmental systems.

During the 1978 city-county consolidation fight, members of the city commission lined up on different sides of the fence. Mayor Wilson and Commissioner Jess Agraz both announced themselves strongly in favor of consolidation. Commissioners Glen Greener and Jennings Phillips opposed the change. Though the evidence is confused on the issue, the Salt Lake Tribune published allegations that Greener secured the support of members of the Salt Lake City fire and police departments in his opposition, and that he solicited $5,000 from the firemen for anti-unification fund. The allegations included charges that Greener promised raises to the city police officers and firemen that would have placed their salaries on a par with the better-paid county sheriff and fire departments in return for opposition to or neutrality on unification.

The unification election failed, but the issues did not fade. On January 12, 1979, apparently at Greener's instigation, commissioners Phillips and David Campbell agreed to appoint Chief of Police Bud Willoughby as city personnel director in place of Robert T. Mullally, who was then in the hospital. Mullally had previously been involved in conflicts with other city employees over hiring policies and other matters. After learning of the appointment and of the allegations against Greener, Mayor Wilson secured the appointment of a three-person investigating committee headed by former Third District Judge Stewart M. Hanson, Jr. and including Marjorie Thomas, former chairwoman of Utah Common Cause, and Max T. Nichols, purchasing manager for the LDS church. After the committee issued its report, Wilson called for Greener's resignation as public safety commissioner, saying that he had used Phillips to achieve his ends, and implying Willoughby's appointment was designed to pave the way to pay off the policemen and firemen.

This unfortunate series of events, perhaps more than anything else, contributed to the change in governmental form. The Hanson committee report charged that the commission form fostered special interests and inefficiency and urged its change. On February 16, 1979, the day following the public revelation of the Hanson committee's findings, the *Salt Lake Tribune* called editorally for the abolition of the council system, which it called "archaic."

After this so-called "Citygate" affair, the movement for change went rather smoothly. Mayor Wilson had previously announced that he planned to retire, but a groundswell of support, which the *Tribune* considered a genuine draft, surfaced in the summer of 1979 and he decided to run again. In May 1979, the people of the city voted by a five to one majority to change the form of government. In the November election, Wilson was reelected to a second term as mayor under the new government.

In January 1980, the city inaugurated the strong mayor-council form of government. The mayor became the chief executive officer of the city, responsible for the day-to-day operation of the government as well as the ceremonial duties he previously performed. The city council was made up of part-time representatives elected as a city legislature but who retained their occupations and professions.

To a large extent, the new mayor-council form was a reincarnation of the system which had existed prior to 1912. As such, the system had its advantages and disadvantages. Mayor Wilson admitted that the council was slow, especially in the first six months, in keeping the wheels of government moving. Since the legislature and executive functions were divided, the new system frustrated some people, for the council was often quite deliberate in making its decisions. Instead of meeting three days a week for legislative work, the council met one day each week to legislate and another to hold hearings. Wilson believed, however, that on the whole such deliberation made for better decisions. The system also provided a more unified administration. As Wilson once put it, if the council decided to limit the number of cars employees were allowed to take home, the decision could not be undercut by one commissioner deciding that for his department the general practice was not applicable. The councilors now legislated, they did not execute as well.

Some people disagreed. Jennings Phillips, for instance, who opposed the change, continued to argue that the new form did not increase the efficiency and economy of city government. His major criticism was that the new system slowed things down because the council took longer to make decisions than did the commissioners who were faced not only with legislating but with the pressure to solve problems. Since the new council members did not have to execute their own decisions, they were not in a great hurry. The major exceptions to Phillips's views would undoubtedly be during times of serious internal conflict like the Jenkins administration of the 1940s when commission business ground to a halt during conflicts between members of the commission.

Perhaps the major problem the Wilson administration had to cope with, up to 1984, was rezoning. That fight began during the Harrison administration, in 1975, when central city rezoning disputes began. It was completed in 1980 when the council finished rezoning the east bench. In general, the conflict was between neighborhood groups who generally owned single family houses and developers who favored high-density residential housing or shopping centers. Often the disputes came before the commission in the form of a proposal to "down zone" an area. The restrictive zoning proposals were designed to make it more difficult to place high-density housing in the neighborhood. Over the five years between 1975 and 1980, the city went through five or six major rezoning battles. Each was accompanied by hearings which can be characterized as explosive confrontations between developers and neighborhood residents.

Typical, perhaps, was the rezoning battle over the Avenues, which led to the creation of a new type of district in the city. By the late 1960s the physical deterioration of the Avenues became quite pronounced. Most homes dated from the period between the 1880s and the 1920s, and as the area deteriorated, many buildings were renovated into multiple family dwellings, owned by absentee landlords who seemed to take little pride in the upkeep of their property. These property owners were often able to escape tax increases simply by failing to improve their property, since property taxes were based on the fair market value of the property and improvements.

By the late 1960s, the movement for historic preservation had begun to develop in the United States. Urban renewal advocates of building destruction were being effectively challenged by advocates of restoration. Increasingly, younger, wealthier, and more culturally aware professional people began to look at the houses in the Avenues area. They recognized the quality of the construction, often disliked the suburban syndrome associated with commuting, station wagons, and shopping malls, and began to purchase and restore the fine old homes.

By the mid-1970s, pressure from these people made change a necessity. Focusing their efforts through the Greater Avenues Community Council, they moved to try to restore the historic character of the neighborhood. Their aim was to change the 1967 Salt Lake City master plan by down zoning the area and by blocking condominiums and shopping centers. They succeeded in securing creation of the Avenues Historic District covering the area from A to Virginia Streets and First to Sixth Avenues. In 1979, the down zoning process was completed by the adoption of the revised Avenues master plan by the Salt Lake City Planning Commission. No longer could developers hope to move in on the Historic District.

This is not to say that Salt Lake City in general did not begin to change with the rest of urban America. Increasingly, during the 1970s apartment houses on South Temple were converted to condominiums, and new and renovated condominiums appeared on North Main, on the southwest side of Capitol Hill, on Thirteenth East, and in other areas of the city.

The historic preservation movement of the 1970s had other effects as well. Buildings scheduled for demolition on South Temple and other streets were subjected to adaptive renovation instead. Many companies found an older home on "Brigham Street" a prestigious address from which to do business. The conversion of the old streetcar barns on Seventh East into the Trolley Square shopping center helped bring business back into the city as the construction of the ZCMI Mall and Crossroads Mall on opposite sides of Main Street, south from South Temple. The historic Hotel Utah was renovated and a new wing constructed in the same architectural style as the original. In addition, new hotels such as the Hilton, the Marriott, and the Tri-arc Travelodge were built in the downtown area. Revitalization of the city's west side went ahead with the renovation of the old Denver and Rio Grande depot at the foot of Third South as a home for the Utah State Historical Society, and with the start of the billion-dollar Triad Center. Perhaps most important, Governor Scott Matheson chose to move back into the city, and the Thomas Kearns mansion on South Temple, which formerly housed the Historical Society, was restored as the official governor's residence.

It would be a mistake, however, to paint too rosy a picture of the success of historic preservation. Numerous buildings were destroyed and urban planners and other citizens raised questions about the adaptive reuse of some of the others. In the construction of the ZCMI Mall, for instance, questions arose about the destruction of the architectural integrity of the building and the retrofitting of the ornate nineteenth-century cast iron facade designed by William Folsom and Obed Taylor. A number of nineteenth-century apartment and office buildings in the downtown area were destroyed. Some concern was raised about the adaptive reuse proposed by Triad Utah of the Deveraux House as a restaurant. Of seventy-seven buildings listed by Margaret Lester in her *Brigham Street* as historically important structures on South Temple Street, thirty-five were demolished by 1979.

The question of urban revitalization was closely connected to the larger issue of city interest groups. Historic preservationists themselves constituted one such group. Led by the Utah Heritage Foundation, this lobby pressed for preservation of historic buildings and ambience. Traditionally, much of the city's business was done in response to interest and pressure groups. Each group had its own interests and they often conflicted with those of other groups. The Utah Taxpayers Association represented members of the business community and attempted to counterbalance any movements to increase taxes. Utilities companies had their own interests, particularly in the area of taxation. They constituted the major group opposing a utilities franchise tax. Contractors wanted as few regulations as possible in building homes and other structures. During the early 1970s poor people's advocates, such as the Community Action Program and the Crossroads Center, were quite powerful, though by the 1980s, they became less so.

Organized labor was an interest group of particular importance, though it declined somewhat after World War II. In 1979, labor unions pressed the city, with little success, for higher wages and benefits. The city had a work force of 2,200 to 2,300 employees at the time, and with high inflation it was difficult to find money to meet increasing salary, wage, and benefit demands. Budgets were still tight by 1982, but the number of employees had declined to about 1900, and those remaining seemed to understand the budgetary pressure under which the city operated. Beyond this, increasing unemployment in Utah and the nation in the early 1980s sent clear signals about the need for stable employment as opposed to demands for large salary and benefit increases.

The Church of Jesus Christ of Latter-day Saints continued to play a unique role in its relationship to Salt Lake City administration. Both as a large property owner and as the religious institution representing the ideals of the majority of Salt Lake's citizens, it was vitally interested in the welfare of the city. For nearly two decades, until late 1969, President David O. McKay continued to hold regular weekly breakfast

Nathan Eldon Tanner. Member of the LDS Church's First Presidency, Prominent Civic Leader, and a Driving Force Behind Downtown Redevelopment.

meetings with Gus P. Backman, secretary and chief executive officer of the Salt Lake Area Chamber of Commerce, and John F. Fitzpatrick (until his death in 1960) or John Gallivan (after 1960), publisher of the *Salt Lake Tribune*. After his appointment as executive vice-president of the chamber of commerce, Fred S. Ball met regularly with Nathan Eldon Tanner, a counselor in the church's First Presidency who died in 1982, or Gordon B. Hinckley, who became a member of the First Presidency in 1981, to discuss city affairs. These meetings helped the church and civic officers understand each other's concerns, and led to many important areas of agreement.

The relationship between the church and the city administration was, and is, reciprocal. Jennings Phillips, a non-Mormon, reported that he often consulted with Gordon B. Hinckley (then a member of the Council of the Twelve) on pornography, which both wanted to control. Ted Wilson, an active Mormon, developed a positive consulting relationship with the church's special affairs committee, consisting of President Hinckley and Elders Neal A. Maxwell, James E. Faust, and David B. Haight. He began paying a visit at least once a year to show them the city's budget, especially because of the church's interest in fire protection and law enforcement. The church-owned Zion's Security Corporation, one of the largest property owners in the city, likewise had particular interests in city planning and development. So also did the late President Tanner, who became one of Salt Lake's most highly respected citizens and who before his death received numerous public recognitions for his important civic contributions. In a recent interview, however, Wilson emphasized that he never had a phone call from the church office building asking him to do particular things. The reciprocal arrangement was based on mutual understanding of common concerns rather than on pressure.

Wilson also reported that this arrangement was very beneficial to Salt Lake City, for at times he went to the church for help in matters concerning the interest of the city. When church-owned Zion's Securities considered tearing down the Eagle Gate apartments on State Street, he spoke with President Hinckley about the matter, since he believed it would be a serious error. Preservationist groups also addressed the question. In this case, historic preservation won a temporary victory and the apartment house was left standing. In 1984, however, a final decision was made to demolish it. Wilson also spoke with church officials on the construction of the church's new Historical and Arts Museum west of Temple Square. He was particularly interested that the design be open enough to allow a passageway to the development and preservation surrounding the historic Devereaux House to the west.

If the LDS church was careful to act as a concerned citizen with a major interest in the city rather than a heavy-handed pressure group on issues of development and city priorities, it took a more active and overt stance on issues of personal morality. The major examples were pornography and liquor-by-the-drink. Jack Gallivan of the *Tribune* and a number of businessmen connected with the tourist, restaurant, and public accommodations industries considered Utah's liquor laws archaic. In the early 1960s, patrons could purchase liquor only in large bottles from state liquor stores or they could buy drinks in private clubs. Gallivan had a bill drafted which he hoped a statewide referendum would pass, since he was sure the predominant Mormon sentiment would block it in the legislature. Gallivan thought he had assurances that the church would not openly oppose the bill, but his expectations proved wrong. Church leadership mounted a strong campaign against the proposal and it was soundly defeated in 1968. Eventually, the public accommodations lobby succeeded in securing the adoption of a mini-bottle bill, which allowed the state to open liquor stores in restaurants and to sell miniature bottles of liquor with meals. This was not entirely satisfactory to the public accommodations groups, but it was probably the best that could be achieved given the sentiment of the Mormon majority and the church leadership on the issue.

Most important for Salt Lake City in the years between 1960 and 1983 were its expanding and changing economic base. Smelters, which dominated the Salt Lake County skyline early in the century, were replaced by high technology electronics businesses like Sperry Univac Communications and Terminals Division, which located in Utah in 1956, and Litton Systems, which began Utah operations in 1958. The construction of the Salt Lake International Center near the airport helped in the city's development by expanding it toward the west, and the modern new terminal buildings at Salt Lake International Airport, completed in the early 1980s, represented the city's growing importance as a center for air travel. Western Airlines and American Express both located central offices in Salt Lake in recent years. The expansion of the tourist industry, and particularly of the ski industry, made Salt Lake an important destination for visitors during all seasons of the year.

Indeed, one might argue that Salt Lake City's economy became virtually post-industrial. At the time of this writing, employment data for Utah from the 1980 census had not yet appeared, but in 1970 nearly forty-nine percent of those employed in the Salt Lake Standard Metropolitan Statistical Area (SMSA) worked in professional, sales, managerial, clerical, and service occupations. Undoubtedly, this increased significantly during the next decade. The city was also the nerve center of Utah's energy-related industries like petroleum and coal, since most of the major companies active in Utah had their offices in Utah's capital city.

In addition to serving as the center of the Intermountain West's economic life, Salt Lake City was also the focus of its cultural activities. In 1974, the National Academy for Educational Development named the University of Utah as among the thirty-six leading research universities in the nation. The University's medical school became a leading research institution, especially in the field of heart surgery, and in 1982 it was the first institution in the world to implant an artificial heart in a human being.

Other cultural institutions made Salt Lake justly famous as an arts center. The Mormon Tabernacle Choir continued to enjoy a reputation as one of the premier religious choral organizations in the nation. A combination of civic and state pride joined to open Symphony Hall north of the Salt Palace in 1979 as the new home of the Utah Symphony. The symphony had some difficulties, however, as relationships between the members and its new director, Varujan Kojian, who replaced Maurice Abravanel in 1980, became strained. The symphony board voted not to rehire Maestro Kojian for another season, but to replace him with Joseph Silverstein, formerly with the Boston Symphony. In 1984, Kojian became orchestral director of Ballet West.

Dance grew to take on particular importance to Salt Lake City. In 1963, the Utah Civic Ballet became a professional company under the aegis of the University of Utah. The Ford Foundation provided a $175,000 grant to enable the company to professionalize and, in 1968, the name changed to Ballet West to indicate its broader Western interest. Other dance companies, including the Ririe-Woodbury Dance Company and the Repertory Dance Theatre, provided expanded and more avant garde dance programs.

In the field of the performing arts, Salt Lake City led the way in the Intermountain West. A replica of the old Salt Lake Theatre was constructed on the campus of the University of Utah. The LDS church sponsored a full season of legitimate theatre in the Promised Valley Playhouse in downtown Salt Lake. As part of the development of Salt Lake's west side, the Capitol Theatre on West Second South became an important spot for theatrical and operatic productions.

The visual arts also had their champions in Salt Lake City. The University of Utah Museum of Fine Arts and the Salt Lake Arts Center, housed in the Salt Palace complex, became the leaders in this regard. Salt Lake also boasted a large number of private galleries featuring the work of local and internationally known artists.

At the same time, Salt Lake City faced many challenges as it entered the last quarter of the twentieth centry. In 1979, the median income of

297

Salt Lake City households, at $13,211, was 74.8 percent of the state average of $17,673. Unemployment was slightly above the state average. Salt Lake City had a larger number of disadvantaged ethnic groups than any city in the state, and these tended to show the most serious patterns. of unemployment. Nearly half of the housing units in Salt Lake were renter-occupied. In Utah as a whole in 1979, 10.3 percent of the population was under the poverty level of $5,787 for an average family of three. In Salt Lake City, that percentage was 13.6. More than 39 percent of Salt Lake City's housing was constructed before 1939, as compared with 18.8 percent in the state as a whole. Much of this old housing was not the newly renovated units of affluent Avenues families, but substandard housing on the city's west side and in the central city.

As much as anything else, the ethnic makeup of the city created particular problems. Salt Lake City had generally the highest concentration in the state of those groups traditionally most discriminated against and with the least training for available, well-paying jobs. In the state as a whole the 1980 census showed that 0.6 percent of the population was black, 4.1 percent of Spanish origin, 0.4 percent Japanese, 0.2 percent Chinese, 0.1 percent Filipino, and 2.8 percent other groups, largely southeast Asians. Of just over 2,108 Vietnamese who lived in Utah, 1,501, or more than half, lived in the census's Salt Lake City urbanized area (not to be confused with the larger Standard Metropolitan Statistical Area which includes the greater Ogden area as well) in 1980. That area also contained 44 percent of the state's black population, 44 percent of its Japanese, 42 percent of its Filipino, 54 percent of its Korean, 60 percent of its Vietnamese, and 68 percent of the Samoan. Of 60,302 persons of Spanish origin in Utah, 31,364, or 52 percent lived in the Salt Lake urbanized area in 1980. Only the Ogden urbanized area had a higher population of blacks, and no urbanized area had a higher population of any of the other ethnic groups. Twenty-three percent of the state's 19,158 American Indians lived in Salt Lake City. Salt Lake County's urbanized area had a larger native American population than any other county in the state, including San Juan, where the large Navajo reservation is located.

A study made in 1969 and 1970 indicated that medical and health care for Salt Lake City's poor was inadequate. According to the report, a third of the medical community refused to treat new welfare patients, and the system provided inadequate information on the health care available. Attacks on services for the poor by conservative groups, together with unemployment nearing ten percent in 1982, undoubtedly exacerbated this situation.

Salt Lake women, like others around the country, were experiencing both difficulties and progress in their bid for acceptance in positions not traditionally held by women.

A story told by a twenty-five-year-old male law student who had been hired as a clerk by a firm in Salt Lake will serve to illustrate the continuing problem of stereotyping. He stepped on to an elevator and smiled at a pleasant-looking young woman, obviously an employee in the building. His question to her revealed his prejudice: "Whose secretary are you?" he asked. Her look made him realize that he had made an enormous mistake. In fact, she was an attorney in the same building. In discussing the incident with *Network* columnist Marj Bradley, he admitted that that incident had made him more aware of his prejudices. Moreover, he realized, thirty percent of the graduates of the University of Utah Law School are women.

Over the years, women moved into the labor force in greater numbers. Specific figures for Salt Lake City are not available, but the trends in Utah as a whole were indicative of changes in the city. In 1890, 12 percent of Utah women worked outside the home; by 1920, that had increased to 21 percent. In 1980, more than 50 percent found themselves in the labor force. Between 1950 and 1980, the rate of increase in labor force participation of women in Utah was greater than the national average, so that the percentage of women employees in Utah was approximately equal to the national average. Between 1950 and 1980, the population of Salt Lake County increased from 274,895 to 619,066, or 125.2 percent. At the same time, female participation in the labor force increased from 94,553 to 216,021, or 128.5 percent. Moreover, the reasons given for participation by Utahns, both Mormon and gentile, were essentially the same. They included meeting family goals, being widowed or divorced, and experiencing a need for self-expression outside the home.

In 1981, General Mills commissioned a national Lou Harris poll on attitudes toward women working in the labor force. It showed that seventy-eight percent of the people believed that women should be able to work even if they had a husband to support them. Most (eighty-five percent) opposed federally funded day care, because they believed that employers should make it easier for working parents to care for their children with flexible time, shared employment, and other similar concessions. After the poll was released, a panel discussion made up of prominent Utahns, most of them from Salt Lake City, demonstrated that Salt Lakers generally held similar views. Barbara B. Smith, general president of the Relief Society of the LDS church, indicated that she had conducted her own informal poll before participating on the panel. She found that most of those she interviewed agreed essentially with the findings of the Harris-General Mills study.

Still, sexual discrimination was apparent in the labor market, particularly in wages and salaries. Such discrimination tended to be less pronounced in Utah between single men and women than between married men and women. A number of things seemed responsible for this condition. Married women tended to be less well educated than their husbands, and they also tended to work discontinuously. The wage differential was also attributable, in part, to the type of work women tended to do. Between 1940 and 1980, for instance, the range of kinds of professional and technical positions held by women in Utah tended to narrow, until by 1980 two-thirds of women professionals were in relatively low-paying technical and health-care jobs. In 1980, the median income of Utah women aged fifteen and older was $4,120, which was 31 percent of the median income of men. Moreover, this ratio had remained virtually unchanged since 1969, and the ratio for Utah women tended to be lower than in the United States as a whole. The only category in which Utah women were paid at a higher ratio than the national average was among women with a graduate education, who received 70.3 percent of the salaries of similarly educated men. The national ratio in this category was 65.4 percent.

Nevertheless, women had achieved a great deal in Salt Lake City, and some of their achievements deserve attention as examples of their expanding role and visibility. Judy Ann Dencker, for instance, a detective with the Salt Lake City Police Department and instructor in the police academy, was named Outstanding Young Woman of the Year in early 1983 by the Salt Lake Women's Jaycees. She had worked as a patrol officer, traffic accident investigator, youth officer, and as a homicide/sex crime detective. She received a unit citation in 1980 for successful work in connection with a sniping incident at Liberty Park. In 1981, she prepared a case resulting in Utah's first felony child abuse conviction, for which she received a special commendation. In 1982, she received another commendation for her role in the investigation and conviction of a series of robberies, sexual assaults, and kidnappings.

De Ann Evans was appointed managing editor of the *Deseret News* in 1981. The first woman to be appointed managing editor of a major daily in Utah, she was born in Idaho and educated at the University of Utah and at Northwestern University. Prior to accepting a position at the *Deseret News* in 1967, she had worked for Congressman George Hansen of Idaho and in Boston.

Virginia "Jinnah" Kelson was the founder of the Phoenix Institute, a private nonprofit organization providing job training for disadvantaged women. Kelson was formerly human relations trainer for the Department of Justice. She recognized a need, and in 1971 set up the Phoenix Institute to assist women in training themselves for useful work in the community.

In many instances, a wife and her husband worked out successful careers together. This was true in the case of Christine Meaders Durham. A graduate of Wellesley, she married George Durham, a Harvard graduate and successful Salt Lake pediatrician. Active in the LDS church, particularly in working with young women, she shared household responsibilities with her husband. She made lunches, drove the carpool, took her daughters to music and dancing lessons, and did the shopping. Her husband came home at 3 p.m., fixed dinner, and cared for the kids. At times while she was a district court judge, she took a sick child with her to court and kept the child in the jury room while she presided on the bench. In 1982, following a controversy between Governor Scott M. Matheson and the legislature over the governor's appointment power, Durham was appointed as the first female supreme court justice in the history of the State of Utah.

In the early 1980s, Salt Lake City was clearly following patterns much like those of other major western cities. As the center of a large metropolitan area, it provided services for most of the Wasatch Front, and the interests of its citizens stretched well beyond Utah's borders. It faced the same sort of problems that other large cities faced, but had a number of things going for it that some cities did not. Impressive civic pride and a population with religious leaders interested in the city's future promised much.

One thing that many Salt Lake citizens realized was that the change in the form of government would not immunize the city from future difficulties, nor would it necessarily provide more rapid solutions to the city's problems. Since the Progressive Era, it has been recognized that structural reform might give the illusion of change because the change itself provides improved morale and new dedication to try to solve problems. Any change, however, will present its own problems which the structure of government itself will not solve. So while Salt Lake's future seemed bright, and progressive leadership had done much that was commendable, leaders were still attempting to find innovative and effective ways to deal with the city's pressing problems.

Artist's rendering of the proposed siting of the new Triad Center in Downtown Salt Lake City. Courtesy of Triad Utah.

———11———

From Today to the Future: The View from 1984

Perhaps no city in the United States has been as difficult to characterize as Salt Lake. Viewed as the center of a worldwide conspiracy in Sir Arthur Conan Doyle's *A Study in Scarlet*, it was also the home town to which Wallace Stegner's main character returned with nostalgia in *Recapitulation*. The multiple images include the prophetic vision of Brigham Young's "Temple City," the Tabernacle Choir's "Crossroads of the West," Gunther Barth's "Instant City," John McCormick's "Gathering Place," Chauncy Harris's "Regional Capital," and others not so complimentary, such as iron-fisted religious domination of politics in Sam Taylor's *Rocky Mountain Empire*, lack of attention to modern planning techniques, harem-like households of multiple wives, and the scam capital of the United States.

Salt Lakers are undoubtedly bemused by these images, but they no doubt understand how so much diversity can abound. As they look to the future, they are concerned about where their city is going—will it provide a healthy family environment and at the same time deal effectively with problems inherent in the urban situation? Historians can hardly expect to predict the future, but current trends and existing patterns provide us with data that can give some idea of the direction the city, planned for the nineteenth century, may be going as it approaches the twenty-first.

For one thing, it is certain that the LDS church will continue to demonstrate a vital interest in the city. Its ownership of large blocks of land, especially in the downtown area, its desire to maintain a positive image for its worldwide capital, its concern with the elimination of vice and crime, and the fact that the city itself is still about fifty percent Mormon

303

all assure that interest. Early in 1984 the church opened an impressive new historical museum west of Temple Square that is designed not only to attract tourists but also to tell the story of Mormonism more fully than ever before. It will display some of the best of the visual arts—including such things as painting, weaving, sculpture, pottery and basketry—produced by Mormons from throughout the world. Historical displays will tell the story of the Latter-day Saints through the use of artifacts from the Mormon culture. Rotating exhibits will focus on prominent Mormon civic, political, business, and cultural figures. Moreover, it will attempt both to educate the public and to provide the specialist with facilities for studying the Latter-day Saint past.

Anticipating the new facility created major concerns for city planners as they considered such problems as traffic flow, congestion, and public services. The solutions were positive examples of city-church cooperation, and there is no reason to suppose that such cooperation will not last.

The church will continue to affect the landscape as well as the economic configuration of the city. In recent years church-owned business enterprises have been responsible for the renovation of ZCMI, the construction of the impressive ZCMI Center shopping mall, the expansion of the Hotel Utah, and in part, the redesign of Main Street between South Temple and Third South into an attractive pedestrian mall and shopping area. At present the church is completing a large building on the same block as its new museum, to house the offices and library of its world-famous genealogical society, and it has announced plans for a new office and retail complex downtown. The new landscaped plaza will occupy a quarter of an acre and contain a twenty-two story tower, named Eagle Gate Tower, and a smaller building, and it is expected to be completed by 1986.

At the same time, it is virtually certain that the gentile community will continue to increase its political and economic influence. Non-Mormon mayors, businessmen, and other civic leaders are proportionally no less common than Mormon, and religious differences seem to affect the city's business climate no more than in other large cities. In the blocks west and southwest of the LDS historical museum, Triad Utah is constructing the Triad Center. A twenty-six-acre mixed-use urban development in the so-called "Gateway District," it will require ten years to complete. It is, however, the largest single development ever attempted in Utah, and is expected to cost in excess of $600 million. When completed it will provide 4.5 million square feet of office, residential, retail, hotel, historic, entertainment, and recreational space. Moreover, unlike much of the slash and burn urban renewal of the past, this project will incorporate existing architectural gems like the historic Deveraux House, a park-like atmosphere, and homes for city people.

Artist's Sketch of Restored Devereaux House. Courtesy of Triad Utah.

An important business venture, it is as much a symbol of Mormon-gentile cooperation as anything undertaken in the city in recent years.

This is not to say that tensions do not exist, but they manifest themselves at a different level than the city's political and business leadership. They often take the form of attacks on the Latter-day Saints by dissidents or avowed anti-Mormons. At times they are directed at the church because individual members identify their particular political positions or personal causes with church doctrines or practices. At other times issues like welfare reform, regulation of cable television, metropolitan consolidation, or urban planning will appear to be evidence of Mormon-gentile strain when, in actuality, representatives of both communities will line up on both sides.

Questions have arisen about the nature of downtown development. Some have wondered whether the construction of both the ZCMI Center and the Crossroads Mall on the north end of the business district would undermine development south of Third South. Others have raised questions about the Triad Center. Some believe that its construction will provide far too much office space for the city to absorb and they are concerned about the cost of that space. State representative Mac Haddow, hardly an advocate of historic preservation, questioned the cost to the state of office space to be rented in the Triad complex.

At the level of organized religion, however, cooperation is, and will likely continue to be, the norm rather than the exception. Thriving congregations of Catholics, Protestants, Jews, Buddhists, and other religions exist in Salt Lake City, and Latter-day Saint representatives regularly participate in the meetings of the Utah Conference of Christians and Jews.

If cooperation is the norm in business and government, and formal cordiality is the tendency in relations between religious groups, in social and cultural matters Salt Lake is really two cities. It seems to us an overstatement to call Salt Lake generally "a city of two selves, a double personality: one loyal to the ideals of the pioneers, the other scorning or blushing for the past," as Nels Anderson did in the 1920s. The business and political communities are too well integrated for that. As Dale Morgan once pointed out, the LDS church has made its peace with the world of business and politics. Morgan was somewhat critical of that change, but it is a fact of life that has made Salt Lake City work on the political and economic level.

It is rather on the social and cultural level that the cleavages remain. The problem is that people who come to Salt Lake City and whose attitudes and life styles have represented the majority opinion in other areas of the United States find themselves instantly in a social and cultural minority in Salt Lake City. As one University of Utah professor and former Mormon bishop put it in an interview for *Utah Holiday*, "It's painful for a WASP to be a minority anywhere in the United States."

Many people who move to Salt Lake City are not used to a culture in which religion is central to the lives of intellectuals, professionals, and business people. They are surprised when they find that in a large urban area a religious institution like the Mormon ward should form such a cohesive community. Mormons share a sense of identity into which it is difficult for others to break.

At the same time, stereotypes held by non-Mormons often exclude otherwise interested Latter-day Saints from social and cultural activity. An LDS professor visiting at the University of Utah reported that other department members regularly visited a private club each week. The others knew he was a Mormon, and did not extend the invitation to him. At times this attitude can become vicious, as in derisive references to "garment wearers," an uncomplimentary reference to religious under-clothing worn by practicing Latter-day Saints, or in the Baptist declaration that the LDS church is a cult, unworthy of fellowship by true Christians.

Most serious is the cleavage drawn within those areas where the two societies must meet. In some schools, PTA officers will alternate between predominantly Mormon and predominantly non-Mormon parents. Children will be drawn into or excluded from particular groups because of their religious connections. Parents often expect their religious beliefs to be enacted into school policy. In nominally secular institutions with LDS connections, like the Promised Valley Playhouse, professional actors and actresses can be shocked because they are expected to refrain from drinking tea and to wear brassieres. Such cultural differences are likely to continue.

So far as future development is concerned, since Salt Lake City's economy has been affected by national trends, the problems that the city confronts now will undoubtedly reflect those of the remainder of the nation. The current recession has affected Salt Lake City less than cities of the East and Midwest, and virtually all sources indicate that the city's future seems quite promising. In 1984 Utah's unemployment rate stood approximately two percentage points below the national average, and the hardest hit areas in Utah are rural counties like Juab, Duchesne, and San Juan rather than the highly urbanized Wasatch Front. More to the point, both Salt Lake City and the larger metropolitan area have experienced a rapid growth in the recent past and the companies spearheading that growth expect to continue their expansion. In mid-1984 it was reported that the cost of living had fallen below the national average. Only in the cost of health care did it exceed the average.

Policies of the Reagan administration have created potential problems. Under the "New Federalism," many programs heretofore funded by the national government are being turned back to the states and cities. Most people in Salt Lake seem to believe this is all right, so long as the revenue sources needed to fund those programs are also returned. At present it is not certain that this will be done. If it is not, the city will be faced with some difficult choices in the allocation of its revenues.

A major advantage that Salt Lake City enjoys in planning for its future is the broad level of agreement in Utah regarding future growth. Several years ago, Governor Scott Matheson appointed an Agenda for the Eighties Commission to solicit testimony throughout the state and to report on citizen attitudes concerning the future. The consensus in the state seemed to favor growth, but at a controlled rate. As one member of the commission put it, "so it doesn't eat us up."

Achieving this goal will undoubtedly prove difficult. The Salt Lake City-Ogden Standard Metropolitan Statistical Area (SMSA) has the second highest birth rate in the United States at 27.1 per 1,000 population. It is exceeded only by the adjoining Provo-Orem SMSA with 37.4.

Both are far above the national rate of 15.9 per 1,000. At the same time, while the average income per worker in Utah ranks about in the middle of the fifty states at 26th, its per capita income ranks very low, at 78.9 percent of the national average because of the large size of Utah families. In fact, in 1981, only four states, all in the South, ranked below Utah in per capita income.

There is, nevertheless some room for optimism. In 1981, the latest year for which we have complete figures, the mining industry led all others in income growth. In second place stood the service industry, which includes such businesses as restaurants, hospitals, hotels, and accounting firms. During the current recession, the decline in demand for oil, coal, copper, and other minerals has had an impact on income in the state, but service industries and trade have been hurt less than most others. This is undoubtedly part of the reason for the relative prosperity in urban compared with rural areas. Salt Lake particularly is most dependent on these post-industrial businesses.

One of the problems Salt Lake City has confronted in securing industry in the past has been its relatively isolated location. It is quite far from the nearest population concentrations on the West Coast. This was, of course, an advantage during the Second World War when the federal government needed a secure location for military installations. Salt Lake was then and still is a major transportation center. If anything, its position has been enhanced by the recent expansion of the Salt Lake International Airport and the decision of Western Airlines to move its Rocky Mountain hub from Denver to Salt Lake City. In 1982 3.2 million people passed through the Salt Lake airport. The completion of I-80 west to Nevada and of I-15 south toward Las Vegas should also improve this condition.

For some industries, nearby population concentrations of the magnitude of the East and West coasts may be irrelevant, provided certain other necessary features are present. As long as an adequate infrastructure and an excellent quality of life exists in a particular community, distance from other population centers may be an unimportant consideration. This is particularly true of services that rely principally on electronic communications or air travel rather than land transportation to serve their clients.

The example of American Express is instructive. American Express decided to move its Travelers Cheque processing center from New York City because of unfavorable rent, utility, and tax rates there. Salt Lake City provided the infrastructure needed, through its Branch Federal Reserve Bank and major banking facilities, its sophisticated telecommunications equipment, and transportation facilities. In addition, the city offered a family-oriented atmosphere combined with a cosmopolitan life style, including recreational facilities, cultural amenities, and a good educational system.

This analysis suggests that, in the future, citizens of Salt Lake City can expect certain types of industry to locate there. First should be those for which distance from other population centers may not be a particularly important consideration. Banks and financial services, the broadcasting industry, and telecommunications all fit this category.

Next should be those businesses producing items with relatively high value in comparison to their size for which other considerations such as the labor force, cost of rent and taxes, and the business climate might be more important than distance from markets. This would include firms producing electronic equipment, drug companies, and companies producing medical and dental instruments. Between 1970 and 1980 electronics employment in Utah—much of it in Salt Lake City—grew 177 percent from 4,700 to 13,000 employees.

The third category should be companies whose operations are dependent upon resources found in Utah. These would include oil and natural gas, synthetic fuels companies, companies mining or processing minerals, and companies servicing those firms.

Fourth should be those businesses with a historical interest in Utah. Perhaps the best example here is defense-related businesses, such as contractors supplying defense installations, or the installations themselves. Others include mining companies and companies providing goods and services for the Latter-day Saint market.

There are, of course, problems with the expansion of some of these industries. While Utah's electronic components industry, which requires minimally trained electronics technicians, has grown more rapidly than that of the nation as a whole and is larger than those in states like Colorado and New Mexico, its computing machines industry has grown only slightly faster than the national average. Projections by the University of Utah's Bureau of Economic and Business Research indicate that unless the State of Utah is willing to spend more on the education of computer scientists, a well-trained labor force will not be present to attract such companies.

A number of changes in recent years lead to the impression that Salt Lake City is on the verge of important breakthroughs in its development. One of these is the interest shown in recent years in Salt Lake by the Saudi Arabian Khashoggi family, especially Essam Khashoggi, chairman of the board of the Triad group of companies, and his brother Adnan, founder of the group. In 1974, the family acquired more than 650 acres of land adjacent to the Salt Lake International Airport. Subsequent acquisitions have placed 900 acres of land in the family's possession. They soon began the development of a project which they and others associated with them believe may reorient the city from a north-south axis along the Wasatch Front to an east-west axis along I-80. In Janaury 1983, the Salt Lake City commission approved annexation of land west of the International Center, which has increased the area of the city by twenty-five percent.

Another problem will be the development of a transportation system capable of providing services for the new area. Most people today still drive their cars to work in Salt Lake Valley, in part because of the relatively inconvenient public transportation service. As one of our sources put it, if someone lives in West Jordan and wants to commute to his job at the Salt Lake International Center, he does not want to have to ride downtown first, then transfer to a bus going to the center. It seems probable that Salt Lake City will not in the near future have the sort of mass transit system characteristic of extremely dense population areas like the San Francisco Bay area or New York City. The information we have, however, suggests that the Salt Lake Valley must address more fully its transportation needs within the next ten years.

Salt Lake City faces another major problem in dealing with the larger metropolitan area. The interests of the citizens of Salt Lake City are not separate fom those of South Salt Lake, Midvale, or other communities in Salt Lake Valley. Yet the valley is honeycombed with small independent communities through which the unincorporated areas of the county form a matrix. To the present time, problems relating to the independent governments have been addressed by agreements affecting single services. The ultraconservatism of the people of the county outside Salt Lake City, however, has militated against the inauguration of any metropolitan government. As a result, economies of scale cannot be achieved in services such as police and fire, since each jurisdiction has its own department. Some agreements have been made to share these services on a limited basis, but the overall problem has not been addressed.

The fragmented jurisdictions also created a public relations problem for the chamber of commerce and businesses like Triad that are trying to entice other companies into the valley. Anyone who picks up a general reference work learns that Salt Lake City has a population of 160,000. In fact, as any Wasatch Front resident could explain, the population of the greater Salt Lake area is closer to 700,000, but some prospective businesses never learn that before they are discouraged at the prospect of moving their company to such a small city.

The problem may also be compounded by a generally conservative attitude presently held by many members of the LDS church. Often, it appears, they perceive conservative political signals emanating from some church leaders as justification for opposing almost all change. In reality, there is a tendency among Mormon leaders to separate political conservatism from ultraconservative attitudes towards growth, economic development, and economies of scale. The LDS church leadership, for instance, stood squarely behind downtown redevelopment, construction of the Salt Palace and Symphony Hall, and inauguration of the Triad Center by making both land and moral support available. Similar progressive attitudes toward regulated growth do not always filter down to lay members.

It is also often difficult to communicate to members the sense of cosmopolitanism felt in church headquarters. Church leaders like President Spencer W. Kimball, President Gordon B. Hinckley and the late President Nathan Eldon Tanner, together with business and community leaders close to the church leadership, have little trouble seeing the need for growth to generate jobs and the desirability of making newcomers, whether Latter-day Saints or not, comfortable in the city.

According to most sources, many companies and individuals fear that they will not fit into what they perceive as a unitary and predominantly Mormon culture. Even if the fear proves to be unfounded, it is a factor in the decision to locate in Salt Lake. Nevertheless, stories continually creep out of the city of neighbors bringing loaves of bread over to newcomers, then never returning when they learn that the newcomer is not a Latter-day Saint.

Another problem in connection with the Latter-day Saints in Salt Lake City has to do with their famous welfare plan. The church operates an extensive welfare system in which volunteers work on farms, in canneries, and on other projects to provide the necessities of life for those too unfortunate to care for themselves. Access to the products of the system is through the bishops, who decide whether to provide assistance to ward members or not. In addition, they have the prerogative of providing help to nonmembers should they decide to do so. The existence of this system and the injunction to church members to avoid public welfare, together with some statements by general and local church leaders opposing public assistance, have led some members to exhibit hostility to those receiving public assistance. In December 1982, at a post-mortem on the recent senatorial election, LaVarr G. Webb, political editor of the LDS church's *Deseret News*, said that Mormons would not rejoin the Democratic party unless it changes its image or unless they decide that government should take a basic role in helping people.

Moreover, many Latter-day Saints themselves receive assistance from public and other private agencies. Some may be inactive, many do not ask for church assistance, others may be denied church help while they are eligible for public relief. Some of these denials may be made by local bishops whose attitudes are more harsh than church policy would dictate. In Salt Lake City, the nonsectarian Crossroads Urban Center provides food for 10,000 persons per year, nearly half of whom are Latter-day Saints.

It should be understood, however, that the aloofness shown at times by Latter-day Saints derives from a long history of persecution, shunning, and hostility from other denominations. During the nineteenth century, the federal government and Evangelical Protestants conducted an extensive campaign against Mormon beliefs and practices, which eventually led to the confiscation of the church's property and the jailing of numerous Latter-day Saint leaders. In recent years, that campaign has continued as various anti-Mormon and fundamentalist groups have picketed the church's conferences, distributed pamphlets attacking church leaders and doctrines, and urged Latter-day Saint exclusion from the community of Christians. As recently as 1982, the Baylor University administration agreed with militant Baptist ministers that they would no longer hire Mormons on their faculty. Even though Baylor is in Texas, many Salt Lake City Mormons feel put upon when anything like this happens to their members.

All of this takes place at a time when the city needs, perhaps more than ever before, the combined efforts of all in the community to help in solving problems. In December 1982, for instance, Mayor Ted Wilson testified before a congressional committee that the number of Salt Lake City's homeless had more than doubled over the past year, largely as a result of the current recession. The city opened a new transient shelter late in 1982, but that did not solve all the problems, and the city's west side is still littered with the derelicts of economic, social, and cultural disaster.

Beyond this, the city faces other problems in its attempt to meet the challenges of the 1980s. Although Salt Lake City has not experienced the fiscal strain of some cities, it has nevertheless continued to encounter some difficulties. The administration faces enormous capital requirements over the next few years, not the least of which will involve the renovation of the city and county building, which is deteriorating from neglect both inside and out. The north end of the building has been shut down because large chunks of sandstone fall off during rainstorms. The city will also incur additional expenses for roads, curbs, gutters, sewers, and water systems. The city, the county, and the state must work together in dealing with problems caused by the backing up of the Jordan River.

Another serious financial problem has been created by recent flooding. A record snowpack during the winter of 1982–1983, coupled with rapid warming in May and June, led to flooding that surpassed even 1952. On May 5, 1983, Thirteenth South became the first of several streets used as rivers. On May 28, waters rushing down City Creek Canyon

Mayor Ted Wilson, Current Mayor of Salt Lake City and a Leader in the movement for the Mayor-Council System.

turned State Street into a sandbag-lined canal. Later in May and into early June, North Temple Street and Walker and Cottonwood Lanes were also turned into rivers. The work of city crews and volunteers recruited principally from Mormon wards and stakes prevented the flooding from becoming an unmanageable disaster. Nevertheless, the expense of handling the water constituted a major financial concern for the city, and capital outlays during the winter of 1983–1984 to deal with further flooding added an additional burden.

The mountain snowpack that winter was just as severe as the year before, and the runoff was nearly as heavy. New storm drains and other preparations, however, made the damage to Salt Lake City much less severe. At the same time, the runoff pushed the Great Salt Lake to its highest level since 1878, causing severe property and highway damage in the vicinity. It also added to the dilution of the lake's famous salinity. The salt content dropped from 28 percent by weight in the early 1960s to less than 10 percent in 1983 and 6 percent in July, 1984. Ocean water has a 3.5 percent salinity. Whatever this may mean for the effort to revive tourism on the shores of the lake, it is virtually certain that the whims of nature will continue to affect both Salt Lake City and the body of water for which it was named.

This is not to say that the city is without resources or that these problems will prove insuperable. Continued growth, the obvious good will of the majority of citizens, and the interest in urban beautification and the environment on the part of the LDS church leadership are all in the city's favor. Salt Lakers have proved themselves enormously resilient over the past 130 years and they will undoubtedly continue to survive and flourish. Most analysts seem to believe that it is one of the cities of the future rather than of the past.

The city's cultural and educational resources are still attractive. The Utah Symphony, Ballet West, and the University of Utah are all institutions of national prominence. During the latter part of 1982, and into early 1983, the University was constantly in the news owing to the implantation there of a mechanical heart in Dr. Barney Clark. It was the first time in history such an operation had been performed on a human patient.

Since World War II, the University has striven for excellence. A report early in 1983 indicated that a number of the University's graduate programs in the physical sciences were among the best in the nation. The Conference Board of Associated Research Councils rated chemistry, computer science, geology, geophysics, mathematics, and physics second in the nation in overall improvement in the past five years. This was a considerable achievement, since the graduate school had only been in existence since World War II. James L. Clayton, dean of the

The Honorable Christine M. Durham, Associate Justice, Utah State Supreme Court. Courtesy, Utah State Supreme Court.

graduate school, opined that the success had come because of a strong policy of freedom of inquiry in research. He said that such progress would have been impossible without such a commitment. Moreover, the University has announced stiffer entrance requirements for undergraduates, including stronger preparation in English, mathematics, history, and foreign languages.

At the same time, University of Utah President David P. Gardner had been appointed as chair of the National Commission on Excellence in Education. The *Salt Lake Tribune* of April 27, 1983 announced the report of that commission entitled "A Nation at Risk: The Imperative for Educational Reform." The report called for an increased emphasis on English, mathematics, science, social studies, computer science, and foreign languages.

Nevertheless, the University faces some serious problems in the future. Enrollment in fall 1982 stood at its highest ever at 24,364 students. At the same time, federal grants, which have gone in the past to help fund research, have been cut from a high of $60.1 million in fiscal 1981 to $58.3 million in fiscal 1982. In response to the Gardner Commission report, the Reagan administration has emphasized such matters as tuition tax credits, educational savings accounts, and abolition of the federal Department of Education, hardly propositions that can be expected to provide the increased funding needed to meet the problems faced by public institutions like the University of Utah. Moreover, the state legislature has put education on notice, not only at the University of Utah

315

but throughout the state, that it is reluctant to appropriate money to pay the cost of continued excellence.

In spite of all these problems and challenges, however, the quality of life in Salt Lake City is good, and the indicators seem to bode well for the future. Even though Utah divorce rates are higher than the national average, the family is still generally idealized and family activities provide much of Salt Lake's social life. The traditional Mormon "family night" (Monday) is often capitalized upon by the Salt Palace and other commercial entertainment centers as they offer special rates to families. The Hogle Zoo has become a major attraction for families, and Salt Lake City's numerous parks and playgrounds are constantly filled. Sports enthusiasts find municipal golf courses in or near the city, as well as country clubs, racquet clubs and the like, and the city seems enthusiastic about its professional baseball, basketball, and hockey teams. University of Utah sports events, especially basketball and football, are also well attended, and many Salt Lakers regularly travel forty-five miles south to attend Brigham Young University's sports activities.

At a more personal level, the quality of many lives in the city is enhanced by its various religious communities. Over fifty percent of the population still belongs to the Mormon church, and for this group the Mormon ward still constitutes a primary social and religious center. Each ward has definite geographic boundaries, usually encompassing 100 to 150 families. Sunday religious services, ward welfare assignments, ward socials and outings of various sorts, ward-sponsored scout troops and athletic teams, Women's Relief Society activites, monthly visits by "home teacher" to each family: all this and more will undoubtedly continue to make the Mormon ward a major center of focus and loyalty for a large portion of Salt Lake City's citizens. The same is true for Catholic, Protestant, and Jewish congregations: all provide active social as well as religious fellowship for their communicants, and will likely continue to provide newcomers to the city with plenty of options for religious association.

In addition, religious boundaries are increasingly transcended as men and women throughout the city find themselves involved in numerous private clubs and public service organizations. Such diverse groups as the Kiwanis club, the Rotary club, the Lion's club, the Masons, the League of Women Voters, and the National Association for the Advancement of Colored People all provide important outlets for people interested in various public causes.

Utahns, including the citizens of Salt Lake City, are also vitally concerned with education, yet the high Utah birthrate has made it difficult to put as much money per student into education as many other states do. Nevertheless, in 1984 one city high school was rated among the top in the nation for educational excellence.

Another important factor in Salt Lake City's favor is the new image Utah has experienced in recent years. In 1972, John Hunt, director of the Utah State University Institute of Outdoor Recreation and Tourism, completed a study on the image of Utah which indicated that most people outside the state believed Utahns to be closer to the national perception of a frontier rancher or an Amish farmer—conservative and hidebound—than to the image they had of themselves as typical middle-class Americans. Recently, Gary Cadez, senior research associate at the institute, completed a follow-up study which indicated that the image had changed to something "closer to reality."

An article by Robert H. Woody in the January 23, 1983 *Salt Lake Tribune* reported on the two studies and tried to assess the reasons for the changes. He cited Robert Redford and the motion picture industry, and Marie Osmond and her image of wholesomeness. Most important, Woody believes, have been the award-winning "Homefront" television ads sponsored by the LDS church showing average American families trying to solve problems. They present universal messages of patience, love, and forgiveness from people who look like everyone else. Important also seems to have been tourism, and especially the ski industry. The opening of international-class ski resorts like Snowbird in Little Cottonwood Canyon and Deer Valley at Park City, both within minutes of Salt Lake City, has added a dimension to Utah's image heretofore not present. Moreover, visitors representing significant sectors of the business and opinion-molding worlds have reported favorable impressions of the state in general and Salt Lake City in particular. Undoubtedly this trend will continue.

On balance, it seems that Salt Lake City has more going for it than against it. In fact, John Naisbitt, in his recent book *Megatrends: Ten New Directions Transforming our Lives*, rates the city as one of the most promising in the United States. Naisbitt expects Salt Lake to be one of the cities of the future, and Salt Lake's citizens are undoubtedly prepared to meet that future.

Salt Lake City Skyline. April 1982. Courtesy, Deseret News.

Bibliographical Note

It would be impossible in an essay of this sort to review all the literature, but the sources indicated below are those that have proved most helpful to us plus some others we believe the reader will find useful.

Two general histories of the history have been written. They are Edward W. Tullidge's *History of Salt Lake* (Salt Lake City: Star Printing Company, 1886) which provides much valuable information on the nineteenth century, but which is as often a history of Utah as of Salt Lake City; and *Salt Lake City: The Gathering Place. An Illustrated History* by John S. McCormick (Woodland Hills, Calif.: Windsor Publications, 1980), which is valuable for the information and pictures it contains, but which because of its format is limited in its scope.

These should be supplemented by [Everett L. Cooley, ed.] *The Valley of the Great Salt Lake*, revised edition (Salt Lake City: Utah State Historical Society, 1963); Charles B. Anderson, "The Growth Patterns of Salt Lake City, Utah and Its Determining Factors" (Unpublished Ph.D. dissertation, New York University, 1957); Dale L. Morgan, "Salt Lake City: City of the Saints," in Ray B. West, ed., *Rocky Mountain Cities* (New York: W.W. Norton, 1949) pp. 179-207; Nels Anderson, "Salt Lake City: From Brigham Young to Babbitt," *The New Republic* 52 (September 7, 1927): 66-71; and Paul A. Wright, "The Growth and Distribution of the Mormon and Non-Mormon Populations in Salt Lake City" (M.A. thesis, University of Chicago, 1971). Charles S. Peterson, "Urban Utah: Toward a Fuller Understanding," *Utah Historical Quarterly* 47 (Summer 1979): 227-35, introduces a whole issue on urban Utah and places Salt Lake City in that broader context.

Studies have been done on sections of the city and on architectural development which we found extremely useful. They are: Margaret D. Lester, *Brigham Street* (Salt Lake City: Utah State Historical Society, 1979); Karl T. Haglund & Philip F. Notarianni, *The Avenues of Salt Lake City* (Salt Lake City: Utah State Historical Society, 1980); John S. McCormick, *The Historic Buildings of Downtown Salt Lake City* (Salt Lake City:

Utah State Historical Society, 1982); and Peter L. Goss, "The Architectural History of Utah," *Utah Historical Quarterly* 43 (Summer 1975): 208-39.

We found three newspapers to be indispensible for understanding the history of the city. The *Deseret News* and the *Salt Lake Tribune* are perhaps the best continuing sources. For the nineteenth century, the *Salt Lake Herald* proved useful as well. After the turn of the twentieth century, the *Intermountain Republican* and its successor, and successor of the *Herald*, the *Herald Republican*, proved useful. On the relationship of the newspapers to the community we found O.N. Malmquist's *The First 100 Years: A History of the Salt Lake Tribune, 1871-1971* (Salt Lake City: Utah State Historical Society, 1971); Wendell J. Ashton, *Voice in the West: Biography of a Pioneer Newspaper* (New York: Duell, Sloan and Pearce, 1950); and Monte B. McLaws, *Spokesman for the Kingdom: Early Mormon Journalism and the Deseret News, 1830-1898* (Provo, Utah, Brigham Young University Press, 1977) valuable. See also J. Cecil Alter, *Early Utah Journalism: A Half Century of Forensic Warfare Waged by the West's Most Militant Press* (Salt Lake City: Utah State Historical Society, 1938). On the foreign language newspapers see William Mulder, "Through Immigrant Eyes: Utah History at the Grass Roots," *Utah Historical Quarterly* 22 (January 1954): 41-55. In entering the newspapers, since there is no comprehensive index for any newspaper until the 1940s, we found the "Journal History" of the Church of Jesus Christ of Latter-day Saints, LDS Church Archives, Salt Lake City, to be quite valuable. It contains a scrapbook-type collection of newspaper articles, diary entries, and other information organized on a day-to-day basis. After 1940, the *Salt Lake Tribune* index proved indispensable.

The Salt Lake City council minutes proved a mixed source. During the early years they are spotty and sometimes poorly written. The tend to be somewhat better after the commission system was adopted in 1911, but they become quite cursory in their treatment of issues brought before the commission in the period after World War II. Through 1954, the minutes are available on microfilm.

For general statistical data, we found the United States decennial censuses to be indispensable. In this same connection, the various issues of the *Utah Economic and Business Review* provided considerable information on Salt Lake and Utah as did Phillip R. Kunz and Merlin D. Brinkerhof, *Utah in Numbers: Comparisons, Trends, and Descriptions* (Provo, Utah: Brigham Young University Press, 1969). The latter is valuable mainly for the period since 1950, though selected topics are covered for some earlier years. The city directories proved invaluable sources.

Several general histories of Utah, its people, and the Mormons proved helpful as well. Orson F. Whitney's *History of Utah*, 4 vols. (Salt Lake City: George Q. Cannon and Sons, 1893-1904) provided historical and biographical information. B.H. Roberts's *Comprehensive History of the Church of Jesus Christ of Latter-day Saints* (Salt Lake City: Deseret News Press, 1930) contains much on Utah and Salt Lake City. Richard D. Poll, Thomas G. Alexander, Eugene E. Campbell, and David E. Miller, eds., *Utah's History* (Provo, Utah: Brigham Young University Press, 1978) was particularly helpful as a source of social and cultural information and comparative urban development in Utah. Charles S. Peterson's *Utah: A Bicentennial History* (New York: W.W. Norton, 1977) provided insights into the relationship between Utah and national patterns. On ethnic and cultural history, Helen Papanikolas's *The Peoples of Utah* (Salt Lake City: Utah State Historical Society, 1976) proved indispensable. On LDS church history, we found: James B. Allen and Glen M. Leonard, *The Story of the Latter-day Saints* (Salt Lake City: Deseret Book, 1976) and Leonard J. Arrington and Davis Bitton, *The Mormon Experience* (New York City: Knopf, 1979) to be most valuable. For the internal history of one of Salt Lake's most significant ecclesiastical units, see Lynn M. Hilton, *The Story of the Salt Lake Stake of the Church of Jesus Christ of Latter-day Saints; 125 Year History, 1847-1972* (Salt Lake City: Salt Lake Stake, 1972).

For biographical information we found a number of sources most valuable. They include: Whitney; *History of Utah*, vols 2-4; Noble Warrum, *Utah Since Statehood: Historical and Biographical*, 4 vols. (Chicago: S.J. Clarke, 1919), vols 2-4; Tullidge, *History of Salt Lake City;* Andrew Jenson, *Later-day Saints Biographical Encyclopedia*, 4 vols. (Salt Lake City: Andrew Jenson History Company and Andrew Jenson Memorial Association, 1901-1936; and Ralph B. Simmons, *Utah's Distinguished Personalities* (Salt Lake City: Personality Publishing Company, 1933).

For general background reading on American cities, the interpretive literature cited in the following section is most valuable. We also found the following books useful in providing perspective: Howard P. Chudacoff, *The Evolution of American Urban Society* (Englewood Cliffs, N.J.: Prentice-Hall, Inc., 1975); Charles N. Glaab and A. Theodore Brown, *A History of Urban America* (New York: The Macmillan Company, 1969); Constance McLaughlin Green, *The Rise of Urban America* (New York: Harper and Row, 1965); Raymond A. Mohl and James F. Richardson, eds., *The Urban Experience: Themes in American History* (Belmont, Calif.: Wadsworth Publishing Company, 1973). For an interesting comparative study, see Ronald Edwin Thrift, "Two paths to Utopia: An Investigation of Robert Owen in New Lanark and Brigham Young in Salt Lake City" (Ph.D. dissertation, University of New Mexico, 1976), in which the author concludes that Salt Lake City succeeded better than New Lanark, in Scotland, because its common religion united its people in purpose and thought.

Chapter 1

The theoretical literature on the development of cities is quite vast, but we found the items cited here most relevant for us. These include Gunther Barth's *Instant Cities: Urbanization and the Rise of San Francisco and Denver* (New York: Oxford University Press, 1975), which contains a chapter on Salt Lake City as a "Temple City" and which also places the idea of "instant cities" in its broader historical context, ancient and modern. Richard C. Wade's *The Urban Frontier: The Rise of Western Cities, 1790-1830* (Cambridge, Mass.: Harvard University Press, 1959) provides considerable information on the process of urban growth in advance of the agricultural frontier. John W. Reps's work, especially *Town Planning in Frontier America* (Princeton, N.J.: Princeton University Press, 1969) and *Cities of the American West: A History of Frontier Urban Planning* (Princeton, N.J.: Princeton University Press, 1979), provided insight into comparative town planning in Europe and America. Two studies by Sam B. Warner, Jr. also provided comparative insight: *Streetcar Suburbs: The Process of Growth in Boston, 1879-1900* (Cambridge, Mass.: Harvard University Press, 1962); and "If All the World Were Philadelphia: A Scaffolding for Urban History 1774-1930," *American Historical Review* 74 (October 1968): 26-43, which provides a framework for comparative socioeconomic growth. *Streetcar Suburbs* should be read with Fred W. Viehe, "Black Gold Suburbs: The Influence of the Extractive Industry on the Suburbanization of Los Angeles, 1890-1930," *Journal of Urban History* 8 (November 1981): 3-26 as a corrective for western cities built near a base of extractive industries.

Several bibliographical essays provided help in setting the history of Salt Lake in context. The most valuable were: Michael H. Ebner, "Urban History: Retrospect and Prospect," *Journal of American History* 68 (June 1981): 69-84; and Kathleen Neils Conzen, "Community Studies, Urban History, and American Local History," in Michael Kammen, ed., *The Past Before Us: Contemporary Historical Writing in the United States* (Ithaca, N.Y.: Cornell University Press, 1980). Max Weber's ideas are presented in Don Martindale and Gertrud Neuwirth, eds., *The City* (New York: The Free Press, 1958), especially chapter 1, "The Nature of the City," which was first published in 1921 in *Archiv für Sozialwissenschaft und Sozialpolitik.* Two special studies on urban patterns proved useful. On the comparative growth of population and services in western cities see Lawrence H. Larsen, *The Urban West at the End of the Frontier* (Lawrence: Regents Press of Kansas, 1978). For an analysis of the structure of urban reform see Melvin G. Holli, *Reform in Detroit: Hazen S. Pingree and Urban Politics* (New York: Oxford University Press, 1969). The idea of island communities is found in Robert H. Wiebe's *The Search for Order, 1877-1920* (New York: Hill and Wang, 1967). Some aspects of modern city culture are outlined in Gunther Barth, *City People: The Rise of Modern City Culture in Nineteenth-century America* (New York: Oxford University Press, 1980).

For Claude S. Fischer's work see "Toward a Subcultural Theory of Urbanism," *American Journal of Sociology* 80 (May 1975): 1319-41; and *The Urban Experience* (New York: Harcourt Brace Jovanovich, Inc., 1976), which also outlines the competing theoretical constructs. The articles in which those views are represented are found in Richard Bennett, ed., *Classic Essays on the Culture of Cities* (New York: Meredith Corporation, 1969).

The literature on community theory is vast. For a concept useful in analyzing larger cities we found René König, *The Community*, Edward Fitzgerald, trans. (New York: Schocken Books, 1968) most useful. See also David J. Russo, *Families and Communities: A New View of American History* (Nashville, Tenn.: American Association for State and Local History, 1974). Martin Buber's *Paths in Utopia*, R.F.C. Hull, trans. (New York: Macmillan, 1950) and Robert Redfield, *The Little Community: Viewpoints for the Study of a Human Whole* (Chicago: University of Chicago Presss, 1955) present views of the nature of community which are scarcely applicable to cities of the size and complexity that Salt Lake City reached as early as the mid-1850s. Robert V. Hine has placed the idea of community in context in *Community on the American Frontier: Separate but Not Alone* (Norman: University of Oklahoma Press, 1980).

Our approach is different from that of Don Harrison Doyle in *The Social Order of a Frontier Community: Jacksonville, Illinois, 1825-70* (Urbana: University of Illinois Press, 1978) which tests the thesis proposed by Stanley Elkins and Eric McKitrick in "A Meaning for Turner's Frontier, Part I: Democracy in the Old Northwest," *Political Science Quarterly* 69 (September 1956): 321-53. Doyle concludes that the Elkins-McKitrick thesis is less satisfactory than the conflict theories of Allan Bogue in "Social Theory and the Pioneer," *Agricultural History* 34 (October 1960): 21-34 and Robert R. Dykstra, *The Cattle Towns* (New York: Knopf, 1968). We would concur that conflict rather than the emphasis on consensus best characterizes Salt Lake City's development. Conflicts, however, were mediated by subcultures, voluntary organizations, and at times by the federal government, more in line with Fischer's views cited above.

In part the conflicts resulted from differing interpretations of the nature of American society and thus of the American civil religion. On the American civil religion see Robert N. Bellah, *Beyond Belief: Essays on Religion in a Post-traditional World* (New York: Harper and Row, 1970) and "The Revolution and the Civil Religion" in Jerald C. Brauer, ed., *Religion and the American Revolution* (Philadelphia: Fortress Press, 1976).

Chapter 2

The most readily available general background material on pre-Mormon Utah is found in chapters 1-5 of Poll et al., *Utah's History*: "Utah, the Physical Setting," by Robert S. Layton; "The Earliest Peoples," by S. Lyman Tyler; "The Spanish Epoch," by Ted J. Warner; "The Fur Trade and the Mountain Men," by David E. Miller; "Explorers and Trail Blazers," by David E. Miller. In the back of the book are some interesting maps on prehistoric and nineteenth century Indian distribution as well as early Western explorations. Although not discussed in our text, the reader may be interested in further reading on the prehistoric people in the area, some of whom had permanent settlements in Salt Lake Valley until about 2500 B.C. Recommended reading includes Alfred V. Kidder, *An Introduction to the Study of Southwestern Archaeology* (New Haven: Yale University Press, 1962); Jesse D. Jennings, *Danger Cave*, University of Utah Anthropological Papers, No. 27 (1957); and Jesse D. Jennings, "Early Man in Utah," *Utah Historical Quarterly* 28 (January 1960): 2-27. More on the Spanish period is found in S. Lyman Tyler, "The Spaniard and the Ute," *Utah Historical Quarterly* 22 (October 1954): 343-61, and Tyler, "The Myth of the Lake of Copala Land of Teguayo," *Utah Historical Quarterly* 24 (October 1954): 313-29, and Julian H. Steward, *Basin-Plateau Aboriginal Socio-Political Groups*, Bureau of American Ethnology Bulletin 120 (1938). See also Herbert E. Bolton, *Pageant in the Wilderness, the Story of the Escalante Expedition to the Interior Basin, 1776* (Salt Lake City: Utah State Historical Society, 1950); Fray Angelico Chavez (trans.) and Ted J. Warner (ed.), *The Dominguez-Escalante Journal: Their Expedition through Colorado, Utah, Arizona, and New Mexico in 1776* (Provo: Brigham Young University Press, 1976); Ted J. Warner, "The Significance of the Dominguez-Velez de Escalante Expedition," in Thomas G. Alexander, ed., *Charles Redd Monographs in Western History: Essays on the American West, 1972-74* (Provo, Utah: Brigham Young University Press, 1975). An important general source on the mountain men is LeRoy C. Hafen's ten-volume collection of biographies, *The Mountain Men and the Fur Trade in the Far West* (Glendale: Arthur H. Clark, 1965-1972). See also J. Cecil Alter, *James Bridger* (rev. ed., Norman: University of Oklahoma Press, 1962). Other important treatments of pre-Mormon exploration and trails include Gloria Cline, *Exploring the Great Basin* (Norman: University of Oklahoma Press, 1963); David E. Miller, "John C. Fremont in the Great Salt Lake Region," *The Historian* 11 (Autumn 1948): 14-28; John C. Fremont, *Report of the Exploring Expedition to the Rocky Mountains in the Year 1842, and to Oregon and North California in the Years 1843-44* (Washington: Gales and Seaton, 1845); Thomas F. Andrews, "Lansford W. Hastings and the Promotion of the Salt Lake Deseret Cutoff: A Reappraisal," *Western Historical Quarterly* 4 (April 1973): 133-50; George R. Stewart, *Ordeal by Hunger* (Boston: Houghton Mifflin, 1960), which deals with the Donner party; David E. Miller, "The Donner Road through the Great Salt Lake Desert," *Pacific Historical Review* 27 (February 1958): 39-44.

The Mormon migration and general patterns of colonization and early government are found in chapters 6-9 of Poll et al., *Utah's History*, all by Eugene E. Campbell: "The Mormon Migration to Utah," "Early Colonization Patterns," "Governmental Beginnings." Since Salt Lake City was so central to the settlement of all of Utah, much in each of these chapters apply directly to what is discussed here. See also the general histories cited earlier, and especially chapters 2 and 3 of Arrington's *Great Basin Kingdom*, and Dale L. Morgan, *The Great Salt Lake* (Indianapolis: Bobbs-Merrill Co., 1947). A very valuable insight into Mormon impressions of Salt Lake Valley is found in Richard H. Jackson, "Righteousness and Environmental Change," in Thomas G. Alexander, ed., *Essays on the American West, 1973-1974* (Charles Redd Monographs in Western History, No. 5, Provo, Utah: Brigham Young University Press, 1975): 21-42. Most useful also on settlement patterns is Joel E. Ricks, *Forms and Methods of Early Mormon Settlement in*

Utah and the Surrounding Region, 1847-1877 (Logan, Utah: Utah State University Monograph Series, 1964). See also Anderson, *The Growth Patterns of Salt Lake City*.

The founding of the city is covered well in the general works, and especially in Morgan, *The Great Salt Lake*. The traveler's description quoted is found in Burton J. Williams, ed., "Overland to California in 1850: The Journal of Calvin Taylor," *Utah Historical Quarterly* 38 (Fall 1970): 312-49. Others are found in Mulder and Mortensen, *Among the Mormons*. For interesting material on the old fort, see Nicholas G. Morgan, comp., *The Old Fort: Historic Mormon Bastion, the Plymouth Rock of the West* (Salt Lake City: 1964). Among other items, this work provides specific insight into the political and economic activities of the church organization by printing minutes of the Great Salt Lake High Council for 1847 and 1848. The same author's twenty-three-page *The Provisional State of Deseret and the Old Fort* (Salt Lake City: Published by the author, 1966) is also useful. See also Dale L. Morgan's highly important article, "The State of Deseret," *Utah Historical Quarterly* 8 (April, July, October 1940): 65-239, Leland H. Creer, "The Evolution of Government in Early Utah," *Utah Historical Quarterly* 27 (January 1958): 23-44, and Klaus J. Hansen, *Quest for Empire* (Lansing: Michigan State University Press, 1967), chapters 6-7. See also Hilton, *The Story of Salt Lake Stake*; James E. Talmage, "Salt Lake City, the Deseret that has Blossomed as the Rose," in L.P. Powell, *History of Towns of the West* (n.p., 1901): 479-508; and Morgan, "Salt Lake City: City of the Saints." General chronology for this period and some interesting city events may be traced in the "Journal History." For the laws of the period, see the four-page publication, *Ordinances, Passed by the Legislative Council of Great Salt Lake City, and Ordered to be Printed* (Salt Lake City: 1849). The importance of Salt Lake City as a regional influence from the beginning of its history is emphasized in Chauncey D. Harris, *Salt Lake City A Regional Capital* (Chicago: Privately printed, 1940).

The fact that there has been no adequate biography of Brigham Young will soon be remedied by Leonard J. Arrington, *Brigham Young: American Moses*, forthcoming from Knopf. In the meantime, our interpretation is partly based on material graciously shared with us by Arrington. Beyond that, the reader is referred to certain studies that have some significant value. Milton R. Hunter, *Brigham Young the Colonizer* (Santa Barbara: 4th ed. rev., 1940; and Salt Lake City: Peregrine Smith, 1973), is the most comprehensive work dealing with Young's colonizing activities. Ray B. West, Jr., *Kingdom of the Saints: The Story of Brigham Young and the Mormons* (New York: Viking Press, 1957) presents a good overview of the period to the death of Brigham Young in 1877. Morris R. Werner, *Brigham Young* (New York: Harcourt, Brace & Co., 1925), is a well-written though skeptical treatment. There is also material of interest and value in S. Dilworth Young, *"Here is Brigham": Brigham Young, the Years to 1844* (Salt Lake City: Bookcraft, 1964), and in two admiring works by family members: Susa Young Gates, with Leah D. Widtsoe, *The Life Story of Brigham Young* (New York: Macmillan Company, 1930), and Clarissa Young Spencer, with Mable Harmer, *Brigham Young at Home* (Salt Lake City: Deseret Book Company, 1940). A more recent study, Stanley P. Hirshson, *The Lion of the Lord: A Biography of Brigham Young* (New York: Alfred A. Knopf, 1969) is interesting but highly disappointing for it draws too heavily on biased newspaper accounts and the author did virtually no research in the primary sources in Salt Lake City. Equally disappointing is the hagiography by Preston Nibley, *Brigham Young, the Man and His Work* (Salt Lake City: Deseret News Press, 1936), which is largely a "scissors and paste" chronology and does not even mention such controversial subjects as polygamy.

Especially important on early economic development is Arrington, *Great Basin Kingdom*. For more insight into the gold rush and its impact, the reader should also consult Eugene E. Campbell, "The Mormon Gold Mining Mission of 1849," *Brigham Young University Studies* 1 and 2 (Autumn 1959-Winter 1960): 19-31 and J. Kenneth Davies, "Mormons and California Gold," *Journal of Mormon History* 7 (1980): 83-100 Dale L. Morgan, "The Changing Face of Salt Lake City," *Utah Historical Quarterly* 27 (July 1959): 209-32, provides further insight into early business activities.

Chapter 3

In general, the newspapers, especially the Deseret News, and the city council minutes were very helpful for most of the topics covered in this chapter. So were the general histories cited earlier, but Tullige, *History of Salt Lake City;* Arrington, *Great Basin Kingdom;* and Poll et al., *Utah's History* were particularly useful throughout. Ricks, *Forms and Methods of Early Mormon Settlement* was also useful on various topics, and Levi Edgar Young, *Chief Episodes in the History of Utah* (Chicago: Lakeside Press, 1912) will provide the reader with some interesting anecdotal material. There are also a large number of published travelers's accounts that provide some interesting insight into the general development, appearance, and social and economic conditions of the city. Among them are Richard F. Burton, *The City of the Saints and Across the Rocky Mountains to California* (1861; reprint, edited by Fawn M. Brodie, New York: Alfred A. Knopf, 1963); Jules Rémy and Julius Brenchley, *A Journey to the Great Salt Lake*, 2 vols. (1861; reprint, New York: AMS Press, 1971); Horace Greeley, "Salt Lake City and the Mormons...," in W. Tryon, *Mirror for Americans* (Chicago: University of Chicago Press, 1952): 729-45; "Great Salt Lake...," in *All the Year Round* 5 (24 August 1861): 509-11; E.V. Fohlin, *Salt Lake City Past and Present...* (Salt Lake City: Privately printed, 1908); "Salt Lake City and its Environs," in *Harper's Weekly* 2 (15 May 1858): 313-13; Robert G. Athearn, *Westward the Briton* (New York: Scribner, 1951).

Insight into Mormon immigration and Salt Lake City growth in this period may be obtained in Arrington, *Great Basin Kingdom*; Anderson, "The Growth Pattern of Salt Lake City"; Gustive O. Larson, *Prelude to the Kingdom* (Francestown, N.H.: Marshall Jones Company, 1947), which deals in detail with the Perpetual Emigrating Fund Company; Gustive O. Larson, "The Mormon Gathering," chapter 10 in Poll et al., *Utah's History*; William Mulder, *Homeward to Zion: The Mormon Migration from Scandanavia* (Minneapolis: University of Minnesota Press, 1957). The famous city wall is discussed in Howard J. Nelson, "Walled Cities of the United States," *Annals of the Association of American Geographers* 51 (March 1961): 1-22, and "The City Wall," *The Pioneer* 5 (March-April 1953): 15-17. The new buildings erected in this period are described in Lester, *Brigham Street*; Goss, "The Architectural History of Utah"; Paul L. Anderson, "William Harrison Folsom: Pioneer Architect," *Utah Historical Quarterly* 43 (Summer 1975): 240-59; Burton, *City of the Saints*, in which the author shows his particularly keen powers of observation and description; and Hilton, *History of Salt Lake Stake*.

The minutes of the city council provided us with fairly good insight into city government. For general background on church-government relations, with examples from Salt Lake City, see also James B. Allen, "Ecclesiastical Influence on Local Government in the Territory of Utah," *Arizona and the West* 8 (Spring 1966): 35-48, and Eugene E. Campbell, "Governmental Beginnings," chapter 9 in Poll et al., *Utah's History*. An excellent and insightful biography of Salt Lake City's first mayor is Gene A. Sessions, *Mormon Thunder: A Documentary History of Jedediah Morgan Grant* (Urbana: University of Illinois Press, 1982). The administration of justice in these early years is discussed in James B. Allen, "The Unusual Jurisdiction of the County Probate Courts in the Territory of Utah," *Utah Historical Quarterly* 36 (Spring 1968): 132-42; Jay E. Powell, "Fairness in the Salt Lake County Probate Court," *Utah Historical Quarterly* 38 (Summer 1970): 256-62. Opposition to church influence is treated with particularly good insight in Ronald W. Walker, "The Godbeite Protest: Another View," *Utah Historical Quarterly* 42 (Summer 1974): 216-44.

Many aspects of Salt Lake City's economic development may be found in Arrington, *Great Basin Kingdom*, where one also gets a feeling for the regional influence of the city. See also A. Russell Mortensen, "Main Street: Salt Lake City," *Utah Historical Quarterly* 27 (July 1959): 275-84, and Dean L. May, "Economic Beginnings," chapter 11 in Poll et al., *Utah's History*. Malmquist, *The First 100 Years* is also useful; as is Morgan, *The Great Salt Lake*; and Burton, *The City of the Saints*. The city council minutes are somewhat helpful, though not complete, with respect to city income and expenditures. These things should be supplemented by consulting Leonard J. Arrington and Thomas G. Alexander, "The U.S. Army Overlooks Salt Lake Valley: Fort Douglas, 1862-1965," *Utah Historical Quarterly* 33 (Fall, 1965): 326-50, and by reading at least the following additional works by Arrington: "Agricultural Price Control in Pioneer Utah," *Agricultural History* 30 (July 1956): 104-13; "The Deseret Agricultural and Manufacturing Society in Pioneer Utah," *Utah Historical Quarterly* 24 (April 1956): 165-70; "The Deseret Telegraph—A Church-owned Public Utility," *Journal of Economic History* 11 (Spring 1951): 117-39; "Banking Enterprises in Utah, 1847-1880," *Business History Review* 29 (December 1955): 312-34; "The Mormon Tithing House: A Frontier Business Institution," *Business History Review* 28 (March 1954): 24-58; "Coin and Currency in Early Utah," *Utah Historical Quarterly* 20 (January 1952): 56-76. Information on income and wealth was kindly provided us by Professor Larry T. Wimmer of Brigham Young University from a major study conducted by himself and professors Clayne R. Pope and James R. Kearl. Other specialized aspects of the economy may be seen in Arrington, Fox, and May, *Building the City of God;* J. Kenneth Davies, "Utah Labor Before Statehood," *Utah Historical Quarterly* 34 (Summer 1966): 202-17; and Fisher Sanford Harris, *100 Years of Water Development* (Salt Lake City: Metropolitan Water District, 1942); Hynda Rudd, "Auerbach's: One of the West's Oldest Department Stores," *Western States Jewish Historical Quarterly* 11 (April 1979): 234-38; Ronald B. Watt, "Dry Goods and Groceries in Early Utah: An Account Book View of James Campbell Livingston," *Utah Historical Quarterly* 47 (Winter 1979): 64-69.

The Utah War, the Mountain Meadows Massacre, the Civil War, the coming of the railroad and the Mormon-gentile conflict are all treated in this chapter as interrelated parts of a larger theme: the integration of Salt Lake City and Utah into the larger American scene. Various aspects of this theme are treated in Arrington, *Great Basin Kingdom*, chapters 8 and 9; Alter, *Early Mormon Journalism*; A. Russell Mortensen, "The *Deseret News* and Utah, 1850-1867" (Ph.D. dissertation, University of California at Los Angeles, 1950); A. Russell Mortensen, "A Pioneer Paper Mirrors the Breakup of Isolation in the Great Basin," *Utah Historical Quarterly* 20 (January 1952): 77-92; Richard D. Poll, "The Mormon Questions Enters National Politics, 1850-1856," *Utah Historical Quarterly* 25 (April 1957): 117-31; and James Richard Greenwell, "The Mormon-Anti-Mormon Conflicts in Early Utah as Reflected in the Local Newspapers, 1850-1869" (Ph.D. dissertation, University of Utah, 1963). The most well-balanced treatment of the Utah War is Norman Furniss, *The Mormon Conflict* (New Haven: Yale University Press, 1960), but see also LeRoy R. Hafen and Ann W. Hafen, *The Utah Expedition, 1857-58: A Documentary Account...* (Glendale, Calif.: Arthur H. Clark Co., 1958), for some very useful documents pertaining to the war and to some activities in Salt Lake City; and A. Russell Mortensen, "A Local Paper Reports on the Utah War," *Utah Historical Quarterly* 25 (October 1957): 297-381. Albert R. Zobell, "Thomas L. Kane, Ambassador to the Mormons," *Western Humanities Review* 1 (October 1947): 320-46, is also useful for this period. The Civil War is dealt with very adequately in Gustive O. Larson, "Utah and the Civil War," *Utah Historical Quarterly* 33 (Winter 1965): 55-77; and E.B. Long, *The Saints and the Union: Utah Territory During the Civil War* (Urbana: University of Illinois Press, 1981). For commentary on the public image of the Mormons in this and later periods see Leonard J. Arrington and John Haupt, "Intolerable Zion: The Image of the Mormons in Nineteenth Century American Literature," *Western Humanities Review* 22 (Summer 1968): 243-60.

The railroad is dealt with in Arrington, *Great Basin Kindgom,* as well as in the following works: Robert G. Athearn, *Union Pacific Country* (Chicago: Rand McNally & Company, 1971); and his "Opening the Gates of Zion: Utah and the Coming of the Union Pacific Railroad," *Utah Historical Quarterly* 36 (Fall 1968): 291-314; Leonard J. Arrington, "The Transcontinental Railroad and Mormon Economic Policy" *Pacific Historical Review* 20 (May 1951): 143-57; Grenville M. Dodge, *How We Built the Union Pacific Railway* (Washington: Government Printing Office, 1910); and David H. Mann,"The Undriving of the Golden Spike," *Utah Historical Quarterly* 37 (Winter 1969): 124-34.

The literature on Mormon polygamy is profuse, and the best guide to that literature is Davis Bitton, "Mormon Polygamy: A Review Article," *Journal of Mormon History* 4 (1977): 101-8. Mormon apostle Orson Pratt, who gave the first public address on the doctrine, published the earliest public defense of it in *The Seer* (Liverpool, 1853-54), and the reader will find these articles important to his understanding of this aspect of Mormonism for that period. The leading statistical analysis of plural marriage is Stanley S. Ivins, "Notes on Mormon Polygamy," *Western Humanities Review* 10 (Summer 1956): 229-39. The most well-known sociological analysis is Kimball Young, *Isn't One Wife Enough?* (New York: Henry Holt, 1954), but for more recent research on polygamous families as well as other aspects of Mormon family life one should also consult Vicky Burgess-Olson, "Family Structure and Dynamics in Early Utah Mormon Families, 1847-1885" (Ph.D. dissertation, Northwestern University, 1975). Perhaps the best general article on polygamy is Lawrence Foster, "Polygamy and the Frontier: Mormon Women in Early Utah," *Utah Historical Quarterly* 50 (Summer 1952): 268-89. The problem of divorce is treated in a very interesting manner in Eugene E. Campbell and Bruce. L. Campbell, "Divorce Among Mormon Polygamists: Extent and Explanations," *Utah Historical Quarterly* 46 (Winter 1978): 4-23. See also, Stephanie Smith Goodson, "Plural Wives," chapter 9 of Claudia L. Bushman, ed., *Mormon Sisters: Women in Early Utah* (Cambridge, Mass.: Emmeline Press Limited, 1976), and Arrington and Bitton, *The Mormon Experience*, chapter 10.

A more general view of Mormon women in the nineteenth century has been the topic of much recent research, though a great deal more remains to be done. Two important books are Bushman, *Mormon Sisters*, and Vicki Burgess-Olsen, *Sister Saints* (Provo: Brigham Young University Press, 1978). Both of these books have essays by Maureen Ursanbach Beecher on Eliza R. Snow: "Eliza R. Snow," in *Mormon Sisters*, pp. 25-41, and "The Eliza Enigma: The Life and Legend of Eliza R. Snow," in *Sister Saints*, pp. 1-20, which appeared first in Thomas G. Alexander, ed., *Essays on the American West, 1974-75)* (Provo: Brigham Young University Press, 1976). Other important recent studies include: Leonard J. Arrington, "The Economic Role of Pioneer Mormon Women," *Western Humanities Review* 9 (1955): 145-64; Maureen Ursenbach Beecher, "Under the Sunbonnets: Mormon Women with Faces," *Brigham Young University Studies* 16 (Summer 1976): 471-84, and "Women's Work on the Mormon Frontier," *Utah Historical Quarterly* 49 (Summer 1981): 276-90; Jill Mulvay Derr, "Women's Place in Brigham Young's World," *Brigham Young University Studies* 18 (Spring 1978): 377-95; Ann Vest Lobb and Jill Mulvay Derr, "Women in Early

Utah," chapter 18 of Poll et al., *Utah's History*; chapter 12, "Mormon Sisterhood: Charting the Changes," in Arrington and Bitton, *The Mormon Experience*; chapters 7 and 8 of Kenneth W. Godfrey, Audrey H. Godfrey, and Jill Mulvey Derr, *Women's Voices: An Untold History of the Latter-day Saints 1830-1900* (Salt Lake City: Deseret Book Co., 1982). For a very early treatment of women, see Edward W. Tullidge, *The Women of Mormondom* (1877; reprint, Salt Lake City: n.p., 1966).

Many of the works previously cited deal with aspects of the Mormon family, but the reader should also consult chapter 10 in Arrington and Bitton, *The Mormon Experience*; Bruce L. Campbell and Eugene E. Campbell, "Pioneer Society," chapter 15 in Poll et al., *Utah's History*; Davis Bitton, "Zion's Rowdies: Growing Up on the Mormon Frontier," *Utah Historical Quarterly* 50 (Spring 1982): 182-95.

Other aspects of social and cultural life in Salt Lake City are touched on in a variety of studies. See especially Papanikolas, *The Peoples of Utah*; Juanita Brooks, *The History of the Jews in Utah and Idaho* (Salt Lake City: Western Epics, 1973); Norton B. Stern, "The Founding of the Jewish Community in Utah," *Western States Jewish Historical Quarterly* 8 (October 1975): 65-69; Leon L. Watters, *The Pioneer Jews of Utah* (New York: American Historical Society, 1952); Mulder, "Through Immigrant Eyes," and also his "Utah's Ugly Ducklings: A Profile of the Scandinavian Immigrant," *Utah Historical Quarterly* 23 (July 1955): 233-59; Arrington and Bitton, *The Mormon Experience*, chapters 7 and 10; Bruce L. Campbell and Eugene E. Campbell, "Early Cultural and Intellectual Developments," chapter 16 in Poll et al. *Utah's History*; Joseph Heinerman, "Early Utah Pioneer Cultural Societies," *Utah Historical Quarterly* 47 (Winter 1979): 70-89; Myrtle E. Henderson, *A History of the Theater in Salt Lake City from 1850 to 1870* (Evanston, Ill.: Published by the author, 1934); Joseph Heinerman, "The Mormon Meeting House: Reflections of Pioneer Religious and Social Life in Salt Lake City," *Utah Historical Quarterly* 50 (Fall 1982): 340-53; Hilton, *The Story of Salt Lake Stake*; Gustive O. Larson, "The Mormon Reformation," *Utah Historical Quarterly* 26 (January 1950): 45-63; Stanley S. Ivins, "The Deseret Alphabet," *Western Humanities Review* 1 (July 1947): 223-29; S. George Ellsworth, "The Deseret Alphabet," *American West* 19 (November 1973): 10-11.

Chapter 4

The general sources mentioned above form much of the basis for the narrative. Especially useful were: Whitney, *History of Utah*; Roberts, *Comprehensive History of the Church*; Tullidge, *History of Salt Lake City*; Anderson, *Growth Patterns*; and newspapers, census reports, the city council minutes, and city directories. The latter proved extremely valuable for determining the ethnic makeup of the city, economic activity in and around Salt Lake City, and the patterns of population distribution. Unfortunately, they were available only for 1869, 1874, 1879–1880, 1884, 1885–1886, 1888, 1892–1893.

A number of travel accounts provided descriptions of the city. The most useful were: Charles Marshall, "Salt Lake City and the Valley Settlements," *Fraser's Magazine* 84 (July 1871): 97-107; and "Salt Lake City," *Harper's Magazine* 69 (1884): 388-404. Isaac M. Wise's "Rabbi Wise: By Parlor Car Across the Great American Desert [1887]" *Pacific Historian* 11 (Fall 1967): 71-72, provides information on the Jewish community. On new buildings see Anderson, "William Harrison Folsom."

On aspects of economic development see: Arrington, *Great Basin Kingdom;* Robert G. Althearn, *Rebel of the Rockies: A History of the Denver and Rio Grande Western Railroad* (New Haven, Conn.: Yale University Press, 1962); and idem., *Union ̄Pacific Country* (Chicago: Rand McNalley, 1971). On the influence of mining see the Summer, 1963 issue of the *Utah Historical Quarterly*; and Richard W. Sadler, "The Impact of Mining on Salt Lake City," Ibid., 47 (Summer 1979): 236-53. On the Emma Mine, see Clark C. Spence, *British Investments and the American Mining Frontier, 1860-1901* (Ithaca, N.Y.: Cornell University Press, 1958), and W. Turrentine Jackson, "The Infamous Emma Mine: A British Interest in the Little Cottonwood District, Utah Territory," *Utah Historical Quarterly* 23 (October 1955): 339-62.

On politics, in addition to the general sources cited above, see: Robert J. Dwyer, *The Gentile Comes to Utah: A Study in Religious and Social Conflict (1862-1890)*, 2nd ed. (Salt Lake City, Utah: Western Epics, 1971); Robert G. McNiece, "The Exciting Situation in Utah," *In Our Day* (No. 4, 1889): 518-22; and "The Gentile Triumph in Salt Lake City," *Harper's Weekly* 34 (February 22, 1890): 143-44. On the Godbeite movement see: Ronald W. Walker, "The Liberal Institute: A Case Study in National Assimilation," *Dialogue: A Journal of Mormon Thought* 10 (1977): 74-85; idem., "The Commencement of the Godbeite Protest: Another View," *Utah Historical Quarterly* 42 (Summer 1974): 16-44; and idem., "The Godbeite Protest in the Making of Modern Utah" (Ph.D. dissertation, University of Utah, 1977).

On the relationship with the federal government see: Thomas G. Alexander, *A Clash of Interests: Interior Department and Mountain West, 1863-96* (Provo, Utah: Brigham Young University Press, 1977); idem., "'Federal Authority Versus Polygamic Theocracy': James B. McKean and the Mormons, 1870-1875," *Dialogue* 1 (Autumn 1966): 85-100; idem., "Charles S. Zane: Apostle of the New Era," *Utah Historical Quarterly* 34 (Fall 1966): 290-314; and idem., "A Conflict of Perceptions: Ulysses S. Grant and the Mormons," *Newsletter of the Ulysses S. Grant Association* 8 (July 1971): 29-42.

On the granting of woman suffrage see: T.A. Larson, "Woman Suffrage in Western American," *Utah Historical Quarterly* 38 (Winter 1970): 7-19; Beverly Beeton, "Woman Suffrage in Territorial Utah," *Utah Historical Quarterly* 46 (Spring 1978): 100-20; and Thomas G. Alexander, "An Experiment in Progressive Legislation: The Granting of Woman Suffrage in Utah," *Utah Historical Quarterly* 38 (Winter 1970): 20-30.

The data on wealth holding and nationality of heads of household comes from the manuscript census. It was collected and tabulated by Larry T. Wimmer, Clayne R. Pope and James R. Kearl of the BYU Economics Department.

Information on the labor movement comes from several sources. The most important were J. Kenneth Davies, "Utah Labor Before Statehood"; and Sheelwant Bapurao Pawar, "An Environmental Study of the Development of the Utah Labor Movement, 1860-1935" (Ph.D. dissertation, University of Utah, 1968).

On the urban united order movement see: Arrington, Fox, and May, *Building the City of God*.

Some material on the city is found in the Francis Armstrong papers at the Utah State Historical Society library, though the material in the papers is principally concerned with his financial affairs.

On urban services see Arrington, *Great Basin Kingdom*, for a general overview. On transportation see in addition, C.W. McCullough, "The Passing of the Streetcar," *Utah Historical Quarterly* 24 (April 1956): 123-29; and "From Mules to Motorcars: Utah's Changing Transportation Scene," *Utah Historical Quarterly* 42 (Summer 1974): 273-77. Water development is discussed in Harris, *100 Years of Water Development*. Medicine and hospitals are considered in Joseph R. Morrell, "Medicine of the Pioneer Period in Utah," *Utah Historical Quarterly* 23 (April 1955): 127-44; and John Bernard McGloin, "Two Early Reports Concerning Roman Catholicism in Utah 1876-1881," *Utah Historical Quarterly* 29 (October 1961): 333-44. These should be supplemented by newspaper reports, city council minutes, and the city directories.

Information on education comes from a number of sources. See Jill Mulvay, "The Two Miss Cooks: Pioneer Professionals for Utah Schools," *Utah Historical Quarterly* 43 (Fall 1975): 369-409; Stanley S. Ivins, "Free Schools Come to Utah," *Utah Historical Quarterly* 22 (October 1954): 321-42; Joseph A. Vinatieri, "The Growing Years: Westminster College from Birth to Adolescence," *Utah Historical Quarterly* 43 (Fall 1975): 344-61; and Ralph V. Chamberlin, *The University of Utah: A History of Its First Hundred Years, 1850-1950* (Salt Lake City: University of Utah Press, 1960).

On the foreign language press see: Thomas L. Broadbent, "The Salt Lake City Beobachter: Mirror of an Immigration," *Utah Historical Quarterly* 26 (October 1958): 328-50; other newspapers; and the city directories.

On the non-Mormon churches see: Francis J. Weber, "Father Lawrence Scanlan's Report of Catholicism in Utah, 1880," *Utah Historical Quarterly* 34 (October 1966): 283-89; Dwyer, *Gentile Comes to Utah*; and the city directories.

There are a number of valuable sources on popular and formal culture. On the various literary and cultural organizations see: Joseph Heinerman, "Early Utah Pioneer Cultural Societies," *Utah Historical Quarterly* 47 (Winter 1971): 70-89; Walker, "Liberal Institute"; William Mulder, "Through Immigrant Eyes: Utah History at the Grass Roots," *Utah Historical Quarterly* 22 (January 1954): 41-55; Ronald W. Walker, "Growing Up in Early Utah: The Wasatch Literary Association, 1874-78," *Sunstone* 6 (November/December 1981): 44-51; in addition to the city directories and newspapers. Lila Carpenter Eubanks, "The Deseret Museum," *Utah Historical Quarterly* 50 (Fall 1982): 361-76, discusses a significant educational and cultural institution of this period. On baseball see Kenneth L. Cannon II, "'The National Game': A Social History of Baseball in Salt Lake City, 1868-1888" (M.A. thesis, Brigham Young University, 1982). The best source on the Pratt-Newman debate is Whitney, *History of Utah*. See also Larry R. Gerlach, "Vengeance vs. the Law: The Lynching of Sam Joe Harvey in Salt Lake City" (unpublished paper presented in the Charles Redd Center lecture series and scheduled for publication in the center's monograph series).

Chapter 5

Much of the information for this chapter, especially for urban services and utilities, city departments, and the activities of voluntary organizations, comes from the newspapers. The city council minutes proved less helpful. General information is also found in E.V. Fohlin, *Salt Lake City Past Present....*

A number of valuable sources exist on politics and administration during the 1890s. Both the *Salt Lake Tribune* and the *Deseret News* supply important information. See also Jean Bickmore White, "Utah State Elections, 1895-1899" (Ph.D. dissertation, University of Utah, 1968). Additional material is found in Leonard J. Arrington, "Utah and the Depression of the 1890s" *Utah Historical Quarterly* 29 (January 1961): 3-18; Lauren H. Dimter, "Populism in Utah" (M.A. thesis, Brigham Young University, 1964); and David B. Griffiths, "Far Western Populism: The Case of Utah, " *Utah Historical Quarterly* 37 (Fall 1969): 396-407.

A number of valuable sources exist on economic development and those involved in it. See especially Leonard J. Arrington and Gary B. Hansen, *The Richest Hole on Earth: The History of the Bingham Copper Mine* (Logan, Utah: Utah State University Press, 1963); and Arrington's *Beet Sugar in the West: A History of the Utah-Idaho Sugar Company, 1891-1966* (Seattle: University of Washington Press, 1966). On Thomas Kearns and his associates see Kent Sheldon Larsen, "The Life of Thomas Kearns" (M.A. thesis, University of Utah, 1964). On Samuel Newhouse see Hynda Rudd, "Samuel Newhouse: Utah Mining Magnate and Land Developer," *Western States Jewish Historical Quarterly* 11 (July 1979): 291-307.

On the development of architectural styles and the urban elite in Salt Lake, in addition to the sources cited in the general bibliography, see Franz K. Winkler, "Building in Salt Lake City," *Architectural Record* 22 (July 1907): 15-37.

On the immigrants we found Papanikolas's *Peoples of Utah* to be indispensable. Particularly useful for the Southern and Eastern European immigrants were the articles by Papanikolas and Philip F. Notarianni. On the blacks, the article by Ronald G. Coleman proved helpful. See also Michael J. Clark, "Improbable Ambassadors: Black Soldiers at Fort Douglas, 1896-99," *Utah Historical Quarterly* 46 (Summer 1978): 282-301.

On labor organization, in addition to Pawar, "Utah Labor," see Joseph C. Clark, Jr. "A History of Strikes in Utah" (M.S. thesis, University of Utah, 1953).

A number of valuable sources exist on women in Salt Lake City. See two articles by Miriam B. Murphy: "The Working Women of Salt Lake City: A Review of the Utah Gazetteer, 1892-93," *Utah Historical Quarterly* 46 (Spring 1978): 121-35; and "Women in the Utah Work Force from Statehood to World War II" *Utah Historical Quarterly* 50 (Spring 1982): 139-59. See also Bushman, *Mormon Sisters*, Burgess-Olson, *Sister Saints*.

A number of important sources exist for the American party administration and the movement for commission government. See Reuben Joseph Snow, "The American Party in Utah: A Study of Political Party Struggles During the Early Years of Statehood" (M.A. thesis, University of Utah, 1964); John S. McCormick, "Red Lights in Zion: Salt Lake City's Stockade, 1908-11," *Utah Historical Quarterly* 50 (Spring 1982): 168-81.

On the general movement for commission government in the progressive era see Bradley Robert Rice, *Progressive Cities: The Commission Government Movement in America, 1901-1920* (Austin: University of Texas Press, 1977). On the Utah commission government movement in Salt Lake see Isaac B. Humphrey, "Commission Government in Salt Lake City" (M.A. thesis, University of Utah, 1936). On the reaction of the LDS church see Milton R. Merrill, "Reed Smoot, Apostle in Politics" (Ph.D. dissertation, Columbia University, 1950); the Journal of Anthon H. Lund, LDS Church Archives, Salt Lake City; the Diary of Reed Smoot, Special Collections, Brigham Young University Library, Provo, Utah; the Nephi L. Morris papers at the University of Utah Library; and the John Henry Smith Journal in the Smith Family Papers at the same place.

On the general prohibition movement see Joseph Gusfield, *Symbolic Crusade: Status Politics and the American Temperance Movement* (Urbana: University of Illinois Press, 1963); James H. Timberlake, *Prohibition and the Progressive Movement, 1900-1920* (Cambridge, Mass.: Harvard University Press, 1963); and Norman H. Clark, *Deliver Us from Evil: An Interpretation of American Prohibition* (New York: Norton, 1976). On the situation in Utah see: Bruce T. Dyer, "A Study of the Forces Leading to the Adoption of Prohibition in Utah in 1917" (M.S. thesis, Brigham Young University, 1958); and Brent C. Thompson, "Utah's Struggle for Prohibition, 1908-1917" (M.A. thesis, University of Utah, 1979). See also the Journal of Heber J. Grant, Archives of the Church of Jesus Christ of Latter-day Saints, Salt Lake City.

There are a number of sources on the importance of religion in social and political culture during the late nineteenth century and early twentieth century. See especially: Carl V. Harris, *Political Power in Birmingham, 1871-1921* (Knoxville: University of Tennessee Press, 1971); Richard J. Jensen, *The Winning of the Midwest: Social and Political Conflict, 1888-1896* (Chicago: University of Chicago Press, 1971); and two books by Paul Kleppner: *The Cross of Culture: A Social Analysis of Midwestern Politics, 1850-1900* (New York: Free Press, 1970); and *The Third Electoral system, 1853-1892: Parties, Voters and Political Cultures* (Chapel Hill: University of North Carolina Press, 1977).

A number of sources exist on water development in Salt Lake. The most important is Harris, *100 Years of Water Development.* On water development during the period see George Frederic Stratton, "Watering a Great City Without Pumps," *Technical World Magazine* 19 (July 1913): 672-75.

Though there is a great deal on the LDS church, studies of the work of non-Mormon churches leave much to be desired. The best sources on the history of the LDS church during the period include: Roberts, *Comprehensive History,* and Allen and Leonard, *The Story of the Latter-day Saints.* On the Episcopal church see James W. Beless, Jr., "The Episcopal Church in Utah: Seven Bishops and One Hundred Years," *Utah Historical Quarterly* 36 (Winter 1968): 77-96. On anti-Mormon mission activity see Arlow W. Anderson, "The Norwegian-Danish Mission in Utah", *Utah Historical Quarterly* 25 (April 1957): 153-61.

The best contemporary information on education is found in Fohlin, *Salt Lake City Past and Present.* On the University of Utah see Chamberlin, *University of Utah.* On LDS post-elementary education see D. Michael Quinn, "The Brief Career of Young University at Salt Lake City," *Utah Historical Quarterly* 41 (Winter 1973): 69-89. On some of the activities of the school board see Eugene Young, "The Revival of the Mormon Problem," *The North American Review* 68 (April 1899): 476-89, and Frank T. Morn "Simon Bamberger: A Jew in a Mormon Commonwealth" (M.A. thesis, Brigham Young University, 1966).

The newspapers provide the best information on both formal and popular culture. On Saltair see: John D. Gadd, "Saltair: Great Salt Lake's Most Famous Resort," *Utah Historical Quarterly* 36 (Summer 1968): 198-221. On social activities at Fort Douglas see Arrington and Alexander, "The U.S. Army Overlooks Salt Lake Valley."

Chapter 6

A great many sources are to be found on progressivism in the United States. Those we found most useful for studying urban progressivism in Salt Lake in addition to Rice, *Commission Government,* included Holli, *Reform in Detroit*; Wiebe, *The Search for Order*; and John D.

Buenker, *Urban Liberalism and Progressive Reform* (New York: Norton, 1973). On the city beautiful movement see William H. Wilson, *The City Beautiful Movement in Kansas City* (Columbia: University of Missouri Press, 1964).

On the operation of commission government see the sources cited for chapter 5, especially Humphrey, "Commission Government." A great deal of information was found in the Samuel C. Park papers at the Utah State Historical Society library, especially in Park's scrapbooks. For a contemporary view from a national perspective of Salt Lake City's experiment see Oswald Ryan, *Municipal Freedom: A Study of the Commission Government* (Garden City, N.Y.: Doubleday, Page and Co., 1915).

Much of the material on the conflict between the Ferry administration and the Civic Betterment Union is found in the city commission minutes. See also "Salt Lake City Adopts Plan for Parking," *National Municipal Review* 1 (1912): 491. See also "An Anti-fly Campaign," *National Municipal Review* 4 (October 1915): 674. *The Progressive*, organ of the Progressive party in Utah, was particularly helpful in the early years of the Park administration. On the water supply see, in addition to the sources cited in the previous chapter, Sylvester Q. Cannon, "Doubling the Water Supply," *American City* 15 (October 1916): 410-11. Some of the biographical information on Sylvester Q. Cannon was supplied by Winfield Q. Cannon. On the streetcar and bus system see C.W. McCullough, "The Passing of the Streetcar."

A number of sources exist for politics during the period. See especially: Brad E. Hainsworth, "Utah State Elections, 1916-1924" (Ph.D. dissertation, University of Utah, 1968); Dan E. Jones, "Utah Politics, 1926-1932" (Ph.D. dissertation, University of Utah, 1968); and Ellen Gunnell Callister, "The Political Career of Edward Henry Callister, 1885-1916" (M.S. thesis, University of Utah, 1967); Frank W. Fox, *J. Reuben Clark: The Public Years* (Provo and Salt Lake City: Brigham Young University Press and Deseret Book, 1980); and Larry R. Gerlach, *Blazing Crosses in Zion: The Ku Klux Klan in Utah* (Logan, Utah: Utah State University Press, 1982). For political problems as well as anti-Mormon activity, see *The Utah Survey* (various issues during 1913), published irregularly by the Episcopal church.

Beyond the perennial problem of a water supply, perhaps the most significant progress was made in air pollution control. See George W. Snow, "Smoke Elimination in Salt Lake City," *The American City* 13 (September 1915): 196-97; "Subscriber from Salt Lake City, Utah to Editor," *The Outlook* 109 (1915): 652-53.

A number of sources exist for popular and formal culture in addition to those cited in the general bibliography and in the bibliography for the preceding chapter. Some include: Chris Rigby, "Ada Dwyer: Bright Lights and Lilacs," *Utah Historical Quarterly* 43 (Winter 1975): 41-51, and Lucile M. Francke, "Salt Lake City, A Music Center," *New West Magazine* 7, no. 3 (1916): 63-65. On radio see Pearl F. Jacobsen, "Utah's First Radio Station" *Utah Historical Quarterly* 32 (Spring 1964): 130-44. On the Italian fraternal organizations see Philip F. Notarianni, "Italian Fraternal Organizations in Utah, 1897-1934," *Utah Historical Quarterly* 43 (Spring 1975): 172-87.

On children and youth see Arthur L. Beeley, *Boys and Girls in Salt Lake City: The Results of a Survey...* (Salt Lake City: University of Utah, 1929).

A great many sources exist for economic development. See Donald Q. Cannon, "The History of the Trucking Industry in the State of Utah" (M.A. thesis, University of Utah, 1962); *Come to Salt Lake City: The Center of Scenic America* (Salt Lake City: Chamber of Commerce and Commercial Club, [ca. 1923]). On Salt Lake's economic growth and its relationship to Utah see: Leonard J. Arrington and Thomas G. Alexander, *A Dependent Commonwealth: Utah's Economy from Statehood to the Great Depression*, Dean May, ed. (Provo, Utah: Brigham Young University Press, 1974). See also: Harold J. Shepstone, "The Mormons of Today: How They Have Solved Social and Economic Problems," *The Millgate Monthly* (April 1921): 76, 403-08. On workers and their problems, including the Utah Associated Industries, see: Pawar, "Utah Labor."

For Utah during World War I see Warrum, *Utah Since Statehood* and idem, *Utah in the World War* ([Salt Lake City]: State Council of Defense, 1924).

On the IWW and radicalism see: Glenn V. Bird, "The Industrial Workers of the World in Utah: Origins, Activities, and Reactions of the Church of Jesus Christ of Latter-day Saints" (M.A. thesis, Brigham Young University, 1976). On other radical groups see: John S. McCormick, "Hornets in the Hive: Socialists in Early Twentieth Century Utah," *Utah Historical Quarterly* 50 (Summer 1982): 225-40. On the Joe Hill case see: Gibbs M. Smith, *Joe Hill* (Salt Lake City: University of Utah Press, 1969). This should be read against the point of view of Leonard J. Arrington and William Roper, *William Spry: Man of Firmness, Governor of Utah* (Salt Lake City: Utah State Historical Society, 1971).

On women see Bushman, *Mormon Sister*, and Burgess-Olson, *Sister Saints*, especially Loretta L. Hefner "Amy Brown Lyman: Raising the Quality of Life for All," pp. 96-116.

Chapter 7

The newspapers, especially the *Salt Lake Tribune* and the *Deseret News*, were most helpful for this chapter, for they paid special attention to the New Deal programs in Salt Lake City. A scrapbook kept by Mayor Louis Marcus contains a very useful collection of newspaper clippings, and this was kindly shared with us by his son, Howard Marcus. City council minutes were also very useful, as was Malmquist, *The First 100 Years*. We also had access to an oral history interview with former Mayor John M. Wallace by Harvard Heath, August 18, 1982.

The regional economic impact of Salt Lake City in this era is seen very well in Harris, *Salt Lake City A Regional Capital*. For other economic and political factors, including the programs of the New Deal, the following sources were also useful: John F. Bluth and Wayne K. Hinton, "The Great Depression," chapter 26 of Poll et al., *Utah's History*, which contains some excellent bibliographical references for more information on Utah as a whole during the New Deal; Wayne K. Hinton, "The New Deal Years: A Political History of Utah 1932-1940" (M.A. thesis, Utah State University, 1963); chapter 8 of McCormick, *The Gathering Place*. Water development is handled in detail in Harris, *100 Years of Water Development*, but see also Leonard J. Arrington and Thomas G. Alexander, *Water for Urban Reclamation: The Provo River Project* (Logan, Utah: Utah Agricultural Experiment Station, 1966). The origin of the Mormon welfare program is discussed in Leonard J. Arrington and Wayne K. Hinton, "Origin of the Welfare Plan of the Church of Jesus Christ of Latter-day Saints," *Brigham Young University Studies* 5 (Winter 1964): 67-85, and Paul C. Child, "Physical Beginnings of the Church Welfare Program," *Brigham Young University Studies* 14 (Spring 1974): 383-85.

Unfortunately, the rapidly growing studies on women have not included specific studies on women in Salt Lake City. For a general view of women in Utah in the period, see Maureen Ursenbach Beecher and Kathryn L. MacKay, "Women in Twentieth Century Utah," chapter 31 of Poll et al., *Utah's History*. Some statistical data on employment of women in the period is given there, but the authors' conclusions are reported slightly differently from ours—possibly because we used different criteria in analyzing the United States census materials. Miriam B. Murphy's important article, "Women in the Utah Work Force From Statehood to World War II," presents a fine interpretive generalization for the state as a whole over four decades, but not much specific information on Salt Lake City for this period. For further insights on women from a national perspective, see William C. Chafe, *The American Woman: Her Changing Social, Economic and Political Roles 1920-1930* (New York: Oxford University Press, 1972). The life of Utah's first woman judge is reported admiringly, and very interestingly, in Beverly B. Clopton, *Her Honor, The Judge: The Story of Reva Beck Bosone* (Ames: Iowa State University Press, 1980).

Some interesting social statistics may be found in Owen F. Beal, *Social Characteristics of Salt Lake City* (Salt Lake City: University of Utah, 1943). For some aspects of Salt Lake City's social history see Violet Walker, "A History and Analysis of Recreation in Salt Lake City" (M.A. thesis, University of Utah, 1934); Wright, "The Growth and Distribution of Mormon and Non-Mormon Populations"; Miriam B. Murphy, "'Of Benefit and Interest to the Children of Salt Lake City'—The Tracy Aviary," *Utah Historical Quarterly* 48 (Summer 1980): 261-70; and various chapters in Papanikolas, *The Peoples of Utah*, where at least a few comments are made about some ethnic groups in the 1930s.

Chapter 8

As with so much of the twentieth century, Salt Lake City newspapers were especially rich for this period, and the city council minutes were also helpful. Chapter 9 of McCormick's *Salt Lake City* is a nice overview. Statistical data for this chapter was derived from the United States census reports. See also John E. Christensen, "The Impact of World War II," chapter 17 in Poll et al., *Utah's History*, as well as other chapters in the book that cover various topics; "Salt Lake City," in *Holiday* 4 (September 1948): 46-50; James L. Clayton, "An Unhallowed Gathering: The Impact of Defense Spending on Utah's Population Growth, 1940-64," *Utah Historical Quarterly* 35 (Summer 1966): 227-42; Leonard J. Arrington and Anthony T. Cluff, *Federally-Financed Industrial Plants Constructed in Utah During World War II* (Logan, Utah: Utah State University Monograph Series, 1969); Leonard J. Arrington and George Jensen, The Defense Industry of Utah (Logan, Utah: Utah State University, 1965); Leonard J. Arrington and George Jensen, *Impact of Defense Spending on the Economy of Utah* (Logan: Utah State University, 1967); and Thomas G. Alexander and Leonard J. Arrington, "Utah's Small Arms Plant During World War II," *Pacific Historical Review* 18 (May 1965): 185-96. The information on wartime housing was based on James B. Allen, "Crisis on the Home Front: The Federal Government and Utah's Defense Housing in World War II," *Pacific Historical Review* 38 (November 1969): 407-28.

Some interesting material on education in Salt Lake City was obtained from the biennial reports of the State Superintendent of Public Instruction. See also LeRoy E. Cowles, *The University of Utah and World War II* (Salt Lake City: Deseret News Press, 1949). Other social data is discussed in Louise Browning, "The Effects of War on Children and Family life in Metropolitan Salt Lake" (M.A. thesis, University of Utah, 1949). Much of this thesis is similar to the report of the Utah Preparatory Commission (Arthur L. Beeley, Convener, and Louise Browning, Secretary) submitted to the International Congress on Mental Health, London, 12-21 August 1948, and published under the title *Impact of War on the Family and Children in Metropolitan Salt Lake* (Salt Lake City: University of Utah Press, July 1948). See also Murphy, "Of Benefit and Interest to the Children of Salt Lake City."

For material on women, see Ursenbach and MacKay, "Women in Twentieth Century Utah;" Edith Berghout, "The Effect of War upon the Employment of Women with Special Reference to Utah" (M.A. thesis, University of Utah, 1944); Hefner, "Amy Brown Lyman." Information on ethnic groups is found in various chapters in Papanikolas, *Peoples of Utah*. Our source for the Hashimoto story is chapter 10 in that book, "Japanese Life in Utah," by Papanikolas and Alice Kasi. For a fine treatment on the Japanese experience at Topaz, see Leonard J. Arrington, *The Price of Prejudice* (Logan, Utah: Utah State University, 1962). See also Elmer R. Smith, "The Japanese in Utah," *Utah Humanities Review* 2 (April and July 1948): 129-44, 208-30; and Brooks, *The History of the Jews in Utah and Idaho*.

Chapter 9

The greatest general help in this chapter came from oral history interviews. They are: Jennings Phillips, former city treasurer and city commission member, interviewed by Harvard Heath on March 30, 1982; Grant Burbidge, former city commission member, interviewed by Harvard Heath on July 31, 1982; L.C. Romney, former city commission member interviewed by Harvard Heath on May 11, 1982; and William Smart, editor of the *Deseret News*, interviewed by Harvard Heath, August 5, 1982.

In addition, we found considerable help from several other sources. Most information came from the newspapers, particularly the *Salt Lake Tribune*, since it was indexed for this period. Also the Louis Holley Collection at the University of Utah library helped considerably. Holly, a former city auditor kept an extensive clipping file which helped considerably in understanding the city's financial problems. The city commission minutes also provided valuable information.

On the war industries converted to peacetime use see: Arrington and Cluff, *Federally-financed Industrial Plants Constructed in Utah During World War II*; "Brigham Young Wouldn't Recognize it" *Business Week* (September 1, 1951): 80-82; and Alexander and Arrington, "Utah's Small Arms Ammunition Plant During World War II." The newspapers also proved valuable for this sort of information. On Geneva Steel see in addition, Thomas G. Alexander, "Utah War Industry During World War II: A Human Impact Analysis," *Utah Historical Quarterly* 51 (Winter 1983): 72-92.

The *Utah Economic and Business Review* provided considerable information. We found particularly helpful: Douglas F. Bennett and James W. Woolley, "Mass Transit in the Salt Lake Valley: 1872-1960," *Utah Economic and Business Review* 37 (September 1977): 1-13; and James W. Woolley and Douglas F. Bennett, "Mass Transit in the Salt Lake Valley: 1960 to 1978," *Utah Economic and Business Review* 38 (January 1978): 1-7.

An analysis of population changes will be found in Wright, "The Growth and Distribution of Mormon and non-Mormon Populations in Salt Lake City."

The home rule controversy produced a number of sources. J.D. Williams summarized it from his point of view in *The Defeat of Home Rule in Salt Lake City* ([New York]: Holt, Rinehart and Winston, 1960). This should be read against the interviews mentioned above, particularly those with Romney and Phillips, and the newspaper reports.

On the police department under W. Cleon Skousen see: Dennis L. Lythogoe, *Let 'Em Holler: A Political Biography of J. Bracken Lee* (Salt Lake City: Utah State Historical Society, 1982).

On the newspaper consolidation and the development of the McKay-Fitzpatrick-Backman triumvirate see Malmquist, *The First 100 Years*, and the interviews.

Chapter 10

The major sources for this period include the interviews cited in the bibliography for chapter 9 plus the following additional interviews: interview with Senator E.J. "Jake" Garn, former mayor of Salt Lake City, on April 7, 1982 by Harvard Heath; interview with Conrad Harrison, former commissioner and mayor, on August 4, 1982 by Harvard Heath; interview with Mayor Ted Wilson, March 16, 1982 by Harvard Heath; interview with Fred S. Ball, executive secretary of the Salt Lake Area Chamber of Commerce, December 3, 1982 by Harvard Heath; and an interview with Emanuel A. Floor, president and chief executive officer of Triad Utah, December 7, 1982 by Harvard Heath.

A number of books also proved useful. Most helpful were the biography of J. Bracken Lee by Dennis Lythgoe, and Peter Wiley and Robert Gottlieb, *Empires in the Sun: The Rise of the American West* (New York: Putnam, 1982). For a general study of the problems associated with urban renewal in the United States see: Martin Anderson, *The Federal Bulldozer: A critical Analysis of Urban Renewal, 1946-62* (Cambridge, Mass.: MIT Press, 1964). On the development of condominiums in Salt Lake City see various stories in *Utah Holiday*, especially: Eileen H. Stone,"Condominium Conversions: High Rise, Low Rise" *Utah Holiday* 13 (July 1979): 66-67, 73.

The most valuable papers were those of E.J. "Jake" Garn and J. Bracken Lee in the University of Utah Library, especially the former, since Lythgoe summarized most of the material valuable for the mayorship in his biography of Lee.

We found a number of important works on specific topics. See E. Woodrow Walton, "A City Regains Lighting Greatness," *American City* 79 (March 1964): 131-33; Dennis L. Lythgoe, "Political Feud in Salt Lake City: J. Bracken Lee and the Firing of W. Cleon Skousen," *Utah Historical Quarterly* 42 (Fall 1974): 316-43; Hilton, *The Story of Salt Lake Stake;* D. Michael Stewart, "Local Government Modernization: Reflections on Salt Lake City-County," *National Civic Review* 66 (1977): 291-99, and the Salt Lake Chamber of Commerce Legislative Subcommittee's "Modernizing Local Government" (n.p., n.d. [Salt Lake City: Chamber of Commerce, ca. 1968]), which deal with the problem of city-county consolidation and governmental modernization; Harry Waters, "Urban Shadows Fall on Sunny Salt Lake City," *Newsweek*, March 15, 1971; Hynda Rudd, "Congregation Kol Ami: Religious Merger in Salt Lake City," *Western States Jewish Historical Quarterly* 10 (July 1978): 311-26; Mark Rindflesh, "And the Poor Get Poor Care," *Alumni*

Emphasis [University of Utah Medical Center] (Spring-Summer 1971): 6-9; Goss, "Architectural History of Utah;" Mike Korologos, "Salt Lake City," *Western's World* 13 (May/June 1982): 40-49; Linda Sillitoe and David Merrill, "Freeman America," *Utah Holiday* 10 (February 1981): 34-36, 38, 40, 42-43, 66-67; and David Merrill and Linda Sillitoe, "Freeman America [part 2]," *Utah Holiday* 10 (March 1981): 33-40, 52, 54.

The best source on the Citygate affair is the *Salt Lake Tribune*. See also Marshall Ralph and Jeff Williams, "The Last Commissioner," *Utah Holiday* 8 (June 1979): 59-66.

On changing population patterns, see Wright, "The Growth and Distribution of Mormon and non-Mormon Populations in Salt Lake City."

On the movement of historic preservation, in addition to the works on various districts in Salt Lake City see: John W. Haggerty, "Historic Preservation in Utah, 1960-80" (M.A. thesis, Brigham Young University, 1980); Mark Hafey, Kevin Kurmada, Paul Shapiro, Bill Stehlin, and Robert Wood, *Historic Preservation: The South Temple Historic District* ([Salt Lake City: privately printed], 1975); and Laurel Friel, "All Fall Down: Money Wins and History Loses at Canyon Road," *Utah Holiday* 10 (December 1980): 42-58.

Perhaps the best single source for the condition of women in Salt Lake City is: *Network*, a "newspaper for women who live and work in Utah and the men who work with them." We found particularly useful Jean Shaw's column, "New Landings" in addition to several feature stories. Some of the most useful were: Marj Bradley, "Where Have All the Feminists Gone.... Or Have They," 6 (April 1983): 12; Karen Shepherd, "Editorial, With or Without Permission," 4 (July 1981): 3; Ralph Marshall, "Phoenix Institute: Still Flying After Ten Years," 4 (July 1981): 8; and Elaine Jarvik, "The Life and Complicated Times of Judge Christine Durham," 10 (January 1982): 10-11. In addition, we secured basic statistical information from the Utah Department of Employment Security's *Women in Utah's Labor Force, 1950-1980*, ([Salt Lake City]: Department of Employment Security, 1981).

Chapter 11

On the place of Salt Lake City in changes projected or the future see: John Naisbitt, *Megatrends: Ten New Directions Transforming Our Lives* (New York City: Warner Books, 1982).

In addition to the sources cited above, for the image of Salt Lake City see: Arthur Conan Doyle, *A Study in Scarlet; The Sign of the Four* (New York: Harper, 1904); Wallace Stegner, *Recapitulation* (Garden City, New York: Doubleday, 1979); Samuel W. Taylor, *Rocky Mountain Empire: The Latter-day Saints Today* (New York: Macmillan, 1978); and "A Reputation for Fraud: Utah Courts Flooded with Proliferation of Ponzi Schemes," *Utah Holiday* 9 (December 1981): 16-18.

The information on the LDS historical museum comes from an interview with Glen M. Leonard, February 22, 1983 by Thomas G. Alexander.

The interviews cited in chapters 9 and 10 were particularly helpful, especially those with William Smart, Ted Wilson, Fred Ball, and Emanuel Floor.

Information from the newspapers proved particularly helpful. See especially, the *Salt Lake Tribune,* Empire Edition, February 20, 1983; Robert H. Woody, "Utah's Image Across A Nation May Be Changing for Better," *Salt Lake Tribune*, January 23, 1983; Jeff Mapes, "Provo-Orem Births Rate Leads U.S." (Provo, Utah) *Daily Herald*, December 13, 1982; Dan Bates, "Mayor Wilson Not Ready to Announce Re-election Plans," *Salt Lake Tribune,* December 10, 1982; Don McLeod, "Congress Called On to Help Nation's Homeless," *Salt Lake Tribune,* December 16, 1982; Mara Callister, "Wilson Couldn't Win, Says Panel," *Daily Herald,* December 10, 1982; Bob Gottlieb, "There's Negative Side to Mormon Welfare System" *Daily Herald,* January 2, 1983; Robert H. Woody, "New Pipeline Acquisition Lets Firm Put Alaska Plan on Hold," *Salt Lake Tribune,* February 6, 1983; "A Heartbeat Heard 'Round the World," *University of Utah Review* 16 (December/January 1982-1983): 1-3; and "Five Graduate Programs are Among the Best" *University of Utah Review* 16 (December/January 1982-83): 4.

On changing attitudes toward Mormons and gentiles see Phyllis Barber, "Culture Shock," *Utah Holiday* 11 (November 1981): 31-40. We appreciated also the insights of John McCormick and Ronald Walker on this matter.

On changing industrial patterns see: Ronda Brinkerhoff, "From Apparel to X-Ray Tube" *Utah Economic and Business Review* 40 (November and December 1980): 1-7; James A. Wood, "The Electronics/Information Processing Industry in Utah" *Utah Economic and Business Review* 42 (October 1982): 1-9; and the Emanuel Floor and Fred Ball interviews.

On important construction which has taken place or is taking place by Triad see: *Salt Lake International Center: The West's Prestige Address* ([Salt Lake City: Triad Utah],n.d.); *Triad Center: A Triad America*

Index

Abravanel, Maurice, 253
"Ackerbügerstadt", 3
Affleck, David A., 266
Air pollution, 109-10, 151, 180-82, 243-44
Airbase Village, 243
Airport, 198, 212, 213, 256, 279, 285, 296, 308
Agenda for the Eighties Commission, 307
Agraz, Jess, 289
Ambassador Gardens, 242
American civil religion, 11
American Express, 296, 308
American party, 140-42
American Smelting and Refining Company, 233
Amusements, 117
Anderson, Nels, 306
Anderson, Thomas J., 99
Angell, Mary Ann, 97
Angell, Truman O., 58
Anti-fly campaign, 177
Anti-mask ordinance, 186
Anti-Mormonism, 157, 305, 312
Anti-polygamy legislation, 77
Anti-rat campaign, 177
Anti-Saloon League of America, 150
Anti-union campaign, 190
Apartment House Association, 269
Architecture, 58-60, 88, 131, 132, 279
Armstrong, Francis 91, 107, 172
Army Ninth Corps Area, 241
Arrington, Leonard, 37
Arts, 58, 83-84, 186, 253, 297, 314
Ashton, Wendel J., 14
Association of City Clubs, 174
Auerbach, Frederick, 68

Auerbach, Herbert S., 222
Auerbachs, 68
Aviation Village, 242
Babcock, O. E., 85
Backman, Gustave "Gus" P., 14, 200, 226, 235, 241, 253, 263, 268, 295
Badger, Carl. A., 150
Bales, M. P., 190
Ball, Fred S., 14
Ballet West, 297, 314
Bamberger, Clarence, 186
Bamberger, Ernest, 13, 184
Bamberger, Mrs. Simon, 144
Bamberger, Simon, 129, 166
Banking, 68
Banks, 91
Baptist church, 198
Barker, James L., 282, 289
Barney, E. S., 110
Barnes, Arthur F., 168, 172
Barth, Gunther, 2, 8
Bartleson, John, 18
Baskin, Robert N., 91, 100, 125
Bear River, 17
Beautification, 56, 176
Beecher, Maureen Ursenbach, 75
Beeley, Arthur, 187
Bellah, Robert 11
Benevolent organizations, 193
Bennett, William H., 176
Bernhisel, John M., 83
Bikuben, 115
Bird sanctuaries, 176
Black, George A., 93
Black, Parnell, 225
Blair, S. M., 82
Blood, Henry H., 213, 222
Board of health, 109

Board of Park Commissioners, 175
Bock, E. A., 168, 172
Bonneville, B. L. E., 22
Book of Mormon, 20
Borg, Grant, 255
Bosone, Reva Beck, 215-217, 228, 243
Bowery, 42
Bowman, John F., 172, 202, 203, 207-08, 223
Bradley, Marj, 299
Brannan, Samuel, 31-32
Bransford, John S., 142, 146
Brassfield, S. Newton, 54
Brewster, Sheldon, 263, 279, 283
Bridger, Jim, 17, 22
Brigham Young Express and Carrying Company, 63
Brown, Hugh B., 225
Buber, Martin, 10
Buchanan, James, 65
Budget system adoption of, 171
Buenaventura River, 18
Building codes, 170
Building Trades Council, 138, 190
Burbidge, Grant, 255, 266, 267
Burbidge, Joseph E., 169, 223, 224
Burroughs Nature Study Association of Utah, 176
Burt, Andrew H., 119, 120
Burt, Homer P., 145
Burton, Sir Richard, 63, 82, 83, 84
Burton, Theodore T., 176, 180, 181, 186
Business district (see also Main Street), 87, 90, 254
Byhower, Nicholas, 164, 176
Bywater, William H., 164, 169

Cache Valley, 22
Caine, John T., 115
Calder, David O., 113-14
California gold rush, 39-40
Camp Douglas (see Fort Douglas)
Camp Floyd, 66, 73
Campbell, David, 289
Cannon, Angus M., 140
Cannon D. James, 283
Cannon, Georgae Q., 13, 114
Cannon, Martha Hughes, 110, 140

Cannon, Sylvester Q., 169, 171, 178, 202
Careless, George, 114
Carnegie Corporation, 177
Carrington, Albert, 31
Cathedral of the Madeleine, 157, 198
Central Pacific Railroad, 71, 88
Chamber of Commerce, 105, 180, 204, 240, 263, 295
Chapman Branch Library, 177
Charities, 156-157
Chautauqua, 117
Chicago Bridge and Iron Company, 252
Chorpening, George, 63
Christensen, C.C.A., 84
Christensen, Joe L.,266
Church of Jesus Christ of Latter-day Saints, 127, 157, 203, 209, 235, 237, 263, 293, 303, 304
    information bureau, 157
    office building, 131, 279
    origin and doctrine, 20-21
    welfare program, 213-14, 311
Church-state relations, 49
Cigarette prohibition, 185
Citizens Alliance, 138
Citizens Defense Corps., 235
Citizen's party of 1909, 145
Citizen's Reform Ticket of 1897, 126
Citizen's Training Camp, 189
City
    nature of, 3-4
City and County building, 130-31
"City Beautiful" movement, 155
City-county consolidation
    movement for, 288-89
City-county cooperation and
    conflict, 284, 285
City Creek, 25, 27
City elections, 98. 125, 141-42, 146-48, 274-75
City government
    early, 29-30, 32, 47
City Hall, 58, 93
City Manager system, 268
The City of the Saints, 63
"City of Zion", 25
City planning, 23, 25, 28, 56, 171, 249, 280, 304

Citygate, 290
Civic Betterment Union, 166, 168
City improvement, 218
City Improvement League, 144,
    145, 146, 164
Civil Planning and Art Commission,
    176, 181
Civil Defense Council, 235
Civil service commission, 171
Civil War impact, 67-68
Civil Works Administration, 210
Clark, J. Reuben, Jr., 184, 213
Clark, John, 126
Clark, William A., 129
Clawson, Hiram B., 103
Clawson, Spencer, 100
Clayton, James L., 314
Clayton, William, 22, 66, 83
Clift House Hotel, 96
Clinton, Jeter, 55, 97
Clinton v. Engelbrecht, 95, 97
Clubs, special interest in 1890s, 116
Commercial Club (see Chamber of
    Commerce)

Commission government, 142-48,
    163, 164, 244-46, 268
Committee on City Planning and
    Capital Improvements, 277
Community, 10, 11, 62
Community Action Program, 293
Comprehensive Employment
    Training Act, 284
Comprehensive History of the
    Church, 158
Comrade Girls, 189
Condominiums, 292
Congregation of the Holy Cross, 113
Congregational church, 112
Conner, Patrick Edward, 67
Conservatism, 1890—1900s, 125
Continental Bank and Trust
    Company, 134
Cook, Ida Ione, 114
Cook, Mary Elizabeth, 114
Corless, John S., 185
Corruption, 12, 223
Cosgriff, James E., 134
Cottrell, Wendell L., 266
Council House, 58, 93
Council of Fifty, 22

Crabbe, A.H., 169, 172
Cricket plague, 27-28
Crime (see also law enforcement),
    162, 258, 281
Critchlow, George A., 222
Crossroads Center, 293, 312
Crossroads Mall, 305
"Crossroads of the West", 62
Cowley, Matthew, 224
Cultural activities (see also arts), 9,
    41-42, 117, 158-59, 314
Cumming, Alfred, 65
Curbs and gutters, 179

Daily Reporter, 73
Daly, John J., 130
Darlington Place, 152
Deer Creek project, 201, 221, 255
Defense spending, 232-33
Dencker, Judy Ann, 300
Denver and Rio Grande depot, 292
Denver and Rio Grande Western
    Railroad, 91, 129, 181
Depression of 1919-1922, 188
Derks field, 256
Dern, George H., 130
Dern, John, 130
Deseret Academy of the Arts, 84
Deseret Agricultural and
    Manufacturing Society, 60, 80
Deseret Dramatic Association, 83
Deseret Hospital, 110
Deseret Literary and Musical
    Association, 83
Deseret Musuem, 117
Deseret National Bank, 91, 102, 103
Deseret News, 54, 55, 57, 60, 62,
    68, 73, 82, 83, 84, 114, 122,
    198, 211, 311
Deseret Philharmonic Society, 83
Deseret Theological Association, 80
Deseret Theological Class, 81
Devereaux House, 59, 293, 295
Dilworth, Mary Jane, 41
Dininny, J. J., 164
Discrimination against blacks,
    262-63
Diseases (see under specific disease)
Divorce rate, 237
Dominguez-Escalante expedition,
    17

Donner party, 18-20
Dooly Building, 131
Dooly, John E., 91, 99
Doremus, Abraham F., 109, 126
Double taxation, 288
Douglas Arms Corporation, 241
Doyle, Sir Arthur Conan, 303
Droubay, C. Edson, 170
Drug busts, 165
Drummond, W. W., 65
Dunbar, David C., 148
Durham, Christine Meaders, 301
Dye, Melvin L., 254

Eagle Emporium, 68-102
Eagle Gate apartments, 295
Early, J.S., 226
Ecclesiastical wards, 31,51, 71,
    79-80, 314
Economic activity, 4, 5, 38-41,
    60-61, 66-68, 90, 105, 127, 188,
    197-98, 200-14, 217, 231-233,
    251-253, 296, 298, 308-311
Economic regulation, 39, 60, 68-70
Edmunds Act, 99
Edmunds-Tucker Act, 99
Education, 42, 82-83, 111-13, 236,
    314-16
Eighteenth Amendment, 225
Eitel McCullough Radio Tube Plant,
    233, 252
Eldredge, Horace S., 103
Eldridge and Clawson, 70
Electric lights, 107
Elites, 113, 100, 130, 132-34
Ellerbeck, Thomas W., 107
Emery, C. Frank, 185
Emigration Square, 45
Emma Mine, 103
Employment patterns, 47, 214-15,
    232
Endowment House, 58
Engelbrecht, Paul, 97
Erwin, E. B., 225, 226-27
Ethnic groups (see also immigration
    and immigrants), 134-35, 189,
    192-93, 239-40 298
Evangelical Protestants, 312
Evans, De Ann, 300
Evans, John Henry, 168
Expansion, 188

Fair Labor Standards Act impact on
    Salt Lake City, 285
Fairbanks, J. Leo, 176
Family Life, 74, 237-38
Faust, James E., 295
Federal agencies (see also specific
    agency), 199
"Federal Bunch", 145
Federal Emergency Relief
    Administration (FERA), 211
Federal Heights, 152
Federal Housing Administration,
    211, 254
Federal Reserve Bank, 4, 188
Federation of Women's Clubs, 215
Fehr, Charles N., 172
Fergo, A.M., 276
Ferry, W. Mont, 144, 146, 166,
    168, 172
Fifteenth Ward, 157
Figlia D' Italia, 193
Finch, Harry L., 172, 186, 226
Fire alarm system, 156
Fire department, 107, 156, 169, 170
Fire fighters union, 170
Fischer, Chaude, 9
Fitzpatrick, John F., 14, 183, 263,
    264, 295
Flooding, 259, 317-19
Floor, Emanuel A., 14
Fly abatement program, 174
Flynn, J. E., 164
Folsom, William H., 58, 88
Ford Foundation, 297
Fort Bridger, Wyoming, 65
Fort Douglas, 57, 67, 73, 96, 189,
    200, 232, 241
Foster, Warren, 129
Frederick, David, 103
Freed, Robert E., 262
Fremont Island, 18
Fremont, John C., 18, 22
Fuller, Louis S., 150

Galigher, Joseph E., 184
Gallivan, John W., 14, 295, 296,
    295, 296
Gambling, 149, 165
Gardner Commission, 315
Gardner, David P., 315

Gardo House, 58, 134, 188
Garn, E. J. "Jake", 280, 283-84, 285
Gates, Crawford, 253
Gates, Susa Young, 144
General Mills, 299
General Tithing Office, 61, 69
Geneva Steel Plant, 252
Gentiles, 15, 72, 92, 99
Geographic Expansion, 57
German Turnverein, 117
Germania Smelter, 102, 103
Geurts, Theodore, 275, 280, 289
Glade, Earl J., 247, 249, 255,
    258-59, 263, 265, 266, 267
Glendale Gardens, 241
Glendinning, James J., 125, 126
Glenn, Hugh L., 165
Godbe, William S., 68, 73, 88, 95,
    129

Godbeite movement, 92
Gold mission, 39-40
Good Government Ticket, 147
Goodwin, George F., 176
Goodyear, Miles, 22, 31
Gorham, Mrs. A. J., 176
Governmental offices
    location of, 93
Grant, Brigham F., 164
Grant, Heber J., 13, 105, 150, 164,
    185, 187, 219, 220
Grant, Jedediah M., 13, 47, 49, 57,
    81, 172
Grant, Ulysses S., 93
Great Depression, 199 ff
Great Salt Lake, 23, 314
Greater Avenues Community
    Council, 292
Greek Orthodox church, 136
Greely, Horace, 58
Greener, Glen N., 289
Groves, William S., 157

Haddow, Mac, 305
Hafen, John, 84
Haight, David B., 295
Haight, Golden, 258
Hammond Hall, 112
Hampton, Brigham Y., 12, 98
Hanson, Stewart M., Jr., 290
Harding, Richard F., 241

Harms, Herman, 164
Harper's Weekly, 57
Harries, Benjamin R., 185
Harriman, Edward H., 153
Harris, Carl, 159
Harris, Chauncey, 197, 303
Harris, Fischer, 220, 222, 227
Harrison, Conrad, 276, 283, 287
Harrison, E. L. T., 73
Harvey, Sam Joe, 119
Hashimoto, Edward D., 135
Hashimoto, Edward Ichiro, 239-40
Hastings, Landsford: Emigrant
    Guide to Oregon and California,
    22
Health and health care, 109-10, 151,
    177, 182, 298
Hempstead, Charles H., 73
Henry, Matthew, 103
Herald, 73, 96, 115, 122
Hickman, William H., 95
Hill, Joe, 191
Hills, Lewis S., 103
Hilton Hotel, 292
Hilton, O.N., 192
Hilton, Thomas H., 155
Hinckley, Gordon B., 13, 295, 311
Historic preservation, 291, 292
Historical and Arts Museum, 295
Hogensen, Herman J., 288
Hogle Gardens, 205, 218, 256
Holladay and Warner, 62
Holley, Louis E., 266, 276
Holli, Melvin, 7
Holmes, Susanna Bransford Emery,
    134
Holy Cross Hospital, 110, 279
Holy Trinity Church, 136
Home Dramatic Company, 117
Home Owner's Loan Association,
    211
Home rule movement, 268-70
Hooper, William H., 102
Hooper and Eldridge, 67
Hoover, Herbert, 202
Hopkins, Harry L., 210
Horne, William W., 266
Horticultural Society, 80
House Wives League, 174
Housing, 240-43, 254
Howard, E. O., 200

Howard, William, 56
Howe, Alan T., 282
Hunt, Duane G., Most Reverand, 219
Hunt, John, 316
Hyde, Orson, 24, 82

Ickes, Harold L., 210, 211, 222
Immigration and immigrants, 8, 45, 105, 134-36, 189, 193
Independence, Missouri, 20
Independent Order of Odd Fellows, 116
Industrial Christian Home, 111
Industrial Workers of the World, 191
Influenza, 182
Inland Crystal Salt Company, 130
Inspector of Provisions, 126
Intermountain Advocate, 129
Intermountain Stock Exchange, 4
International Center, 296, 310
International Smelting and Refining Company, 233
"Instant City", 2
Ireland, E. A., 120
Irrigation, 34
Island communities, 8
Isn't One Wife Enough?, 79
Italian Mothers Club, 193
Ivins, Anthony W., 265

Jack, James, 107
Jackling, Daniel C., 130, 133
Japanese-American Citizen's League, 239, 240
Jeff's Grocery Store, 282
Jenkins, Ab, 229, 231, 234, 244, 246-47, 266
Jenkins, Bruce, 274, 280
Jennings, William, 13, 59-60, 67, 68, 70, 91, 102, 103, 120, 172
Jensen, Richard, 159
Jessen, H.C., 182

Jewish community, 88
Johnston, Albert Sidney, 66
Juvenile delinquency, 159, 177, 187-88, 258
Juvenile Instructor, 115

KSL Radio, 198

Kane, Thomas L., 65
Kearns Army Air Base, 232
Kearns, Jennie Judge, 133
Kearns, Thomas, 13, 129, 130, 133, 141, 146
Kessler, George E., 170
Keith, David, 13, 130
Kelsey, Eli B., 82
Kelsey, Louis C., 145
Kelson, Virginia "Jinnah", 300
Kennecott Copper Corporation, 233, 252
Kennecott Copper Building, 279
Kerens, R. C., 129
Keyser, George D., 147, 164, 220, 235
Khashoggi family, 309
Kimball, Heber C., 37
Kimball, Spencer W., 263, 311
King, William H., 144, 184
Kingsbury, Joseph T., 194
Kirtland, Ohio, 20-21
Kleppner, Paul, 159
Kletting, Richard K. A., 131
Knerr, William M., 191
Knight, Newell, 266
Knight, Walter S., 170
Kojian, Varujan, 297
König, Rene', 10
Korns, William H., 147, 164
Ku Klux Klan, 185-86
Kurumada, Jan, 239

Labor, 106, 138, 293
Ladies Literary Club, 174, 180
Lagoon, 159
Lake Phoebe-Lake Mary Reservoir, 178
Lambourne, Alfred, 84
Land distribution, 26-27
Lane, Elwood, 166
Laney, Francis G., 168
Langton, William, 221
Lannan, Patrick L., 105
Latter, Fullmer H., 268
Latter-day Saints Hospital, 157
Law enforcement (see also crime), 52-54, 179-80, 223-25, 236
Lawrence, George N., 184
Lawrence, Henry, W., 70, 95, 105, 129, 147, 164

League of Women Voters, 269
Leatherwood, Elmer O., 147
Lee, Harold B., 213
Lee, J. Bracken, 256, 274, 275-76,
  279, 283, 289
Liberal Institute, 117
Liberal party, 92, 99, 100, 125
Liberty Park, 155
Liberty State Betterment League,
  165
Libraries, 118
License fees, 95-96
Lincoln, Abraham, 67
Lingenfelter, Ben E., 266
Lion House, 58
Liquor regulation (see also
  prohibition), 55, 165, 296
Literary organizations, 117
Little, Feramorz, 91, 111
Litton Systems, 255, 296
Livingston and Kinkead, 41, 62
Lodges and secret societies, 116
London, Belle, 149
Los Angeles and Salt Lake Railroad
  Company, 129
Lowrey, Irvin, L., 166
Lund, Anthony C., 187
Lyman, Amasa, 39
Lyman, Amy Brown, 183, 203,
  238-39
Lynch, William J., 141

Mack, M.J., 109
MacNeill, Charles M., 130
Maeser, Karl G., 113
Mail service, 63
Main Street, 66, 68, 197, 304
Marcus, Louis, 205-10, 212, 220,
  221
Marriott Hotel, 292
Marriott, Dan, 282
Martin, Lewis D., 149
Masonry, 185
Matheson, John B., 235, 243
Matheson, Scott M., 14, 258, 301,
  307
Maw, Herbert B., 235
Maxfield, Jollie Ellen, 138
Maxfield, Lois, 138
Maxwell, George R., 96

Maxwell, Neal A., 295
Mayor, shift in characteristics of,
  171-72
McCarty, Daryl, 282
McConkie, Oscar W., 235, 246
McCormick, John, 199-200, 303
McCornick and Company, 91
McCornick, William S., 13, 91, 99,
  103, 105, 129
McKay, Ambrose Noble, 183, 265
McKay, David O., 13, 14, 263, 264,
  265, 293
McKean, James B., 95
McKinney, J. W., 147
Merrill, Joseph F., 181
Methodist Church Home Missionary
  Society, 165
Methodist Episcopal church, 112
Metropolitan Hall of Justice, 277,
  279
Metropolitan Water District, 221
Miner's National Bank, 68
Mining, 68, 90, 129, 308
Minorities (see also ethnic groups),
  217, 239
Modern city culture, 8
Moench, Louis F., 114
Monnett, Osborn, 181
Moral reform, 8
Moran, Patrick J., 172, 186
Morgan Commercial College, 113
Morgan, Dale, 51, 306
Morgan, James F., 191
Morgan, John, 113
Mormon Reformation, 81
Mormon Tabernacle, 58, 253
Mormon Tabernacle Choir, 187, 297
Morman Tribune, 73
"Morman underground", 78
Mormans (see Church of Jesus
  Christ of Latter-day Saints)
Morris, Nephi L., 145, 150, 190
Morris, Richard P., 13, 126, 141,
  142, 147, 164
Morrison, Arling, 191
Morrison, John G., 191
Motion pictures, 186
Mountain Dell Reservoir, 178
Mountaineer, 73
Moyle, Henry D., 281
Murdoch, William, 226, 228

Mullally, Robert T., 289
Mulliner, Samuel, 38
Mulvey, Martin E., 149
Municipal improvements, 100
Murdoch, James D., 145
Murray, Eli H., 114
Museum of Fine Arts, 297
Naisbitt, John, 316
National Association for the
  Advancement of Colored People,
  193, 262
National Industrial Recovery Act
  (NIRA), 209, 210
National League of Cities, 285
National Recovery Administration
  (NRA), 210
Nauvoo Legion, 93
Neslen, C. Clarence, 13, 168, 169,
  172, 184, 185, 187
New Deal, 208-13, 232
New Federalism, 307
New West Educational Commission,
  112
Newhouse, Samuel, 13, 130, 133
Newman, John P., 119
Newspapers, 73, 114-15, 198, 262
Nibley, Charles W., 176, 185
Nibley Park, 176
Nichols, Max T., 290
Ninth Corps Area Service
  Command, 232

Oberndorfer, Joseph, 141
Officer's Training Camp, 189
Ogden, Utah, 22, 71
Old City Hall demolished, 254
Oliver, Fred M., 276
Olson, Berkley, 186
Opium dens, 118-19
Oregon fever, 18
Oregon Territory, 17
Oregon trail, 18
Orem, Walter C., 129
Orphan's Home and Day Nursery,
  111, 183
Ottinger, George M., 84
Out migration, 261, 278

Packard, John Q., 155
Paden, William M., 147
Palmer, Ana D., 203

Park, John R., 83, 113
Park, Samuel C., 147, 164, 176
Parking regulation, 180, 217
Parks and Playgrounds Association,
  155
Paul, S. G., 164
Paul, Samuel, 126
Paul, William, 59
Payne, W. L., 224, 226
Peep O'Day, 73
Penrose, Spencer, 130
People's party, 100
Perpetual Emmigration Fund, 45, 80
Phelps, W. W., 82
Phoenix Institute, 300
Phillips, Jennings, Jr., 269, 283,
  287, 289, 291, 295
Phillips Petroleum, Co., 252
Pierce, J. K., 280
Pierce, R. O., 227
Pioneer monument, 219
Pitt, Thomas D., 149
Pitt, William, brass band, 83
Plummer, Charles G., 142
Plural marriage, 21-22, 35, 77-79,
  98
Police department, 107, 227, 258,
  267, 280
Polygamy (see plural marriage)
Polysophical Society, 80, 81
Population, 2, 25, 28, 42, 45, 46,
  87, 219, 278-79
Populists, 126, 129
Pornography, 296
Porter, Sam B., 147
Powers, Orlando W., 144
Pratt-Newman debate, symbolic
  importance of, 119-20
Pratt, Arthur, 126
Pratt, Orson, 24, 26, 74, 77, 82, 119
Pratt, Parley, P., 31
Pratt, Romania B., 110
Prejudice, 27
Preparedness movement, 188
Presbyterian church, 113
Primary Association, 77
Progressive, The, 166, 180
Progressivism, 163 ff., 172-73,
  194-95
  social and structural reform
  under, 7, 163

Prohibition, 150, 169, 223, 224-25
Promised Valley Playhouse, 297, 307
Promontory Summit, 72
Prostitution, 118, 148, 149, 282
Protestants, 150
Public education, 111
Public health, 182
Public market, 174
Public relations, 310
Public schools, 82-83, 194
Public utilities, 107
Public transit, 257
Public Works Administration (PWA), 209, 210, 211

Quorum of Twelve, 25

Racism, 136, 159
Radio broadcasting, 187
Rampton, Calvin L., 285
Rawlins, Joseph L., 113
Read, Charles, 147
Reconstruction Finance Corporation, 202, 208
Record, O. B., 227
Redfield, Robert, 10
Reed, Charles H., 147
Reese, Enoch, 62
Reese, John, 62
Relative inequality, 106
Relief Society, 75, 77, 80, 99, 110, 183, 203, 215, 238, 239
Religion, census of 1890, 115-16
Remey, Jules, 55
Remington Arms Plant, 233, 251
Repertory Dance Theatre, 297
Residential differentiation, 6
Reservoirs, 178
Rezoning movement, 291
Rich, Charles, C., 39
Richards, Stephan L., 165
Rigdon, Sidney, 20
Ririe-Woodbury Dance Company, 297
Riter, Mrs. W.W., 144
Roberts, Boliver, 99
Roberts, Brigham H., 157
Roberts, Paul, 269
Robinson, J. King, 54
Robinson, J. Will, 222

Rocky Mountain Bell, 154
Roman Catholic church, 198
Romney, George, 88
Romney, L. C., 256, 266, 267
Roosevelt, Franklin D., 200, 209, 210, 222
Rosenblatt, Joseph, 268
Ross, C. Ben, 210
Rowland Hall, 112
Royce, Josiah, 11
Russell, Majors, and Wadell, 63

St. Joseph's School, 113
St. Mark's Hospital, 110
St. Mark's School, 112
St. Mary's School, 113
Salt Lake Academy, 112
Salt Lake and Ogden Railway, 129
Salt Lake and Utah Railroad, 129
Salt Lake Aqueduct, 222-23
Salt Lake Army Club, 189
Salt Lake Arts Center, 297
Salt Lake City (see also specific categories)
    as territorial capital, 47
    auditor, 164
    board of health, 152
    bond rating of, 276
    Department of Public Works, 7, 66
    description, 28-29, 57, 63, 87, 197
    finance, 51-52, 56, 259-60, 276-77, 293
    founding of compared to other cities, 25-26
    image of, 316
    name changes, 25
    patent, 97
    regional center, 45, 91, 197-99
    site selection, 23
    wall, 57
Salt Lake City Beobachter, 115
Salt Lake City Clearing House Association, 200
Salt Lake City Gas Company, 107
Salt Lake City-Ogden Standard Metropolitan Statistical Area (SMSA), 307
Salt Lake Collegiate Institute, 113

357

Salt Lake Council of Women, 215, 217
Salt Lake County Almshouse, 111
Salt Lake Daily Telegraph, 119
Salt Lake Dramatic Association, 116
Salt Lake Federation of Labor, 240
Salt Lake Industrial Center, 251
Salt Lake Kindergarten and Graded School, 113
Salt Lake Ministerial Association, 168
Salt Lake Real Estate board, 200
Salt Lake Redevelopment Agency, 286
Salt Lake Seminary, 112
Salt Lake Sketch Club, 158
Salt Lake Telegram, 146, 198
Salt Lake Temple, 37, 58
Salt Lake Theatre, 58, 83,84, 186
Salt Lake Traction Company, 180
Salt Lake Tribune, 73, 114, 115, 122, 125, 141, 146, 158, 158, 166, 198, 199, 223, 244, 246, 264, 295, 296
Salt Lake Valley, 17-20, 23-24, 26
Salt Lake Women's League, 149
Salt Lake Zoological Society, 218
Salt Palace, 159, 186, 277-78, 297, 311
Saltair, 159
Savage, C.R., 35
Scarborough, Louis E., 241
Schreiner, Alexander, 187
Sevens, Order of, 13, 184
Shores, C.W., 166
Scott, George M., 91, 100
Secret societies, 116
Sells, William H., 120
Seventies Hall of Science, 58-80
Seventies Quorum, 81
Shaffer, J. Wilson, 93
Sharp, James, 91, 105
Sheets, George, 156
Sheldon Jackson College, 113
Sheppard-Towner Mother and Child Health Act, 183
Sherwood, Henry, 31
Shipp, Ellis R., 110
Silver King Coalition Mines Company, 130
Silverstein, Joseph, 297

Skidmore, Charles H., 236
Skliris, Leonidas G., 135, 136
Skousen, W. Cleon, 259, 267, 280
Sleator, Robert G., 138
Sloan, Edward L., 96, 115, 119
Smallpox, 151
Bmith, Barbara B., 299
Smith, Emma, 75
Smith, George Albert, 67, 186, 253
Smith, Hyrum, 21
Smith, J. McKinnon, 279
Smith, J.O., 174
Smith, Jedidiah, 17
Smith, John, 29, 31
Smith, Joseph F., 13, 140
Smith, Joseph Jr., 20-21, 49, 75, 77
Smoot, Abraham O., 52
Smoot, Reed, 129, 140, 150, 185, 207
Snow, Eliza R., 75-76, 80
Snow, Herbert A., 229
Snow, Lorenzo, 80
Snow, Zerubabbel, 82
Social Hall, 58, 80, 84
Social Hall School, 114
Social welfare, 8
Socialist Labor party, 126
Socialist party, 190
La Societa'Cristoforo Columbo, 193
Soldier's and Sailor's Employment Commission, 190
Sowles, M. B., 99
Spalding, Franklin S., 144, 183
Spencer, Orson, 82
Sperry Univac, 255, 296
Sports, 117-18, 158-59, 176, 253, 256, 277, 278, 296
Spry, William, 145, 150, 179, 191
Staines, William, 59
Standard Oil of California, 130, 252
Stansbury, Howard, 57
State Board of Health, 152
State Industrial Commission, 191
State of Deseret, 32
Steele, Axel, 191
Stegner, Wallace, 302
Stenhouse, T. B. H., 73
Stephens, Frank B., 144, 145
Stephens, Virginia Snow, 192
Stevenson, C. L., 109
Stewart, Adiel F., 255, 259, 267

Stewart, Frank Page, 225
Stewart, William M., 103
Strong mayor-council form of
  government, 289-90
Subcultures, 9, 10, 193
Suburban growth, 273
Sugar House, 152
Sullivan, Louis, 131
Sunday closing, 150-51
Surplus Commodities Corporation,
  212
Sutherland, George, 145
Swaner, Leland S., 251
Swimming,1880s to 1890s, 118
Symphony Hall, 278, 297, 311

Talmage, James E., 117, 158
Tanner, Nathan Eldon, 13, 311
Taylor, Samuel W., 303
Tadesco, Fred, 235, 246-47, 256
Temple Square, 157, 217
Territory of Utah, 32
Third California Volunteers, 67
"This is the Place Monument", 253
Thomas Kearns Mansion, 292
Thomas, Marjorie, 290
Thompson, Ezra, 126, 141, 142
Tithing house, 61
Tocqueville, Alexis de, 152
Topham, Dora B., 149
Tourism, 5
Transcontinental railroad, 71-72
Transportation, 4, 6, 107, 153, 256,
  310
Treganza, Albert Owen, 131, 176
Triad Utah, 292, 293, 304, 305,
  309, 311
Tri-arc Travelodge, 292
Tullidge, Edward, 67, 73, 119
Turner, Chauncey,32
Turner, David S., 268
Twentieth Ward, 93, 106
Twin Lakes Reservoir, 178
Typhoid fever, 109

Unemployment, 189, 202-05, 307
Union National Bank, 91
Union Pacific Railroad, 71, 88, 129
Union Vedette, 68, 73
United Orders, 106
U.S. Bureau of Mines, 181

United States Steel Company, 252
Universal Scientific Society, 80
University of Deseret (see also
  University of Utah), 42, 57, 75,
  83, 113
University of Utah, 83, 113-14, 194,
  205, 213, 297, 314-16
University of Utah Medical Center,
  279
Urban growth, problems, and
  services, 7, 88, 107, 108, 109,
  152, 154, 177, 179, 255, 277,
  279, 286
Utah Anti-Compulsory Vaccination
  League, 152
Utah Associated Industries, 190
Utah Centennial Commission, 265
Utah Central Railroad, 72, 88, 102
Utah Civic Ballet, 297
Utah Conference of Christians and
  Jews, 306
Utah Congress of Mothers, 174
Utah Construction Company, 191
Utah Copper Company, 191
Utah Expedition, 65
Utah Gas & Coke, 154
Utah Heritage Foundation, 293
Utah Holiday, 306
Utah Humane Society, 158
Utah-Idaho Sugar Company, 130,
  198
Utah Independent, 154
Utah Light and Railway Company,
  153, 154, 177
Utah Magazine, 73
Utah Mining Gazette, 115
Utah Oil Refinery, 233, 234
Utah Oil Refining Company, 251,
  252
Utah Posten, 115
Utah Power and Light Company,
  177, 181
Utah Prepatory Commission, 237
Utah Produce Company, 69
Utah Society of Engineers, 182
Utah Southern Railroad, 91, 102,
Utah State Fair, 159
Utah State Federation of Labor, 138,
  190-91
Utah State Historical Society, 292
Utah State Road Commission, 252

359

Utah Symphony, 253, 278, 297, 314
Utah Taxpayer's Association, 174
Utah Transit Authority, 257
Utah Valley, 22
Utah War, 65-66
Valley Tan, 73
Van Cott, John, 32
Varian, Charles S., 166
Vice (see also prostitution),
    149,165, 166,258, 281-82,
    control, 149, 165, 166
Voluntary organizations, 152,
    173-74, 179
Wade, Richard, 2
Wagner, Act, 211
Walker Brothers, 68, 88, 91, 103
Walker, James R., 105
Walker, Joseph R., 13, 103, 105
Walker Opera House, 117
Wall, Enos A., 133
Wallace, John M., 228, 251
Wallace, Walker, 269
Wallace, Willilam R., 145
Wandamere, 159
Ware, Walter E., 131
Warm Springs Bathhouse, 177
Water system, 34, 57, 107, 108,
    177, 178, 222, 223, 255-56
Webb, Arch G., 254
Webb, LaVarr G., 311
Webb, William C., 228
Weber Canyon, 71
Weber, Max, 3
Weggeland, Daniel, 84, 114
Weggeland, Gordon, 254
Weight, Burtram A., 268
Weir, Thomas, 130, 147
Wells, Daniel H., 13, 46,49, 91, 93,
    95, 107, 172
Wells Fargo and Company, 91
Wells, Heber M., 105, 152
Wells, Rulon S., 151
West, Caleb, 105
Western Airlines, 296, 308
Western Federation of Miners, 191
Westminster College, 113
Whitney, Orson F., 23
Whitaker, George A., 147
Whitaker, John M., 204
White, J. Parley, 166, 168

Widstoe, John A., 194
Widstoe, Osborne J. P., 194
Wilkes, Charles, 22
Williams, J. D., 268, 269
Williams, Parley L., 184
Willoughby, Bud, 289
Wilson, George, 13, 184
Wilson, Ted, 288, 295, 312
Wiscomb, J. E., 164
Woodhull Brothers, 90
Women, 74, 138, 192, 214-15, 234,
    238, 299-300,
Women suffrage, 98
Women's Chamber of Commerce,
    215
Women's Exponent, 77, 115
Women's Rescue Station, 149
Woodson, Samuel H., 41
Woodruff, Wilford, 23, 80, 91, 127
Woody, Robert H., 316
Woolley, Ted. F., 180
Word of Wisdom, 224
Works Progress Administration,
    201, 211, 212, 231, 236, 247
World War II, 231

YMCA, 158
YX Company (See Brigham Young
    Express and Carrying Company)
Young, Ann Eliza, 97
Young, Brigham, 3, 10, 13, 22, 24,
    29, 34, 51, 52, 60, 65, 69, 71,
    72, 74-75, 77, 78, 79, 83, 95, 96,
    97, 106, 107, 303
Young, George W., 150
Young, John, 31, 117
Young, Kimball; 79
Young Ladies' Aid Society, 111
Young Ladies Mutual Improvement
    Association, 110, 117
Young, Mahonri M., 253
Young, Seymour B., 111

Young Women's Journal, 115
ZCMI, 70-71, 103, 304, 305
ZCMI Center, 304, 305
Zane, Charles S., 98, 112
Zion's Cooperative Mercantile
    Institute (see ZCMI)
Zion's Savings Bank and Trust, 91
Zion's Security Corporation, 295